# ARYA DHARM

*Hindu Consciousness in 19th-Century Punjab*

# ARYA DHARM

*Hindu Consciousness in 19th-century Punjab*

KENNETH W. JONES

MANOHAR
2006

First published 1976
Reprinted 1989, 2006



Hb.: ISBN 81-85054-91-6
Pb.: ISBN 81-7304-709-X

*Published by*
Ajay Kumar Jain for
Manohar Publishers & Distributors
4753/23, Ansari Road, Daryaganj
New Delhi 110 002

*Printed at*
Lordson Publishers Pvt. Ltd.
Delhi 110 007

*Distributed in South Asia by*
FOUNDATION BOOKS
4381/4, Ansari Road
Daryaganj, New Delhi 110 002
and its branches at Mumbai, Hyderabad,
Bangalore, Chennai, Kolkata

# CONTENTS

# LIST OF MAPS

# LIST OF MAPS

# PREFACE

Cultural interaction between the British and South Asians, between ruler and ruled, dominates the history of nineteenth-century British India. The conquest of South Asia and the establishment of the British Raj brought Western civilization through the medium of British culture into direct contact with the Indo-Muslim civilization of South Asia. From this confrontation emerged a new colonial culture neither wholly English nor completely South Asian, but a unique way of life peculiar to the British Raj. By the mid-nineteenth century, members of this colonial ruling class saw themselves in terms of the empire. They became "sahibs" and "memsahibs"—social roles explicable to both their countrymen at home and to the conquered peoples of South Asia. Social roles cannot exist without a standardized explanation—that is, without ideology. British imperialism, the mythology of empire, provided the underlying rationalization for British colonial identity. The various historical processes that created social roles and formulated ideology were inextricably bound by mutual reinforcement. Once established, this imperial identity expressed itself daily in the dynamics of colonial culture.

South Asians drawn into the colonial milieu of the British Raj, into daily contact with their English rulers, also were compelled to create a new world of their own. They started from a variety of reference points—from the great tradition of Indo-Muslim civilization, from their own regional culture, and from the specific traditions of their castes and subcastes. Success beckoned as the British empire opened new opportunities for wealth, power, and prestige. Those who could bridge the gap between their own culture and British colonial society, who would learn the ways of the white man and become adept in his language, constituted a new class in South Asian society. The members of this class, educated and anglicized, paid a price for their success. They became both marginal and alienated as they commuted daily from their own cultural environment to the world in which they worked and studied, and back again to their own society. Some felt the pain of psychological separation acutely; others did not; but all were affected and none could escape.

Alienated and marginal men found it impossible to feel comfortable with many of the customs, values, and attitudes of their surrounding society. That nothing in their inherited culture explained their dilemma of alienation or the fact of foreign conquest compounded their sense of disorientation. Nothing held out hope for a better future. Individual thinkers tried to reorder their own sense of identity and relate it to the realities of colonialism, providing new visions of the past, present, and future. This search for self marked the beginnings of a process of cultural adjustment. In its first stages members of the anglicized class were too few and too scattered to support movements of change. Instead, they generated prophets of a new world who existed as loners, voices without an audience. With the first generation of college-educated South Asians, the visions of different individuals provided a variety of bases for social and religious movements dedicated to changing South Asian culture. Alienated and marginal men accepted a particular vision, elaborated it, and produced an ideological explanation of their place in history. Identity for the individual became ideology for the group.

Commitment to a particular ideology not only eased the psychological tensions of anglicized South Asians but also channeled their energies into new patterns of action. The nineteenth century saw an immense proliferation of religious and social organizations dedicated to reviving the "true" past and removing the evils of a degenerate present. Belief in a particular ideology legitimized change; commitment to that ideology bred militancy and radicalism. The more passionate the belief the greater the strength to condemn contemporary custom and to stand against the sanctions of society. Ideological commitment also demanded the defense of one's beliefs against all challenges whether within South Asian society or without. By the end of the century a proliferation of social and religious movements added new unity and new divisions to South Asia, as each group sought to defend its own particular vision of the universe against all who disagreed. The search for identity produced new forms of group consciousness and increasing ideological competition. With the twentieth century, expressions of group consciousness took on political overtones and in the most extreme cases provided the bases for differing forms of nationalism.

This process from the reformulation of identity through political expressions of group consciousness can best be seen in a regional context. Regional culture rather than the great tradition of Indo-Muslim civilization set the frame of reference for cultural interaction. Three regions—Bengal, Maharashtra, and Punjab—contributed heavily to the creation of a modern and modernizing Hindu consciousness. This study focuses on the process of identity reformulation and acculturation among Punjabi Hindus from its beginnings in the 1860s through the creation of a politicized Hindu consciousness in the years prior to World War I. During this half-century Punjabi Hindus led in the founding of a new world, partly British and partly Punjabi. Though the Arya Samaj dominated this process among Punjabi Hindus and dominates this study, this is not the history of a movement; it is instead the history of a process.

The writing of social history in a time and space without even the fundamental structure of chronological fact means the creation of an entire world, a three-dimensional mosaic composed of thousands of discrete facts linked by chronology and historical judgment. The resulting picture is both incomplete and uneven. Some areas of the past are clearly defined, others only sketchily known, while the edges of the picture fade off into darkness. Too much remains unstudied and unknown. More questions are raised than answered, and only more research into the history of Punjab and its geographical neighbors will enable scholars to relate fully the events in this study to the broader picture of nineteenth-century British India. This volume itself is the first of three interlinked studies of Punjabi Hindus during the same period: an examination of the modernization of Hindu orthodoxy will follow and in turn be followed by a study of the changing social structure among Punjabi Hindus. The three volumes together will provide a basic picture of change within one community and one region of British India which, when related to other research, may begin to form a greater mosaic of cultural interaction between South Asian civilization and the West.

Historians who seek to understand the intricacies of cultural interaction and social change are faced with a series of hurdles. First and most fundamental is the complex and extremely diverse nature of the source materials. They are found in a variety of languages, physically scattered and of an extremely diverse nature encompassing government documents, tracts, journals, newspapers, diaries, memoirs, private papers, organizational reports, and records. They are rarely written with objectivity in mind, but more often than not are polemical or propagandistic. They reflect attitudes, values, and beliefs. This raises the second hurdle facing a social historian. He only partially deals with reality, with what happened, but also must focus on "subjective reality"—what people believed happened. Social and cultural history is created out of an interaction between these two forms of reality, the latter often more relevant than the former. For the forces that lie behind human action are most often based on fears and hopes embedded in subjective visions of a real world. Whether the British discriminated against Hindus in the 1890s is a question of reality; whether Hindus believed that such discrimination was taking place is a question of subjective reality. An historian must see both realities and the interaction between the two if he is to understand the dynamics of change and motivation. Lastly, the complexity of this past needs an analytic and conceptual framework if it is to be more than mere chronology. In much of historical writing such frameworks are well established by previous scholarship, but in the area of cultural interaction in a colonial milieu, theory is still in the earliest stages of development. The conceptual framework for this volume has been created from a variety of sources: the work of Erik Erickson on identity and maturation, of Anselm Strauss on the psychological implications of shifts in terminology, Gerald D. Berreman on acculturation among the Aleuts, Wolfram Eberhard with his studies of social change in China and Turkey, David Kopf on the concept of the golden age, John Broomfield on elites, Francis L. K. Hsu on the nature of Hindu society, and M. N. Srinivas on Sanskritization and Westernization. In this volume the theoretical underpinnings must remain implicit; an explicit statement awaits further research, reflection, and writing.

The debts I owe both to individuals and institutions are far too many to list here, but some of them must be acknowledged. First, to Percival Spear, my thanks for introducing me to South Asian

Studies when I was still a raw undergraduate so many years ago, and to Professors Thomas R. Metcalf and Eugene F. Irschick for their patience during the travails of my dissertation. The American Institute of Indian Studies provided the most fundamental assistance to this research by enabling me to work in India on two separate occasions, 1963–1964 and 1968–1969. Without their support this research would have been impossible. The Bureau of General Research of Kansas State University, through its annual grants, made possible continual research and writing. My personal thanks go to Professors N. Gerald Barrier, Ainslie T. Embree, Steven J. Golin, John R. Sisson, who provided criticisms and suggestions for this manuscript, and to Marguerite Jones whose editorial comments were invaluable. The errors, however, are mine alone.

In India many individuals bore patiently with my continual inquiries. The staffs of the Indian National Archives and the Nehru Memorial Museum were extremely helpful. My special thanks go to Dhan Keshwani who introduced me to the collection at the National Archives and to Vijaya Chandra Joshi who did the same for the Nehru Museum. Shri Joshi also introduced me to his many acquaintances among Punjabi Hindus. Perhaps my greatest debt goes to the many officers and members of the Arya Samaj who gave freely of their time and energy to a stranger endeavoring to understand their world. Those who worked at the Sarvadeshak Arya Pratinidhi Sabha, the Dayanand Anglo-Vedic College Trust and Management Committee, the Gurukul Kangri, and numerous other Samaj institutions provided invaluable assistance and access to historical materials. I particularly want to thank Lala Ganpat Rai who along with his family did much to make life in Punjab explicable. The staff of the Chandigarh *Tribune,* the fathers of the Cambridge Brotherhood in Civil Lines, the officers of the Naya Bans Arya Samaj Mandir in Old Delhi, and the staff of the Vishveshvaranand Vedic Research Institute of Hoshiarpur all graciously provided me with assistance and access to their collections of historical data. My personal thanks go to Shri Ram Sharma, Director of the Institute of Public Administration in Una, to Acharya Vishva Bandhu, Director of the Vishveshvaranand Institute, to Shri Dhareshwar of the Gurukul, and Shri Virendra of the *Daily Pratāp;* their encouragement and help greatly aided me in my research. Most of all I would like to thank the people of Punjab and particularly the members of the Arya Samaj who bore patiently and with good humor a stranger in search of their past.

I have used a minimal transliteration scheme in this volume, sufficient it is hoped to enable an individual knowledgeable in any of the relevant languages to recognize a word in its original form. The Punjab is a linguistic nightmare. During the nineteenth century and early twentieth, Punjabis wrote and published in a mixture of languages—Hindi, Urdu, Punjabi, English, and occasionally Persian, Arabic or Sanskrit. Transliterations into English followed little rhyme or reason, and spellings of a given name or term varied widely. When in doubt, I have followed either John T. Platts, *A Dictionary of Urdū, Classical Hindī and English,* or the *Mānak Hindī Kōsh.* With names, I have attempted to use customary patterns whenever possible. Absolute linguistic consistency would only distort historical reality. In writing Punjabi history, it is necessary to proceed firmly, grasping the Persian maxim, *Himmat-i-mardān, madad-i-khudā* (God helps those who help themselves).

KENNETH W. JONES
*Manhattan, Kansas*

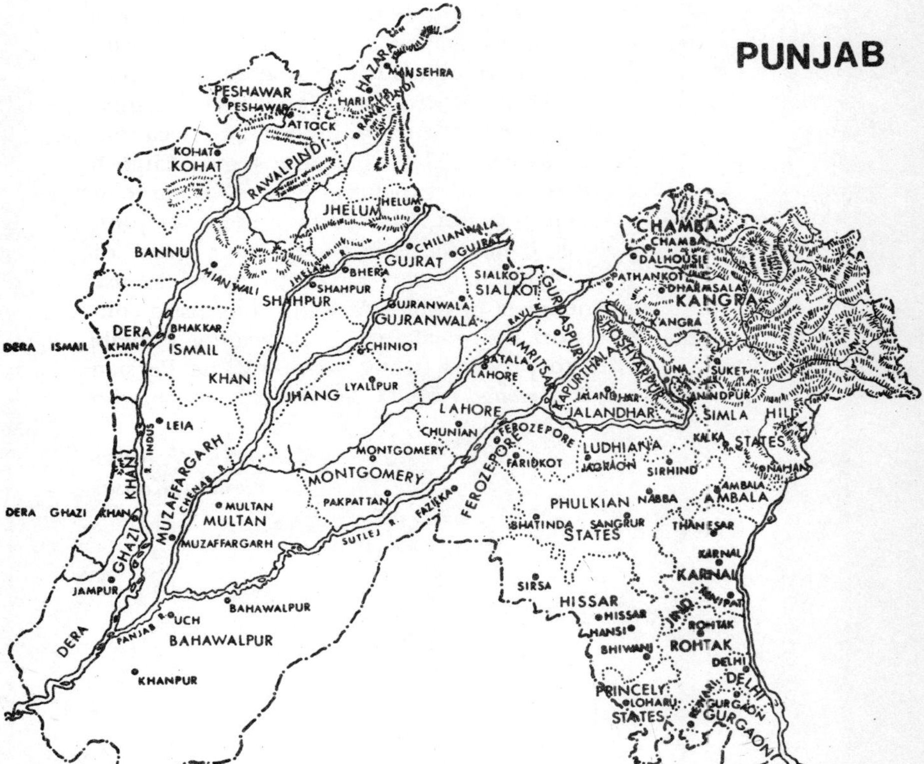


Adapted from the Handbook of The Punjab, Western Raputana, Kashmir and Upper Sindh (London, 1883).

Scale

50 0 50 100 150

# Chapter I

# THE BEGINNING OF CHANGE

We must at present do our best to form a class who may be interpreters between us and the millions whom we govern; a class of persons, Indian in blood and color, but English in taste, in opinions, in morals, and in intellect.

THOMAS BABINGTON MACAULAY

## THE PUNJABI HINDU

The forces of cultural change and modernization unleashed by British conquest swept the South Asian subcontinent. New forms of affiliation and action arose following the establishment of the British Raj and the resultant introduction of a foreign culture. Although the forces behind this conquest remained constant for much of British India, regional patterns of traditional life, of social structure, and of historical experience molded behavior and determined cultural adaptation. It is here in the regional context that one can best see the dynamics of interaction within British India. The Punjab, both as a division of the British administrative structure and as a cultural region within the South Asian subcontinent, provides one such context for the study of cultural interaction. Punjab uniqueness has long been accepted though roughly delineated by both traditional and contemporary stereotypes. Often a corridor of conquest, a pathway to the rich plains and imperial cities of the Gangetic Plain, the Punjab experienced repeated waves of conquerors, would-be conquerors, and migrants. Stasis an impossibility, change became traditional, as survival precluded rigidity.

The original Hindu-Buddhist culture of the Punjab faced Islam and gradually gave way before it. By the mid-nineteenth century Muslim Punjabis accounted for half of the population. Migration and conversion created an Islamic community located predominantly in the western half of the province. Islam flowed from Afghanistan in a great wave down the mountain passes, along the foothills and out across the plains. High ground remained Hindu, as did the eastern and southeastern areas farthest from the Iranian Plateau. All of the province was affected by Islam and in this shared a common experience with Hindustan to the south. The eastern plains possessed a majority of 60 percent Hindus. The hills, east of the Ravi River, contained an overwhelming Hindu community of 94 percent, and only here did Hindu culture survive and dominate.[1] The Rajas and Brahmans of the hills maintained their ancient prerogatives and traditions. The Brahmans retained respect; the Rajput still ruled. On the plains Islam dominated politically for nearly eight hundred years, from the raids of the eleventh century to Ranjit Singh's ascent to the throne in 1799. Hindus might seize power briefly as individuals, they might staff the governments as groups, while petty Rajas survived, isolated and impotent, but Hindus did not rule. Politics became Islamicized and remained so until the late eighteenth century.

Cultural contact between the Islamic world and Hindu tradition created an historical situation similar to that of the nineneenth century. Hindus, who participated in this Muslim world, learned Persian and adjusted to a foreign culture, created new forms of identity, and new concepts of self. Born of such interaction, Sikhism altered the Punjab from within. A quietist movement owing much to Islam, the Sikhs were driven by persecution to militancy and finally to guerilla warfare against Muslim dominance. The Sikhs retained their ties to Hinduism but also converted heavily from it. Faced with two converting religions, the British would add a third; Punjabi Hindus were transformed into a minority. By 1891 they represented merely 40 percent of the province and continued to decline in the following census reports.[2] Theirs was a community on the defensive. Unable to protect themselves from competing religions, Hindus could envision the eventual extinction of their community.

The lack of political power molded the Hindu social structure. Rajputs and Brahmans possessed little leadership within the Hindu community. Muslim and Sikh political dominance under-

1. Government of India, *Census of India, 1891, the Punjab and Its Feudatories, Part I, the Report of the Census*, by E. D. Maclagan (Calcutta: Government of India, 1892), p. 88. [Hereinafter, *Census, Punjab Report 1891*.]

2. *Ibid.*

cut the role of the Rajput and challenged the position of the Brahman on two distinct but interrelated levels. First, Brahmans were denied their monopoly of religious symbols. Islam introduced new religious practitioners, while Sikhism created a new set of scriptures open to all. On the second level, Brahmans found their sources of income diminished. While Muslim rulers might support Hindu temples or ceremonies, such support was spasmodic and rare. Always inherent in the relations between priest and client was an element of subservience, of inferiority. Brahmans might claim superior sacerdotal status, but in the end they depended on the wealth of landowning and commercial castes. Possessed of little wealth and learning, the Punjabi Brahman served more affluent and influential castes, becoming in western areas heavily dependent on his traditional *jajmāns* (patrons). More followers than leaders, the Punjabi Brahmans, the third most numerous caste in the province, were the victims of history, an example of Hindu weakness and political impotence.[3] As with the Brahmans, Hindu Rajputs also held a circumscribed position within Punjab as they too lacked political power. Beyond the Punjab hills Muslim and Sikh aristocrats ruled the plain with but few Hindu exceptions.

The diminution of traditional priestly and ruling functions at the apex of Hindu society allowed for greater leadership in social and religious life on the part of the commercial castes, the Vaishyas. Monied, literate, serving in business, commerce, government and the professions, the Khatri, Baniya, Arora and Sud comprised a sensitive and creative section of Punjabi society. For here in the world of finance and the professions Hindus remained dominant. The inroads of conversion and migration struck the two extremes of Hindu society; the middle levels remained vital and living. Change and stasis interwoven into their heritage, the Punjabi Vaishya, like the Vicar of Bray, retained his position and, if possible, improved it under each political upheaval. The successive governments of the Mughals, Sikhs, British, and independent India have been staffed and, at times, led by men of these castes.

3. Among those who have commented on the peculiar position of the Punjabi Brahman are: M. N. Srinivas, *Social Change in Modern India* (Berkeley: University of California Press, 1966), pp. 9, 18; and Prakash Tandon, *Punjabi Century, 1857–1947* (London: Chatto & Windus, 1961), pp. 76–77.

Seldom at the top of society, the Punjabi Vaishyas allied with their Brahman followers possessed a tradition of innovation, of creative response to cultural and political change.

Creativity and leadership depend on perception and awareness of altered circumstances, capacity to act and the dissatisfaction or disorientation that propel the actor forward against his traditional patterns of culture. To be disoriented and marginal without resources, psychological or societal, to be rejected and made irrelevant, as were many members of the pre-British ruling elites, more often than not prohibited creativity. Lack of involvement, ignorance as to the nature of change, and knowledge that more than merely political power had altered characterized the peasant masses. For rural Punjab interaction with the new British power or the older conquerors was largely limited to problems of land revenue and law. The deeper patterns of life and thought remained unchallenged. It was in the cities, not the villages, that initial cultural interaction took place; there a new world came into being.

Cultural marginality was highly selective, flowing with the patterns of involvement. The classic village moneylender whose economic and cultural spheres remained rural and agriculturally-oriented shared with the village priest and peasant a world of limited cultural change. Only when drawn out of his village context, anglicized and urbanized, would a village literati join those who had gone before him. Leadership then was determined heavily by traditional roles and functions. Among Punjabi Hindus the Vaishyas would lead; among Vaishyas, the Khatri and his associates, the Saraswat Brahmans.[4] The Khatris claimed, with some justice and increasing insistence, the status of Rajputs, of Kshatriyas, a claim not granted by those above but illustrative of their

4. Highest in status among all the commercial groups, the Khatris tended to be ocated in cities, towns and the larger villages, with a concentration in central districts of the Punjab. While a majority of the Khatri caste engaged in trade, business and moneylending, their commercial relations were more often to princes, businessmen and merchants. They tended to support commerce, not agriculture, nor were they restricted to Vaishya occupations. In the districts of Hoshiarpur, Lahore, Gujrat and Gujranwala, Khatris owned land and lived at the level of landlords or petty chiefs, more Rajput in style than Baniya. Participation in past governments, Moghul and Sikh, both as high civil officials and military officers, gave to the Khatri a different tradition and perspective than the more lowly, purely commercial and rural Baniya, Arora or Sud. Denzil Ibbetson, *Panjab Castes* (Lahore: Government Printing, Punjab, 1916), pp. 247–248.

ambiguous position on the great *varna* scale of class divisions and their importance within the Hindu community. Possessed of questionable and flexible status in the traditional hierarchy, literate, urban, and often wealthy, in search of recognition for their achievements and pretensions, the Khatris acted as "traditional innovators," leaders into new worlds.

The restlessness exhibited by Hindu Vaishyas and their Brahman clients, many of whom no longer followed the priestly traditions, was echoed by the lowest level of Hindu society. Outcastes too responded to changed circumstances as they sought to leave their degraded social position through conversion to Islam, Sikhism and later to Christianity. This process of conversion created outcaste groups in all three religious communities. Interaction with new cultures remained limited for most outcastes and resulted in little significant change, for caste prejudice existed within the new world as well as the old. Servants of the foreigner might become minimally anglicized, or as Christian catechists participate in a new religion while a few received education in mission or government schools; but conversion for the majority of outcastes meant little difference in lifestyle or social position. At best they became clients subservient to the paternalism of Christian missionaries. Their new experiences were contained within the bounds of their own subcommunity and did not contribute to the creation of a modernized Hindu consciousness.

Punjabi Hindus would view the British from the perspective of their community, its past successes and contemporary dilemmas. The great Hindu tradition did not furnish them with a valid frame of reference. It was too vague, too universal, and too abstract. The regional stage proved more relevant, particularly as British administration created a concrete expression of that traditional yet imprecise entity "Punjab." Within the region lay a multiplicity of caste and subcaste social norms. Individual Punjabi Hindus found their basic frame of reference in the caste structure. Being not merely a Khatri but a Sarin Khatri provided a sense of place and identity. As reformers discovered, it was this level of the social world which punished deviation by proponents of change. The "specific tradition" of an individual's *jāti* or caste rather than the great tradition of his religion dictated expected social behavior. Here also can be found many of the tensions and ambiguities which determined social status and efforts toward social mobility.

From amidst these complexities of specific and regional traditions Punjabi Hindus viewed the British conquest, and then stepped forward to meet its new complexities.

### ANGREZĪ DHARM KĀ RĀJ (The Rule of English Duty)

British experience in Punjab proved unique. They arrived as conquerors and rulers, possessed of a mature imperial consciousness and lifestyle. From the beginning they were "sahibs," an identity transcending function. Here soldier, administrator, and missionary blended together into a whole, as they had nowhere else in India. British experience in Punjab combined an imperial ideology with the last period of creative administration. The Punjab was a new land, to be ordered and settled, molded by the hands of a chosen few. The Punjab, as a mid-nineteenth century conquest, opened the way to a concrete expression of Victorian imperial dreams. Here was a land of warlike tribes, sturdy peasants, defeated and waiting to be transformed into a model of imperial efficiency and administration. An ideal province that still lives as an image of how the empire was or, at least, how it should have been.

Lord Dalhousie annexed and so founded the famed "Punjab school" of administration. Departing from previous administrative practices, Dalhousie established a three-man board to administer the new territories. He chose the brothers, Henry and John Lawrence, along with Charles Mansell and they, in turn, brought in men of their own choice to staff the new provincial government. Dalhousie and the Lawrences shared certain basic attitudes and presuppositions. All disliked elaborate regulations, courts, judges, and especially lawyers. All preferred, instead of constitutionality and codes of procedures, direct personal rule, with swift, uncomplicated justice. There was in them a strong desire to change and to control. The Punjab system allowed Dalhousie direct detailed supervision of the provincial administration and at the same time created a system of government both economical and efficient.[5] The province was divided into divisions and districts with a corresponding commissioner and deputy commissioner. The latter ruled his district with the combined powers of revenue collector, magistrate and civil judge.[6] Each dis-

5. Eric Stokes, *The English Utilitarians and India* (Oxford: Clarendon Press, 1959), pp. 244–245, 248.

6. *Ibid.*, pp. 243–244.

trict officer was the *mā-bāp,* the patriarchal king of his district. He dominated by his moral force, by *izzat,* or face, the maintenance of which surpassed all other needs.[7]

Ideology and personality meshed. Both the military and civilian traditions of British rule mingled in the Punjab. Paternalism and a strong utilitarian sense of authority, inherited from the work of R. M. Bird and James Thomason in the North-Western Provinces,[8] blended with the military tendency to use force, to reform and govern by the sword. An underlying and ever-present feature of the Punjab administration was its ready use of violence and acceptance of such use as a matter of policy. For they believed in "over-awing, by a prompt and stern initiative," . . . and would brook nothing short of absolute, active and positive loyalty. ". . . Government should not condescend to exist upon the moral sufferance of its subjects."[9] The frontier character of the Punjab, British respect and even fear of the "martial qualities" of Punjabis as well as their later dependence on Punjabis within the British Indian Army, heightened and extended this early use of military force. A strange blend of overt confidence, public righteousness and underlying fear formed the basis for Punjab administration, and produced a brittle, crystalline quality to life in that province.[10]

Manly, courageous, energetic and a lover of sports, the Punjab administrator—soldier- or civilian-bred—was also religious. An atheist "sahib" was as unthinkable as he would have been intolerable. Christianity had been integrated into the identity pattern of the British with the result that Christian missionaries occupied the

7. Norman Gerald Barrier, "Punjab Politics and the Disturbances of 1907," Ph.D. dissertation, Duke University, 1966, pp. 4–5.

8. Stokes, *The English Utilitarians,* p. 246.

9. Philip Woodruff, *The Men Who Ruled India,* Vol. I (New York: Schocken Books, 1953), p. 373, quoting Mr. Frederick Cooper, Deputy Commissioner at Amritsar.

10. One cannot help but be struck by the homosexual and oedipal qualities of many earlier Punjabi administrators. Many were bachelors, completely immersed in their work, apparently without sexual instincts; they seemed dedicated to a severe cult of virility, often tinged with sadism and violence, and found their outlets in pig-sticking, hunting and brotherly comradeship. To be manly was all. Philip Mason gives an excellent picture of this type: "Few of these men were married; they speak constantly of their mothers in terms as emotional as they use of their religion. Passion blazed in them and was harnessed to work and to bodily rigour. A man who wished for marriage before middle-age was frowned on: it was an infidelity to the ideal of work." Woodruff, *The Men Who Ruled India,* p. 325.

land in the wake of British conquest. Their first major station beyond Delhi was Ludhiana, the headquarters for later expansion into the Punjab. In 1834, John C. Lowrie, an American Presbyterian, founded the Ludhiana Mission which rapidly became a center of education, publishing, and proselytization. The Ludhiana Press was established in 1835 and soon produced a stream of tracts, pamphlets and journals in Punjabi, Hindi, Urdu, Persian and Kashmiri.[11] Through their publishing, missionaries both popularized and standardized the northwestern languages Burnt by the Sikhs in 1845 and by the mutineers in 1857, the mission press persisted. Within its first three years, the Ludhiana Press released 68,000 volumes, while other missionary presses soon added to this stream of polemical literature after 1849.[12]

Victory carried both Raj and missionary beyond the Sutlej. In November 1849, the American Presbyterians, led by Rev. John Newton and the Rev. C. W. Forman, arrived in Lahore with a staff of six missionaries. By December they had opened both a station and school.[13] The organizational ability and talents within the mission movement were extensive: so was its support. British officers and officials not only requested money, they donated it in large and consistent sums. Mission stations were brought into being and sustained through the funds and energy given by zealous Englishmen within the province. Whatever differences existed between governmental officials and missionaries remained hidden within the English community. Punjabis rarely, if ever, glimpsed such controversies. Instead, they saw Christianity and British rule as interlinked, the one an attribute of the other.

After the Mutiny of 1857–1858 Christian missionaries greatly extended their system of stations and intensified their proselytization. The 1850s had seen scattered stations established from the Punjabi Hills to Multan in the south and Attock in the west. By the 1880s there existed a network of missions covering the entire province. Missions stretched north of Delhi in a great system, a bent "E." One leg went from Delhi to Ambala, its back curved through

11. Punjab Government, *Gazetteer of the Ludhiana District, 1888–9* (Calcutta: Calcutta Central Press, n.d.), pp. 74–76. [Hereinafter *PG: Ludhiana, 1888–9.*]

12. *Ibid.*, pp. 75–76.

13. C. R. Ewing, *A Prince of the Church in India, Being a Record of the Li : of the Rev. Kali Charan Chatterjee, D.D., for Forty-eight Years a Missionary at Hoshyarpur, Punjab, India* (London: n. pub., 1918), pp. 45–46, and *PG: Lahore, 1893–4*, p. 95.

Lahore along the mountains to Peshawar; the upper leg stretched south along the edge of Afghanistan to Dera Ismail Khan, Tank and Dera Ghazi Khan; and the middle leg ran south to Multan. From the major stations radiated smaller missions in the district or *tahsīl* towns, and from there into the villages. In an arc above the plains, stations were scattered through the Punjab Hills into Kashmir.

Christian missions expanded both geographically and programmatically. Direct proselytizing through street and bazaar preaching, through the publication and dissemination of religious tracts and journals, and through education remained the major forms of Christian evangelism, but missionaries developed new methods and new dimensions of proselytization. In the 1860s the Church Mission Society opened medical missions, particularly along the frontier with its heavily Muslim population. These missions attracted numerous patients but few converts.[14] The *zanāna* mission and the Christian colony extended missionary activities into new directions. A logical outgrowth of proselytizing, the *zanāna* mission attempted to reach women in the seclusion of their homes. The tradition of *pardah*, seclusion, kept most women beyond the reach of Christian preaching until it was decided, in the 1860s, to send female missionaries to individual homes. Visiting during the day when the men were generally in the fields, missionaries succeeded in reaching the unreachable. Boredom was their ally. Conversion under these circumstances produced serious consequences. Punjabis strongly resented *zanāna* missionaries for tampering with their womenfolk and violating the sanctity of their homes. On occasion they accused the missionaries of "kidnapping" and "girl-stealing," when a new Christian convert fled her "heathen" environment for the protection of the sympathetic missionary. The *zanāna* mission produced not merely the cry of "religion in danger," but a more damning one, "subversion in the home."[15]

The Christian colony illustrated the direct links between government and missions. The Church Missionary Society of Lahore founded the first such colony in 1868 when it received a lease on

14. *PG: Dera Ismail Khan, 1883–4*, pp. 56–57.

15. See Government of India, *Selections from the Vernacular Newspapers Published in the Punjab*, volumes for 1888–1902. (Hereafter cited as *SPVP*.)

1,935 acres of land in the Chunian *tahsīl* of Lahore District. Irrigated by the newly-completed Bari Doab Canal, this land was extremely valuable, and Punjabi leaders understood well the significance of its acquisition by Christian missionaries. The Church Missionary Society, led by Robert Clark, established a model village, equipped with well-built cottages, schools, a training center, and an excellent road network. The Society gave converts their own plots to begin life under the direction and discipline of the missionaries. Landless and despised, these converts were largely Churas, outcastes from Amritsar District. The Christian colony, like the Spanish missions of California, grew up as a small community under the control and supervision of white missionaries and with the blessing of the government. Religious paternalism paralleled official policy.

Colonies, stations, schools, publications and preaching comprised the structural elements of the mission system, converts the substance of its success. Punjabis converted, in great numbers or small, depending on the yardstick employed for analysis. By 1881 Christian converts numbered 3,912 and were heavily concentrated in the central districts of Lahore, Amritsar and Sialkot, plus Delhi to the southeast. Together these four districts contained 2,168 converts. Missionaries had less success in the princely states, the west central districts of Montgomery, Jhang and Shahpur, and the border districts of Kohat and Dera Ismail Khan. Within ten years the Christian community expanded to 19,750 members (see map 2 on p. 11). Insignificant numerically, this marked an increase of 410 percent.[16] Though greatly encouraging to the missionaries, such percent of increase proved frightening to many leaders of the Islamic, Sikh, and Hindu communities. Nor were future statistics much more reassuring. By 1901 the convert community totalled 37,980 and by the following decade, 1911, it had grown to 163,994.[17] Still a tiny fraction of the total population, convert gains received considerable publicity and, taken not as an absolute number but as an indication of future trends, they promised the eventual sweeping away of all indigenous religions. Unlikely as such a possibility might be, to those already disturbed by the chal-

16. *Census, Punjab Report 1891*, pp. xliv, 97.

17. *Census, Punjab Report 1891*, p. 93; *Census, Punjab Report 1901*, p. 158; and *Census, Punjab Report 1911*, p. 129.

# The Distribution of Indian Christians in 1891

## by Districts

**Districts by Number**

1. Mandi *
2. Suket *
3. Hoshiarpur
4. Kapurthala *
5. Faridkot *
6. Nabba *
7. Patiala *
8. Jind *
9. Delhi
10. Simla
11. Chamba *
12. Kangra
13. Simla Hill States *
14. Ambala
15. Karnal
16. Rohtak
17. Gurgaon
18. Jullundur
19. Ludhiana
20. Patiala *
21. Hiss–

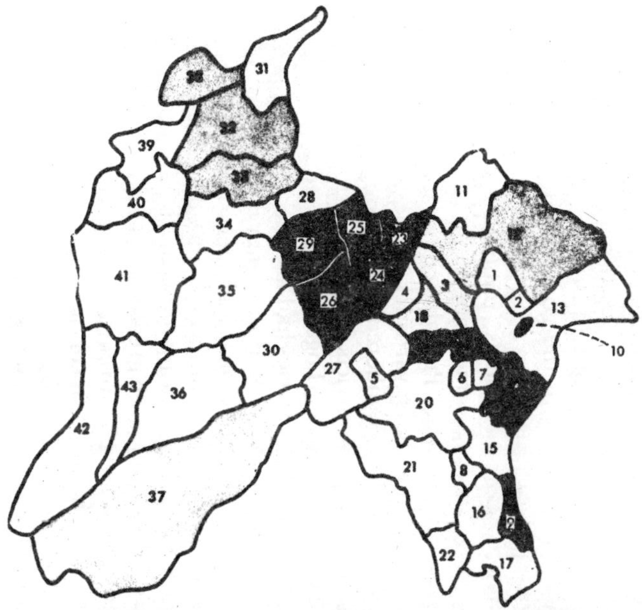

**Districts by Number**

22. Princely States *
23. Gurdaspur
24. Amritsar
25. Sialkot
26. Lahore
27. Ferozepore
28. Gujrat
29. Gujranwala
30. Montgomery
31. Hazara
32. Rawalpindi
33. Jhelum
34. Shahpur
35. Jhang
36. Multan
37. Bahawalpur *
38. Peshawar
39. Kohat
40. Bannu
41. Dera Ismail Khan
42. Dera Ghazi Khan
43. Muzaffargarh

* Princely State or States

1 - 100
101 - 250
251 - 500
501 - 1000
1000 and up

Adapted from the Census, Punjab Report 1891.

MAURICE SCHWANKE

lenges of new ideas introduced since annexation, the Christian threat was real.

Christian conversion followed patterns of previous religious inroads, striking at the two sections of the social structure. Initial conversions came from the upper levels of Punjab society, from the privileged and prestigious. Few in number and won individually, high caste converts accounted for far more public attention and reaction to Christian conversion than the numerically superior successes among the depressed. Repeatedly, conversion or the threat of conversion among students at mission schools, or members of the literate castes, produced a public uproar. For such conversions threatened the small but growing class of educated, sensitive Punjabis already faced with the need to adjust to British rule. The largest number of converts came from the outcastes, particularly the Churas. Among the largest castes numerically, Churas were also one of the lowest in social status. Sweepers, scavengers, and landless laborers, many had already been converted to Islam and Sikhism. They now responded to Christian proselytization as they had previously to those who promised both a changed theology and an altered social status. Missionaries were able to convert outcastes in large numbers. Mass conversion in one decade, 1881–1891, produced an increase of over 3,000 percent in the Christian community of Sialkot District.[18] Youth first, under the pervasive influence of mission and government schools, and outcastes second by mass conversion, it seemed only a matter of time before the British would complete their conquest, sweeping all before them—political, cultural, and religious.

The British in the Punjab presented an exaggerated and more extreme image of their presence elsewhere in the subcontinent. The confidence and enthusiasm of the Dalhousie period was preserved and legitimized by the Mutiny. Earlier attitudes lived on and fused with high imperial emotions of the late nineteenth century. The juggernaut of British rule crossed the Punjab plains to subdue, administer, convert, improve—without halt and without question. English duty, *"Angrēzī dharm,"* gave justification and direction to this new ruling caste. For the recruit from England already imbued with national and class consciousness of his homeland, the imperial subculture of the Raj completed his sense of

18. *PG: Sialkot, 1883–4*, p. 32; and *PG: Sialkot, 1894–5*, p. 46.

identity, supplying him with an ideology to legitimize his position at the apex of Punjab social structure. Above all else he knew who and what he was, and wore the sacred thread of imperial consciousness that set him apart from the "nigger," the "native," who, whatever he might be, could never be English.

## DOMINANCE OF AN IMPORTED ELITE

The inland march of British conquest carried with it both English administration and their anglicized allies. Just as British military strength ultimately rested on the "native" soldier, the government depended on the loyal services of the intellectual sepoy, the Indian clerk, teacher, translator, the "*Bābū*." Bengal, the first major area to be conquered, was also the first to possess an educated, anglicized class, a pool of trained men, willing and able to support the bureaucracy of imperial rule. Bengalis followed British power as it moved up the Gangetic Plain serving both government and non-governmental agencies. Brahmans and Baidyas from Bengal and Kayasthas from both Bengal and the North-western Provinces moved northwest in search of jobs. Annexation of the Punjab created an immediate need for trained subordinates to staff the new provincial government. Even with the exaggerated emphasis on personal rule, on individual decision and initiative, the administration needed an extensive system of clerks. What was true for the government was equally true for the missions. They too needed manpower to undergird expansion into the newly-conquered territory. Both Raj and Church filled their posts with men from Hindustan. Bengalis traveled to the Punjab settling predominantly in the cities, the centers of administration and political power. At home in the Raj, they dominated the social and intellectual world of the Punjab, for they brought with them forms of identity and acculturation, attitudes and ideologies already created in Bengal. The intellectual products of Bengal moved northward as did individual Bengalis from one community to the next. Social, religious and later political ideas passed along this network of human contacts created initially by British imperial expansion.

Punjabis recognized the advanced ideas brought into their province by Bengalis and accepted their leadership. "*Bābū*" was not yet a term of approbation, but an honored title denoting the successful Indian who had adjusted to this strange British-dominated world.[19] The greatest asset to social and religious progress were these "distinguished Bengali gentlemen who came to settle in Lahore, and who actually formed the vanguard of public life" in that city.[20] A small contingent of educated Punjabis and leaders of the Kayastha emigrants from the North-Western Province joined with these Bengalis to create a new "native" elite.[21] If part of the educated Punjabi community was willing to grant leadership and status to emigrant Bengalis, they themselves were acutely aware of their own superiority. "Bengali Babus were to be seen in all the Government Offices, Schools and Dispensaries and a few Punjabis who were in service considered it best to obey and serve them, whom they respected as their leaders and teachers."[22] Punjab was a backward province and those who possessed the light should do all to aid and assist it. S. P. Bhattacharjee described his early attempts to mobilize fellow Bengalis: "I drew their attention to the fact that they were maintaining themselves on the wealth of this province which was in its infancy, where the inhabitants were all raw materials with not mature experience and as they were much more educated and civilized than the Panjabis they should feel themselves in duty bound to lead them to the right path, to enlighten their gloomy minds and to ask them to follow their footsteps."[23] The urge to convert, tutor and instruct the poor Punjabi was not limited to Englishmen; their countrymen too would guide them toward enlightenment.

Bengalis and Hindustanis provided two models of adaptation: Christian and Brahmo. Bengali Christians settled in Punjab in the 1850s. Converted in Bengal they came primarily to staff mission-

19. Prakash Tandon, *Punjabi Century*, p. 17.

20. Bhagat Lakshman Singh, *Autobiography*, ed. Ganda Singh (Calcutta: Sikh Cultural Centre, 1965), p. 45.

21. Babu Pratul Chandra Chatterji, Kali Prosana Roy, Jogindra Chandra Bose, and Novin Chandra Rai were among the most prominent of the Bengalis, while Lala Har Sukh Rai, proprietor of the *Kōh-i-Nūr* newspaper and press, Pandit Gopi Nath and his brother of the *Akhbār-i-'Ām*, represented the Kayastha community of Lahore. See Bhagat Lakshman Singh, *Autobiography*, pp. 45–46.

22. S. P. Bhattacharjee, *Memoirs of the Official Career of S. P. Bhattacharjee, Late Superintendent, Office of the Superintendent Engineer, 3rd Circle, Punjab P. W. Department, Lahore, 1894*, p. 8.

23. *Ibid.*, p. 9.

ary schools and societies. Pandit Golak Nath Chatterji, a Bengali Brahman and the first Indian convert of the American Presbyterian Church, moved north to head the Jullundur mission,[24] while Radha Raman Raha, a fellow Bengali, began his career in the Punjab as a teacher in one of the mission schools.[25] Others soon followed. Kali Charan Chatterjee, the most eminent of all Bengali Christians, came to the Punjab in 1861 at the invitation of Pandit Golak Nath. Kali Charan accepted a position as headmaster of the Jullundur Mission School and in 1862 married Golak Nath's daughter.[26] The flow of Bengali Christians, almost all Brahmans, produced a small but compact community of converts. Tied to each other through religion, regional culture and often by marriage, the Bengali converts found themselves both a part of the white Christian world and their old parent regional culture. They too traveled to Calcutta and in turn hosted Bengalis visiting the Punjab. They too were part of a communications system, stretching up the Gangetic Plain, from Bengal to the Indus. Educated, generally of high caste and closely associated with the new regime, Bengali Christians provided Punjabis with one model of adjustment and accommodation: it was a model that few Punjabis accepted.

The process of alienation and its resulting search for identity which first affected Bengal produced Raja Ram Mohun Roy and the Brahmo Samaj. Roy's attempt to reinterpret Hinduism through a return to Upanishadic rationalism, his simultaneous rejection of popular religious forms and Christian pretensions, set a pattern that reappeared repeatedly through the subcontinent. A new tradition, reinterpreted and refurbished, fused with the institutional and organizational patterns of the Christian church and allied with contemporary forms of communication, marked the beginnings of modern intellectual life in South Asia. Bengalis constructed the first model of successful acculturation and then carried it with them as they spread beyond their home province. If the English brought a form of poison, then Bengalis supplied one antidote, one acculturative pattern that others could accept and call their own.

24. C. R. Ewing, *A Prince of the Church in India*, p. 42.

25. Narendra Nath Gupta, *Reflections and Reminiscences* (Bombay: Hind Kitabs, 1947), pp. 171–172.

26. Ewing, *A Prince of the Church in India*, pp. 67–68.

A small group of Bengalis, with a few Punjabi enthusiasts, founded the Brahmo Samaj of Lahore in 1863.[27] Over the next two decades branches were opened in Rawalpindi, Amritsar, Multan, Rupar, Simla and Dera Ghazi Khan, but only the parent Lahore Samaj and the Simla branch remained active.[28] Both Lahore and Simla contained cohesive and stable Bengali communities which supported the Brahmo Samaj with funds and talent. Here also could be found educated Punjabis who joined the Samaj and accepted Bengali leadership. Bengali Brahmos faced similar problems in attracting Punjabis to their program as did the missionaries. Both possessed an ideology, a message they wished to disseminate among the less enlightened Punjabi. Both were foreign and spoke languages unknown in the northwest. In 1876, the Brahmo Samaj founded a society to translate its literature into Punjabi, Hindi and Urdu. and in 1877 they established one of the few Brahmo presses outside of Bengal. Proselytization rested upon literacy. Brahmo tracts and the monthly journal, *Hārī Hakīkat,* brought their message to the literate few, to the new elites of the Punjab,[29] as did the continued travels of Brahmo missionaries and leaders. From Bengal came Keshab Chandra Sen in 1867 and 1873, Debendra Nath Tagore in 1867, 1872, and 1874, and a series of lesser known Brahmo figures either singularly or in groups.

From the beginning a small but socially significant number of educated Punjabis participated in the Brahmo Samaj and were closely linked to the Bengali community. Primarily Hindus, the four Punjabi founders of the Lahore Samaj were all Hindu clerks; a few Sikhs also allied themselves with the Brahmo Samaj and its Bengali members. Bengalis stood for all that was new or modern. Successful and socially daring, they provided young Punjabis with

27. There is some debate over this. Bhattacharjee gives September 1862 as the founding date, see Bhattacharjee, *Memoirs,* p. 11; also Sivanatha Sastri, *History of the Brahmo Samaj* (Calcutta: R. Chatterjee, 1911), Vol. II, p. 394; while Sophia Dobson Collet gives 1863 in the *Brahmo Year-Book* for 1880.

28. S. D. Collet, ed., *The Brahmo Year-Book for 1876. Brief Records of Work and Life in the Theistic Church of India* (London: William & Norgate, 1876), p. 18; G. S. Chhabra, *The Advanced History of the Panjab Ranjit Singh and Post Ranjit Singh Period,* Vol. II (Ludhiana: Parkash Brothers, 1962), p. 348.

29. S. D. Collet, *The Brahmo Year-Book for 1876,* p. 36; *The Brahmo Year-Book for 1877,* pp. 15, 38; and *PG: Lahore 1893–94,* p. 92.

models for identification and emulation. Few other patterns of life were available except traditional roles which could no longer be accepted. Bengalis offered a lifestyle and, as Brahmos, institutional patterns for adaptation.

If imitation is a form of flattery, opposition is a measure of success. The Brahmo Samaj generated critics among orthodox Hindus, both Punjabi and Bengali. The founding of the Lahore Samaj and the conversion of Babu Novin Chandra Rai produced an immediate drop in the number of subscriptions to the local Kali temple.[30] Orthodox Hindus reacted to this loss of support as they were to react throughout the Punjab to criticism from and demands for religious reform which emanated from the Brahmo Samaj. From its inception the Brahmo Samaj represented a direct challenge to orthodox Hinduism. It was in the eyes of many Punjabis "un-Hindu" and beyond the pale of social acceptance. Yet opposition from those who sought to retain tradition and to deflect the challenges of modernity was both expected and tolerable. Far more ominous for the future of Punjabi Brahmos were points of friction within the movement, between its Bengali and Punjabi members.

Brahmo Samaj ideology combined syncretism with radical reform. Created before Christianity was an integral part of the British government, and when imperial ideology was still unformed, Brahmos expressed a tolerance and appreciation of Christian ethics ill-suited to Punjab of the late nineteenth century. Brahmos sought equivalence with the Christian West, claiming that at their core all religions were good, all strove for the same ends, and utilized much the same methodology. Theistic, rational and syncretistic, Bengali Brahmos tended to be extreme in their rejection of contemporary Hinduism. They proclaimed widow remarriage acceptable, ate communal meals, discarded the thread of orthodoxy, and rejected established forms of Hindu worship. As a consequence, Brahmos generated orthodox opposition and "roused the hatred of the people towards the Brahmo Samaj."[31] Many Punjabis saw Brahmos as apostates who had forsaken the faith of their ancestors. Bengalis might choose this degree of

30. Bhattacharjee remarked that "Wherever Bengali Baboos went and took up service, they established a shrine of Kali for worship and amusement's sake." S. P. Bhattacharjee, *Memoirs*, pp. 220–221.

31. *Ibid.*

radicalism, but few Punjabis followed them. The *Prīti Bhōjan,* or love feasts, held by the Brahmo Samaj proved too daring for many of the Punjabi Brahmos and clearly divided the membership between those who would and would not attend.[32] Similar points of division arose over intercaste marriages sponsored by the Samaj. Punjabis in this movement, as in later social and religious reforms, were unwilling to break with Hinduism, choosing rather to call for change while retaining their caste ties intact.

The tolerant acceptance of other faiths, in particular of Christianity, that characterized Bengali Brahmos found few adherents in mid-century Punjab. Such syncretism gave little support to Punjabi Hindus surrounded by proselytizing religions and fearful of Christian conversion. Brahmo ideology had been formed of a gentler age and mere equivalence no longer sufficed. Brahmo concepts fitted the Bengali experience with its unique regional heritage and historical experience. During the 1860s and 1870s the Brahmo Samaj provided many Hindu and Sikh intellectuals of the Punjab with an acceptable pattern of action and identification. In time they would reject it.

### PUNJABIS IN SEARCH OF THE FUTURE, 1850–1880

The wave of British conquest brought in its wake a secondary wave of cultural change. From Delhi to southeastern Punjab, the Jullundur Doab, and finally Lahore a process of interaction between the alien and indigenous cultures gained momentum throughout the second half of the mid-nineteenth century.

Each community within the Punjab, Muslim, Sikh, and Hindu, met the British conquest and its associated introduction of a new civilization from its own historic perspective. Although the circumstances differed, each community possessed a sense of defeat and frustration. Muslims of Punjab and the entire northwest had the sharpest and oldest awareness of decline from past preeminence. The Moghul collapse followed by a rise in Maratha, Sikh, and finally British power highlighted their own communal weakness. Well before the arrival of the British, Muslim leaders sought to reestablish their community and end its slow degeneration. Muslim thinkers, led by Shah Wali-ullah, hoped to restore Islamic

32. Ruchi Ram Sahni, "Self-Revelations of an Octogenarian," unpublished manuscript in the possession of V. C. Joshi, Nehru Memorial Museum, p. 238.

glory through an end to internal divisiveness and a return to religious purity. Muslims would purge their community of Hindu practices and customs which had crept in over the past centuries. They would also stress the brotherhood of Islam and so dampen the sectarian conflicts which pitted Muslim against Muslim. Only a truly Islamic community could hope to find again its past preeminence.

Under the leadership of Shan Abdul Aziz and Sayyid Ahmad Barelvi this movement for restoration became increasingly political, culminating in the struggle for a new Muslim-controlled state. Beginning in 1826, Sayyid Ahmad Barelvi led a *jihad* or holy war against the Sikh kingdom of Ranjit Singh. Located on the northwestern border of the Sikh domain and largely unsuccessful, this campaign exemplified the determination of Muslim thinkers to reestablish Islamic dominance. After the annexation of the Punjab, the British inherited this war and finally crushed it in 1868. This defeat and the end of the Mutiny plunged the Islamic community into deeper despair. They had failed to revive their communal fortunes by either political or military means. They stood suspect in the eyes of the British and were beset by new threats. Christian polemicists attacked Islamic beliefs, and conversion threatened to diminish the size of the Islamic community. Hindus provided a growing economic competition and also became increasingly assertive. The lines separating Muslim from non-Muslim were sharpened by forces within the Islamic community and without. This demarcation had always been clearest at the level of high religion, in the cities, and among Islamic thinkers, but there had always been points of conflict between Muslim and non-Muslim.

Communal riots and struggles over the protection of kine existed long before the arrival of the British. But they soon added another element to religious competition: the printing press. Muslims and non-Muslims quickly adapted this new technique to their tradition of communal strife. In 1852 Sheikh Salim of Delhi published *Kathā Salvī*, a vicious satire on Hinduism, and by the 1860s tract conflicts appeared between defenders of Islam and Hindu critics.[33] Printing came first to the towns to the southeast of Punjab. Bareilly, Moradabad, Agra, Meerut, and Delhi became centers of

33. Another early example of this trend was Muhammad 'ubaid Allah's *Tohfa-ul-Hind* (A Gift to India) (Ludhiana: 1963). Munshi Inderman of Moradabad car-

publication, of Islamic cultural creativity, and of communal competitiveness. Strangely, during the 1840s and 1850s, printing presses in the North-Western Provinces were located in the western towns with the sole exception of Benares.[34] Prior to annexation, presses also existed in Ludhiana and after 1846 in Simla. By the mid-1850s presses quickly became established in Lahore, Amritsar, Multan, Gujranwala, and Sialkot. The creation of modern publishing brought a new dimension to intercommunal relations and also opened the Punjab to influences from beyond the province, which, in turn, acted upon and modified the internal world of Punjab. Punjabi Muslims possessed a unique heritage which even included limited cooperation with the Sikh kingdom of Ranjit Singh, but after 1849 they would act and react within the broader perspective of subcontinental Islam.

Sikhs, unlike Muslims, were primarily a Punjabi community. They did not possess a broader subcontinental framework, but would live and die by their unique and specific provincial heritage. They were, however, bifurcated between Cis-Sutlej Sikhs, who resided within British territory, and the remainder of the community within the Sikh Kingdom. Annexation ended this division and reunited all Sikhs under the British. Sikhs shared with Muslims and Marathas a heritage of political dominance. They could look back to yesterday when they ruled and see around them in the Sikh princely states evidence of their past dominance. Their heritage was a closely interwoven history of religion and politics cemented by armed struggle against a host of Islamic opponents. Perhaps of all communal divisions those of the Sikh and Muslim were the clearest, hardest, and least ambiguous. As a small minority they had scant choice but to accept British rule for they themselves could do little and no allies stood ready to join with them. But acceptance of English rule was painful for some Sikhs. The nearness

---

ried out a campaign against Islam for nearly a decade, producing a series of tracts which in turn generated further replies by Muslim writers. See Munshi Inderman, *Saulat-i-Hind* (Fury of India) (Moradabad: 1868); also his *Tohfāt-ul-Islām* (Gifts to Islam) (Gujranwala: 1968); and the tract by Muhammad Ali, *Zafar-i-Mubīn* (Victory Clarified) (Bareilly: 1873).

34. This pattern persisted into the 1860s although not with the same degree of exclusiveness. See *Selections from the Records of the North-Western Provinces, Report on Native Presses in the North-Western Provinces* (annual reports published by the Government in Allahabad).

in time of their own political dominance made reduction to an impotent minority status psychologically difficult. They, like the Muslims, would seek answers for their defeat and paths to communal revival. The Namdharis exemplify this search, for they would purify the Sikh faith and create a separate world from the newly-arrived British Raj. Their failure and suppression demonstrated that overt separation was impossible. Leadership within the Sikh community fell to anglicized Sikhs who would find accommodation with the new empire while striving to rejuvenate Sikh society.

Punjabi Hindus, like the Sikhs, were a minority, geographically divided between the small kingdoms of the Himalayan foothills and the greater Hindu community of the Indo-Gangetic plains. The hill Hindus lived in a socio-political environment which had adjusted to and survived under both Islamic and Sikh rule. The British appeared as one more invading power necessitating another round of adjustment for survival. The British conquest swept past the hills creating little need for immediate change in either policy or lifestyle.

The Hindus of the plains, unlike the Sikhs and Muslims, had no political heritage. They had not ruled in Punjab since the thirteenth century and could only turn to their religious and cultural heritage for communal identity and revitalization. Their history was one of dominance by foreigners and representatives of two conversion religions. Their past was one of defeat and slow decline, but against this stood two trends. First, many of the upper caste Punjabi Hindus had been successful in exploiting opportunities for employment and power under non-Hindu states; and second, unlike the Sikhs, they were members of the greater community of Hindus throughout the subcontinent. Provincially in a minority, they were members of the majority community in South Asia. Both Hindus and Muslims possessed majority and minority status depending on how they were viewed. Muslims were a majority in Punjab, a minority in South Asia, and members of a great world community. Hindus were a minority in Punjab, a majority in South Asia, and members of a unique but somewhat isolated community on a world-wide scale. Only the Sikhs retained a consistent minority status whatever yardstick was used to measure them. Yet even the Sikhs could be among a majority if they were considered a subsection of the Hindu community. Majority and minority status then were not determined by statistics but perception, and perception was more often than not shaped by underlying fears. For all three communities the arrival of the British meant defeat and new threats to their security. This threat was not equal. Punjabi Hindus lost the least, adapted the quickest, and became the most successful of all three communities within this new and strange world of the British Raj.

Punjabi Hindu interaction with the British began in 1827 with the introduction of English education in the Old Delhi College. Students came to Delhi from the surrounding area to study, and by the 1830s a small group of educated young men formed the nucleus of a new anglicized elite in that city. One of the most famous, Ram Chandra, traveled to Delhi in 1833 from his home in Panipat in order to join the College. A brilliant student, he became a professor of mathematics at the College soon after his graduation.[35] Yet his academic success pointed to the dangers inherent in Western education, for in the process of his training he converted to Christianity. This and his advocacy of new imported ideas, science and rationalism, created considerable opposition among the local citizens. "We commenced," he wrote, "a monthly magazine at the cheap rate of four-pence a month in which notices of English Science were given. Not only were the dogmas of ancient philosophy exposed, but many of the Hindu superstitions were openly attacked. The result of this was that many of our countrymen condemned us as infidels and irreligious."[36] A second Hindu student, Dr. Chiman Lal, also converted to Christianity, but apostacy had its cost in Delhi. With the Mutiny, Indian Christians became targets of hatred second only to Europeans. Chiman Lal was killed and Ram Chandra barely escaped. Those who had criticized orthodoxy, whether Hindu or Muslim, were suspect. Most of the newly educated left Delhi during or after the Mutiny, bringing to an abrupt end the intellectual ferment of the previous two decades.

Although shattered by the Mutiny, the Delhi experience contributed directly to cultural change within the Punjab proper. A participant in the Delhi Renaissance, Munshi Kanhya Lal Alakhdhari maintained a pre-eminent position in the Punjab as an advo-

35. C. F. Andrews, *Zaka Ullah of Delhi* (Cambridge: W. Heffer & Sons, Ltd., 1929), pp. 37–38.

36. *Ibid.*, p. 40. Ram Chandra founded two Urdu journals for the propagation of his ideas, *Mahbūb-i-Hind* and *Favāid-i-Nazarīn;* Muhammad Sadiq, *A History of Urdu Literature* (London: Oxford University Press, 1964), p. 400.

cate of social and religious reform for nearly three decades, until his death in 1882. He linked the earlier intellectual creativity of Delhi with the rising young educated Punjabis of the 1870s. Kanhya Lal began his career as a Hindu reformer in 1853 with the twin publications of *Chirāg-i-Hakīkat (Light and Truth)* and *Sham'-i-Ma'rifat (Light of Knowledge).*[37] In 1858 he founded the Gyan Press at Agra and began to publish a steady stream of writings on religion, mathematics, physics, household and political economy, social customs and morals. Particularly important for later Hindu thought were Kanhya Lal's translations into Urdu of the *Bhāgavad Gītā, Upanishads,* and *Yōg Vaishistc.*[38] In addition to Hindu scriptures he translated selections from Islamic literature and wrote a sketch of the life of Christ, "so that the Hindus may learn the religious tenets of Mohammedanism and Christianity and be well fortified against their invasions."[39] During the 1860s and 1870s, Kanhya Lal traveled widely throughout the Punjab, a lone reformer with a bitter tongue and sharp pen.

In 1872, after resigning from his position as manager of Khalsia State, friends asked him to start a society similar to Sayyid Ahmad Khan's for the regeneration of the Hindu community. In typically acid style, he replied that "The case of the Mohammedans was far different. They had lost their power only one hundred years ago, while the Hindus had been in this state of imbecility and degeneracy since 800 years. There is no possibility of success in this direction, especially when the unworthy sons of the Aryan rishis preferred the worship of trees, stones, and rivers, and Mohammedan tombs to that of the Almighty Providence and they think themselves bound to observe the popular bad customs instead of those prescribed in the Vedas and Dharm Shastras."[40] In spite of this expressed disillusionment Kanhya Lal founded a reform society, the Niti Prakash Sabha (Society for Moral Enlightenment) in Ludhiana in March 1873. This new society achieved local influence and notoriety by dividing the Hindus of Ludhiana into reformist and orthodox factions, but did not result in any sus-

37. These works were written in Shahpur and printed in Agra, *Arya* (Lahore), August 1882, p. 117.

38. *Ibid.* By 1867 Kanhya Lal had translated the *Upanishads, Tribune,* April 23, 1913, p. 2.

39. *Arya,* August 1882, p. 117.

40. *Ibid.*

tained move toward redefining Hinduism, a judgment that applies equally well to Kanhya Lal's entire career. He was always a loner, an important figure, a catalyst for later change, but never the leader of a movement; the yet fetal nature of the new Punjabi Hindu elite precluded such a role. Individuals might become concerned over the nature of Hindu society or religion, but their efforts to change remained disparate and unconnected. The only center of sustained intellectual questioning was Lahore, with its cohesive Bengali community and its growing numbers of educated Punjabis.

In 1866, Lala Behari Lal and Pandit Bhanu Datta Bassant Ram joined Novin Chandra Rai and S. P. Bhattacharjee to found the Lahore Sat Sabha (Society of Truth), a reform organization focused solely on Punjabi society.[41] The Sabha was dedicated to social reform and education, as was the Brahmo Samaj, but with the one major difference—the Sat Sabha sought to utilize Punjabi as the sole medium of its work. Although Behari Lal publicly opposed the principles of the Brahmo Samaj, the new society followed Brahmo patterns of worship, and clearly adopted its organizational structure. So close were the two societies in form that initially the Sat Sabha was taken to be a branch of the Brahmo Samaj.[42] Besides organizational techniques the Sat Sabha borrowed most of its ideological orientation from the Brahmo Samaj. It too was eclectic and theistic, and in later years came to be criticized for its willingness to borrow from Christianity. Outspoken Punjabis labeled both the Sat Sabha and the Brahmo Samaj as being "tainted with foreignism."[43] The Sat Sabha's lack of an independent ideology precluded success on any significant scale although it succeeded in establishing a school in 1882 and retained some life of its own throughout the 1880s.[44]

Although movements for social change grew from the context of British rule, they were also sponsored by British administrators,

41. S. P. Bhattacharjee, *Memoirs,* p. 12. Lala Behari Lal was manager of the Sat Sabha and Bhattacharjee its secretary.

42. S. Sastri, *History of the Brahmo Samaj,* Vol. II, pp. 395–396; *Tribune,* March 23, 1887, p. 5.

43. Bawa Chhajju Singh, *The Life and Teachings of Swami Dayanand Saraswati* (Lahore: Addison Press, 1903), p. 337.

44. G. W. Leitner, *History of Indigenous Education in the Panjab since Annexation and in 1882* (Calcutta, 1883), p. 98.

particularly during the 1850s and 1860s. The determination of the new government to suppress infanticide led to a generalized attack on a whole series of marriage customs, including the dowry system, elaborate rituals, large wedding parties and lavish rewards to those who performed the marriage ceremonies. British officers attempted to achieve reforms through pressure on the aristocrats as the "natural leaders" of society.[45] Governmental actions also delineated areas of social customs that became approved targets for later reformers whose motivation stemmed from changes within themselves and their communities. Gradually, leadership shifted from the government and its aristocratic clients to the new educated elites, first the Bengalis and afterward the Punjabis.[46]

In 1865, Dr. G. W. Leitner founded the Anjuman-i-Punjab, the most successful of European-led efforts to influence Punjabi opinion. Dr. Leitner had reached Lahore the previous year to take the position of Principal in the newly-organized Government College. He arrived a recognized scholar of Oriental languages and literature, with a reputation in England and Europe. Leitner immediately began to express his views on indigenous, vernacular, and classical education, their intrinsic worth and the need for their revival. The Anjuman, under his leadership, moved to reform educational policy in four directions: (1) the establishment of a University of the Punjab, (2) the revival of Arabic and Sanskrit learning, (3) the introduction of European science to the general population through education in the vernacular languages, and (4) raising the standards of English education.[47]

45. On October 29–31, 1853, a grand *darbār* (reception) was held at Amritsar to abolish infanticide. "The gathering at Amritsar was both representative and impressive. Rajas, especially of Suket, Chamba and Noorpur, many gentlemen of rank and position in the Punjab, Members of the late Durbar, Chieftains from the Kangra Hills, the Bedees of Dera Baba Nanak, Commissioners and landlords and merchants attended. Raja Dinanath and Raja Sahib Dyal presided over the deliberations of the Brahman and Khatree Committees." For an excellent description of this approach, see V. N. Datta, *Amritsar Past and Present* (Amritsar: Municipal Committee, 1967), p. 46.

46. An example of government-inspired reform was the Sikhsha Sabha of Lahore. Founded in response to Sir Robert Montgomery's urging, this Sabha attempted to promote female education, although with little success. Within a few years the Sabha had disappeared, leaving behind as its sole memorial the Sikhsha Sabha Hall, a popular public forum in later years. *Tribune*, May 13, 1893, p. 4.

47. Joachim H. Stockqueler, *A Review of the Life and Labours of Dr. G. W. Leitner* (Brighton: The Tower Press, 1875), pp. 10–11.

Leitner's campaign found sympathetic support from Punjabi aristocrats and some members of the Western educated community. The Anjuman, with its meetings, reading room and lecturers, soon became a powerful voice in local and provincial affairs, as Dr. Leitner's own influence expanded. In 1870, the society began publishing *Akbhār-i-Anjuman-i-Punjāb*, an Urdu monthly, which added an English edition in 1881. During the late sixties and early seventies the Anjuman and Leitner remained at the center of educational and cultural developments, but toward the end of the 1870s a gulf appeared between Leitner, with his insistence on "Oriental" learning, and the rising Punjabi elite, who demanded expansion of English education. This argument between "Orientalists" and "Anglicizers" became bitter, abrasive and public with the opening of the 1880s, as a combination of Bengali and Punjabi leaders challenged Leitner's influence.

Punjabi Hindus in their publications reflected both the forces for continuity and change. Several strands appear in their writings. Reacting to British initiative, Hindus called for an end to infanticide,[48] perhaps the earliest form of social reform, but the bulk of Hindu publications during the 1850s and 1860s was essentially traditional: devotional and didactic literature on popular religious subjects.[49] Religious topics appeared in print along with tracts intended to instruct and uplift the literate Hindu. A few Hindus commented on the new anglicized world and the knowledge it had to impart, but traditional didactic literature dominated.[50] It did not long remain traditional. Those who sought to instruct their fellows began to differ on the nature of their advice. Some writers were content to restate previous religious beliefs unchanged, to write verses in praise of Krishna,

48. See Munshi Diwan Chand, *Sirāt-ul-Mustaqīm* (The Correct Path) (Sialkot: 1850), and Munshi Harasukh Raya, *Tanbīh-ul-Ghafilīn* (Punishment for Negligence) (Lahore: 1853).

49. Examples of this literature include Pandit Vansidhara, *Qissah-i-Dharm Singh* (The Story of Dharm Singh) (Agra: 1855); Pandit Mukand Ram's religious magazine, *Gyān Pradhyānī Patrikā* (Lahore: 1867); Anonymous, *Sangīt Dhurū Jī Kā* (Songs of Dhuru) (Delhi: 1868); and Girdhari, *Krishna kā Bārah Māsā* (A Lament for Krishna) (Delhi: 1868).

50. Among discussions of the new world is a tract by Baldev Singh, *Dāk Bijlī kā Prakār* (The Nature of Electricity) (Agra: 1855); Pyare Lal's periodical, *Atālīq-i-Punjāb* (Tutor of Punjab) (Lahore: 1869); and the *Proceedings of the Debating Club of Delhi,* 1871–1873, published by the Debating Club in Urdu.

Durga or Ram; but others began to attack existing customs and beliefs. Gradually differences appeared, positions solidified, and opposing visions clashed under the stresses of adjustment to the new realities of British rule.

The forces of change—British, Bengali or Punjabi—generated counter pressures by those who would defend their faith from external criticism, be it missionary or reformer. Modern Sanatanist (orthodox) movements in Punjab trace their growth from the career of Pandit Shraddha Ram. Born in 1837 in the town of Phillaur, District Jullundur, Shraddha Ram was raised as an orthodox Brahman, although he later worked for the British. During the 1860s he became involved in the defense of Hinduism through a reaction to the criticism of Novin Chandra Rai of the Brahmo Samaj, the personal crusades of Kanya Lal Alakhdhari, and the persistent anti-Hindu stance of Christian missionaries. In 1867 he founded a school in Ludhiana to teach Sanskrit and moral education to Hindu boys as a counter to the Christian schools of that city. Munshi Yamuna Prasad joined this school as its chief administrator and began a long career of Sanatanist leadership.[51]

With the arrival of Kanhya Lal in Ludhiana, tensions between reformers and orthodox sharply increased. When Kanhya Lal convened a meeting to inaugurate his Niti Prakash Sabha, Shraddha Ram attended with his disciples, Munshi Yamuna Prasad and Munshi Chet Ram Nagar. In the ensuing debate, Shraddha Ram condemned Kanhya Lal and in so doing presented an excellent description of Hindu reform as viewed by the orthodox of that time. After a polite opening Shraddha Ram pointed out that "only those people can provide protection who are themselves firm Hindus. Even though all of us think we are firm Hindus only a person who accepts the teachings of Shruti and Smirti can be a firm Hindu and if he thinks that the Vedas, and Dharm Shastras are the products only of the Brahmans and accepts this as Hinduism, he cannot be a true Hindu." Kanhya Lal Alakhdhari did not, of course, fit the description of a "firm Hindu." He was instead a cultural apostate, ridiculous and offensive in his anglicization.

Mr. Alakhdhari who is against Shruti and Smirti and does not keep a knot on his head and does not wear the sacred thread which is essential for the

51. Tulsī Dēva, *Shraddhā Prakāsh,* (Lahore: Punjab Economical Press, 1896), p. 28; quotes given below from pages 30–31.

Vaishya and who hates to have cow dung paint in the kitchen and uses a dining table and calls *Bhōjan* as *Khānā* and thinks all the caste system is useless, then how is it possible that Hinduism can spread and prosper through his efforts? He also has some ideas that to worship Krishna, Chandar Ramchandar and Brahma and Vishnu and to go on pilgrimage to the Ganges and other rivers is foolishness. He believes that the *Shrāddha* and other customs and religious worship are made or are creations of the Pandits to fool or to cheat others. Then he wears shoes and he wants to listen to the preaching of the Vedas and Shastras in front of Christians and Muslims and he cannot tolerate a mark on the forehead of another person. Then how can he protect the Hindu religion?

To leave the traditions and customs of Hinduism in order to save them seemed to Shraddha Ram and many orthodox Hindus contradictory if not simply insane. It was a self-defeating strategy and would only encourage the work of the "Muslims, Christians and the Brahmo Samaj." Following his condemnation of Alakhdhari, Shraddha Ram gave a learned discourse, an *updēsh,* gathered together his disciples, and left the meeting. But he could not so easily stem the tide of criticism both from within and without.

For the next two decades, until his death in 1882, Shraddha Ram toured, lectured, debated, wrote, founded temples and orthodox organizations in support of the Sanatanist cause. He was joined by Pandit Salig Ram Acharya, head of the Vaishnava Sabha, by his biographer and disciple, Tulsi Deva, by Pandit Gopi Nath and Munshi Yamuna Prasad. In 1874 he toured eastern Punjab and, in spite of his condemnation of conversion, undertook to purify Hindus who had been lost to the faith, a radical step later condemned by orthodoxy as un-Hindu.[52] In the same year Shraddha Ram published his major polemical work, *Dharm Rakshā (The Protection of Religion),* in response to a lecture of Babu Novin Chandra Rai. The three enemies of Hinduism—Brahmos, Christians and Muslims—each came in for criticism and refutation.[53] Returning to Ludhiana, he founded the Hindu Dharm Prakashik Sabha dedicated to the defense of Hindu orthodoxy. By the late 1870s

52. Reconversions were performed in Sialkot, Mian Mir, Jullundur, Phagwara, Phillaur, Ludhiana, Ambala, and in Saharanpur in the United Provinces, Tulsī Dēva, *Shraddhā Prakāsh,* p. 54.

53. Shraddhā Rām *Dharm Rakshā* (Ludhiana: Jamna Prasad Sahib Dharm Sahayak Press, 1876).

Shraddha Ram stood first among the spokesmen of Hindu orthodoxy. Kanhya Lal Alakhdhari and Shraddha Ram typified two divergent responses to Western culture as introduced by the British and to the modernized Hinduism of the Bengali Brahmos. The gulf between these two streams of thought would grow rapidly in the ensuing years

The later 1870s marked a turning point from individual campaigns of change and defense to sustained social and religious movements. Marginality and alienation began to affect a growing number of young Punjabi Hindus sufficiently to produce sustained movements for change. Influences from Bengal, from the remnants of the Delhi Renaissance, from government, missionaries, English educators, and individual Punjabi thinkers created a milieu of intellectual and psychological ferment centered on the city of Lahore. A wandering *sanyāsī*, Swami Dayanand Saraswati, would provide the catalyst for a coalescence of this ferment, a channelling of unrest into organizational action directed at transforming Punjabi Hinduism into a faith capable of commanding the respect and commitment of a culturally lost generation.

## Chapter II

# FROM IDENTITY TO ASSOCIATION: THE FOUNDING OF THE PUNJAB ARYA SAMAJ

**Situated as we of the first generation of University students were, practically without any guidance from our elders even as to the choice of our subjects or of our future careers, we were largely like a boat without a steersman—at the mercy of the current that might be flowing at the time.**

RUCHI RAM SAHNI

### DAYANAND: THE FOUNDING OF A NEW FAITH

Punjabi Hindus did not produce a prophet of their own but found the core of their new identity reordered around the ideas of a wandering holy man from the state of Gujarat, Swami Dayanand Saraswati. One of the most complex and intriguing men of the nineteenth century, Swami Dayanand developed and preached his own brand of reinterpreted and modernized Hinduism. He called for a return to the past based on his belief in the infallibility of the Vedas, the most ancient texts of Hinduism. Dayanand demanded social and religious reform as a reestablishment of past purity. With Dayanand rationalism gave way to faith, equivalence to superiority, and tolerance to militancy. Aggressive and uncompromising, Dayanand's faith fitted the mid-Victorian atmosphere of dogmatic Christianity and imperial arrogance. A restless, questing generation of educated Punjabis needed a new faith and through Dayanand they discovered it. In time they modified his ideas to make them their own, the basis of a new traditionalism, a new concept of self and of the world.

Swami Dayanand Saraswati was born in Tankara, a small town in central Kathiawar, in 1824. Raised in an obscure native state, Dayanand's education was that of a Shaivite Brahman, orthodox and unaffected by the outer world. As a youth Dayanand showed an unwillingness to accept both his family's plans for his future and orthodox Hinduism. Seriously troubled by the practice of idol worship, disturbed by the deaths of his sister and uncle, he left home at the age of twenty-two. Dayanand's family had attempted to end his restlessness through marriage, and instead precipitated a final break. The years from 1846 to 1860 were spent in search of *muktī*, release, the traditional goal of Hindu ascetics. Little is known of Dayanand's activities during this period and there is nothing to indicate an interest in reform, social or religious. Clearly Dayanand did not find satisfaction and solace as a *sanyāsī*. He continued to search for a *guru* who could answer his own internal questing. In November 1860 he found his preceptor, Swami Virajanand Saraswati, a blind ascetic from the Punjab. For three years he studied with Virajanand, accepting not only a new theology but a set of goals which gave redirection to his life. When Dayanand left Virajanand in 1863, he gave as *guru dakshīnā* (a departing gift) the promise to reform Hinduism. Dayanand, the seeker of individual immortality, emerged a reformer challenging the present.

Swami Virajanand and his disciple divided all Hindu scripture into the "*ārsha*" and "*un-ārsha*" texts. The former, the work of *rishis*, divinely inspired saints, were authoritative, the sole source of legitimate teaching and proper practice. *Ārsha* texts included the Vedas and all others written while Vedic scholarship still persisted. All "scriptures" compiled after the degeneration of Vedic studies, which meant after the Mahabharata, the great war of antiquity, and its accompanying destruction, were *un-ārsha*, and unacceptable if they deviated from the Vedas. In post-Mahabharata times the sacred Vedas could not be fully understood; error, corruption, and superstition crept in, as Hinduism declined from its ancient heights. What little Vedic lore was remembered could no longer be properly interpreted. False texts, particularly the popular *Purānās*, came to dominate Hindu thought; decadence followed. Now Vedic truth should be sought, but not indiscriminately. Only Panini's treatise, the *Ashtādhyāyī*, and Patanjali's commentary, the *Mahābhāshya*, could lead to the proper interpretation of Vedic Sanskrit and only such an understanding would make it possible to judge what elements of contemporary Hinduism were *ārsha*, correct, and *un-ārsha*, in error. Meaning became all, and interpretation opened the way to legitimize change through the authority of ancient scripture.

No element of popular religion lay beyond the reach of Virajanand's logic; each was subject to the test of Vedic authenticity, and thus to reinterpretation. Monotheism replaced polytheism; the unity of God was established by redefinition, with the pantheon of Hindu gods becoming merely attributes of one universal God. Idolatry, caste, child marriage, Brahmanical claims of superiority, pilgrimages, horoscopes, the ban against widow remarriage, restrictions on foreign travel—the vast bulk of popular Hindu religious practices—all disappeared with polytheism. Only a rationalistic monotheism remained, supported by a new interpretation of the past. History was rewritten to save the present and make possible the future.

The present degeneracy of Hinduism, like the fact of colonial subservience, had to be explained. How could a people so sublime as the Vedic Aryans, who predated all other men and created civilization, sink to such depths of ignorance and dependency? What cataclysmic event destroyed that "golden age" of Vedic truth? Dayanand found a clear and compelling answer, the *Mahābhārata.* This titanic struggle engulfed the entire subcontinent, beginning a decline into ignorance from which Hinduism could not escape. Truth, the key to all life, was lost. "When men of great learning, princes, kings, sages, saints, were killed in the Great War or died, then the teaching and preaching of the Vedic literature and the Vedic religion became extinct."[1] Following the chaos of this war, "The whole of India was split up into small pieces," and the Brahmans who should have preserved Vedic knowledge did not, with disastrous results. "When the Brahmanas went without education, the condition of the kshattriyas, vaishyas, sudras became unspeakable."[2] War and selfishness on the part of priestly classes destroyed the vitality of Hindu culture. Instead of preserving and reviving this ancient faith, the Brahmans sought to solidify their hold on the Hindu community. "They . . . preach to the kshattriyas, etc., 'We are your objects of worship, without serving us you cannot get heaven or salvation.' If you will not serve us, you will be sent to the terrible hell, the epithets 'Brahmana' and 'venerable,' which according to the Vedas and books of sages, were applicable to only those who were most learned and pious, came to

1. Ganga Prasad Upadhyaya, *The Light of Truth, English Translation of Swami Dayananda's Satyarth Prakasha* (Allahabad: The Kala Press, 1956), p. 392.

2. *Ibid.*, p. 393.

be usurped by these ignorant, sensual, hypocritical, irresponsible and vicious people."[3] Weakened from within, the Hindu community faced the challenges of Buddhism and Jainism, then fell before invading Islam and the Christian British.

The path back to the glories of ancient Arya Varta was clear. Erroneous and evil elements of Hinduism had to be removed. Instead of "false Brahmans" there must arise a new class of religious leaders, Brahmans not by the accident of birth but by merit. A man from the lowest level of society could be a Brahman if he had the qualifications. "Even now only that man is fit to be called a *Brahmana* who is learned and of good habits, and an ignorant man deserves to be called a *shudra.*"[4] Dayanand envisioned an open social system with education and not birth as the determinant of status. Brahmans, particularly Punjabi Brahmans, need not fear such a society, for they would, if they were pure and properly educated, retain superiority.[5] Dayanand's world view appealed directly to the educated elite, drawn as it was heavily from the Vaishya castes. The way to material success, to spiritual status and to social superiority was now one and the same—the path of education. Literacy led to an understanding of Vedic truth, the "golden age" of ancient Hinduism, and a reformed purified future. Literacy became an obligation for all who would follow the new faith, and stemming from this obligation was the rejection of all traditional limitations on learning that barred outcastes and women from hearing or studying the sacred texts. All must read the truth in its pure Vedic form and should the Vedas prove difficult to comprehend, then Arya literature stood ready to explain and interpret them.[6]

3. *Ibid.*
4. *Ibid.*, p. 125.
5. For many Punjabi Brahmans this opened the way to a status that they had not fully possessed in the past. Since large numbers of them had moved into occupations unrelated to their priestly heritage, Arya doctrine opened to them the opportunity of retaining both a new, well paying career, and claims to superior religious rank. One could be a Babu or Munshi in government service, a *vakīl* in the courts and still retain a form of Brahmanhood. They did lose any possible claim to a monopoly of religious symbols and power, but this monopoly had long been shattered by other forces within the province. The untraditional Brahman of the Punjab lost little of actual value.
6. A clear and concise statement on the need for education can be found in Bhagwandatta, ed., *Rishī Dayānand Saraswatī ke Patra Aur Vigyāpan* (Amritsar: Ram Lal Kapur Trust, 1955), p. 127.

Dayanand, the social reformer, did not spring fully formed from the mind of Virajanand or from the dust of his feet. The years from 1863 to 1872 saw an evolution take place that transformed this *sanyāsī* into a social and religious reformer partially modeled after the anglicized Marathas and Bengalis. In his first years of preaching Dayanand retained his *sanyāsī* dress, spoke in Sanskrit, and focused his attention solely on his fellow Brahmans. He would reform the Hindu world from above. Dayanand's travels through upper India brought him face to face first with Christian missionaries and later with a variety of anglicized reformers.[7] From his contacts with Christian missionaries and their literature Dayanand formed his opinions and acquired information used later in attacking both Christian theology and proselytization.

Dayanand's transformation from *sanyāsī* to social reformer was accelerated by his growing interaction with anglicized Indians. From 1868 to 1871, he continued to live as a *sanyāsī* and to employ traditional means of religious reform. The ancient form of public debate, the *shāstrārth,* was his major tool of proselytization. In addition he opened schools to spread his own version of the Hindu faith. The schools failed. He depended on Brahman instructors who taught orthodox ideas to which they were committed.[8] Dayanand's utilization of Sanskrit and reform within the Brahmanical system produced few results except for a certain notoriety. In 1872 he arrived in Calcutta at the invitation of Debendranath Tagore. His visit of four months and his close contacts with Brahmo Samaj leaders produced a radical shift in Dayanand's reform techniques. He emerged from Calcutta visibly transformed. Gone was the loin cloth in favor of contemporary dress; with it went Sanskrit; he now spoke in Hindi to a different audience, the educated non-Brahman.[9] Dayanand's abandonment of Sanskrit, like Luther's re-

7. During the two years, 1866–1868, Dayanand held discussions with several missionaries and received a Hindi copy of the New Testament from Rev. T. J. Scott. Har Bilas Sarda, *Life of Dayanand Saraswati, World Teacher* (Ajmer: Vedic Yantralaya, 1946), pp. 61–62; Reid Graham, "The Arya Samaj as a Reformation in Hinduism with Special Reference to Caste," unpublished Ph.D. dissertation, Yale University, 1942, p. 129.

8. J. N. Farquhar, *Modern Religious Movements in India* (New York: The Macmillan Company, 1919), p. 108; Graham, "The Arya Samaj," p. 131.

9. Dayanand still retained the inner aspects of *sanyāsī,* and adhered to all his earlier vows.

jection of Latin, marked a permanent break with established religion. Still very much a Hindu, he would reform from beyond the limits of accepted dogma and traditional methodology.

In the years 1872 to 1875 Dayanand traveled continually, experimenting with various forms of organization and proselytization. In Mathura he founded an Arya Sabha and a journal, the *Ārya Prakāsh;* neither succeeded.[10] Dayanand did not have at his command either sufficient funds or disciples to carry these efforts to success. In 1873 he met Sayyid Ahmad Khan[11] and also the Aligarh District Collector, Raja Jai Kishen Das. At the latter's urging Dayanand wrote the *Satyārth Prakāsh (Light of Truth),* a statement of his ideas and beliefs. First published in 1875, this book, more than any other, was to influence Hindu thinking in the Punjab and much of northwestern India.[12] Dayanand was in Bombay and his home state of Gujarat in 1874–1875. Here he met with leaders of the Prarthana Samaj, but as in Calcutta, failed to establish a working relation with local reformers. His speeches in Bombay and Poona in which he denounced caste, idol worship, and extolled widow remarriage, created violent opposition. At one lecture in Poona it took a hundred police to restore order and prevent a mob from attacking the outspoken reformer.

Dayanand's lectures attracted disciples as well as opponents, and in 1875 he was able to translate this support into the first successful Arya Samaj. On April 10, 1875, the Bombay Arya Samaj met, adopted rules and elected its officers, thus giving an organizational expression to Dayanand's ideas.[13] In spite of his initial successes neither Maharashtra nor Gujarat responded to his message. A few disciples remained in Bombay, but they had little impact beyond that city.

10. Graham, "The Arya Samaj," pp. 151–152.

11. *Ibid.*, p. 150.

12. Considerable controversy erupted within the Samaj over differences between the first and second editions of the *Satyārth Prakāsh.* For an introduction to these debates, see Yudhīshtīr Mīmāṁsak, *Rishī Dayānand kē Granthōn kā Itīhās* (Ajmere: Vijay Press, 1941), and Har Bilas Sarda, *Works of Maharishi Dayanand and the Paropkarini Sabha* (Ajmer: Vedic Yantralaya, 1942).

13. Dayanand founded the first Arya Samaj at Rajkot, Gujarat, and a second at Ahmadabad, but neither lasted for long. The Rajkot Arya Samaj became involved in local politics and was disbanded by governmental order; the Ahmadabad Samaj apparently withered from lack of support. Graham, "The Arya Samaj," p. 158.

THE SANYĀSĪ IN THE PUNJAB

Dayanand moved north once again and in January 1877 reached Delhi to attend the great Durbar proclaiming Queen Victoria Kaiser-i-Hind. Here he met with other social and religious leaders in an attempt to form a grand coalition of all reform elements. In this he failed, but while in Delhi, Dayanand encountered several prominent Punjabis who urged him to visit Lahore. He accepted and arrived in that city on April 19, 1877.[14] Dayanand remained in the Punjab until July 11, 1878, yet in that period of less than fifteen months he began a radical transformation of the Punjabi Hindu community.

Invited by Punjabi reformers and leading public figures, Dayanand's lectures attracted immediate attention, more than his hosts had expected or desired. His attacks on idol worship, child marriage, traditional death rituals, and food taboos, plus his insistence on Vedic infallibility, proved again highly controversial. Of equal importance was his aggressive, belligerent mode of address and the enthusiastic response he inspired. Opposition mounted as the newly converted threw their idols into the Ravi River or publicly smashed them in the local bazaars.[15] Criticism might affront or even outrage, but the public disgrace of God's images was sacrilege in the eyes of the orthodox. They reacted immediately. Pandit Bhanudatt, the *āchāryā* of the Lahore Sat Sabha, joined Pandit Shraddha Ram in founding the Sanathan Dharm Rakshini Sabha (the Society for the Protection of the Eternal Religion). Pandit Shraddha Ram, a veteran of earlier struggles with Christian missionaries and Brahmo reformers, led in countering Dayanand's challenges to popular Hinduism.

As Dayanand toured the Punjab, Shraddha Ram followed in his wake to strengthen the beleaguered forces of orthodoxy. When Dayanand visited Jullundur the leading Pandits sent a hurried message to Shraddha Ram to come and do battle.[16] Each side, re-

14. The invitation to visit Lahore was extended by Sardar Vikram Singh Aluwalia, Pandit Manphul, Munshi Har Sukh Rai, proprietor of the *Kōh-i-Nūr* press, and Kanhya Lal Alakhdhari. Sarda, *Life of Dayanand,* pp. 162–163. For a complete listing of Dayanand's travels, see Sarda, *Ibid.*, pp. 337–344.

15. Sarda, *The Life of Dayanand,* pp. 179–180.

16. Tulsī Dēva, *Shraddhā Prakāsh* (Lahore: Punjab Economical Press, 1896), p. 55.

former and orthodox, mobilized its resources, as leading Sanatanists quickly joined Shraddha Ram and his disciples. The Sanatanists employed traditional forms of propaganda and the new printing press with equal facility.[17] Lahore quickly became the central point in this controversy following the organization of the Lahore Arya Samaj. Shraddha Ram in turn used the Harī Gyān Mandir of Lahore, which he had founded, as his main platform of anti-Arya propaganda.[18] Dayanand would have his say, and orthodoxy its answer, in this the most basic of all struggles. While Dayanand overtly opposed orthodoxy, he also in an indirect yet more significant way undermined existing reform organizations. The first was immediately apparent, the latter took time to manifest itself.

Following three months of lectures and private discussions, the Lahore Arya Samaj held its first meeting on July 24, 1877. This time had been spent in careful preparation. A committee of three—Lala Sain Das, Lala Jiwan Das, and Lala Mul Raj—rewrote the original principles drafted in Bombay.[19] The lengthy and confused Bombay statement was simplified, with elements of belief separated from the purely organizational. The committee produced a set of ten principles *(Niyams)*, an Arya Samaj creed broad enough to be widely acceptable (Appendix I). Stressing the ultimate authority of one formless, omniscient God, the source of all knowledge, and the authority of the Vedas, Arya principles called specifically for social action. "One should not be content with one's own welfare alone, but should look for one's own welfare in the welfare of all." A doctrinal statement, general yet uplifting, this creed required only that an individual accept the Vedas as the ultimate source of all authority and by implication Dayanand's scheme of Vedic interpretation. The committee next sought to frame by-laws *(Upniyams)* for the new organization. By the end of

17. In 1878, Pandit Govind Ram published his *Dayā Nand Mat Mardanā Nibandh (A Refutation of the Religion Founded by Daya Nand)*, an attack on Dayanand's *Commentary on the Vedas*. Govind Ram intended to reach not the educated elite but the community of Brahmanical Pandits and so wrote in Sanskrit rather than the more popular Urdu. Munshi Yamuna Prasad came to the support of his Guru with a series of anti-Arya articles in *Tuhfa-i-Kashmīr* which he edited, and was in turn attacked by Lala Mathra Das in *Ārya Darshan*.

18. *Regenerator of Arya Varta*, Vol. I, No. 7, September 17, 1883, p. 4.

19. Graham, "The Arya Samaj," p. 185.

July, the Lahore Arya Samaj had elected its officers,[20] acquired a meeting place in Anarkali Bazaar, opened a Sanskrit school, and claimed a membership of 300.[21]

While developments in Lahore remained in the hands of the newly-recruited members, Dayanand traveled throughout the province. His first tour of Amritsar, Gurdaspur, and Jullundur lasted a little over three months and resulted in three new Samaj branches.[22] A distinct pattern developed. Contacts were made between Samaj members and interested citizens of a Punjab town, who, acting as a local reception committee, arranged for Dayanand's accommodations and speeches and publicized his proposed visit. Usually this ad hoc committee was comprised of local reformers, often members of the Brahmo Samaj, along with others of the educated community. Whenever possible, Dayanand stayed with a leading citizen of the town, a *Rai Bahādur* or *Dīwān Sāhab.* In Lahore he was hosted by Diwan Rathan Chand and Dr. Rahim Khan, and in Amritsar by the Sikh philanthropist, Dyal Singh Majithia, who arranged for his accommodation with a prominent Muslim, Miyan Muhammadjan. With advance arrangements completed a section of its leading citizens met Dayanand at the railway station and conducted him through the town. Speeches, debates, and private discussions followed until a Samaj had been organized. Dayanand then moved on to another town and the process was repeated. In all, he founded eleven Samajes stretching from Ferozepore and Jullundur northward to Rawalpindi, with one branch to the south at Multan (see map 3). Each was autonomous. No centralizing or coordinating organization existed save that of Dayanand, the prophet.

Opposition to Dayanand reoccurred in each town he visited and followed much the same pattern as it had in Lahore. Without ex-

20. Officers of the new Samaj were drawn from those close to Dayanand with Lala Mul Raj, President; S. P. Bhattacharjee, Vice-President and Minister; Lala Jewan Das, General Secretary; Lala Koondun Lal, Treasurer; and Lala Bullah Das, Librarian. S. P. Bhattacharjee, *Memoirs of the Official Career of S. P. Bhattacharjee, Late Superintendent, Office of the Superintendent Engineer, 3rd Circle, Punjab P.W. Department, Lahore, 1894*, p. 40.

21. The membership figures were given in the *Kōh-i-Nūr* of July 28, 1877, and quoted in Sarda, *Life of Dayanand*, pp. 181–182; see page 180 for the Sat Sabha controversy.

22. The Amritsar and Gurdaspur Samajes were established during Dayanand's visit, the Jullundur Samaj shortly after his departure from that city.

# Arya Samajes Founded During Swami Dayanand's Tour of the Punjab

Districts by Number

1. Mandi
2. Suket
3. Hoshiarpur
4. Kapurthala
5. Faridkot
6. Nabha
7. Patiala
8. Jind
9. Delhi
10. Simla
11. Chamba
12. Kangra
13. Simla Hill States
14. Ambala
15. Karnal
16. Rohtak
17. Gurgaon
18. Jullundur
19. Ludhiana
20. Patiala
21. Hissar

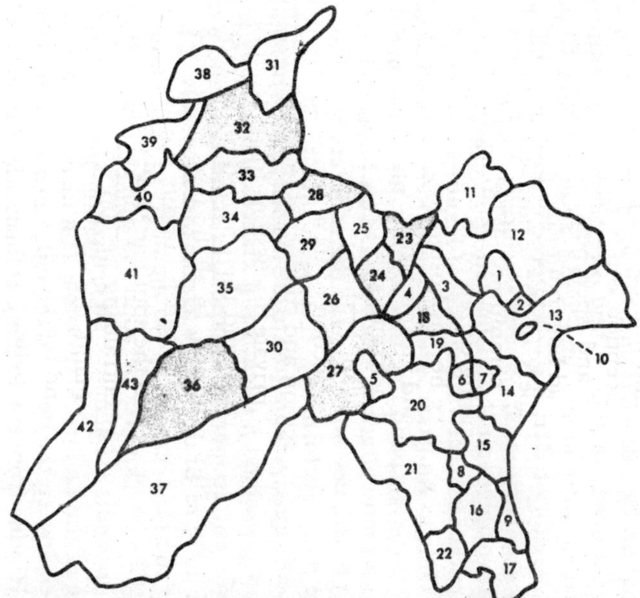


Districts by Number

22. Princely States
23. Gurdaspur
24. Amritsar
25. Sialkot
26. Lahore
27. Ferozepore
28. Gujrat
29. Gujranwala *
30. Montgomery
31. Hazara
32. Rawalpindi
33. Jhelum
34. Shahpur
35. Jhang
36. Multan
37. Bahawalpur
38. Peshawar
39. Kohat
40. Bannu
41. Dera Ismail Khan
42. Dera Ghazi Khan
43. Muzaffargarh

* Only Gujranwala had more than one Samaj with branches at Gujranwala and Wazirabad

Founded Arya Samajes

Adapted from the Census, Punjab Report 1891.

MAURICE SCHWANKE

ception, Dayanand's most violent confrontations were with the forces of orthodoxy. Here lay his sharpest criticisms and the most dramatic responses. In Gujrat District mobs of orthodox supporters, hurling stones and bricks, disrupted one of Dayanand's meetings. His clerk was beaten in Wazirabad, and threats of assassination followed him throughout his travels. Such action was provoked deliberately. In Gujrat Dayanand recited and discussed the *Gāyatrī Mantra,* traditionally heard only by the upper castes, before a mixed audience of Hindus and Muslims. In Multan his condemnation of the Gokula Gossains, the local temple Brahmans, resulted in the most dramatic orthodox response of his entire tour. A mob, armed with knives and clubs shouting "Jai Gopal! Jai Gopal!"—victory to Krishna—scattered one of his public gatherings. By comparison, Dayanand's criticism of Christianity and Islam provoked genteel and limited counteraction. They were secondary targets, receiving far less of his attention or of his sharp tongue. Only in Amritsar, when Dayanand belittled Sikhism, did militant Sikhs respond by threatening his assassination. Orthodoxy, the most attacked, reacted on many levels, but was in fact little hurt by this new voice; instead the sufferers were Dayanand's allies, the Punjab reformers.

For those already committed to the modernization of Hinduism, Dayanand presented a dilemma of choice. Should they join this new movement, cooperate, oppose it, or stand aloof and wait? Initially the Lahore Brahmos saw Dayanand as an ally, a potential leader of their movement, as did members of the Hindu Sabhas. All hope of such close cooperation was quickly lost, as Dayanand insisted on Vedic infallibility and criticized Brahmo beliefs. The founding of the Lahore Arya Samaj gradually forced individuals to choose between the new and the old, a process that drew many Punjabi Hindus from the existing reform organizations. The Sat Sabha was crippled, the Hindu Sabhas eclipsed; only the Brahmo Samaj remained alive and active. Yet it too was permanently changed: already dominated by Bengalis, the Brahmo Samaj became almost totally a Bengali organization. The educated Punjabi Hindu now groped toward a new expression of his own identity, no longer satisfied with an imported Bengali ideology.

Relations between the Brahmos and Aryas settled into a fixed pattern of ideological struggle within the reformist world, and cooperation whenever an issue external to that world demanded it. For one Brahmo leader, Shiv Narayan Agnihotri, this competition became intensely personal. He met Dayanand twice and was humiliated by him on both occasions.[23] Brilliant, eloquent, and a prolific writer, Agnihotri produced a stream of anti-Arya tracts. He initiated this paper war in 1878, with *Pandīt Dayānand Saraswātī kē Vēda Bhāsh par Review* (Review of the Ved Bhashya of Pandit Dayanand Saraswati), a critique of Dayanand's basic philosophical interpretation of the Vedas, and followed with a series of Urdu pamphlets expounding Brahmoism.[24] In the process of attack and counterattack, Aryas and Brahmos clarified and elaborated their respective ideologies. They made explicit and distinct the position of each group on specific issues, their methods of advocating and legitimizing change, and their respective degrees of social radicalism.

Brahmo insistence on the truth of all religions and the greatness of all religious leaders appeared to many Punjabis as apostacy. They reacted with horror. "I wish to emphasize, [recalled Ruchi Ram] as the plainest of plain facts that I myself noticed, *scores of times,* that the mere mention of Christ or Mohammad with respect as a great religious teacher, immediately led to the emptying of the Samaj hall of practically everybody excepting the few Brahmos. How many times have I not heard people exclaim as they rushed out of the hall, 'Oh, they are Christians,' 'they are followers of Mohammad,' 'they have no faith of their own,' 'they are denationalized people,' and a dozen other similar opprobrious epithets."[25] Punjabis not only disapproved of Brahmo ideology but socially boycotted leaders of the movement, especially

23. Sarda, *The Life of Dayanand,* pp. 176, 179.

24. Pandit Shiv Narayan Agnihotri's *Dayānand Saraswātī kē Vēda Bāsh par Review* (Lahore: Victoria Press, 1878); then came *Mazhab aur 'Aql* (Religion and Reason) (Lahore: Victoria Press, 1882); *Bunyād-ul-Īmān-i-Brahmāh Dharm pahlā hissā*(Principles of the Brahmo Religion) (Lahore: New Imperial Press, 1883); *Brahm Dharm kē Vikhyān* (Sermons on the Brahmo Religion) (Lahore: New Imperial Press, 1883); *Asrār-i-Dīnīyāh* (The Mysteries of Religion) (Lahore: New Imperial Press, 1884); *Brahm Dharm Sanghita* (The Doctrine of the Brahmo Religion) (Lahore: New Imperial Press, 1885), one of the few tracts in Hindi; and, *Dayānandī Kalyugī Mazhab* (The Iron Age Religion of Dayanand Saraswati) (Lahore: Brahm Prachar Press, 1887).

25. Quotes given below from Ruchi Ram Sahni, "Self-Revelations of an Octogenarian," unpublished manuscript in the possession of V. C. Joshi, Nehru Memorial Museum, pp. 131–132.

Brahmos from their own province. Those who joined the Samaj "were looked upon as the most hateful of persons and . . . mere public profession of the faith was enough to seriously lower a man in the eyes of his community."

The heroic stance of the Brahmos appeared to the Aryas as unwise tactically and as culturally treacherous. "No doubt the Brahmos paved the way to reform, but their business ended there. They could not touch our houses, and hence they could not introduce reform into it. They shunned the society of those whom they wanted to reform, and people naturally shunned theirs."[26] By contrast to Brahmo elitism, Aryas pointed to the completely Hindu character of Dayanand and to his use of scriptural authority. "In this state of things a leader appeared in the person of Swami Dayananda Saraswati, Pandit. His ways of thinking, his moves of life, and his lines of action were quite national and free from those objections that people complained of in the Brahmos. He did what no Brahmo could ever dream of. He entered our very homes, roused us from our beds, upbraided the priesthood that had allowed us to lie in bed so long after sun-rise. And he did all that not cryingly and with entreaties, but with an authority that none could question for a moment." The power of Dayanand's arguments, drawn from the most ancient Hindu texts, offered protection to those who accepted them. Change could be advocated with the hope that social punishment might be mitigated if not entirely escaped. "Formerly when any person attempted celebrating widow marriage, there was always a fear of excommunication, that horror of horrors to a Hindu, but now things are different. People are told that it is in their own Shastras, in fact in the very Vedas, that widow marriage is sanctioned, and this makes them hesitate a little before questioning its propriety." Brahmos with their indiscriminate attacks on tradition had little in their ideology which could or would protect them from the anger of orthodoxy.

Arya writers repeatedly stressed the alien nature of Brahmos and held their anglicization up for ridicule much as Shraddha Ram had scoffed at the cultural borrowing of Kanhya Lal Alakhdhari,

Some of them took unhesitatingly to coats, hats, and pants without any censure from their co-labourers. Thus indirectly encouraged they went further, and began to indulge freely in the habit of resorting to hotels and

26. Quotes given below from *Arya Magazine*, June 1882, pp. 142–145.

> eating with forks and knives on tables. In a word they commenced to imitate the customs and manners of Europeans. Some showed so much anxiety in leaving off their own customs, etc., that they actually adopted European habits and manners, in lieu of national ones, although the latter could be retained with much more advantage in every respect. They declaimed the observance of Durga Puja festival as unfit to be reformed, and began to exchange presents in Christmas, to which they saw no objection. They thus saw all evil in everything national, and all good in everything European.[27]

Brahmo acceptance of European culture and social forms proved a tactical error cutting them off from the "confidence of the public."

The Lahore experience repeated itself throughout Punjab. The establishment of each new Arya Samaj forced a series of individual and occasionally group choices. The Ferozepore Hindu Sabha joined en masse and simply changed its name to the Ferozepore Arya Samaj, while in Multan, Brahmos deserted the older organization for a newly-established Arya Samaj. By the 1880s only the Lahore and Simla Brahmo Samajes remained vigorous and active organizations, both supported by local Bengali communities. In this first joust between the imported Bengali elite and a newly-emerging Punjabi leadership, organizational victories by the Punjabis meant only a partial diminution of Bengali social and intellectual leadership. Bengalis retained positions in education, government service and journalism won in the post-annexation years. They retained also their links to the more sophisticated and advanced homeland of Bengal. First to export its concepts of social and religious change, Bengal would later disseminate political consciousness through its expatriates in the north. Bengalis in the Punjab, as interpreters of modernity, found their social position temporarily sustained against competition from an emerging elite. This competition between Bengalis and Punjabis would be decided in the 1880s, as the first generation of college-educated Punjabis made their appearance and chose between the older models of self and the new, between Brahmo and Arya.

### THE ARYA SAMAJ AND THE ABSENT SWAMI

In the months that followed Dayanand's visit to the Punjab a strange relationship developed between the Swami and his follow-

27. *Arya Magazine*, May 1882, pp. 60–62.

ers. On leaving the Punjab, Dayanand toured the North-Western Provinces with considerable success. By 1881, he could view with pride a flourishing revivalist and reform movement covering much of northern India. Yet the Arya Samaj was not enough for Dayanand. Its existence did not end his wanderlust nor dominate his energies. He visited Bombay in 1881 and then spent the last year and a half of his life, June 1882 to October 1883, in a vain attempt to achieve his Vedic society through the Rajput princes. Dayanand never questioned his belief in the classic Hindu polity. It alone was truly Hindu and should be the vehicle for the rebirth of past glories. Here he failed again, for the traditional Rajputs, like the Brahmanical priests, showed a distinct unwillingness to be reformed into greatness. Honor they gave Dayanand, but not the power he needed.

During the years before his death Dayanand inspired his educated followers from his written works but gave them little leadership. His letters show a preoccupation with technical and financial questions rather than with issues facing the new movement.[28] Each Samaj depended on its own talents and resources. Leadership developed within the Lahore Samaj as the largest, wealthiest, and most talented of the new societies. Patterns of worship and proselytization utilized in Lahore became models for the outlying Samaj branches. Dayanand did not leave detailed instructions as to what or how the Samaj should carry on its activities; Aryas looked instead to the Brahmo Samaj and the Protestant church for their models. In time they created their own forms of worship.

The Arya service as J. C. Oman, a sympathetic Englishman, witnessed it in 1879 consisted of four elements: a *Hōm* or Vedic fire ritual, hymns, a lecture or sermon, and again hymns which closed the meeting.[29] Though somewhat elaborated, this pattern exists today. When Oman visited, singing was performed by Muslims hired for the occasion.[30] Congregational singing soon replaced these professionals, leaving an Arya service which closely paralleled that of the Protestant church. The sermon delivered at this

28. See both Bhagwandatta's *Dayānand Saraswatī kē Patra aur Vigyāpan* and his *Rishī Dayānand Saraswatī kē patra aur vigyāpanōn kē parishishta* (Amritsar: Ram Lal Kapur Trust, 1957).

29. J. C. Oman, *Indian Life, Religious and Social* (London: T. Fisher, Unwin, 1889), pp. 95–98.

30. Traditionally outcaste Muslims sang at Hindu ceremonies.

meeting stressed many of Dayanand's favorite themes: the evils of child marriage and the traditional ban on widow remarriage, the uselessness of ignorant *sanyāsīs*, the need for education, including technical training, and the decadent practice of idol worship. "In denouncing idolatry the lecturer stated that in Vedic times men who bowed down to images made of wood or stone would have been punished like ordinary malefactors—in fact, like thieves and robbers."[31] As was typical of much Samaj writing, the enlightened past condemned a degenerate present.

Oman attended the anniversary celebration of the Lahore Samaj three years later, in November 1882. He found little changed. The same hall was somewhat more finely decorated, with a larger audience, and those conducting the service showed a slightly more aggressive attitude. "There appeared to be a controversial tone in the addresses delivered, and it was considered desirable to affirm frequently (evidently in reply to objectors) that the *Hom* was not a religious observance, that it was not a worship of Agni (fire); but was carried out from purely sanitary considerations; since the products of the combustion of the particular substances used diffused through the atmosphere of a crowded assembly were of a distinctly healthful character."[32] Science would support this new Hinduism, not challenge it, for those constructing Arya ideology saw no contradiction between the two forms of knowledge. "Thus the highest speculations of modern science dovetail very wonderfully with the ancient Aryan belief which asserted that all [the] universe has come into existence out of one primal element, the *Akas.* True, this theory of our ancient rishis when first known to the western world was ridiculed and set down as another example of the diseased imagination of the Asiatics. But the arguments above clearly show that far from being a subject of contempt, this ancient theory of evolution of matter is amply justified by the researches of modern science."[33] Arya rejection of contemporary superstition, added to this ancient rationalism, produced a system of thought modern and compatible with the new knowledge, science.

31. Oman, *Indian Life,* p. 99.

32. *Ibid.,* p. 101.

33. From an article entitled "The Theory of Evolution from an Aryan point of View" in the *Arya,* March 1882, pp. 6–11.

Lahore's contribution to ritual innovation was matched by developments in the fields of communication and ideology. Pamphlets and later journals published in Lahore were utilized by Aryas in their struggles with orthodoxy and the Christian missions. Aryas looked to Dayanand for inspiration, to the Lahore Samaj for assistance. The primary need at this time was for some form of communication which would strengthen the faith of those already committed and win new converts. Individual Samajists published tracts and pamphlets on specific issues and in explanation of general Samaj ideology,[34] but effective communication came only with the establishment of Arya periodicals.

Lala Rattan Chand Barry of Lahore started the first Samaj paper, the *Arya,* in March 1882. Barry devoted his journal "to Aryan philosophy, art, science, literature, and religion, embracing the views and opinions of the present Aryans on Social, Religious and Scientific subjects" whose purpose was "to correctly represent the views and opinions of the Arya Samaj . . . ."[35] Lala Rattan Chand, in his first issue, referred to the numerous misunderstandings about the goals of the Samaj and hoped that his new paper would "if possible, blunt the shaft of our detractors."[36] While the *Arya* generally expressed Samaj views, Barry often took decidedly individual stands that conflicted increasingly with one or another Samaj faction.[37]

Early in 1882 Lala Salig Ram, proprietor of the Arya Press, suggested the establishment of one English and one Urdu journal. A group of young students, including Lala Lajpat Rai, Lala Hans Raj, Lala Shiv Nath, and Pandit Guru Datta, responded and together started the *Regenerator of Arya Varta,* an English weekly and the official voice of the Lahore Samaj. Lala Hans Raj and Pandit

34. Among the first such tracts was Bawa Narain Singh's *Vēaō tō Budhan dā Dharm Sambandh* (Conversation on religion between Veda and Budhan) (Amritsar: Chashma-i-Nur Press, 1878), in Punjabi; and his *Dharm Vichār* (Thoughts on Religion) (Lahore: Arya Press, 1882), in Urdu.

35. An advertisement in the *Tribune,* January 13, 1882, p. 11.

36. *Arya,* March 1882, p. 1.

37. Debates over contents of the *Arya* caused its editor to declare that "Various communications have been received by us and the Arya Samaj Lahore enquiring whether the *Arya* is a private enterprise or undertaken by the Lahore Samaj as a body. To be clear we have to observe that the paper is a private enterprise and is published in the interest of the Arya Samaj." *Arya,* August 1882, p. 136.

Guru Datta jointly edited the *Regenerator* which lasted for nearly two years. Newspapers and journals tended to have short unstable lives, but from this period onward the Arya Samaj always possessed several periodicals. As soon as one collapsed another was founded. Lahore became and remained the center of Samaj publications, the point of dissemination of Arya news and new ideological issues. Other towns produced their own publications in later years, but Lahore dominated.

The need for papers paralleled the need for *prachār* (preaching) and *updēshaks* (missionaries). As the Samaj grew, new units needed assistance to strengthen their own members, to win converts, to defend themselves from orthodoxy and from opposing religions.[38] The Lahore Samaj called for a Vedic Missionary Fund on July 6, 1882.[39] This was followed by the suggestion of an Arya Tract Society. In August a group of Lahore Aryas took the first concrete steps in organized proselytization by founding the *Ārya Updēshak Mandalī* (Aryan Missionary Circle) "with the special object of dealing a death blow to Christianity with weapons of reason and fair argument."[40] Not general need, but a specific incident—the intention of a young student to convert to Christianity—generated this missionary group. They attacked the Christians as they had been attacked by them. "Every evening they walk out to the Anarkali [Bazaar] in singing bands where they stop and preach for a while against Christianity after which they return to the city singing hymns and prayers to the deity. The band appears just like the Salvation Army marching with the difference that its members have no uniforms."[41] The Aryas now took to street preaching, a favorite Christian technique. In the years that followed, the streets of Lahore became dotted with preachers—Christian, Arya, Brahmo, Sikh, Muslim—each extolling his particular cause and condemning all others. With street preaching, Aryas began to exhibit a new sense of militancy. The older members of the Samaj felt uncomfortable with such tactics, but as younger men of a new generation entered the society, these inhibitions disappeared as increasingly the Samaj experimented with new techniques of proselytization.

38. *Arya Magazine,* June 1882, pp. 83–85.
39. *Arya,* September 1882, p. 159.
40. *Regenerator of Arya Varta,* Vol. I, No. 7, August 20, 1883, p. 3.
41. *Regenerator of Arya Varta,* August 20, 1883, p. 4.

Samaj militancy grew on the twin pillars of belief and fear. To understand the genesis of social or religious movements is to comprehend their basis in fear. With the Aryas—as with the educated Hindus of Punjab—they feared above all else the *kirānīs,* the missionaries. "They are prepared to use every foul and unchristian means to convert the people to Christianity. At present boys of tender age are mostly their victims. These boys know nothing of their own religion; they have not even read their alphabet . . . . In short, they are utterly in the dark as to what religion is. Being furnished with no counter force to counteract the pernicious and unhealthy influence of the Christian doctrine, their minds are the most ready to imbibe any impression, however detrimental to their happiness and to the happiness of their relations."[42] The vision of young Hindu boys submitting to daily Christian indoctrination haunted Aryas. English education remained the key to worldly success, but conversion to Christianity was a terrible price for that success. "The boys who read in the mission schools rarely avoid catching the disease with which their masters are afflicted and which, though a disease, is put by those masters in the most favorable light. For six mortal hours daily have they to remain in the society of their Christian masters and how is it possible for the poor things not to accept as truth whatever is said by them . . . . Whatever kind be the ideas you infuse in their minds in their infancy, they will retain it to the end of their life and their conduct, while living, will be according to them unless some timely measures are taken to nullify their influence." Christianity would sweep the younger men away and through conversion win the future.

While mission schools subverted the educated young, the poor and illiterate were won by baser means.

> The number of Protestant Christians . . . has doubled in the last ten years. What is the cause of this increase? . . . Was there any thirst for salvation at the bottom of their conversion? We answer no because it is impossible that so many illiterate persons be attracted to Christianity by the local Christ which they had, as if contracted, at the time of reading the word of God revealed to [the] apostles. We repeat—no, no, no! The real cause of the increase in the number of Protestant Christians was the dreadful famine of 1874. It was the physical necessity—bread—which

42. Quotes given below from *Regenerator of Arya Varta,* September 3, 1883, p. 3.

induced these persons to adopt Christianity rather than the spiritual yearnings for salvation.[43]

Fear of Christian conversion was tinged with hope—they could be stopped, Hinduism protected, and then revitalized. "India has been conquered by England. The religions of England also want to [conquer] the religions of India; but alas! it is not in its power to do so. . . . Hinduism, though most seemingly a tissue of most absurd superstitions, is not really so. It has [the] Vedas for its source and the water, however muddily in its course, can be easily cleared of those impurities which had made it so unwholesome, it contains the highest truths of philosophy compared to which the narratives of the Bible are mere fiction."

The same forces which brought Christianity had freed Hindu thought and made possible a purification of the present state of degeneracy. "Brethren, when I think over the social condition of my motherland—India—believe me that my heart sings within me . . . . Enlightenment is fast dislodging the superstitions which people had fallen in, being persuaded to do so by the so-called Brahmans. The flood of western education is sweeping away before [a] remorseless tide the accumulated filth of ages."[44] Replacing the centuries of decadence, a new age of progress and enlightenment dawned. Aryas accepted the most unique of Western concepts, progress, and believed fully in it. "Brethren now the time has come when we can openly discuss matters—religious as they are—which we dared not give out in time gone by for fear of being considered liable to penalties of excommunication and the like. Now as the people advance morally and intellectually they can thoroughly understand the motives which actuate the popes of forcing us to undergo certain ceremonies. . . . Let us establish [a] good and virtue inculcating society. Let us come forward with our purse if need be and protest against the ravages of priestly caste." Change would come and with it bring a new purified society—strong, rational, and free both from external challenges and internal abuses. This society would also be free from Brahmanical domination, from the "popes" who had, through their own selfishness, destroyed the noble life of ancient Aryavarta.

43. Quotes given below from *Regenerator of Arya Varta,* February 19, 1883, p. 3.
44. Quotes given below from *Regenerator of Arya Varta,* October 8, 1883, p. 4.

Defeats, first to the priestly castes and later to the Muslim conquerors, explained the present state of subservience to the British. But history held more than defeat; past glories and greatness were there as well, and could be revived. The essentially positive nature of Arya ideology appealed to this new generation of educated Hindus, the first generation in Punjab to acquire an advanced education in English colleges.

### NEW LEADERS, NEW LOYALTIES—FOUR WHO CHOSE

Competition between the Aryas and Brahmos for the loyalties of Punjabi reformers represented merely the first round. In 1880, a far more serious struggle began for the allegiance of this new generation of educated Hindus. Victory or defeat in this contest determined organizational dominance among Punjabi Hindus. The careers of four young men—Pandit Guru Datta, Lala Hans Raj, Lala Lajpat Rai, and Lala Munshi Ram—illustrate the victory of the Arya Samaj over its rival Brahmos. For this struggle for the loyalties of a generation meant that the victor won the energies and talents of the newly educated.

Pandit Guru Datta was born in Multan on April 26, 1864, of a wealthy Arora family. His father, Lala Ram Kishen, a Persian scholar, was then in the service of the Punjab Education Department. The young Guru Datta received an education typical of the cultural melange of Punjab. He studied English, Persian, Sanskrit, some Arabic, and Urdu. To the Persian poets of his early education, Maulana-i-Rumi, Shamas Tabrez, and Diwan-i-Hafiz, he later added the works of John Stuart Mill and Jeremy Bentham.[45] While still a student in Multan he became interested in questions of religion, which he discussed with two close friends, Pandit Remal Das and Lala Chetan Anand, already convinced Aryas. Under their influence Guru Datta read the *Satyārth Prakāsh* and on June 20, 1880, joined the Multan Arya Samaj. His initial enthusiasm led him to study the *Ashtādhyāyī* with a local pandit. A brilliant but somewhat erratic student, Guru Datta saw little future in Multan and so in June 1880 left to continue his studies at the Government

45. Guru Datta, *The Works of the Late Pandit Gurudatta Vidyarthi, M.A., with a Biographical Sketch,* 3rd ed. (Lahore: The Arya Printing, Publishing & General Trading Company, Ltd., 1912), p. 6; Ruchi Ram Sahni, "Self-Revelations of an Octogenarian," p. 117.

College in Lahore. Once a student there, Guru Datta quickly established himself as a leader. His obvious academic ability, plus an excellent command of both spoken and written English, placed him at the center of intellectual activities amongst his fellow students. He did not immediately join the Lahore Samaj, but instead became attracted first to atheism and the Brahmo Samaj. By the time he had finished college in 1882 Guru Datta resolved his doubts and became an enthusiastic Arya.[46] His choice drew with him other students from the College, including several who later became important leaders within the Samaj.[47]

A young Bhalla Khatri, Lala Hans Raj joined the Government College, participated with Guru Datta in his Free Debating Club, and followed him into the Arya Samaj. Born on April 19, 1864, Hans Raj was just one week older than Guru Datta; but where the latter was dramatically able, Hans Raj showed his academic ability through disciplined hard work and a maturity of purpose. Hans Raj's family was poor and only his ability to win a government scholarship and the sacrifice of his elder brother, Lala Mulk Raj, made his education possible. Never prosperous, his family found life increasingly difficult after his father, Lala Chuni Lal, died on February 14, 1876. Chuni Lal began his career as a moneylender, but with the establishment of the British administration he became an Appeal *Niwās*, a drafter of legal documents. When Hans Raj was seven his father's increasing illness brought the family back from Lahore to Hoshiarpur where Chuni Lal became an assistant to a Bengali *vakīl* or lawyer practicing at the local bar.[48] Chuni Lal influenced the family both as a participant in the new anglicized world of law and in the traditional world of Islam. He had studied Persian and showed a deep interest in Islam by in-

46. Ruchi Ram Sahni, "Self-Revelations of an Octogenarian," p. 81

47. Guru Datta had founded a Free Debating Club which included Lala Shiv Nath, Lala Lajpat Rai, Lala Hans Raj, Dewan Narendra Nath, Lala Sada Nath, Lala Chetananda, Lala Ruchi Ram, Pandit Hari Kishen, and Pandit Raneshar Nath. While the students explored and discussed a wide variety of religious and social ideas—from atheism to Aryanism—several of the key figures in Samaj history participated and later followed Guru Datta into the Samaj. Guru Datta, *The Works of the Late Pandit Gurudatta*, p. 20; and Guru Datta, *Wisdom of the Rishis or Works of Pt. Gurudatta Vidyarthi, M.A.*, ed., Pandit Chamupati (Delhi: Sarvadeshik Pustakalaya, n.d.), p. iii.

48. Sri Ram Sharma, *Mahatma Hans Raj, Maker of the Modern Punjab* (Jullundur: Arya Pradeshik Pratinidhi Sabha, 1941), pp. 4–8.

viting local Muslims to his house and celebrating Islamic festivals.[49] Hans Raj grew up then in a multi-cultural home, open to influences from Islam, Hinduism, and the West. In 1879 the family moved to Lahore after Lala Mulk Raj secured a position in the Post Office. Hans Raj joined the mission school and in December 1880 passed the Calcutta University Entrance Examination. He quickly demonstrated his academic ability at college, receiving his B.A. in History in 1885. Hans Raj stood second in the college examinations, an achievement which opened the way to a successful and lucrative career in government service, should he choose it.

A year younger than Guru Datta and Hans Raj, Lala Lajpat Rai joined the college in February 1881,[50] after several unsuccessful attempts to pass the entrance examination. Unlike his two classmates, Lajpat Rai demonstrated only minimal ability at college, hampered as he was by ill health and a chaotic educational background. Lajpat was born in the village of Dhudike in the Ferozepur District in 1865, a Baniya of the Aggarwal *jāti*.[51] He received his early education in Rupar, where his father was an instructor in Persian, but his education was almost continuously interrupted by illness and travel.[52] His peripatetic father moved the family from Rupar to Simla, then Ambala City, and back to Jagraon.[53] Added to this familial wandering, Lajpat found himself caught in a religious conflict. His grandfather had been a Swatembara Jain,[54] and his father, Lala Radha Kishen, nearly a Muslim. "For the first twenty-five or thirty years of his life he [Radha Kishen] was a believer in Islam, according to the Suni School. He used to recite *namaz* and to observe the *ramzan* fast; and he cultivated acquaintance among the Ulemas and Maulvis. When Sir Syed Ahmad started his socio-religious mission, he read Sir Syed's works and became a follower of his. Up to the fortieth year he was a

49. *Ibid.*, p. 7.

50. Lajpat Rai, *Autobiographical Writings*, ed., V. C. Joshi (Delhi: University Publishers, 1965), p. 21.

51. N. B. Sen, ed., *Punjab's Eminent Hindus* (Lahore: New Book Society, 1944), p. 96.

52. Lajpat Rai, *Svargīya Lālā Lājpatrāy jī kī Āthmakathā*, ed., Bhīmsēn Vidhālankār (Lahore: Navyug Granthmālā, 1932), p. 27.

53. *Ibid.*, pp. 27–30.

54. Lajpat Rai, *Autobiographical Writings*, p. 11.

Muslim of the Syed Ahmad School."[55] Lajpat's mother found this Islamic influence almost unbearable. "I remember full well that whilst I was yet a child she used to shed tears over my father's religious 'improprieties' for hours. Sometimes she would not taste food for days together, and would keep heaving sighs of sorrow all the time with her children in her lap."[56]

A continual struggle developed between the parents with the children caught between. Lajpat watched his mother practice her Hinduism in semi-secret, always fearful of her husband's censure. "The observances, the *poojahs,* the *shraddhas,* she neglected none of these. Generally she did all this without my father's knowledge. Sometimes she would shut all doors in his absence and be through her orthodox observances before his return. But occasionally she might be taken unawares, or our father might gather from our talk that in his absence she had been occupying herself with idol-worship; on such occasions he would lose temper and administer her a scolding. Poor creature, she put up with everything; she would weep and suffer in silence."[57] Over the family hung the threat of conversion and an ensuing disintegration of the home. "Our father knew if he turned Mussalman, our mother would take her children with her and live either at his father's or at her own father's." Lajpat grew up amidst this religious tug of war, in a house with little money and constant tension.

Lala Lajpat Rai arrived in Lahore an insecure youth of barely sixteen. Here he met two of his father's friends, Pandit Shiv Narayan Agnihotri and Lala Bhawani Das, and at the urging of Pandit Agnihotri joined the Brahmo Samaj. His father thought well of the Brahmos and had on occasion contributed to the Brahmo journal, *Birādar-i-Hind* (Brother of India), edited by Agnihotri.[58] But his close friendship with Pandit Guru Datta, Lala Chetan Anand, and Lala Hans Raj proved more decisive. In December 1882, they persuaded Lajpat to attend the Arya Samaj anniversary, and in spite of his father's strong opposition he joined and immediately became involved in Arya affairs.[59] In February

55. *Ibid.*, p. 13.
56. *Ibid.*, p. 15.
57. Quotes given below from *Ibid.*, p. 15.
58. *Ibid.*, p. 23.
59. Within one week of joining the Samaj, Lajpat departed on a tour of the

1882 Lajpat passed his *mukhtārī* examination for a junior pleader license. His failure to pass the *vakālat* (lawyer's) examination later that year led him to leave college and return to Jagraon. Here he began his law practice after a mediocre college career. Lajpat was, at best, an indifferent student who tended to follow the lead of others more able or more self-confident than himself.

In 1882 Lala Munshi Ram, the last of this quartet, arrived in Lahore to begin law classes at the Government College. Older than most students at the college, Munshi Ram was born into the Khatri caste in Talwan, Jullundur District, in 1856. His background, life-style and relative wealth set him somewhat apart. Like Lajpat Rai, Munshi Ram had a peripatetic youth, traveling with his father who served in the police but was unable to settle long in any one place. Munshi Ram's parents taught him a rigid orthodoxy. His father, a devout Shaivite, insisted that his son follow scrupulously all religious rituals. Munshi Ram also was urged by his father to be physically aggressive, as befitting a Kshatriya. At home his mother demanded as well that the small child carefully observe the taboos of touch and purity. "At the time of answering the calls of nature, the child had to fully undress himself, even during the cold months. Only after getting himself cleaned with a bath, he could dress again. Even the very touch of drains cost him a bath. If, in his wanderings, he came to touch any water, he had to take a bath and wash himself."[60] Munshi Ram rebelled from such strictness, turning his energies to sports and liquor. He studied at Banda in the North-Western Provinces where he received his middle school education, entered Queen's College in Banaras and later continued his education in Allahabad. While living in Bareilly he met Swami Dayanand and although he was impressed with Dayanand, he did not join the Samaj or change his rather dissolute life. Through his father's influence he received a post as Naib Tahsildar at Bareilly, but soon clashed with his English superior and left government service.

Munshi Ram seemed destined to drift without purpose or suc-

---

United Provinces to collect money for a publishing fund. He went to assist Bhai Jawahir Singh, then secretary of the Lahore Samaj. For the young Lajpat, this trip marked the beginning of his public life; he made his first speeches and came into contact with other members of the Samaj outside of the Punjab. Lajpat Rai, *Āthmakathā*, p. 45.

60. M. R. Jambunathan, ed., *Swami Sharddhanand* (Bombay: Bharatiya Vidya Bhavan, 1961). See the first sixty-six pages for an account of his early life.

cess. Restless and troubled by a strong conscience, he possessed neither personal nor professional goals. After his father was posted to Kurji, Jullundur District, the family decided to send Munshi Ram to Lahore for legal study. Once there he rented a house and settled uneasily into the role of a student. Munshi Ram soon met members of both the Brahmo Samaj and the Arya Samaj, becoming particularly close to Bhai Jawahir Singh and Bhai Ditt Singh, then both Aryas. Following an initial failure, he passed his *mukhtārī* examination, returned to Jullundur, and then to Phillaur to begin his law practice. His first stay in Lahore gave Munshi Ram a beginning in law and heightened the tensions within himself, between conscience and conduct. After a severe personal crisis brought on by his drinking, Munshi Ram returned to Lahore for his *vakālat* examination. In this he succeeded, but more significantly he began to solve his internal struggles through an acceptance of Aryanism. In 1885, Munshi Ram returned to Jullundur a lawyer and the President of the new Jullundur Arya Samaj.

Munshi Ram's acceptance of Samaj doctrines clearly stemmed from a deep personal crisis. The slow process of questioning society or a desire for reform mattered less to Munshi Ram than his own moral condition. Aryanism was for him a religious belief, deeply held and at the core of his being. Thus, he brought to the Samaj an element of strong, passionate commitment which he maintained until his assassination in 1926. His conversion to vegetarianism was typical of this attitude·

When I was thus engaged in reading the tenth chapter of the *Satyarth Prakash* the servant announced that supper was ready. I rose with deep thought and getting my hands and legs cleaned, I went into the dining room for supper. To my sorrow I found there was a flesh curry. I hated it so much that I took the bowl containing flesh and threw it against the wall. It broke to pieces. My friends got excited. "What, any flies in the curry? What is this? Why did you throw it? What is the matter?" were the various queries. Silencing all of them, I said, "Don't you speak without thinking. It is one of the great sins for Aryans to eat flesh. I could not bear the sight of it at my table." All my brothers were startled. They kept quiet at the moment, but some time afterwards asked me why, instead of handing it over to others, I broke the bowl into pieces. I did not reply them and perhaps it was due to my timidity. How can the fetters forged by custom and tradition of the world be silently broken? I could only eat a little that day.[61]

61. *Ibid.*, p. 53.

Similar emotional clashes took place between Munshi Ram and his father over the performance of orthodox rituals. The new convert remained true to his faith, a faith which he transmitted to the young and struggling Jullundur Samaj. Here in the Jullundur Doab, Munshi Ram made his leadership felt.

For Munshi Ram, as for Lajpat Rai, their experiences in Lahore and conversion to the Samaj represented only the first phase of their new lives. After the Lahore experiences, each left to begin his career in law and Aryanism in the *mofussil.* Lajpat would later settle in Lahore; Munshi Ram did not. His world remained the Doab, and after 1902, Hardwar and Delhi. Thus, Lajpat Rai and Munshi Ram typified a process that became increasingly important during the 1880s and 1890s, by which young men traveled to Lahore for education, became imbued with the culture of that city, then left and spread its lifestyle throughout the Punjab. Some returned in later years, as success or retirement brought them back. Lahore, the magnet, dominated the entire northwestern area from Kashmir to Sind until it was torn asunder in 1947.

## EMERGENCE OF THE PUNJABI HINDU ELITE: THE 1880s

For a few brief years, in the early 1880s, youth broke through the traditional domination of age and seized a degree of creative leadership seldom seen throughout the past or in years hence. The heightened change and awareness of that change, existent during these years and especially in Lahore, gave stature to the student generation. ". . . As we college students, belonged to the first generation of English knowing Punjabis, we were much flattered by the older men of the Province. We were often spoken of as the 'hopes' of the country. On our own part, we were also led to think that we should try to deserve at least a little of the nice things that were said about us."[62] Old answers no longer satisfied, no longer appeared relevant to contemporary problems. The "hopes" of this new generation would find new paths toward the future. Yet this meant that a generation had little of the past to guide them, to support them in their quest for a purpose in life or on the more mundane level of day-to-day decision making.

The alienated and marginal students of the 1880s shared a common confusion and a generational perception of events. They

62. Ruchi Ram Sahni, "Self-Revelations of an Octogenarian," p. 117.

also shared a search for some systematic explanation of their experiences. Ruchi Ram Sahni, looking back on his own years in Lahore, remembered that an "intellectual isolation filled us with a feeling of our own importance, not a very enviable position for a youth who was standing on the threshhold of life but did not know [on] his own what pitfalls lay in front of him or his own capacities and limitations, intellectual, social and spiritual."[63] Students sought answers to their dilemma of identity through their studies and through a variety of movements and allegiances. They attempted to comprehend their surroundings—to understand even vaguely the strange and perplexing varieties of concepts filtered through the new, English education and its accompanying linguistic confusion. "The remarkable books, as they appeared both to Guru Datta and myself [Ruchi Ram Sahni] we also read together in our spare hours in the College verandah. . . . These were Mill's *Utilitarianism* and Bentham's *Theory of Legislation.* They were, of course, not included [in] the college 'course,' but that was of little consideration for both of us."[64] Driven by curiosity and the need to understand the new anglicized world, these two students struggled with strange concepts in a completely foreign tongue. "We read and re-read Mill's small book line by line, or paragraph by paragraph, discussing, arguing, differing or agreeing in the end, as we went along Now and again. we could not 'do' more than a sentence or two in the course of an hour, for either we could not agree as to what the author's real meaning was or, for some other reason, the whole time was taken up with the discussion about all the implications of the passage or how far we could ourselves accept his lead." This new knowledge could only be gained with difficulty—even in its simplest sense—while the meaning and implications of English thought eluded all but the most brilliant and determined.

Ideology cannot be created in a vacuum. By its very nature it is the product of group action and elaboration. Answers that explain a new universe, a new historical situation, must inevitably be produced in cities, through the interaction of intellects sharing a similar perception of events. Symbols, if they are to have meaning, can only be given that meaning through dialogue and a common acceptance of their representational content. Lahore became the

63. *Ibid.*, p. 76.
64. Quotes given below from *Ibid.*, p. 75.

crucible for such a dialogue. Here the students drawn out of their small towns and rural environments found a window to the world.

"Thankful as I am to my teachers, I wish deliberately to record that on coming to Lahore, my eyes were for the first time opened to the immense treasures of knowledge that were readily available to any one who could care to take advantage of them. . . . The only Arts College that the capital of the Province could boast of was the Government College and all the books it possessed were shown on the shelves of not more than fifteen almirahs resting against the walls of the big hall. But even so, for a man who had never seen even a school library and was hungry for knowledge the small library in the Government school and the bigger one at the Government College looked like an ocean with precious pearls . . . available to anyone who would dive for them."[65]

Lahore became the center of new learning, of political power, of intellectual and cultural ferment, and, above all else, the gateway to success. Delhi, after the closure of Delhi College, slipped into second place only to be rescued by the establishment of the imperial capital in 1911. Ludhiana and Jullundur lost much of their importance after annexation of the Punjab and even Amritsar followed Lahore. By the end of the 1880s the pattern of occupational distribution showed Lahore's growing place in the new anglicized world. Of all the cities of the Punjab, Lahore had the highest percent of strangers, of citizens born outside of the city and district. Delhi and Amritsar, by contrast, remained heavily populated by their own people. They attracted fewer emigrants and played correspondingly lesser roles in social and cultural change.[66]

Lahore's dynamic nature and steady growth throughout the nineteenth century produced a unique lifestyle. Prakash Tandon described accurately the creation of "old-boy" Lahoris who by the end of the nineteenth century had taken on the characteristics of a class, both economically and culturally. "Each generation, my grand-uncle, father, uncle and we ourselves, studied at Lahore. When you settled in a profession or service, most of your colleagues were old friends from Lahore; you married into some family whose sons and daughters had been to Lahore. Thus Lahore came to acquire a very special position in our society. There was an overall class of Punjabi professionals who had been educated at

65. *Ibid.*, p. 63.
66. *Census, Punjab Report 1911*, p. 24.

Lahore, and this was not a 'caste of birth or inheritance,' for in many colleges, especially those started by charitable trusts, there was a large number of students from humble homes in towns and villages."[67] The two forces, British policy and traditional social dynamics, combined to determine the configuration of this new class, the English-educated Punjabi.

British introduction of Bengalis and Kayasthas from beyond Punjab could only meet the immediate needs of post-annexation manpower. It was a temporary solution. The new provincial government sought through its educational policies to create a pool of educated Punjabis sufficient to staff their expanding provincial bureaucracy. The government encouraged secondary and higher education while allowing students to study through the medium of Urdu rather than the more difficult English. By 1855, Urdu had replaced Punjabi and Persian as the official language on the lower levels of administration. As the availability of educated and literate manpower increased, the government introduced educational qualifications for its employees. By 1865, a "broad vernacular education" became necessary for any position paying over Rs. 20 a month. In 1874 the educational qualification for promotions to Rs. 25 per month or more required a middle school examination.[68] These standards were adjusted from time to time depending on the availability of educated personnel. For the higher positions English literacy and a college education became the prerequisites.

Response to the opportunities created under the British followed existing occupational patterns of the province. The traditionally literate castes moved swiftly into schools and from there into new occupations demanding literacy. Among Hindus this meant the Brahmans, and the commercial castes, Khatris, Aroras and Baniyas, plus a few of the smaller commercial and artisan groups. By the 1870s occupational patterns were clearly visible. At the lowest levels of government service, below Rs. 15 per month, the number of Hindus and Muslims was nearly equal. But in the middle and upper levels the pattern shifted to a nearly total dominance by the Hindu priestly and commercial groups. Together they accounted for over 80 percent of the "superior appoint-

67. Prakash Tandon, *Punjabi Century, 1857–1947* (London: Chatto & Windus, 1961), p. 192.

68. Norman Gerald Barrier, "Punjab Politics and the Disturbances of 1907," Ph.D. dissertation, Duke University, 1966, pp. 12–13.

ments."[69] This pattern of Hindu dominance extended to the professions outside of government service, medicine, law and engineering.[70]

The nature of the student community mirrored occupational patterns. "Although the number of Hindu and Muslim students in primary schools was approximately the same, Hindus shot ahead in secondary and higher education. In 1871, for example, there were only 6 Muslims in college compared with 93 Hindus; in higher schools, 1,658 Muslims and 4,468 Hindus; middle schools, 2,200 Muslims and 5,433 Hindus. The Muslim position was made worse by their tendency to enroll in the vernacular branch of education, while most of the Hindus preferred the more westernized English branch."[71] Literacy followed education. Here too the Hindus led: 65 percent of the total literate male community were Hindus,[72] and among the Hindus the commercial castes prevailed. "The three great trading castes, the Khatris, the Baniyas and the Aroras contributed over 40 per cent. of the literate population."[73] An examination of those literate in English shows similar patterns. Of the 19,274 Punjabis literate in English in 1891 the Khatris stood first followed by the Brahmans, Sheikhs, Aroras and Baniyas.[74] Knowledge of English went overwhelmingly to the Hindu commercial castes with the Khatris far outdistancing all others within the traditional social system.

69. *Ibid.*, p. 17.

70. N. G. Barrier gives the following figures: among 67 assistant surgeons employed by the British, for example, there were 9 Muslims and 52 Hindus. The Hindus included 20 Khatris, 7 Aroras, 13 Brahmans, and 7 members of minor trading castes. By 1885, there were 48 first-class pleaders (29 Hindus, 4 Muslims, 7 Bengalis) and 160 second-class pleaders (129 Hindus, 20 Muslims, 4 Bengalis). Although identification of the second-class pleaders is impossible, among the 29 Hindu first-class pleaders there were 4 Brahmans, 11 Khatris, 4 Aroras, 3 Baniyas, and 2 members of minor trading castes. N. G. Barrier, "Punjab Politics and the Disturbances of 1907," pp. 17–18.

71. *Ibid.*, p. 16.

72. *Census, Punjab Report 1891*, p. 250.

73. *Ibid.*, p. 252.

74. In 1891 the major literate castes were as follows: Khatris, literate 99,405, knowing English, 4,221; Brahmans, literate 116,542, knowing English, 2,697; Sheiks (Muslims), literate 23,181, knowing English, 1,338; Aroras, literate 138,928, knowing English, 1,313; and Baniyas, literate 103,928, knowing English, 1,153. *Census, Punjab Report 1891*, p. 253 and p. lxix, Appendix C, Abstract 61.

The elites in formation would be "new" in certain specifics, but would also represent pre-British social and cultural realities Possession of literacy and a tradition of cultural adjustment marked the Hindu commercial, priestly and, to some extent, artisan castes. In the past they had survived and at times flourished under both Islamic and Sikh rule. The process of learning a new language and of adapting to a conquering civilization existed as a precedent in Punjab as throughout much of northern India. The forms of adjustment, dictated by the nature of each conquering civilization, would change; the nineteenth century experience represented something "new" as did the modernity of British rule. The link between scientific and cultural change in the Western world brought continual change to Punjabis as it did to their foreign rulers. "Newness" became a permanent feature of life affecting all strata of society, although with distinctly different rates of impact. Placing—social, geographic, and occupational—determined exposure to change and thus cultural creativity. The English-educated Hindu sensed that British rule meant not merely the replacement of one political power with another, but a fundamental challenge to the existing order and to the presuppositions on which that order rested. The expanding awareness of change can be seen not only in institutional innovation but in the growth of public opinion, itself a product of both group consciousness and the rapid development of modern communications.[75]

New forms of communication, primarily in printing and journalism, allowed for the expression of public opinion, meaning the views and attitudes of the literate elites. The anxieties of these elites first focused on two areas, education and employment, both interlinked and supporting the very existence of this class. These were class interests affecting all whose careers depended either directly or indirectly upon governmental policy.

Punjabis voiced concern over the rather poor development of the Government College. The number of students enrolled in the college grew slowly, almost painfully. Yet the college and Dr. Leitner received continual public support. Leitner dreamed of an

75. The number of newspapers waxed and waned according to a variety of factors, but the years 1880 to 1904 showed a dramatic increase indicative of an expanding literate community and the rising effectiveness of public opinion. In 1880–1884 the average number of newspapers was 39.20, in 1900–1904 it rose to 141.80.

"Oriental University of Upper India" which would revive traditional learning and bring Western enlightenment to all through the vernacular languages.[76] In 1870, he succeeded in opening the Punjab University College with an Oriental College as an integral part of this "University-to-be." Leitner's leadership, highly appreciated by the aristocrats and the more traditional sections of Punjabi society, was opposed by the educated community. Toward the close of the 1870s Leitner became a target of public opinion, as the man who would hinder the growth of English education, Western learning, and higher education. The newly educated suspected his emphasis on "Oriental" learning. Leitner maintained that the Oriental College would be "the model indigenous teaching University in the Punjab for all the indigenous educational elements of the Province, Hindu, Muhammadan and Sikh. It combines modern requirements with the traditional learning of the Maulvis, Pandits, Munshis and Bhais, which is imparted on a more critical system than is generally pursued in indigenous institutions."[77] Should Leitner succeed in his goals, English-speaking Punjabis felt their roots would be cut and entrance to the new occupations clearly inhibited. In 1881, Dyal Singh Majithia, a Sikh aristocrat, philanthropist and close friend of the Bengali Brahmos of Lahore, founded the *Tribune,* an English-language newspaper. Throughout 1881 the Lahore *Tribune* condemned "the anti-higher education policy of government," and the "sham orientalism" of Dr. Leitner.[78] This newspaper, staffed almost completely by Bengali Brahmos, expressed opinions accepted by the majority of educated Punjabis. Brahmos, Aryas, and orthodox among the Punjabi Hindus demanded the extension of English education, damned Orientalism as obscurantism, and complained that Leitner's policies, if followed, would suppress and inhibit the growth of a Punjabi elite.[79] Educational politics had arrived and soon became a permanent feature of Punjabi life.

76. J. P. Bruce, *A History of the University of the Panjab* (Lahore: n. pub., 1933), p. 11.

77. G. W. Leitner, *History of Indigenous Education in the Panjab since Annexation and in 1882* (Calcutta: n. pub., 1883), p. 102.

78. *Tribune,* April 9, 1881, p. 9; and Special Supplement, *Tribune,* June 25, 1881, p. 7.

79. The *Tribune* was not alone; the *Kōh-i-Nūr, Akbār-i-Ām, Nasīm-i-Hind, Punjābī Akhbār, Patiāla Akhbār,* and even the *Civil and Military Gazette* joined in criticiz-

In the 1880s Punjabis reacted to a series of issues brought to their province from the more politically advanced areas of Hindustan and Bengal. The Punjab gradually became integrated into the general world of British India. Surendra Nath Banerjea's visit in 1877 brought Bengali politics up the same line of communication that had already introduced Bengali concepts of social and religious change. Bannerjea's career received continual publicity throughout the cities of Punjab, particularly since the *Tribune* remained directly under his influence. The Idol Contempt Case of 1883 and Surendra Nath's subsequent imprisonment made him a martyr in the eyes of educated Punjabis. Meetings of indignation and sympathy for the "imprisoned patriot"[80] were held throughout the major cities of Punjab. The Ilbert Bill provoked similar political action—meetings, articles, and pamphlets discussed the issue, praised Lord Ripon and condemned "Anglo-Indian" racism. While the Ilbert controversy tended to unify Punjabis, to bring about cooperation among the major religious communities, other issues proved divisive and for Punjab far more significant.

The introduction of local government in 1881 politicized the educated elites and created an arena for communal competition. Hindus, Sikhs, and Muslims fought for control of the new structures. Victory meant prestige and patronage; defeat—loss of influence and "face."[81] The Hindu elite quickly mobilized. "We read the discussions in the *C[ivil] and M[ilitary] Gazette* on the one side and the *Tribune* on the other. The two vernacular papers, the *Koh-i-noor* and the *Aftab-i-Punjab,* were considered of no account. We also attended the public meetings in support of the Resolution [on local government]. We also held our own meeting in the Boarding House at which we resolved to go round to the nearby towns and villages and address public meetings explaining the objects and importance of the reforms. This was the first time I [Ruchi Ram Sahni] took active interest in a public movement of any

---

ing Leitner and the Punjab University College. Outside the Punjab, such prominent papers as the *Pioneer, The Bengalee,* the *Indian Mirror* and *Bombay Gazette* expressed similar sentiments. *Tribune,* June 25, 1881, p. 7; also issues for July 9, p. 9; July 30, p. 8; June 18, p. 8, April 30, 1881, p. 8.

80. *Regenerator of Arya Varta,* May 28, 1883, p. 6.

81. N. G. Barrier, "The Punjab Government and Communal Policies, 1870–1908," *Journal of Asian Studies,* XXVII, No. 3 (May 1968), p. 529.

kind."[82] Political agitation, a new and strange activity, often followed existing lines of social communication within a given community and also heightened divisions between religious groups. "During the vacation when I went to my native town, Behra, I got together three or four meetings, mostly of shop-keepers along with a few school teachers, and set out to them as well as I could, the aims and objects of the new reforms, and what good it was going to do the people. I also went round to some of the villages in the neighbourhood and addressed similar meetings. It was a novel experience both for me and my audience." Overlapping the question of local government came an issue which struck Punjabi sensibilities with great force, the Hindi-Urdu controversy.

The question of which language should be utilized in education and administration became serious first in the North-Western Provinces. Echoes of this debate affected Punjabis as early as the 1860s, but it was not until the government appointed the Hunter Commission on Indian Education that the question became serious for Punjab. Each major community, Muslim and Hindu, mobilized in the hope that they could influence the Commission's decision.[83] The resulting clash began a period of increasing intercommunal rivalry which waxed and waned but remained a fact of Punjabi life until partition. Hindus strove to replace Urdu with Hindi, a campaign that saw a high degree of unity among all segments of their community—Brahmo, Arya, and orthodox. The Brahmos, led by Babu Novin Chandra Rai, Sitala Kanta Chatterjee, and Kali Prosanna Chatterjee, wrote and spoke in support of the *Dēva Nāgrī* script, the promotion of Hindi literature and particularly for its acceptance as the medium of instruction in government schools. Novin Chandra Rai was the most persuasive of the three. As an educator and outstanding public figure, he commanded widespread public attention. Novin Chandra's experience in translating Brahmo literature from Bengali and English into one of the languages current in the Punjab[84] convinced him

82. Ruchi Ram Sahni, "Self-Revelations of an Octogenarian," pp. 117–118.

83. Barrier, "Punjab Politics and the Disturbances of 1907," pp. 28–29.

84. *Tribune*, February 22, 1897, p. 4; June 5, 1900, p. 3; and Ruchi Ram Sahni, "Self-Revelations of an Octogenarian," pp. 238–239; Collet, *The Brahmo Year-Book for 1877*, p. 15.

that Hindi should be the language of communication throughout the Punjab.

Aryas recognized Brahmo contribution to the cause of Hindi. As Lajpat Rai noted, "Although Brahmo literature did not very much glorify Hinduism, its atmosphere was not free from Hindu nationalism. The Brahmos were much enamoured of the English people and English culture, but as compared with Islam they respected pristine Hinduism. They were votaries of Sanskrit and Hindi, and in the Urdu-Hindi controversy they advocated the cause of Hindi."[85] Arya publications and pamphlets devoted themselves to the question of language and script throughout the years 1881–1883. The arguments centered around the question of which language could be considered the true vernacular of the province and which of the competing scripts, the Perso-Arabic or *Dēva Nāgrī*, was the best suited for primary and secondary education. The Commission approach to decision making in this issue, as in many others, represented an open invitation to agitational politics. Whatever group could mobilize effective public opinion might succeed in influencing the bureaucracy. Defeat with one commission need never be permanent; another commission, another round of agitation, held the hope of redress and final victory.[86] This debate over language continued, becoming a permanent aspect of communal politics in the Punjab.

In December 1882, the Hindus of Lahore, spurred on by the successful organizational activities of Sayyid Ahmad Khan and by the general political excitement of the times, founded the Lahore Hindu Sabha. Led by Raja Harbans Singh, the Sabha hoped to protect Hindu interests by: "I. Adoption of measures calculated to promote and enhance brotherly feelings among the different sections of the Hindu community and to effect the removal of those obstacles which stand in the way of their union. II. Advocacy of political rights and privileges of the Hindu community at large by constitutional means. III. The establishment of schools for education of Hindu children and encouragement of Hindi, the vernacu-

85. Lajpat Rai, *Autobiographical Writings*, p. 79; also see Leitner, *History of Indigenous Education in Panjab*, p. 45.

86. See Barrier, "The Punjab Government and Communal Politics," pp. 529–530.

lar of the country."[87] Lala Sangam Lal, writing in the *Arya*, justified this new organization as a necessary defense against organized Islam. "The existence of such a Society as the Mahomedan Association, which has already made many unworthy and unreasonable attacks against the Hindus as a body, in the way of sending out Memorials to Government, praying for special privileges over Hindus, and accusing the latter of undue partiality to persons of their own creed, and which in the absence of any similar Society amongst Hindus, have up to this time remained unanswered, adds pre-eminently to that necessity."[88]

By the mid-1880s both the Hindu and Muslim communities had taken their first steps toward communal organization. Yet the period of deepening ideological and religious controversy, of fierce struggle, and finally the institutionalization of communal tensions lay ahead. The immediate future offered wealth and increased social status for those literate in English. Many Punjabi Hindus saw the world as a positive place of opportunity and hope. Arya ideology filled the psychological vacuum felt by marginal and alienated Hindus striving to relate both to their parental world and the new anglicized reality of British India. The class interests of an emerging Hindu elite converged with Arya ideology which stressed literacy and the need for Vedic knowledge. Both focused on education as the path to spiritual and worldly success. It lay at the nexus of their hope and fear. The threat of apostasy cast gloom over the rewards inherent in the new economic opportunities. Aryas would provide an answer to this dilemma, a chance to acquire English education without fear of conversion, of the loss of one's soul to Christianity or godless materialism.

87. *Regenerator of Arya Varta*, December 10, 1883, p. 5.

88. The *Arya*, December 1882, pp. 221–222. For similar statements of support and news of the Sabha, see *Arya*, October 1882, p. 181. *Regenerator of Arya Varta*, February 26, 1883, p. 6 and May 28, 1883, p. 6.

## Chapter III

# IN SERVICE TO THE COMMUNITY: THE ARYA SAMAJ AS ANGLICIZER

No one can know God, *Dharma* and the sciences without knowing the meaning of the Vedas, because the Vedas are the basis of all the sciences. Without knowing the Vedas no one can acquire true knowledge . . . . The light of truth, wherever and in whatever quantity it has shone, has issued from the Vedas. For this reason, all men should endeavour to know their meaning and teachings.

SWAMI DAYANAND SARASWATI

### EDUCATION: THE TWO-EDGE SWORD

On October 30, 1883 Swami Dayanand Saraswati died in Bhinai House, Ajmere. His demise left Aryas without their *guru,* the central figure of this entire movement. Dayanand had no spiritual heir to insure ideological continuity, no bearer of gnostic knowledge to reinterpret doctrine, nor any institutional structure to proclaim proper and official dogma. Only his diverse writings remained to guide the faithful, and these were open to interpretation by each Samaj and each Arya. This potential ideological anarchy was matched by a complete absence of any coordinating or controlling body. Each local Samaj was free to act and believe according to its own conscience. Yet a rough consensus existed both in belief and goals, and rather than paralysis, Dayanand's death supplied a stimulus to new growth and dynamism. In death he proved a more flexible and inspiring figure than during the last few years of his life. He and his writings could be interpreted to fit local needs and yet still remain the symbol of reverence and respect for all Samajists. Samaj leadership now operated on a local and provincial level without the impeding shadow of a distant prophet.

The initial responses of Aryas to Dayanand's passing proved quite uniform. In meeting after memorial meeting speakers urged the founding of a school or college in honor of the departed prophet. Memorial meetings in Lahore, Ferozepore, and Multan simultaneously passed resolutions calling for the establishment of a Dayanand College,[1] "where Vedas might be taught side by side with other learning."[2] The idea of founding such a college seemed daring almost beyond belief, but reformist Muslims had succeeded in creating their own college, so why not Aryas? "All difficulties will give way if we have recourse to labor and perseverance. Look at Maulvi Sayyed Ahmed Khan, the great founder of Aligarh College who single handed, with the aid of perseverance, brought about such wonderful results." Arya emotions were heightened by the return of Lala Jiwan Das and Pandit Guru Datta from Ajmere. Fresh from the deathbed of Dayanand they related the story of his last hours before a meeting of Aryas held on November 8 at the Lahore Samaj. They closed their dramatic and heartrending tale with an appeal for funds. The audience responded enthusiastically: "All present were moved and everyone came, everyone from the young students to the aged sire came forward with their mite to raise up the proposed memorial. Some of the poor shopkeepers and menials who have to live from hand to mouth could be seen pressing forward to add what little they could to the funds."[3] Aryas raised Rs. 7,000 in this one gathering. The meeting passed a formal proposal to found a Dayanand Anglo-Vedic College and then dispersed with declarations of enthusiasm for the new cause and hope for the future.

The concept of a school which would teach both the new knowledge of the anglicized world along with Vedic truth offered the best of two worlds, opportunity with safety. Dayanand himself had experimented unsuccessfully with schools to teach his reformed Hinduism, and various Samajes in Punjab had organized small schools. Yet a college, staffed and supported solely by Indians, seemed an immense undertaking. Only a combination of fear and hope, of economic opportunity and cultural anxiety, would produce sufficient drive to achieve this goal. Aryas began in the eighties to articulate their educational needs. "If the fair garden of

1. Dayanand Anglo-Vedic College Society, *First Annual Report of the Dayanand Anglo-Vedic College Society for the Year 1886–87* (Lahore: Public Advocate Press, n.d.), p. 3. [Hereinafter, *College Report, 1886–87*.]

2. Quotes given below from *Regenerator of Arya Varta*, Vol. I, No. 7, November 5, 1883, pp. 4–5.

3. *Regenerator of Arya Varta*, November 12, 1883, p. 5.

Aryavarta is now being overwhelmed by weeds of materialists, atheists, sectarians, heretics and unbelievers the cause may be traced to the want of Vedic Schools, the absolute necessity of which is daily being keenly felt by us. If the Vedic Schools were established, all the evils that arise from early marriages, premature deaths, prohibition of widow marriage and excessive expenditure incurred in marriages, would have been put a stop to. Were our children acquainted with the Vedas, they would never have fallen prey to Buddhism, Christianity, Mohammedanism, licentiousness and drunkenness."[4] Proper knowledge meant salvation, both personal and national, while education provided that knowledge. This would not be an obscurantist education as envisioned by the "Orientalist" Leitner, who yearned for a rebirth of the classical languages.

Aryas recognized the new world's demand for English literacy and sought that literacy within a milieu of revived Hinduism. This would provide Punjabi parents with an ideal educational situation. "When people will find no difference between the Anglo-Vedic, Government and mission schools as regards English education, and see in the former additional advantages of Vedic instruction, the Vedic schools will be crowded with boys and I trust will do substantial good to the sons of Aryavarta. The English language will also be a medium of comparison of the Aryans to the Modern Science and enable the boys to be acquainted with the manners and ideas of the greatest nations of the modern world."[5] Teaching through English, the new schools would further anglicization while simultaneously introducing a countervailing force of revived Vedic life.

Punjabi Hindus' acceptance of British culture and its role in the new government created the possibility of rejecting another "foreign" civilization—the Islamic. Persian and Arabic went first; Urdu remained, but under increasing attack by Aryas and others among the newly-mobilized Hindu community. "The Arya Samaj contemplates establishing an Anglo–Aryan School in which English and Sanskrit will be taught with very little or no Persian at all."[6] The revival of Sanskrit paralleled the abandonment of Per-

4. *Arya Magazine*, May 1882, pp. 1–2.
5. Lala Ganeshi Lall, writing in the *Arya Magazine*, May 1882, pp. 2–3.
6. *Regenerator of Arya Varta*, September 3, 1883, p. 3.

sian. Although English opened the door to the future, Sanskrit remained the key to the Vedic past. Aryas supported both, though in practice the former more than the latter. "Before the advent of the British in India no one knew—or even cared to know—what Sanskrit was save a handful of Brahmans . . . . But since the English flag was planted on Indian soil, Sanskrit began to be patronized and recognized even by those who had a natural hatred of it, I mean, the Mohammedans."[7] Exaggerated as this statement may be for India, it is only partly so for the Punjab. Few Punjabi Hindus, including the Brahmanical castes, knew Sanskrit or cared to know it. Both Sanskrit and the *Dēva Nāgrī* script commanded little attention in pre-British Punjab.

The relative ignorance of Sanskrit among orthodoxy aided Aryas in their struggles with contemporary Hinduism. So rare was this knowledge that Aryas quickly found that with even a small knowledge of Sanskrit they could easily defeat orthodox Pundits in public debates. At times Aryas won through a combination of knowledge and bluff. "As Guru Datt knew Sanskrit well, he would sometimes commit a Sanskrit speech written out by himself to memory and then he would be taken round to a few muffassil stations to hold Shastrarth [debates], generally on idol-worship, with the orthodox Pandits. A public challenge would be thrown out for any Pandit to join him in discussion in the Sanskrit language. As no one could come forward to speak in Sanskrit, the Arya Samaj party would return from the 'field' and pass through the streets with bands playing triumphantly, the processions stopping here and there for short speeches to proclaim the defeat of the orthodox party."[8] In spite of their conflicts with the Samaj, both Brahmo and orthodox leaders aided Arya advocacy of Sanskrit, the *Dēva Nāgrī* script, and Hindi. The Hunter Commission left in its wake a sensitized Hindu community eager to challenge and, if possible, change the existing dominance of Urdu in both education and administration.

Arya educational experiments found a general acceptance among the Hindu community. The disenchantment with governmental educational policy and particularly over the role of Dr.

7. *Regenerator of Arya Varta*, October 29, 1883, p. 1.

8. Ruchi Ram Sahni, "Self-Revelations of an Octogenarian," unpublished manuscript in the possession of V. C. Joshi, Nehru Memorial Museum, p. 81.

Leitner had already reached its height in 1880-1881. Added to the older fears of conversion and alienation, now it appeared that the government was determined to restrict higher education and thus limit the growth of the new elite. This uncertainty over higher education in the Punjab accounted for much of the encouragement received by Aryas in their attempt to found an Anglo-Vedic college. Widespread sympathy existed, but the transformation of that emotion into donations of cash or labor sufficient to establish and sustain a school or even more ambitiously a college proved a difficult task.

The first outburst of enthusiasm which followed the meeting of November 8, 1883, lasted through the remainder of that year. The Antarang Sabha (Executive Committee) of the Lahore Arya Samaj met on December 6 and chose a subcommittee to take charge of collecting and depositing funds.[9] Lala Lal Chand presided over this subcommittee, with Bhai Jawahir Singh as secretary. The committee appealed to "our princes and chiefs, to nobility and gentry, higher and lower dignitaries of the realm, to the people at large, without distinction of creed and color to help us in our great undertaking."[10] Fund raising remained the central task of this group, but little could be accomplished without clarifying the goals of the educational movement. Consequently, Lala Lal Chand prepared a draft scheme and sent it to the various Punjab Samajes for their comments and suggestions. The scheme stressed previous thinking on the question of education, but it also showed a keen awareness of the problem of cultural marginality and alienation created amongst the English-educated elite. "The rush of foreign ideas, by the introduction of English literature into this country, has had no doubt the effect of enlightening and improving many thousand minds, of a few of whom the country may well feel proud. But foreign education has produced a schism in the society which is truly deplorable. An educated class has been created, a class which moves by itself, a class incapable of materially influencing, or being influenced by, the uneducated masses, and a class without precedent in any country on the earth."[11] Lal Chand's

9. *Regenerator of Arya Varta,* December 10, 1883, p. 8.

10. *Regenerator of Arya Varta,* December 10, 1883, p. 7.

11. Quotes given below from Sri Ram Sharma, *Mahatma Hans Raj, Maker of the Modern Punjab* (Jullundur: Arya Pradeshik Pratinidhi Sabha, 1941), pp. 36–38.

restructured educational system proposed ending this separation of "class" and "mass," creating a unified revived Hindu community. "The primary object will, therefore, be to weld together the educated and uneducated masses by encouraging study of the national language and vernaculars; to spread a knowledge of moral and spiritual truths by insisting on the study of classical Sanskrit; to assist the formation of sound and energetic habits by a regulated mode of living, to encourage sound acquaintance with English Literature and to afford a stimulus to the material progress of the country by spreading a knowledge of the physical and applied sciences." English language for adjustment, Hindi for communication with the masses, Sanskrit and the works of Dayanand for moral uplift, and science for material progress—Aryas offered answers to the most acute dilemmas of occupational mobility and cultural adjustment.

As the months passed into 1884, initial enthusiasm waned. The faithful still supported the educational movement, but much of the money already promised never arrived; other donations were paid only slowly. The more than Rs. 7,000 collected on November 8, 1883, increased to only Rs. 8,097 by December 10. With the passage of time it became evident that the aristocracy and wealthier among Punjabi Hindus would not contribute large sums to the movement. The work of raising funds fell on a few dedicated members of the Samaj, who collected money almost solely from the newly educated and the traditional commercial castes.[12] Aryas concentrated their efforts in the major cities, particularly Lahore, but also experimented with techniques, reaching beyond their existent centers of strength. "Other measures were also adopted for making the movement popular and for engaging public sympathy on its behalf by sending out members in deputations to the mofassil stations. These members with the assistance of local dignitaries and the local Samajes held public meetings at the several stations to which they were deputed, and by their lectures and advice greatly contributed in raising local subscriptions and in spreading a knowledge of the objects of the movement."[13]

By mid-1885, a new vigor became apparent. Aryas raised nearly Rs. 11,000 by July. The Lahore Fund Committee decided to invest

12. *Regenerator of Arya Varta,* March 4, 1884, p. 3.
13. *Arya Patrika,* July 25, 1885, p. 3.

this capital at 4 percent interest in the Agra Bank, but much of the money was not in their control. Samajes in Rajasthan, the North-Western Provinces, and Sind, as well as throughout the Punjab, held donations. They were under no obligation to forward them to Lahore, particularly as the location of the proposed college remained undecided. The question of location became heated during 1885, and some Samajes threatened to suspend further collection until a site could be chosen. Along with this question, the equally serious problem of control over the new institution remained unanswered.[14] These dual problems became more divisive. As the funded capital grew and the reality of a school drew closer, Arya leaders struggled to create some form of control and supervision that would satisfy the various Samajes involved in the educational movement.

As Samaj leaders considered Lala Lal Chand's draft scheme of organization, an event took place which drove the educational movement forward with increased vigor. On November 3, 1885, the Antarang Sabha received a letter from Lala Hans Raj in which he offered to serve as principal of the proposed school indefinitely and without pay.[15] Aryas reacted with renewed enthusiasm. The Antarang Sabha of the Lahore Samaj met nine times during November to work out details of the constitution of a new educational society. Lal Chand, in his proposal of September 7, 1885, outlined the basic problem facing the Samaj: "Until present there exists no effective organization, no systematic effort for exhausting the various resources available for attaining success in this great cause for utilizing the scattered amount uselessly held in deposit in different localities. It is believed, therefore, the time has now arrived for combining these isolated efforts, and for placing the scheme on a permanent and effective footing."[16]

British law, with its concept of registered societies, partly dictated a solution to this problem, but the details could only be determined through a lengthy period of debate and discussion within the Samaj. "How this society and committee are to be constituted is the all important question. What interests should be represented on the committee, whether any interests should have an

14. Sri Ram Sharma, *Mahatma Hans Raj,* p. 45.

15. *College Report, 1886–87*, p. 8.

16. *Proceedings, Dayanand Anglo-Vedic College Managing Committee,* Vol. I (a), from 1885. [Hereinafter, *Proceedings, DAVCMC, 1885.*]

executive control, what classes should be excluded, and if there is to be any compromise of interest, then on what grounds; these are all intricate problems which require solution at the very outset."[17] After lengthy discussion, but only minor modification, the Lahore Samaj passed Lal Chand's scheme. In order to secure approval of the major Samajes, the Antarang Sabha asked each to send a representative to Lahore at the time of the anniversary celebrations in December.[18] Each year the Lahore Samaj held a day or two of meetings to commemorate its founding. The Lahore anniversary functioned as an unofficial convocation of Samaj leaders from Punjab and the adjoining provinces. These celebrations became the earliest centralizing force after Dayanand's death. Following the festivities, the visiting delegates returned to their respective Samajes. On January 31, 1886, they reconvened in Lahore and approved the new educational scheme.[19] After this meeting, the Dayanand Anglo-Vedic Trust and Management Society was duly registered as the sole legal body controlling all funds and, in time, all property of the college movement.

Although the Society held legal responsibility, de facto and considerable de jure power rested with the Managing Committee. The right to representation on the Managing Committee was based on wealth. Each Samaj, which had donated Rs. 1,000 to the college movement, earned one seat on the Managing Committee. The representatives themselves were required to be Aryas of good standing. This limited membership to Aryas from the more active or at least wealthier Samajes. Non-Aryas could be appointed to the Managing Committee and thus gain entrance to the Society through several special constituencies. "Besides the Samajic interest, there are several other interests which require to be represented on the committee. For instance, the engineering, the medical, the educational, etc. It would be most unfortunate if in

17. Quotes given below from *Proceedings, DAVCMC, 1885*.

18. *College Report, 1886–87*, p. 8.

19. Representatives from six Samajes with supporting letters from three others traveled to Lahore for this gathering. They included: Lala Lal Chand, Lahore; Lala Sain Das, Lahore; Lala Jiwan Das, Lahore; Pandit Shiv Dat Ram, Amritsar; Lala Kashi Ram, Multan; Lala Jiwan Kishan, Gujranwala; Lala Ralla Ram, Gujranwala; Lala Shiv Saran Das, Ludhiana; and Lala Lajpat Rai, Rohtak. Letters approving the scheme came from Dehra Dun, Sukkar in Sind, and Simla. *College Report, 1886–87*, p. 9.

selecting representatives these interest selections were necessarily and perforce, confined within the Samajic circles."[20] In the approved constitution, "interest representation" included one member each for: education, medicine, engineering, nobility, law and service, appointed by the Managing Committee. Three other rules determined membership and power on the Managing Committee. First, members held seven-year terms and, second, representatives of a given Samaj need not be members of that Samaj. Thus, an outlying Samaj might, and often did, choose someone living in Lahore to act as its representative. The Managing Committee met monthly, making it extremely difficult for many Aryas to attend regularly. Third, Samajes that donated over Rs. 5,000 to the college fund earned additional representatives. This meant that the Lahore Samaj, with its wealth and strategic location, tended to dominate the Managing Committee. The "interest representatives" inevitably lived in Lahore and were close friends if not active members of the city Samaj.

The Managing Committee held its first meeting on February 27, 1886, but little was accomplished until its second meeting on March 20. The committee chose its first officers: Lala Lal Chand as president and treasurer, with Lala Jawala Sahai vice-president and secretary. It next decided to open a high school as soon as feasible and to temporarily locate it in Lahore until the question of a permanent site was settled. These decisions plunged the group into a series of meetings throughout the spring in order to complete the plans necessary to open the new school on June 1, 1886.[21] Subcommittees began work on a variety of problems, detailing rules for the conduct of business in the Managing Committee and in the proposed school, drafting a scheme of studies for each class, considering the question of appointment of the school's teaching and menial staff—the tasks seemed endless, particularly since the committees and subcommittees tended to employ the same individuals repeatedly.[22]

Of the young men only Pandit Guru Datta served on the Manag-

20. *Proceedings, DAVCMC, 1885.*

21. The date was decided upon in the Managing Committee meeting of April 24, as was the scheme of studies.

22. Lala Lal Chand carried the greatest responsibility, followed by Lala Sain Das, Lala Ishwar Das, Lala Madan Singh, Lala Jawala Sahai, Lala Mul Raj, and Lala Jiwan Das.

ing Committee and took a significant part in the initial planning. After receiving his M.A. in 1886, Guru Datta was appointed assistant professor of science in the Government College, enabling him to speak as a faculty member of the most prestigious college in the province. The following year, when J. C. Oman went on leave, Guru Datta replaced him as acting professor of science. Guru Datta's educational success legitimized his role in the college movement, the first of his generation to be accepted by the Arya leadership. Lala Hans Raj closely followed Guru Datta. A far less colorful person, Hans Raj by his dedication to the movement and his professional involvement in the school gained power over the years that seconded only Lala Lal Chand's position as president of the Trust and Management Committee. Hans Raj showed an amazing capacity for discipline and efficient work. He was in fact the ideal school principal, austere, responsible, puritanical--dedicated to the cause of Arya education. Lala Mulk Raj, his elder brother, exhibited a similar determination. It was Mulk Raj's decision to support his younger brother that enabled Hans Raj to devote himself to the college. Mulk Raj pledged to give half of his earnings of Rs. 80 per month to Hans Raj. This sum had to serve for the two households, plus the remainder of their father's family.[23] The decision of these two brothers should not be underrated. During the 1880s job opportunities for educated Punjabis were plentiful. Not only was Hans Raj offering to serve without remuneration, but he abandoned the chance of a lucrative career which could easily have resulted in wealth for himself and for his poverty-stricken family.

Hans Raj's altruism served to inspire others and to rekindle enthusiasm. Early in 1886 a wealthy contractor from Multan, Lala Jawala Sahai, donated Rs. 8,000 to the Anglo-Vedic College. This donation, the largest single amount received, made it possible to open the Dayanand Anglo-Vedic High School, but was not sufficient to maintain it. Consequently, in February 1886 the Lahore Samaj launched a drive for monthly subscriptions. They estimated that Rs. 400 per month would be sufficient to cover expenses of the new school until a capital fund could generate the needed income from interest.[24] Additional revenue would be raised from tuitions; but in order to encourage education, the

23. Sri Ram Sharma, *Mahatma Hans Raj*, pp. 40–41.
24. Sharma, *Ibid.*, p. 48.

Managing Committee decided on low, fixed fees. Unlike the government and mission schools, which charged on a sliding scale according to each family's capacity to pay, the Dayanand Anglo-Vedic schools would have one set of fees for all, but would at the same time keep them as minimal as possible.[25] Low fees encouraged even the poorest of the clerks and shopkeepers to send their children for education; in turn, they provided much of the financial support which maintained the Dayanand Anglo-Vedic schools. Along with the announcement of the fee schedule, the Managing Committee published a scheme of studies, including the pattern of classes, language of instruction, and projected curriculum. Aryas accepted the existing structure of the government schools with the addition of Vedic studies (see Appendix II). By May, Aryas completed plans for the new school. Yet underneath their excitement ran a current of anxiety. Would the school succeed or fail, and in failing destroy their dream of a safe, Hinduized education? Only an uncertain future would tell.

### THE DAYANAND ANGLO-VEDIC SCHOOL IN OPERATION

On June 1, 1886, the Dayanand Anglo-Vedic High School opened its doors. The public responded enthusiastically. By the end of the first week 300 students had enrolled.[26] The staff quickly organized classes from the first grade through the college entrance level, while the press of students made it necessary to subdivide some classes into sections.[27] The number of students swelled to 550 by the end of June.[28] This surprising enrollment indicated faith in the Samaj and hope for its success, as well as the disillusionment

25. The final fee schedule announced in the school prospectus was as follows:

*Admission Fees*

From students admitted in the Lower Primary Department . . . . . . . . . . . . As 4
From students admitted in the Upper Primary Department . . . . . . . . . . . . As 8
From students admitted in the Middle and Upper Departments . . . . . . . . Rs 1

*Monthly Fees*

Lower Primary Department . . . . . . . . . . . . . . . . . . . . . . . . . . . . . . . . . . As 2
Upper Primary Department . . . . . . . . . . . . . . . . . . . . . . . . . . . . . . . . . . As 4
Middle Department . . . . . . . . . . . . . . . . . . . . . . . . . . . . . . . . . . . . . . . . As 8
Upper Department . . . . . . . . . . . . . . . . . . . . . . . . . . . . . . . . . . . . . . . . Rs 1

26. *Tribune*, June 5, 1886, p. 7.

27. *College Report, 1886–87*, p. 13.

28. *Arya Patrika*, June 22, 1886, p. 6.

and fear associated with government and mission schools. Within one year hope turned to confidence as the new school demonstrated its ability. At the end of the academic year, students from the Dayanand Anglo-Vedic School competed successfully in the annual round of examinations. "We are extremely glad to hear of the signal success which the D.A.V. School has achieved in the last Entrance Examination of the Calcutta University, four boys were sent up, and all four of them passed. One passed in the first division, two in the second, and one in the third. The result speaks for itself."[29] The school also managed to pass fourteen out of twenty-six in the middle school examination.[30] This initial showing solidified public confidence and during the next few years the school maintained a high percentage of passes throughout the examination system. Not only was the Dayanand Anglo-Vedic School culturally safe, it offered an excellent chance for success in the new world. In 1888, the government recognized this excellence: "The D.A.V. School which receives no grant-in-aid deserves special mention as it has supplied nineteen successful candidates for the Entrance Examination or more than any other school in the Province. The proportion of successful candidates also, which was 41 percent, was higher than most other institutions."[31] The government followed its praise by official recognition. Academically secure, the school's rapid expansion threatened to undermine and exhaust its financial foundations.

The Samaj had developed considerable sophistication in collecting and accounting for funds, but with the rapid growth of the school, a new urgency drove Samaj leaders to search for additional revenue and to experiment with new methods of mobilizing financial strength. As early as June 1885, a list of donations to the College Fund appeared in the *Arya Patrika* and in April 1886, the Managing Committee began publishing them in the *Tribune.*[32] These lists provided recognition to the donors, accountability of the funds received, and publicity for the educational movement.

29. *Arya Patrika,* June 7, 1887, p. 6.

30. *College Report, 1886–87,* p. 13.

31. Quoted in Shri Ram Sharma, *Mahatma Hans Raj,* p. 51.

32. *Arya Patrika,* June 27, 1885, p. 8. These lists were published in the *Tribune* from April 3, 1886, through December 18, 1889, and listed some 1,302 donations including individual gifts, monthly subscriptions, receipts from special fund drives, receipts from local Arya Samajes and interest from bank deposits.

In addition, the Management Society issued periodical financial reports both in the *Tribune* and Samaj journals. In May 1887 they published the first annual report of the Trust and Management Society. Reports, articles, and donation lists kept the literate community continually informed on the financial progress of the Dayanand Anglo-Vedic School, while Aryas used a variety of methods, some traditional, others adopted from the outside world, to mobilize resources.

Initially Aryas employed a combination of public meetings and deputations to raise funds. Beginning with the first memorial gatherings following Dayanand's death, Aryas held meetings throughout the Punjab to stimulate donations and publicize the educational movement. Both Arya and non-Arya papers reported each event, and listed the donors with the amounts given or pledged. Throughout the latter half of the 1880s, these occasions became a regular part of Punjabi Hindu life. They not only provided funds for Arya schools but a social forum for the educated elite. The Dayanand Anglo-Vedic School became an all encompassing "cause" for many Punjabis. Their time outside their profession was absorbed by the Samaj and its activities. Aryas traveled in deputations to the North-Western Provinces, to Sind, and Rajasthan, seeking donations for the school, usually with success. Groups also traveled throughout the Punjab in an endless search for funds.

Delegations of Aryas traveled to the various Samaj anniversaries. In emulation of the Lahore anniversary festivities, each Samaj began to celebrate its own founding. These anniversary ceremonies became occasions for the local Aryas to draw together, and also for provincial leaders to lend their own prestige to the local festivities. The number of dignitaries and the amount of money raised at an annual celebration indicated the relative importance of each Samaj. With the smaller and newer Samajes results might be quite modest. "Several members of the Daya Nand Anglo Vedic College Committee had gone to Sialkote on the occasion of the last anniversary of that Samaj. A number of gentlemen of the Sialkote cantonment waited upon the members with an address expressive of their sympathy with the cause the Members had undertaken and assuring them that they [the deputation] were ready to sacrifice their wealth, mind and body in the sacred cause and as a proof of that they had there and then collected a purse of Rs. 85 in aid of this institution which they presented together with an address written in a highly eulogical style to the Members."[33] Although the deputations traveled by train and were reported in the press, Aryas incorporated many traditional elements in their pattern of action. Here the presentation of a purse and a eulogistic address stem from the past while serving contemporary needs.

Anniversary celebrations proved a major source of income from the wealthier Samajes. The *Arya Patrika* of June 7, 1887, reported "the sum of Rs. 1,300 collected in aid of the D.A.V. College on the occasion of the last anniversary of the Peshawar Arya Samaj."[34] The Amritsar Samaj raised Rs. 1,300 at its anniversary in 1889, with an additional Rs. 1,900 pledged by the membership; in the same year the Gujranwala Samaj realized Rs. 1,300 in cash and Rs. 1,500 in pledges.[35] During 1890, anniversary celebrations accounted for Rs. 7,245 out of a total of Rs. 12,322 in funded capital collected that year.[36] While Aryas amassed impressive sums on special occasions, much of their income came from small amounts given by thousands of Punjabis with an amazing regularity and faithfulness.

The harnessing of small donations on a regular basis started with the Lahore Samaj's establishment of a monthly subscription system. At that time the capital of the Trust and Management Society stood at Rs. 36,000 invested in Government Promisory Notes bearing 4 percent interest. This returned only Rs. 120 per month, not enough to cover the daily expenses of the projected school. Monthly subscriptions would have to cover the expected deficit, while the school's supporters began the drive for a "Permanent Fund" sufficient to sustain the school out of its earned interest.[37] Various Samajes quickly responded with promised monthly donations totalling over Rs. 250 per month. Although this system dealt with very small sums, it spread and gradually created significant sources of income. Both individuals and groups donated, as social pressure aided enthusiasm. At times, it was no doubt difficult not to donate and still live and work comfortably with one's peers. "It is

33. *Arya Patrika,* August 23, 1887, p. 7.
34. *Arya Patrika,* June 7, 1887, pp. 6–7.
35. *Tribune,* October 12, 1889, p. 5 and February 27, 1889, p. 4.
36. *College Report, 1889–90,* p. 12.
37. *College Report, 1886–87,* p. 26.

a matter of great pleasure to see that gentlemen from all places are coming forward to help the D.A.V. College movement. The clerks of the Railway Station, Bhatinda have volunteered to pay 3 pies per rupees from their salaries every month in aid of the D.A.V. College Fund. Their contributions in this way will amount of Rs. 2/10 per month."[38] Group donations came from clerks and the staffs of various offices, from students, teachers, and businessmen.

Punjabis also gave to the college movement from beyond the province. Individuals sent contributions from every part of India and in time from all areas of the world. Particularly strong and consistent assistance came from the areas west and south of Punjab, from the northwest frontier, Baluchistan and Sind. Punjabis had followed British expansion in these directions, securing lucrative jobs in government service, as businessmen, pleaders, and teachers. Punjabis traveled west and south in much the same way as Bengalis and Kayasthas had moved northwest to the Punjab. The transplanted Punjabi—generally an educated Hindu—often proved a loyal and dedicated supporter of the Samaj and its causes.[39] Hindus in the western and northwestern areas of British India found themselves surrounded by a sea of Muslims and reacted with a heightened awareness of their religious identity. Separated from their social milieu, from ties of caste and the associations of youth, they turned to the Arya Samaj as a replacement for all they had left behind. Many who supported and participated in Arya causes found a place there for themselves and their families.

The pattern of Samaj funding shows clearly that the school was supported by the literate, commercial groups and the newly anglicized. "It is a pity our Rajas, Maharajas and Sirdars and Jagirdars have practically kept themselves aloof from the Anglo-Vedic

38. *Arya Patrika*, December 14, 1886, p. 7.

39. The Sukkur Arya Samaj provided leadership in Sind, while the local College Committee, Bolan Pass, successfully mobilized Hindu clerks and government contractors working on the Bolan State Railway, and members of the Hirok Arya Samaj in Baluchistan. For information on the Sukkur Arya Samaj, see the *Arya Patrika*, May 4, 1886, p. 5; June 29, 1886, p. 6, and various donation lists in the *Tribune* throughout the 1880s. The Bolan Committee is mentioned in the *Arya Patrika* issues of October 5, 1886, p. 5; October 12, pp. 5–6; June 15, p. 7; and the Hirok Samaj in October 5, 1886, p. 7 and October 12, 1886, p. 6.

College movement."[40] The aristocracy had little interest in or sympathy for the Samaj or its educational programs. Only rarely did they donate and then usually in response to a deputation of leading Aryas who approached them as traditional supplicants. More often than not, it was the educated elite who went asking for funds from their less prestigious or more traditional peers—they turned quite naturally to the market place.

> Gentlemen of good position, who have themselves given liberal donation[s] go to *bazar's* to ask for contributions from the common people. An institution can truly be called national when all people from highest to the lowest join in establishing it. That is the cause of the Dayanand Anglo-Vedic College will be readily admitted by all. The splendid sum of about Rs. 45,000 in hard cash which has been realized up to this time [June 1886], has all been subscribed by common people and gentlemen of the middle class. No Raja and Maharaja has yet been appealed to. This is the reason why so much general interest is shown in the progress of the College movement.[41]

Samajists saw themselves as living in a "pauper province" which necessitated unusual methods to collect the needed funds. They recognized and alternately praised or denigrated the fact that their members were mostly clerks, "pen pushers," who could contribute only small amounts.[42] Arya genius lay in the sophistication of their methods for realizing large sums through small donations.

With the success of the school and its parallel rising expenses, Aryas developed a host of new techniques for fund raising. The tradition of giving gifts to Brahmans on important occasions became an important source of revenue, once Aryas modified it for their own uses. From 1886 on sympathizers and members of the Samaj marked happy events with a donation to the College Fund. These occasions varied widely, including "Rs. 200 on his son's marriage," "Rs. 8/- on birth of a son," "Rs. 6/- on recovery of wife's health," "Rs. 1/- on having passed the telegraphic examination," and "Rs. 2/- by four clerks, on the increase of their pay."[43] Not all such donations were as small. One Arya, Lala Parmanand, a pleader from Multan, gave Rs. 200 on the birth of his son.[44] As this

40. *Tribune,* September 15, 1888, p. 2.
41. *Arya Patrika,* July 20, 1886, p. 6.
42. *Tribune,* September 15, 1888, p. 2.
43. *College Report, 1886–87,* pp. 24–25.
44. *Arya Patrika,* November 2, 1886, p. 7.

form of donation grew in popularity, various *jātis* decided to give to the College Fund on the occasion of marriages within their group.[45]

Other traditional festivals served to stimulate donations as the educated Punjabi Hindu moved further in lifestyle from the norm of surrounding society. "Dear Brother,—I am directed to inform you that at the late 'Magh i' it was proposed in the 'Samaj' that the members should pay something at the usual 'Teshars' holidays in aid of the Daya Nand Anglo-Vedic College Fund. As it is an old custom here amongst the so-called Hindus to distribute raw Kichhari (mixture of rice and Mung) to Brahmans it was thought necessary that we should also give our quota of Kichhari to the College Fund. This was unanimously passed and about Rs. 2 was collected on account of 'Kichhari.'"[46] The giving of alms, first employed by Bhai Nehal Singh in street begging, also proved exploitable in other terms.

> In the summer months, at one of the weekly gatherings of the Lahore Arya Samaj, a simple and weak Sadhu made his appearance. At the end of the discourse on *Satyārth Prakāsh* he delivered an inspiring lecture which suggested that other Samajs also should go begging every Sunday for a handful of flour from each house to be used for the Samaj work. Accordingly, in every house a "Dharm Pot" was kept, in which ladies of the household used daily to put a handful of flour. This had become so popular and useful that it contributed its mighty share towards the founding of the Dayanand Anglo-Vedic College.[47]

The *ātā* (flour) fund spread from Lahore throughout the Punjab, becoming a regular source of income. Lala Munshi Ram and Lala Dev Raj of Jullundur both accepted and then elaborated it, adding a "rag fund." "It was meant that the Samaj servants should collect all the torn clothings from the houses and the proceeds realised out of their sales should be added to the Samaj Fund."[48]

45. "Some of the most important biradaris of the Panjab, viz., the Aror Bans of Lahore, and some Khatri Biradaris of Chakwal, Rawalpindi, Behra and Gujerat who have passed resolutions to the effect that on the occasion of marriages something will always be donated for the D.A.V. College. They have fixed the least sums to be donated on these occasions." *College Report, 1891–92*, p. 15.

46. *Arya Patrika*, March 15, 1887, p. 7.

47. M. R. Jambunathan, ed., *Swami Shraddhanand* (Bombay: Bharatiya Vidya Bhavan, 1961), p. 78.

48. Jambunathan, *Ibid.*, p. 79.

The *ātā* system appealed to Aryas as part of their traditional world. In all matters, organizational, ideological, and financial, they stressed their adherence to the past, the correct and true past of Hinduism, and whenever existent customs could be adopted to fit contemporary needs, the tension between modernity and tradition diminished. "Our readers will be glad to learn that the Abbotabad Arya Samaj also is now taking active steps to collect subscriptions in aid of the D.A.V. College Fund. The members have also adopted the *Dharm Ghat* or atta system, and have sent Rs 4 to the Managing Committee as the income of three weeks . . . . The system is the more commendable because it is in accordance with an old practice and custom of the country and is not a new thing."[49] *Ātā* and rag funds, monthly subscriptions, donations on festivals and important occasions, gifts collected during the anniversary celebrations—small and large donations—all added to the growing monetary base for continual expansion of the Dayanand Anglo-Vedic School.

The Dayanand Anglo-Vedic College Trust and Management Society became both a financial as well as an educational institution. Before the development of Punjabi banking, the Society gained control of a significant pool of capital.[50] Initially the Managing Committee invested its funds in Government Promisory Notes, the Agra Bank, Ltd., and the Bengal Bank in Calcutta.[51] They next purchased Municipal Debentures issued by the Calcutta City Corporation. The beginning of the 1890s saw a shift of investment patterns as the committee began placing money in Punjabi institutions. By February 1892, the Alliance Bank of Simla had become a regular depository for Samaj funds. In May of that same year the committee deposited Rs. 10,000 in the Punjab Banking Corporation.[52] In addition to supporting local banks—a function which would take on increased importance during the later 1890s—the Managing Committee began investing in land, espe-

49. *Arya Patrika,* August 17, 1886, p. 4.

50. Funded capital rose as follows: December, 1886, Rs. 50,000; January, 1889, Rs. 105,406; December, 1892, Rs. 190,000; and July, 1893, Rs. 203,000. Sri Ram Sharma, *Mahatma Hans Raj,* p. 54; *Tribune,* December 14, 1892, p. 4 and July 22, 1893, p. 4.

51. *College Report, 1886–87,* p. 28.

52. *Proceedings, DAVCMC,* Investment Sub-Committee, February 8, 1892 and May 1, 1892.

cially mortgages, and occasionally granting loans, both to individuals and to local Arya Samajes. The Managing Committee, with its capital accumulation, played the role of Samaj banker. By 1894, it became necessary to delegate several members of the Sub-Committee to investigate and report on individual loan requests.[53] The growth of capital created an increasingly complex financial role for the Managing Committee, a role which tended to further centralize an expanding movement. The Samaj now had its banker and the educated elite a new source of capital and the beginnings of an educational system.

Confidence in the new school, both within the Samaj and among the general public, created an internal crisis early in 1888. By this time 697 students had enrolled, and the question arose as to the possibility of opening intermediate or college classes. A sharp division developed between those led by Lala Lal Chand, who felt this to be a premature step, and those who wished to move ahead toward completion of the Arya dream of an independent college. In the ensuing debate, Lala Sain Das, Lala Lajpat Rai, and Pandit Guru Datta persuaded a majority of the Managing Committee to proceed as soon as possible. The Committee announced that first-year Intermediate Classes would be opened on June 1, 1888.[54] Irregular college classes commenced as scheduled. By 1889, college classes were fully organized and the Punjab University granted affiliation to the new college on May 18, 1889.[55] Aryas proved as successful in operating a college as they had with their school. Yet this decision opened a rift in the ranks of college supporters that led to an internal struggle for control of the entire Samaj movement and finally to its division into two separate orgnnizations.

Once the Managing Committee had decided to open a college, they faced the question of who should head the new institution. It was not easily answered. Two candidates immediately came under consideration: Pandit Guru Datta and Lala Hans Raj In many ways Guru Datta appeared to be the most logical choice. His position on the faculty of Government College, his obvious brilliance and participation in all spheres of the college movement, argued

53. See *Proceedings, DAVCMC,* Investment Sub-Committee, Vol. I, July 6, 1894; also for one of the earliest loan requests, see *Proceedings, DAVCMC* (Hindi), Vol. I, November 18, 1887.

54. Sri Ram Sharma, *Mahatma Hans Raj,* p. 53.

55. Sharma, *Ibid.*, p. 54.

for his appointment as principal of the new college. Guru Datta, however, had become increasingly erratic. Looking back, Ruchi Ram Sahni described him in these words: "I do not exactly know under what influence he was brought towards the end of his short life, but it is a fact that not long after leaving college in 1886, Guru Datta became very eccentric in his ways and habits . . . . He was rather too readily impressionable. At the time I am speaking of he became a great believer in what he called *'Hardening Theory.'* He would go about in the coldest season clad in thin cotton clothes, while in the summer months he would be seen walking about dressed in thick woolen winter garments."[56] Guru Datta's odd appearance matched his strange behavior. "I have seen him walking in the streets of Lahore with his University gown on. I was also told that, occasionally, he appeared on the Arya Samaj platform habited in his gown and hood as if he was attending a University Convocation." Peculiar in his habits, Guru Datta showed disinterest, if not disdain, for public opinion. "He would sometimes sleep for two working days and nights together, while, at other times, he was found working day and night without a wink of sleep. He became irritated at friendly advice. I cannot say for certain, but it was commonly believed that at this time he was suffering from T. B."

Estranged from the dominant group within the Managing Committee, Guru Datta's personality moved toward *Bhakti,* devotionalism. He envisioned the Samaj as a religious movement, not as primarily educational or social. His fascination with Aryanism finally led him to question English education and Western knowledge. "By and by he took up the extreme attitude that learning English was useless. He is reported to have expressed once the wish that he could forget all his western learning and become an unalloyed Sanskritist."[57] Pandit Guru Datta's drift toward Sanskrit and Vedic studies worried Lal Chand, Sain Das, and Hans Raj, "who did not share these views. They did not like his extremist preachments."

Lala Hans Raj, by contrast, methodical, competent, and a strict disciplinarian, seemed the model schoolmaster. He shared much

56. Quotes given below from Ruchi Ram Sahni, "Self-Revelations of an Octogenarian," pp. 82–83.

57. Lajpat Rai, *Autobiographical Writings,* ed. V. C. Joshi (Delhi: University Publishers, 1965), p. 49.

the same temperament with Sain Das. Neither was very "religiously minded," and both "believed that to wean the people from all western learning and to substitute it by Sanskrit grammar would do great harm."[58] Lala Sain Das strongly favored Hans Raj, an opinion which carried great weight in the Managing Committee. Sain Das was in the word of Lajpat Rai, "a sort of autocrat. He disliked extremist dogmas and did not regard those people as safe leaders of the nation who become inordinately long-winded when leading congregational prayers, or who always kept talking of God and *dharma.* He did not want to banish religion *(dharma),* but he did want to emancipate people from religious subtleties, religious fuss and superstition. He loved Guru Dutt deeply, and regarded him as his own child. But he loved his own ideas and mission even more than that."[59] Sain Das followed his greater love and led the Managing Committee to reject Guru Datta and choose Hans Raj as the principal of the new college. This decision disappointed Guru Datta and angered many of his close associates. The resultant bitterness did not quickly dissipate; instead, it heightened existing differences within the college movement and throughout the Samaj.

Under Hans Raj the new Dayanand Anglo-Vedic College prospered. Enrollment grew in both the school and college, but it tended to level off after 1889. By 1890, thirty-eight students were on the rolls of the college and in 1893 the college opened its first B.A. degree classes. The Managing Committee could claim to have succeeded in its basic goal of creating a college in memorial to Dayanand. The school and college were both recognized by the general public and the government. In fact, they had become models for others, both within the Samaj and without. Individual Samajists, local branches, other reform groups and opponents of the Samaj began to organize schools throughout the province. Aryas who had concentrated their energies on education in Lahore now turned to the *mofussil,* (the countryside). In 1888 Lala Jawala Sahai started an English school in Lun Miani (Shahpur District), while the Arya Samaj of Jullundur Cantonment founded a school which enrolled 300 students by the following year.[60] Aryas also turned to the problem of female education. By 1889 the

58. Lajput Rai, *Ibid.*, p. 50.
59. Lajpat Rai, *Ibid.*, pp. 50–51.
60. *Tribune*, September 25, 1889, p. 5.

Ferozepore Samaj had organized a successful girls' school.[61] The Samajes of Gujrat and Jullundur districts quickly followed the Ferozepore model.[62] Even one of the smallest and poorest Samajes, that of Baghbanpura, managed to maintain both a boys' and a girls' school by sending delegations throughout Punjab and North-Western Provinces.[63] Education became one of the major preoccupations of the Aryas. During the 1890s Aryas would build an educational system throughout the entire province, from the primary grades through college.

### STRUCTURE, FUNCTION AND IDEOLOGY

The growth of the educational movement and the parallel expansion of the Arya Samaj brought both complexity and diversity to the original organizational structure of the Dayanand Anglo-Vedic Society. Initially the Society and Managing Committee showed a high degree of unanimity. Enthusiasm for a school held supporters and leaders together in a common cause. Each could imagine the proposed school developing along his desired pattern of education. Potentiality allowed for flexibility, reality did not. Once the school existed, it could not in concrete form satisfy the variety of expectations expressed by the increasingly diverse Aryas who supported it. Yet while expansion created centrifugal forces, the functioning of the Dayanand Anglo-Vedic College organizational structure moved toward the centralization of power. The two processes created tension within both the educational movement and the Arya Samaj as a whole.

The formal organization of the Dayanand Anglo-Vedic College Trust and Management Society was highly centralized. The Society, which met only once a year, exercised little power; instead, the Managing Committee and its subcommittees decided questions of both policy and administration. Here power lay with those who regularly attended meetings and formed an inner ring around the central figure of Lala Lal Chand. The office of president quickly accrued power. All decisions and problems flowed through it. Hans Raj, as headmaster and later principal, communicated through Lal Chand to the Managing Committee, as did the lowest

61. *Tribune,* November 27, 1889, p. 5.
62. *Tribune,* July 23, 1890, p. 5.
63. *Tribune,* August 13, 1890, p. 4.

peon. The president might give a decision himself, refer the matter to a subcommittee or to the Managing Committee. He would then transmit final decisions to the petitioner. Immensely able, Lal Chand dominated by his energy and his near omnipresence. He rarely missed a meeting of the Managing Committee or of its associated subcommittees. His defeats in committee meetings were even rarer. Lal Chand's power also rested on his alliance with other strong personalities. Until his death in 1890, Lala Sain Das shared Lal Chand's conception of the proposed school and as president of the Lahore Samaj wielded considerable influence on the Managing Committee. Lala Ishwar Dass, M. A., a pleader from Rawalpindi, provided both support and leadership from 1886 through 1911. He served repeatedly as vice-president and secretary to the Managing Committee and participated in a variety of subcommittees. Similarly, Lala Ralla Ram, a clerk at the Public Works Department Office in Lahore, joined the Managing Committee in 1888 and remained an active member until 1910. He too participated as an officer and member of various subcommittees, and voted consistently with the Lal Chand group. Lala Sukh Dyal showed similar dedication, serving both as an officer and committeeman from 1886 to 1914 and after. Beyond the most active members who provided support and leadership were several Aryas who could be counted on to vote with the educational establishment on any controversial issue.

The first of the young men to join Lal Chand's circle was Lala Hans Raj. Normally considered as "the" leader of the Dayanand Anglo-Vedic College movement, he tended to wield far less power than Lal Chand, especially during the first few years of his service to the school. Hans Raj only entered the decision-making process in 1888, but with his selection as principal and with the deaths of Guru Datta and Sain Das, he emerged second only to Lal Chand. He too served on the Managing Committee and the various subcommittees. He followed the lead of Lal Chand, as did another of the younger Aryas, Lala Lajpat Rai. Lajpat devoted much of his time and energy to raising funds for the school. After he returned to Lahore in 1892 Lajpat participated actively in the Managing Committee and voted with the Lal Chand faction. Not all of the early college supporters found themselves in agreement with Lal Chand and Sain Das, either on specific questions or in the general conceptualization of the school and college. Two men, Pandit

Guru Datta and Lala Jiwan Das, provided alternate leadership for those not satisfied with the educational philosophy of the dominant group. Lala Jiwan Das served the Managing Committee as secretary from its inception. He consistently attended meetings of the Managing Committee and several subcommittees through 1894, but increasingly disagreed with college policy. His disillusionment with the school and college led him, as it led others, to ally with Pandit Guru Datta against the Lal Chand faction.

Little dissension appeared in the movement prior to the debate over the college principalship. But from as early as 1883 differences existed, particularly in the mind of Guru Datta, as to the desired nature of Arya-sponsored education. The most basic issue to Guru Datta and others was the degree to which the school should be "Aryan" or "Vedic." Correspondingly, how far should it be "Anglo," and would it be in the last analysis simply another version of the government college. Underlying this debate were clashing conceptualizations of the Samaj, its meaning and the nature of Dayanand's mission.

The struggle for control of the school began at the annual Society meeting of January 31, 1889. Lala Ralla Ram,[64] representing the Jhelum Arya Samaj, proposed and Guru Datta seconded an elaborate scheme of Sanskrit, Hindi and Vedic studies.[65] All students would study Sanskrit and *Ārya Bhāshya* (Hindi), beginning in the 4th primary grade, take up various writings of Dayanand, including the *Satyārth Prakāsh* and his *Rigvēdādī Bhāshya Bhūmikā,* and finish with extensive study of Panini's *Ashtādhyāyī.* Ralla Ram also called for the establishment of a Vedic Library with an initial grant of Rs. 5,000 and an annual expenditure of Rs. 1,000. In order to further the religious nature of the school, the Dayanand Anglo-Vedic College Boarding House would be operated according to a rigid set of rules, with scheduled activities throughout the day supervised by one assistant superintendent per twenty students. Lala Narain Das and Rai Ganga Ram amended the proposal to the effect that the "Committee should decline to discuss the proposals brought by the Jhelum members of the Society: First, because the letter which accompanied the above

64. Lala Ralla Ram, the critic, should not be confused with the Lala Ralla Ram who served on the Managing Committee, worked in Lahore, represented the Ludhiana Samaj, and was a close associate of the Lal Chand group.

65. Quotes given below from *Proceedings, DAVC Society,* January 31, 1889.

proposals was in intemperate language; second, that the proposals were an attack on the Managing Committee and third, that they were aimed at discrediting the Managing Committee." The amendment won, 31 to 10, and the Society adjourned.

The Sanskritists' challenge to the Managing Committee became a regular feature of the Society's meetings. In 1890, Lala Parmanand attempted to delay approval of the budget until it included "encouragement to the study of Hindi and classical Sanskrit and the Vedas." He lost, 33 to 2. Although similar attempts failed by various one-sided votes, the pressure by the pro-Sanskrit group proved sufficient to force a compromise accepted by the Society on June 1, 1890. "The Society desires that the *Satyartha Prakasha* and *Rigvedadi-Bhashya Bhumika* (Hindi portion only) of Swami Dayanand be introduced, in portion or portions as the circumstances may suggest to the Managing Committee, in the curriculum of study in the Primary and Middle Departments of the Institution and the Sanskrit portion of the *Rigvedadi Bhashya Bhumika* be introduced in the curriculum of study in the Upper and the College Departments of the Institution in portion or in portions as the circumstances may suggest to the Managing Committee."[66] Like most compromises it satisfied few people. The struggle continued, but with one major change in leadership. Pandit Guru Datta's health finally collapsed in the last months of 1889. He died on March 9, 1890, but his place as leader of the Sanskritist group did not remain vacant long. Lala Munshi Ram of the Jullundur Samaj quickly established himself as the prime critic of the Managing Committee.

During the annual Society meetings of 1891 and 1892, Lala Munshi Ram, Lala Parmanand, and Lala Ralla Ram led repeated attacks on the establishment under the banner of furthering religious and language training. In 1891 they called for the creation of a Vedic Department and moved that both science and English be made optional subjects. Both motions failed, but their voting strength had increased in the meantime to approximately one-third of the Society.[67] At the Society meeting of May 20, 1892, the

66. Sri Ram Sharma, *Mahatma Hans Raj*, p. 62.

67. The core of the Munshi Ram-Sanskritist faction was made up of: Lala Ralla Ram, Jhelum; Durga Prasad, Lahore; Jewan Das, Lahore; Lala Parmanand, Lahore; Pandit Dharm Chand, Amritsar; Janmejaya, Jullundur; Ram Krishna, Jullundur; Lala Dev Raj, Jullundur; Lala Jaya Chandra, Lahore; Kedar Nath

entrenched powers attempted to strike back by tightening requirements for membership on the Managing Committee. This proposal lost and the status quo remained, but with ever-growing tension.[68] This contest for power within the Society and Managing Committee was mirrored by a similar struggle within other Samaj organizations. By 1893, differences of belief created open criticism of the opposing Samajists on a personal level. Indirect criticism became direct, and the loyalty of Aryas to the College proved insufficient to neutralize existing anger.

The Society meeting of May 27, 1893, opened with an attack on the Managing Committee, referred to as "a loose, unwieldy, unmanageable body of members including men who may not be able to command confidence from either worldly point of view or the force of their education or character."[69] The *Proceedings* describe the rest of the meeting: "Another important proposal was put forth by Lala Tola Ram who proposed that the following clause be added to the report: 'That some religious books are taught, yet there is no systematic religious training in the College.' The anti-Management Committee group was defeated on all its amendments in a series of votes. Then another struggle developed over the question of membership to the Managing Committee. Once again the majority of the votes went to the pro-Managing Committee group who wanted to maintain the level of Rs. 1,000 from a given Samaj in order to have representation on the Managing Committee." After losing consistently, the Sanskritists called for a year's postponement of the meeting. In this too they failed, and the ensuing debate broke through the bonds of parliamentary decorum, becoming a bitter, personal quarrel. "Lala Amolk Ram in reply to someone's remark said that they were not without bad motives. Raizada Bhagat Ram observed that this might be true in his case, but there were others who voted 'with bad motives.' That proceedings were not carried out in [an] upright manner. When his attention was drawn to this point by some members, Bhagat

---

Thapar, Lahore; and, Lala Khushi Ram, Lahore; plus Lala Chetanand, Multan Leadership in the meetings tended to be in the hands of Lalas Munshi Ram, Parmanand, and Ralla Ram, while centers of regional strength could be found in Jullundur, Jhelum, Gujranwala, and part of the Lahore Samaj. See *Proceedings, DAVC Society,* May 30, 1891, and *College Report, 1891–92,* pp. 9–11.

68. See *Proceedings, DAVC Society,* May 20, 1892.

69. Quotes given below from *Proceedings, DAVC Society,* May 27, 1893.

Ram said, 'I repeat the remarks.' As this reflected disrespect on the whole Society and not [a] particular member, cries of shame, shame were uttered by most of the members." With the eruption of open animosity, all hope of compromise ended. "Lala Munshi Ram then stood up and said, 'You can turn us out of the Samaj, you can turn us out of the building, but you cannot deprive us of the Vedic love within our hearts.' Having said these words, he left the meeting with several others; most of them belonging to the Jullundur Samaj. Lala Durga Prasad, Lala Khushi Ram and some others of the Lahore Samaj followed his example. Following their departure a series of measures were taken to control voting of the members of the Society." Munshi Ram's walk-out left the Managing Committee faction in complete control which they would maintain in spite of one more concerted attempt to seize power by the dissidents at the next Society meeting. The year 1893-1894 brought an end to the unity of the Punjab Arya Samaj only sixteen years after its founding in Lahore. Success of the movement, its rapid expansion and ideological development created tensions too severe for containment in the older structures.

In the years prior to this schism Aryas faced a series of challenges even as they succeeded in the realm of education. Dayanand's vision now found concrete expression in the Samaj and its adherents, who in turn redefined and elaborated this vision, producing in its stead a complex ideology created by Arya thinkers. Aryas were forced to define themselves and their ideology through interaction in the real world. They faced the most fundamental task of clarifying their relationship with Hindu orthodoxy, with the world of tradition from whence they arose and which in turn they would remold in their own image. This process of interaction, both within and beyond the Hindu community, further accelerated differences among Aryas and finally created the division of 1893-1894.

## Chapter IV

# ON DEFINING THE GROUP: THE ARYA POSITION IN THE HINDU WORLD

> The 11th chapter of the *Satyārth Prakāsh* will briefly treat of the beauties and defects of the Indian religions, based as they are upon the *Purāṇas* and their subsidiary works. The reader should not take it amiss or misunderstand me, if they are not charitable enough to consider this attempt of mine to be a positive service done to their fallen cause, for it is never my object to injure or oppose the interests of anybody; but, on the contrary, the purpose of my life is to put them on the path to the discernment of truth.
>
> SWAMI DAYANAND SARASWATI

### FROM IDEOLOGY TO CUSTOM: THE SEARCH FOR A HINDU LIFESTYLE

The Arya Samaj would find itself through the continual interaction of two levels of existence, the ideological and functional. Action and the word determined the place of the Samaj in the Punjabi world—its place within the Hindu community and its relations with those beyond. Ideology enhanced the possibility of certain types of action while it circumscribed others; action, in turn, necessitated further ideological elaboration. Aryas evolved along the path of their commitments and in the process defined the nature of the Samaj. The first task of the Samaj—as any sect—was to separate itself from parental orthodoxy. The iconoclastic criticisms of Dayanand provided a separate ideological base, but as long as Samajists accepted and practiced the rituals of orthodox Hinduism in their daily life, they could not break free of the past nor rid themselves of Brahmanical influence. To preach change meant little when no birth, death or marriage ceremony could be performed outside of the world of orthodoxy. Aryas refused to follow the Brahmo Samaj and move beyond the limits of Hinduism. They wished instead to find a place compatible with Dayananda's severest criticism yet still within the Hindu world.[1] This they did through a slow, piecemeal process of experimentation. They moved forward in an uneven rhythm of boldness and timidity, of accommodation and innovation.

At the most superficial level Aryas attacked various local customs which they believed immoral or indecent—in this they found support among a wide variety of groups, even leaders of orthodoxy. Aryas condemned the singing of indecent songs on ceremonial or festival occasions, excessive mourning, public bathing, liquor and meat-eating—all sins against their puritanical code. They attempted to replace the traditional and to them obscene songs popular among Punjabi Hindus with their own purified versions.[2] Criticism had its practical limits, as in the case of certain festivals where outright abolition proved impossible. *Hōlī*, the great spring festival of fertility, could not be wished away; instead, Aryas purified it and turned the occasion to their own ends. In 1886 and 1887 various local Samajes began to observe *Hōlī* in its Aryan form. "On the 9th March, 1887, the festival of Holi was celebrated in Lahore Arya Samaj. The building, as usual, was canopied and hung with evergreens. The invitation cards were issued over-night to respectable people to request their presence. Not withstanding the general licentious merriment outside, the audience was comparatively large. Hymns and *holies* were sung. After a short but impressive prayer performed by Lala Hans Raj, B. A., the *havan* ceremony was gone through."[3]

The purity and sobriety of these Aryan rituals contrasted sharply with the popular and degenerate *Hōlī* celebrations then in practice. "Whatever may be the origin of this disgraceful festival as explained by the vulgar, it is certain that the obscene songs and foul shameless abuses uttered at the top of voice in the streets of Indian cities, are mere outcome of man's unchecked ignorance,

1. *Arya Patrika,* July 4, 1885, p. 6.

2. See Pandit Bhaj Datta, *Gain Sanskār* (Rites of Passage) (Amritsar: Chashma-i-Nur, 1890), and the numerous publications of Mai Bhagwati. She was an Arya *updēshak,* one of the very few women missionaries then preaching. In this volume she expressly intended to replace the traditional women's songs used at the time of Hindu marriages.

3. Quotes given below from *Arya Patrika,* March 15, 1887, p. 2. Also see the description of an Arya *holi* celebrated at Ferozepore in the year previously, *Arya Patrika,* March 30, 1886, pp. 4–5.

which delights in wickedness." Ancient scriptures described no such festival and instead pictured a *Hōlī* both beneficial and scientific.

The ancients performed *havans* at the time of harvest on a very grand scale offering the new cereals at the blazing altar. The reason is that the cold stagnant air of the past winter being rarefied by the vernal sun, strong currents of air are set in motion, and are, therefore, very appropriate means of carrying wholesome and purifying substances in gaseous forms to the hungry mouths of vegetation, which is revived under the genial influence of the sun returning from the southern regions. . . . In short, it is simply the festival of the sun, the source of life, and is, therefore, especially fitted for the learned people to observe it in the ancient ways.

Aryas based their rejection of unwanted customs on an appeal to ancient authority, the modern truth of science, and contemporary life in the more advanced countries if such seemed valid. These sources of legitimization need not conflict since the underlying truth was universal.

When Arya criticism moved to reform the more fundamental rituals of the life cycle—birth, death, marriage—they lost all orthodox allies, creating instead implacable opponents. Arya replacement of life-cycle ceremonies not only threatened existing beliefs, but also struck at the economic position of the Brahmanical castes. Arya ceremonies did not employ Brahmans but were conducted by Arya pandits or even Samaj members, if they knew the proper ritual. Dayanand's *Sanskār Vidhi* provided a series of ceremonies complete with instructions and the Sanskrit text for each of the life-cycle ceremonies. Readily available to Samajist, each could if he chose conduct these rituals. In practice few did. The Samaj tried to provide Arya pandits or leading officials in the place of the traditional Brahman. With its own rituals and priests, the Samaj began to separate itself from the world of the orthodox, although the process was both long and difficult.

By 1887 Aryas increasingly utilized their own rituals. Death came first. Young members of the Samaj found themselves forced to choose between the traditional and the revived forms upon the death of a relative, usually a wife or parent. This choice was often painful, between conscience and society. Pandit Guru Datta was one of the first to follow his beliefs against the wishes of his community. Guru Datta's announced intentions to use Aryan rites created immediate social pressure from relatives and members of his caste. Social radicalism, when actually carried into practice, required courage, conviction, and a deep sense of faith. "His Bradri which contains in its ranks some of the most influential inhabitants of Mooltan, threatened to cast him off for ever and ever, but he paid not the slightest attention to their impotent vociferations. He told them to go and do their worst, and for himself, he said, nothing could shake him out of the resolve, he had taken, of conducting the obsequies of his parents on Vedic principles. The Bradiri stormed and threatened over and over but to no purpose. He would not shift an inch from his position, and he did every thing as became an Aryan, in utter defiance and contempt of the formidable host of caste-men, who wanted to intimidate him by their threats."[4]

The funeral ceremony attracted a large crowd of Hindus—some curious, many hostile, and a few admiring; but it was successfully completed in spite of a threatened social boycott. Not only did Pandit Guru Datta prevail but in doing so gave meaning to the name Arya, as did others who took a similar stance. "The manly and uncompromising behavior of the Pundit on the occasion demonstrated to the nominal Arya that the name Arya had some significance, that its adoption, on a man's part, entailed on him certain duties, and chalked out for him certain course of procedure, in matters both public and private, which he must pursue at all hazards, and, to the outsiders, it proved that an Arya had strength of character in him and knew how to uphold truth when truth was to be upheld."[5] The use of Arya death rites clearly differentiated the Samajist from surrounding Hindu society. During the 1880s and early nineties this act remained a radical step, an ideal that only the most dedicated dare take, but by the turn of the century, it no longer shocked the orthodox nor created significant social opposition.

4. *Arya Patrika,* November 15, 1887, pp. 4–5.

5. *Arya Patrika,* November 15, 1887, pp. 4–5; also see similar reports of Arya death ceremonies in the *Arya Patrika,* January 4, 1887, p. 4; two accounts; March 20, 1888, p. 6 and November 8, 1887, p. 3; and in the Lahore *Tribune* for September 4, 1889, p. 5 and September 11, 1889, p. 5. Those who would reject the traditional death rituals found justification for their decisions in such Arya tracts as Durga Prasad, *The Shrāddha* (Lahore: Virajanand Press, 1892), and Swatma Nand, *Mritak Shrāddha Khandan* (Refutation of the Shrāddha Ceremony) (Lahore: Virajanand Press, 189[illegible]).

Although the issue of death rituals angered traditional Hindu leaders and served to separate Aryas from their contemporaries, it did not touch the core of social and cultural organization; it did not cause the fundamental challenge created by Ayra attempts to alter marriage rites and patterns. The question of marriage reform was linked to two problems: first, the role of women in Hindu society and, second, the degree to which the Arya Samaj would separate itself from existing social groups. The reformation of marriage rituals, the remarriage of widows, the campaign against child marriage, and the question of educating women formed a cluster of causes at the heart of Arya relations with the Hindu community. Like other social reform organizations, Aryas worked to change the role of the Hindu woman. ". . .these days are the days of progress and reform. The time is advancing with rapid strides. Every obstacle in the way will be sooner or later cleared up when women will have equal rights with men."[6] Though seldom expressed in such absolute terms, Aryas, if successful, would create a modernized woman markedly different from the traditional Hindu wife.

Between 1886 and 1890, Aryas began to adopt the marriage rituals in the *Sanskār Vidhi* instead of the more elaborate and expensive forms of popular Hinduism.[7] Unlike the question of death rituals which could be altered by one man if he was sufficiently strong-minded, marriage required the agreement of the two contracting families, who in turn needed to face the wrath of their respective lineages. More often than not the decision lay with the groom's family while the bride's relatives acquiesced.[8] The Arya

6. *Regenerator of Arya Varta,* Vol. I, No. 7, August 20, 1883, p. 5.

7. The Aryas in their tracts, journals, and speeches, sought to popularize and explain their own rituals while condemning traditional custom. The change in rituals was an integral part of their critique of social and religious life. For general statements on the problem of rituals and popular Hinduism, see Devi Dayal Varma, *Guldasta-i-Islāh* (Nosegay of Correction) (Ferozepore: Gouldsbury Press, 1890), Lala Jiwan Das, *Islāh-i-Mu'āsharat-i-ahl-i-Hanūd* (Improvement of the Social Life of the Hindus) (Lahore: Koh-i-Nur Press, 1885), and his *Sawāl-o-Jawāb Mutazammin hāl-i-Ārya Samāj* (Questions and Answers on the Condition of the Arya Samaj) (Lahore: Mufid-i-Am Press, 1891). Occasionally Samaj writers chose to attack a single Hindu ceremony or ritual that they deemed useless or the product of mere superstition. Lala Bataliya Ram, in *Gangā Ashnān,* rejected ritual bathing in the Ganges as a foolish superstition (Amritsar: Chashma-i-Nur Press, 1887).

8. See the marriages described in the *Arya Patrika,* June 15, 1886, p. 8 and August 17, 1886, pp. 3–4.

press reported Samaj marriages in the Punjab and beyond. Each incident provided both a model for others and encouragement to those contemplating such a step. The marriage, in 1888, of a prominent Arya's daughter created just such an example.

> The marriage ceremonies as might have been expected from a man of Lala Amir Chand's determined character and true Aryan views, were performed in thorough conformity with the directions of the Sanskar Vidhi. The outsiders who were present on the occasion were agreeably surprised with what they saw. All the malicious and distorted accounts which they had heard of the Aryan customs and institutions proved to be utterly groundless and they said as much. The correspondent remarks justly that one deed is worth a thousand lectures, and it is deeds which will win us the sympathy and cooperation of the people and not empty lectures.[9]

Arya rituals had their practical as well as ideological aspects. They could be performed with much less expense. Aryas emphasized the "pure and simple Vedic rites,"[10] without fireworks, dancing girls, or the elaborate rituals of orthodox Hinduism.

For those who wished to marry their children with Ayra rites to other Samaj families, or within the expanding educated community, the location of suitable mates became a serious problem. Separated from their families either by distance or ideology, Aryas developed a new marriage institution—the newspaper advertisement. Beginning in 1883, the Samaj press carried requests for an "Arya gentleman, who should be sound in health, good character and gives the pledge to never enter into bigamy or polygamy;"[11] a bride, "desirous of getting married in strict accordance with the Vedic rites;"[12] and for "an able and educated Kshatri belonging to the Chohan and Ratur families."[13] The traditional arrangers of marriage, the barbers and priests, could no longer be depended on and so the marriage advertisement provided an alternative.[14] By 1884, the "matrimonial notice" was a standard item in many Samaj publications. In addition to the traditional values of family, wealth, and color, these notices stressed new qualifications: English education for the child, or a family dedicated to Samaj ideals. Proficiency

9. *Arya Patrika,* March 27, 1888, pp. 6–7.
10. *Arya Patrika,* July 20, 1886, p. 8.
11. *Arya,* February 1883, p. 262.
12. *Arya-Patrika,* May 4, 1886, p. 8.
13. *Arya Patrika,* February 1886, p. 6.
14. See comment in *Regenerator of Arya Varta,* September 24, 1883, p. 3.

in the anglicized world did not replace older criteria of status, but added new personal or familial dimensions to that status.[15]

Aryas began a more radical marriage reform with the advocacy of widow remarriage. Munshi Jiwan Das, in his tract *Sādah-i-Haqq* (The Plain Truth), and Pandit Lekh Ram in *Risāla-i-nawīd-i-begwān* (A Treatise Containing Glad News for Widows),[16] stated the Samaj arguments for the remarriage of widows by all Hindus regardless of past customs or present social status. By 1882, Arya journals began carrying accounts of widow remarriages.[17] Yet instances of such marriages remained rare, as example fell far behind precept.

Aryas found support for their cause among non-Arya Hindus. The beginnings of public opinion strengthened Arya will to put their doctrine into practice. Difficulties intervened here as they had with the use of reformed marriage ritual. How did one locate widows willing to enter into a marriage? *The Social Reformer and Marriage Advertiser* offered a practical solution and Aryas greeted this new publication with enthusiasm. "We welcome the appear-

15. At times, individuals attempted to retain the benefits of both the old and new orders. Arya criticism of child marriage did not deter one Samajist from entering the following matrimonial notice. "I have got 3 unmarried brothers 16, 14 and 12 years old, all being brought up in the 4th, 5th and 7th classes of Government College, Ajmere. I being backed by the will of my parents and uncle I have an interest to give them full religious and literary education and they shall have to continue their studies till their 25th year, the lowest stage of brahmacharya according to the laws of the greatest law giver, Manu. But everyone is aware of the delicacy of the times—the present reforming time, especially when we have that recently been delivered from "ignorance" and "degradation"—by our Lord Swamiji Dayanand Saraswati who disappeared too soon and untimely. So at the present time I wish that their betrothals be made (to the satisfaction of my family members) among my Aryan caste fellows the Sukhe Sens Kayastha (I mean by Aryans those belonging to the Arya Samaj). My father's name Lala Futteh Lal is the Amin of 12 villages of Udaipur on a salary of Rs 80 per mensem and the same amount is drawn by my uncle, Behari Lal, the Deputy Inspector of Schools of the Merwaraj District. Full particulars will be afterwards given on the communication being made to us. Those wishing to communicate should address thus: Lala Ram Gopal, c/o Lala Futteh Lal, Purani Mandi, Ajmere." *Regenerator of Arya Varta*, August 11, 1884.

16. *Sādah-i-Haqq* was published in Lahore: Koh-i-Nur Press, 1882, and *Risāla-i-nawīd-i-begwā* appeared in 1883, published by the same press, both were reprinted in later years.

17. See *Arya*, March 1882, p. 19. This marriage was between two Khatris and was solemnized by the Lahore Arya Samaj.

ance of the Social Reformer and Marriage Advertiser and sympathize heartily with its aims and objects . . . . To give currency to widow marriage in Punjab, [is] a very noble undertaking, which must command itself to every right thinking man, those who seek for matrimonial alliance with Hindu widow[s] must refer to it, for nearly a full page is given through the advertisements of widows who are willing to remarry."[18]

The Amritsar Arya Samaj led in this drive for the acceptance of widow remarriages. Not only did they assist in the performance of widow marriages, they did so in a grand, public manner, giving maximum publicity to each event. "The opponents of the Arya Samaj . . . will be greatly surprised to hear that another widow marriage has been celebrated under the auspices of the Umritsar Arya Samaj, on the 10th September 1885. This is the second widow marriage which has taken place at Umritsar through the efforts of the local Ayra Samaj. In the present case the pair belonged to the Arora caste, one of the high castes of the Punjab . . ."[19] The practice of Arya social concepts proved fascinating, as hundreds crowded in the Samaj *mandir* (temple). Social radicalism created controversy and high entertainment. "All the balconies and roofs of the neighbouring houses were crowded by ladies who assembled in great numbers to witness the ceremony. . . . But the majority of the people approving the action of the Samaj took no active step against that departure from the common custom of the day. All persons present on the occasion seemed to take great interest in the matter." The Amritsar Samaj continued to provide leadership in the widow-remarriage movement. In 1886, they sponsored the marriage of a Brahman widow, the daughter of a village priest. In the same year the Lahore Arya Samaj and the Samaj at Kohat joined the Amritsar Samaj in conducting widow remarriages.[20] Samaj-sponsored remarriages and tracts led to greater public approval of "virgin widow" remarriage;[21] but the

18. *Regenerator of Arya Varta,* February 11, 1884, p. 5.

19. *Arya Patrika,* September 12, 1885, pp. 6–7.

20. See *Arya Patrika,* August 24, 1886, p. 8; *Tribune,* August 28, 1886, p. 7; *Arya Patrika,* August 31, 1886, p. 8; *Tribune,* September 4, 1886, p. 7; and *Arya Patrika,* September 7, 1886, p. 5.

21. Arya tracts on the question of widow marriage and child marriage include: Ama Ram, *Masalā-i-Niyōg* (Principles of Widow Marriage) (Lahore: Mufid-i-'Am Press, 1888); Munshi Chatar Bihari Lal, *Risāla-i-Dharm Mitra* (The Friend of Reli-

acceptance of the remarriage of widows who had children came much more slowly.[22]

Arya pamphlets proved effective in reaching the newly educated. Often dramatic in its presentation, this literature presented Samaj ideology in numerous forms—lectures, dialogues, moral tales, poetry—offering didatic entertainment to the literate Hindu. Lal Jiwan Das in his *Dō Hindū Bēwā Auratōn kī Bātchīt* (A Discussion between Two Hindu Widows), recasts an earlier remarriage sponsored by the Amritsar Samaj into a message of hope for two lamenting Hindu widows, Radha and Jasoda.

As the talks between Radha and Jasoda came to an end, an Arya, who had been listening to this talk secretly standing nearby, spoke out thus: Listen you Radha, and you Jasoda, some followers of Swami Dayanand Saraswati, i.e., the Arya Samajists, who had been trying for long to ameliorate the sad plight of widows, have after all shown some courage. The fact is that on January 21, 1885, A.D., they performed the remarriage of a widow in the Arya Samaj mandir of Amritsar, and it is very gratifying that this marriage was performed according to the Shastras and in this marriage several Raises or well-to-do men, of the city as well as several Pandits also took part besides hundreds of people who had gathered together in this function including many women, and everybody present appeared to be very happy about the entire proceedings.
Jasoda: Is it a fact? To which caste and varna did the girl and boy belong? At what age had this girl become a widow? And, at what age had she been remarried?
Arya: A detailed account of this marriage has already been published in Urdu and English newspapers and this is a topic of discussion in many cities and towns. The girl was a Malhotra Char Ghar Khattri, and she too was named Jasoda. She had been married for the first time at the age of nine and she had become a widow two years later. Her father was already dead but her mother was alive. Because her mother had herself suffered the pangs of widowhood in her own life, she would not tolerate that her child widow daughter should also suffer all through her life, and because she had already heard of this view of the Arya Samaj that widow remarriage was perfectly permissible according to the Shastras, she kept search-

gion), an anti-child-marriage tract (Sadhaura, District Ambala: Bilain Press, 1893); and Bawa Chhajju Singh, *Brahmacharya versus Child Marriage*, Tract No. 1 (Lahore: Aror Bans Press, 1893).

22. One such remarriage occurred in 1894 when the Lahore Arya Samaj sponsored the marriage of "an elderly couple. Both bridegroom and the bride are of a mature age and the latter has a child by a previous husband." *Tribune*, February 17, 1894, p. 4.

ing for a suitable boy for her. In the end, she succeeded after three years and taking shelter in the Arya Samaj, she remarried her widow to a young man who is Chopra Khattri by caste and his name is Lala Radha Kishen. And it had been stated that this boy also was a widower. Thus, the two were bound in wedlock in accordance with the Shastras.[23]

In spite of Arya tracts and publicizing of actual remarriages, such instances remained relatively rare throughout the remainder of the nineteenth century. The Samaj did provide, however, in its doctrines and rituals a place of refuge within Hinduism for those who wished to remarry as well as for those who would marry against prevailing familial and social opposition.

Associated with the general "betterment" of women was the cause of female education, which received fitful support by Aryas during the early 1880s. Aryas had founded schools for girls in Lahore, Jullundur, and Amritsar, but had met with only indifferent success. A lack of teachers, textbooks, and public support was compounded by differing views of the content and scope of girls' education. Almost all writers within the Samaj recognized the need to change the status and role of women, and with this to educate girls in some manner, but exactly how remained open to considerable debate. A vagueness in thinking dominated the subject and was undergirded by little in the way of commitment or urgency. Various social reform organizations, including the Samaj, had experimented with female education, but with limited success.[24] Significant progress in women's education had to wait upon the development of leadership within the *mofussil* Samajes.

By 1885, the Amritsar Samaj began to devote its energy and wealth to the construction of girls' schools, and to the problem of their continuing financial support.

Our brothers of the Amritsar Arya Samaj are, of course, working very zealously and steadily. We have the pleasure of announcing the establishment of two girls' schools at that place through the exertions of the local Samaj. A similar good news again comes from that quarter. A third girl's school has been started by that body in Kutra Dula from Sunday, the 20th ultimo. The cause of female education through indigenous agency has received great encouragement in the city of Amritsar.[25]

23. Lala Jiwan Das, *Dō Hindū bewā Auratōn kī Bātchīt*, trans. H. L. Saxena (Lahore: Arya Pustalakaya, 1891), pp. 14–15.

24. *Arya Patrika*, September 12, 1885, p. 3.

25. *Arya Patrika*, October 3, 1885, p. 4.

During the years 1885–1888, the Amritsar Samaj provided continual leadership, while the Lahore Samaj concentrated on the Dayanand Anglo-Vedic schools. They too maintained a girls' school, but the most successful institution in Lahore, the Anglo-Vernacular Girls' School, was a project of the Lahore Brahmo Samaj. Patronized by the educated community, this school attracted students from "well to do families."[26] The students were taught a limited curriculum in Hindi. "Besides reading and cyphering, the girls are taught the useful arts of sewing and knitting."[27] Girls' education remained limited in scope and importance until the Jullundur Samaj provided new patterns of motivation and leadership. Lala Munshi Ram, Lala Dev Raj, and the militant wing of the Samaj would make female education their special cause.

In 1888, Lala Munshi Ram started a campaign to open a girls' school in Jullundur City, not out of idealistic concern for the status of women but out of fear of Christian conversion.[28] Munshi Ram recalled:

On my return home from court, Vedakumari came running with this newly learnt message, "Christ is the Prophet. No price is required to mention his name. Christ is my anchor. He is my Krishna, etc., etc." I was startled to hear this and, on enquiry, I learnt that they were taught even to detest our holy Sastras. I realized then that an Aryan Girls' School was an absolute necessity

As usual, on the next Sunday we went to the Arya Samaj Mandir. Rai Bahadur Bakshi Sohanlal, Pleader, was also present. We had interesting talk there, after which we all went to my house. I opened the topic of having a Girls' School of our own. Bakshiji was all willing and agreed to

26. *Tribune,* December 22, 1886, p. 5.

27. See *Arya Patrika,* December 28, 1886, pp. 5–6, for report of the schools; also *Tribune,* December 22, 1886, p. 5 and June 20, 1888, p. 5.

28. Similar undercurrents of anxiety appeared in earlier accounts of the women's educational movement. After praising the work in Amritsar, the *Arya Patrika,* of October 3, 1885, p. 4, remarked: "We are, however, very sorry to remark that this endeavour of the people to take the education of their girls in their own hands does not find favour with Christian missionaries, because they fear that the girls' school set up by them, mainly with object of alluring native girls to their own faith, will be left by Hindu girls in time, and thus their baptising mission among Hindu females will be greatly checked. These efforts in the cause of female education on the part of the Amritsar Samaj, will, we are certain receive great encouragement from our benign Government and public."

do his best for the school. That very night I drafted an appeal for subscriptions.[29]

In 1890, the Jullundur Samaj succeeded in opening a girls' school, the Arya Kanya Path Shala.[30] The Path Shala began life with a student body of eleven and a staff of three teachers. Success came only a year later with the appointment of a woman headmistress, Bibi Guru Devi, who quickly provided leadership for the teaching staff.

Lala Dev Raj, a close associate of Munshi Ram, took the position of school manager, while two local Aryas—Master Hira Singh and Master Sant Ram—agreed to serve as school inspectors. The school prospered in spite of some opposition and the number of students steadily rose from its original eleven to fifty-five by the end of 1892.[31] The Jullundur Samaj found success of the Path Shala increased their financial problems. Lala Munshi Ram and Lala Dev Raj turned their creative energies to fund-raising projects for the Path Shala. They employed the techniques already used for the Dayanand Anglo-Vedic School, including a "Refuse Fund," patterned after the earlier *ātā* fund, and street begging.[32] Confidence bred a willingness to test further the limits of public tolerance. In 1891, the school accepted widows as well as unmarried girls and, in 1892, Lala Dev Raj announced that the Samaj intended to establish a girls' high school, a Kanya Maha Vidayalaya, at a projected cost of Rs. 250,000.[33] Not only did this announce-

29. M. R. Jambunathan, ed., *Swami Shraddhanand* (Bombay: Bharatiya Vidya Bhavan, 1961), pp. 100–101.

30. This was their second attempt. The first school founded in 1886 failed for the lack of a woman teacher and accompanying pressure against female education by the Hindu community.

31. The early development of the Arya Kanya Path Shala can best be followed in the *Digest of the Kanya Maha Vidalaya Reports* for the years 1890–1896, 1898, 1899, and 1905, which have been inserted on two fold-out pages of the bound volume, *Kanya Maha Vidyalaya Annual Reports*. These are handwritten sheets and the digest reports are not necessarily for the same years as the bound reports. Both the digests and bound reports are in Urdu. See *Digest Reports, 1891, 1892*. The struggles which accompanied Arya attempts to found and promote female education in Jullundur are described in the biography by Satya Dev Vidhyalankar, one of its major proponents, *Lālā Dēv Rāj* (Jalandhar: Kanya Mahavidyalaya ki Svarn-Jayanti, 1937).

32. *Tribune*, March 16, 1892, p. 4 and April 23, 1892, p. 4. Lala Dev Raj took up begging in the streets to raise funds for the Path Shala.

33. *Tribune*, July 6, 1892, p. 4.

ment seem grand beyond possible realization, it also represented a goal which found little approval among advocates of the Dayanand Anglo-Vedic College. This debate over the proposed high school demonstrated differences of opinion as to the advisability of giving higher education to women as well as the general tensions existent in the Samaj by the early 1890s.

The question of higher education for women did not divide reformers from the orthodox as much as it set one reformer against another. In 1894, a series of letters appeared in the *Tribune* arguing the merits of "Primary vs. High Schools for girls." Lala Lajpat Raj began the debate by questioning the advisability of female education. "I maintained and do so still, that the spread of education among males had some strong and important inducements to back it, while the education of girls cannot necessarily derive any support from the same motives for education."[34] He did not reject female education, but instead wanted only primary education for girls. Lala Lal Chand joined Lajpat in calling for caution and continued broadening of primary education.[35]

The advocates of female education, Lala Sundar Dass, Lala Kashi Ram and Lala Ralla Ram, found themselves caught between the desire to educate women and the fear, which they shared with others, of the possible impact education might have on women and their relationship with the dominant males. Sundar Das Suri, in answer to Lal Chand and Lajpat Rai, showed the ambiguity that surrounded female education and the fears it created even among those who called for its extension. ". . . I hold that the character of girls' education should be different from that of boys in many essential respects. The Hindu girl has functions of a very different nature to perform from those of a Hindu boy and I would not encourage any system which would deprive her of her national traits of character. A smattering of reading and writing, the most that can be expected for some time in many cases, would be a poor substitute. We cannot be too cautious in this matter. The education we give our girls should not unsex them."[36] Caution, opposition, the lack of trained female teachers, of textbooks and school facilities, and the difficulty in raising funds, all inhibited the movement for

34. *Tribune*, March 23, 1894, p. 5.
35. *Tribune*, March 28, 1894, p. 5.
36. *Tribune*, April 11, 1894, p. 5.

female education, but they did not halt it. The Jullundur Samaj pushed ahead with its goal of higher education for girls.[37] Practical considerations entered the controversy, as it appeared that the drive for a women's college might compete with the Dayanand Anglo-Vedic College for Arya contributions.[38] It is not accidental that the supporters of women's education tended to be the critics of the Dayanand Anglo-Vedic College Managing Committee—those who would by 1894 break with Lal Chand and his associates. Lala Munshi Ram, Lala Dev Raj, and other militant Aryas increasingly identified with the women's movement in all its aspects, particularly education.

The advocates of the Kanya Maha Vidyalaya found allies among the newly-organized women's auxiliaries to the regular Samaj. A Stri Samaj (women's society) existed in Ludhiana, maintaining there both a Female Vedic School and an Ashram (home) for widows.[39] Even more surprising, female *updēshaks*, missionaries, began to travel throughout the Punjab. Women lecturers were unique and rare, yet they appeared in such divergent places as Jullundur, Hariana, and the heavily Islamicized district of Dera Ghazi Khan.[40] The early nineties witnessed an increase in activities for women's rights and female education. Various local Samajes founded girls' schools and sponsored lectures on the status of women.[41] The Jullundur Doab led all other areas in this movement, while it in turn followed the leadership provided by the Jullundur Samaj.

At the most fundamental level the tensions between the alienated modernizing male and his female relatives propelled the

37. Various Samajes supported the cause of higher education for girls. See Lala Dev Raj, *Kanyā Mahā Vīdyālaya Jālandhar par Ārya Samājon kī Resolution,* a collection of resolutions from local Samajes on the opening of the Kanya Maha Vidyalaya (Jullundhur: Sat Dharm Pracharak Press, 1893).

38. See letters in *Tribune,* by Ralla Ram, April 25, 1894, and letter by Lala Lal Chand, May 16, 1894, p. 5.

39. *Tribune,* October 24, 1891, p. 4.

40. One Shrimati Mai Bhagwanti spoke in Hariana before a large public gathering, while in Dera Ghazi Khan it was necessary to hold meetings with women speakers in private houses. See *Tribune,* January 13, 1892, p. 5.

41. See Kenneth W. Jones, "The Arya Samaj in the Punjab: A Study of Social Reform and Religious Revivalism, 1877–1902," unpublished Ph.D. Dissertation, University of California, Berkeley, 1966, p. 170.

former to attempt to modernize the latter. No basic change in lifestyle or values could take place without changing women, for they linked the individual house to the greater world of social conformity. A husband who dared to innovate too strongly, to alter existing mores, would answer to his wife and through her to both groups of relatives and, if the issue became too public, to his *birādarī*. The wife also linked the present to the future through her influence over the children. Only a truly strong male could prevail against his wife, his female relatives, and his castemen. Conversely, if a couple stood united, their household could exist to a far greater degree as a separate unit, a law unto itself. Aryas and their educated peers recognized this problem. ". . . women should be educated to the highest level they were capable of . . . because it is the women who stand most in the way of social reform."[42] Yet to change the nature of women, to emancipate them, to educate them beyond the most limited of knowledge, opened up possibilities truly frightening in a society which still lived in the shadow of *pardah*. The Hindu woman, as etched in literature and in male minds, stood for submissiveness and obedience, whatever reality might be, an ideal seemingly incompatible with higher education. Only those who wished passionately to change society remained willing to fight for a modernized Hindu woman. For all, ambiguity dominated. The ideal Sita, the traditional Hindu wife, lived uneasily with the concept of a modernized, educated woman striding forward into the Vedic past.[43]

### SANĀTAN DHARM: ARYAS VERSUS ORGANIZED ORTHODOXY

The Aryas, with their modernized and de-Brahmanized rituals, their restructured conceptualization of the female role, had achieved an increasingly separate identity from the orthodox and traditional world around them. Their defense of this new lifestyle and aggressive condemnation of the old created an institutionalized opposition. The personal campaigns in defense of tradition of the 1860s and 1870s gave way to new organizations

42. Lala Harkishen Lal, in a letter on "Female Education," in *Tribune*, May 9, 1894, p. 5.

43. The dangers of liberating women were clearly indicated by the impact of Mai Bhagwati on the town of Hariana. ". . . of late, a correspondent says, it has been difficult to get well-cooked dishes at any house at Hariana, and few people stop at Hariana for fear of indigestion . . . ." *Tribune*, July 13, 1892, p. 3.

with all the techniques of modernity. Much as missionary proselytization forced the establishment of aggressive reform groups, which in turn adopted the style and tactics of their enemy, orthodoxy too borrowed from its opponent, the Arya Samaj.

In the middle 1880s orthodoxy still fought primarily with the traditional weapons, the *shāstrārth,* and the *updēsh* or public lecture. Sanatanists did not hesitate to use the press, although the great mass of their literature came after 1889.[44] By 1887 a Sanatanist organization, the Bharat Dharm Maha Mandal (Great Society for Indian Religion), entered the field of combat. Led by its secretary, Pandit Din Dayal, the Maha Mandal sponsored debates, lectures and publications in defense of orthodoxy. Pandit Din Dayal proved an effective, dynamic leader of the Mandal. Even Arya reports of the Pandit's activities admitted his ability. "One Pundit Din Dyal . . . is reported to be staying at present at Ferozepur where he is delivering lectures on diverse subjects to the great satisfaction of the idolatrous portion of the community of that place. . . . He is reported to have directed his battery of flowing eloquence and his unanswerable arguments solely against the Arya Samaj in his various discourses."[45] Pandit Din Dayal also turned to scriptural sources for legitimization in arguments paralleling those used by Aryas. "In the lecture he is said to have proved by quotations from the Vedas, the Puranas and the Smritis, that the worship of idols alone is the means of finding God. In order to impress the truth of his remarks upon his hearers, he adduced proofs from Arithmetic, Mathematics, Medical Science, Geography, History, Natural Philosophy, Chemistry, Metaphysics, Logic, etc., in support of his position."

The struggle between the Arya Samaj and the Maha Mandal soon developed a personal note with attacks on Din Dayal and Pandit Gokal Chand, "'the seven-tongued' spokesman of the

44. For two earlier examples of Sanatanist tract literature, see Lala Salig Ram's *Qawā'id Ārya Granth Shōdhak Sabhā* (Rules for the Corrections of Books issued by the Arya Samaj) (Amritsar: Chashma-i-Nur Press, 1885), and Kishen Singh, *'Ambar-i-irfānī, radd-i-'Itr-i-Rūhānī* (Refutation of the Doctrines of the Arya Samaj); Salig Ram published many of the Sanatanist tracts prior to the establishment of the Anglo-Sanskrit Press of Lahore.

45. Quotes given below from *Arya Patrika,* December 27, 1887, pp. 3–4. For a general critique of the Maha Mandal, see Lala Duni Chand, *Mahā Mandal kī Jhūthī Shaikhī* (The False Boast of the Maha Mandal) (Gujranwala: Khadim-ut-Ta'lim Press, 1889).

Mandal."[46] Aryas painted Din Dayal as an ill-educated failure before he took up the cause of orthodoxy,[47] while Gokal Chand, as a lapsed Arya, drew criticism for his apostacy.[48] Debates between Sanatanists and Aryas centered heavily on idolatry, the role of Brahmans, Arya interpretations of the Vedas and their concommitant rejection of Puranic scriptures.[49] The question of idol worship, from the very onset, sharply divided Aryas from orthodoxy.[50]

Even more central arguments arose over the position of Brahmans both within the caste structure and as mediators between man and God. Here the Samaj denied all Brahmanical claims to superiority and also sought to fasten on them the historic guilt for contemporary Hindu degeneracy. To the Aryas, Brahmans were "popes," an epitaph of condemnation assimilated from the Protestant missionaries.[51] Aryas also spent considerable effort in denigrating Vedantic philosophy as the basis of contemporary Hinduism.[52] Sanatanists responded in kind In the later 1880s they began to produce a stream of literature in defense of their

46. *Arya Patrika,* April 17, 1888, p. 4.

47. *Arya Patrika,* February 28, 1888, p. 5.

48. *Arya Patrika,* April 17, 1888, pp. 4–5.

49. See Pandit Lekh Ram, *Purān kisnē banāē* (Who made the Puranas?) (Lahore: Virajanand Press, 1891).

50. The Sanatanist tracts, *Risāla tā'īd But Parastī* (A Treatise in Support of Idolatry) (Lahore: Khai Khuwah Press, 1888), and *Risāla-i-Tardīd-i-Dalīl-i-But Parastī* (Refutation of Reasons for Idolatry) by Lala Dev Dayal (Amritsar: Boz Bazar Press, 1890), produced a counter series of Arya tracts starting with Pandit Lekh Ram's *Murtī Prakāsh* (Exposure of Idolatry) (Amritsar: Chashma-i-Nur Press, 1888), and followed by Pandit Kishan Narayan, *Likchār nambar ēk Murtī Khandan ya'nī but prastī kē tardīd* (Lecture No. 1, Refutation of Idolatry, that is the Impropriety of Idolatry) (Multan: Nar Singh Press, 1889), and Lala Durga Prasad, *Murtī Pūjā Khandan* (Refutation of Idolatry) (Lahore: Virajanand Press, 1891).

51. See Lala Chiranji Lal, *Pōpe Mukh Chaper* (Rebuke to Brahmans, satirically called Popes) (Lahore: Anglo-Sanskrit Press, 1889); Varma Nar Singh, *Ārya Jajmān aur Pōpe Pandhē kī bāt chīt* (Dialogue between an Arya and his Pope Pandha) (Sialkot: Zafr-ul-Matabi Press, 1890); Lala Kashi Ram, *Sawāl-o-Jawāb Bāp Bētā wa Ta'rīfāt-i-Pōpan wa Barahān Mah* (A Dialogue between the Father and a Son, or a Satire on the Brahmins and the Twelve Months) (Sialkot: Mirza Press, 1890); and Lala Mul Raj, *Pōpe Nāsh Mālā* (A Rosary of the Destruction of the Popes) (Ludhiana: Dabdaba-i-Iqbal-i-Rabbi Press, 1890).

52. See Mani Ram, *Vēdānt Kathā* (The Story of Vedanta) (Lahore: Virajanand Press, 1889), and Badri Datt, *Manas Vinōd* (Amusement of the Mind) (Lahore: Virajanand Press, 1890).

own beliefs and critical of Arya claims to represent true Hinduism. The teachings, as well as the personality, of Swami Dayanand remained for Sanatanists a prime target of criticism.[53] Beyond personalities, Sanatanists struggled to refute Arya ideology and simultaneously to create in their fellow Hindus a sense of alarm over Arya threats to orthodoxy.[54] Occasionally orthodox speakers attacked the Arya position on widow marriage or child marriage,[55] but idolatry and the role of Brahmans remained the central points of conflict.

Gradually the orthodox created a network of local Sanatan Dharm Sabhas throughout the province, but here again progress was slow and fitful. Outside of Lahore, the major area of Sanatanist support was the Jullundur Doab, particularly the cities of Jullundur, Ludhiana, Hoshiarpur, and the town of Phillaur. This area, the previous base of Shraddha Ram, had active Sanatan Dharm Sabhas by 1890.[56] The spread of Sanatan Dharm Sabhas intensified the struggle between orthodoxy and Aryas. Existing forms of competition were augmented by law suits, organized

53. Kaka Ram, in *Bhajan Sanātan Dharm Updēsh* (A Song Sermon of the Eternal Religion), ridiculed both Swami Dayanand and his followers for their folly and ignorance (published in Lahore at the Anglo-Sanskrit Press, 1889); also see Pandit Thakur Das, *Dayā Nand kē ghalat tāwīlen namber-i-awal Niyōg* (Wrong Interpretations of Daya Nand, No. 1, Regarding Widow Marriage) (Lahore: Narankari Press, 1890), and Shiv Naran Parshad, *Risāla Ma'sūm bā Srī Swāmī Dayānand Saraswātī kī Mahimā* (A Treatise called for the Glory of Swami Dayanand Saraswati) (Lahore: Vilasa Press, 1892).

54. See Pandit Nana Lal, *Ārya Samājiōn kē Likchār kā Jawāb* (Reply to a Lecture of the Arya Samajists) (Lahore: Anglo-Sanskrit Press, 1889); Lala Kidari Mal, *Musaddas-i-Vīr Bhāī Parkāsh* (Stanzas Manifesting Fearlessness) (Delhi: Iftikhar-i-Delhi Press, 1890), an exhortation to the orthodoxy to rise and defend themselves; and Pandit Kaka Ram, *Sanātan Dharm Updēsh aur Pakhandī mat Līlā* (The Teachings of the Sanatan Dharm and the Doings of the False Creeds) (Lahore: Victoria Press, 1892).

55. *Tribune*, May 29, 1889, p. 4.

56. *Tribune*, March 1, 1890, p. 4; and August 12, 1893, p. 4. Tracing the growth of the Sanatan Dharm Sabhas and Arya Samajes can prove difficult, since both claimed they were the "eternal," i.e., Sanatan religion. "A correspondent from Patiala states that a Sanatan Dharm Sabha has been established there. He also adds that the aims and objects of the Dharm Sabha are those of the Arya Samaj. We quite agree with the correspondent in thinking if the objects of the Dharm Sabha are identical with those of the Arya Samaj, the distinction of name is not only useless, but inconvenient and even positively illegible." *Arya Patrika*, November 21, 1885, p. 6. By the end of the 1880s, such points of confusion disappeared with clarification of the doctrines of both the Sanatanists and Aryas.

proselytization, and the development of publications through both periodical and tract literature.

Frustrated opponents of the Arya Samaj turned to the civil authorities and to the caste brotherhoods for assistance against the reformers. Attempts to outcaste Aryas rarely succeeded, nor did the civil authorities care to enter into what was essentially a religious debate. Orthodox opponents of the Arya Samaj persuaded local officials to ban Arya missionaries from street preaching in the Kapurthala State, but the ban was short lived and ineffective.[57] Increasing controversy and acrimonious debate between Aryas and Sanatanists did not preclude some sympathy on points of mutual concern. The encouragement of Sanskrit both in literature and education remained a shared goal, although for somewhat different reasons. Aryas reluctantly admitted the "good works" of Sanatanists. "The Dharam Maha Mandal is not altogether a sham. It has some redeeming features about it. It is trying to do something in the direction of reviving the study of Sanskrit. If instead of wasting its sum and substance in fruitless efforts to revive idolatry, if instead of crying hoarse over the supposed want of religious faith in the natives, they devoted their time and energies to the revival of Sanskrit, the richest storehouse of truth in the world, they would be conferring an inestimable boon on their countrymen."

By the mid-1890s, defenders of orthodoxy had organized to combat Aryas, whom they saw as enemies from within the world of Hinduism. Clearly different from the norm of society, Aryas were not generally perceived as beyond Hinduism, as having broken with their religion, but as existing somewhere at its edges, at one with those who freely criticized existent practices and beliefs. This perception of Aryas as reformers and critics posed another difficulty for members of the Samaj. If they were not orthodox, were they then Brahmos; and, if they were not latter-day followers of a Bengali heresy, how did they differ, and where did they stand in relation to existing movements for change and reform?

## REFORMING THE REFORMED: ARYAS VERSUS BRAHMOS

The process of differentiating Aryas from Brahmos continued during the 1880s with increasing vehemence, only to dissipate by

57. *Tribune*, September 3, 1890, p. 5. Also see accounts of attempts to outcaste Arya Samaj members in the *Tribune*, May 4, 1890, p. 4; and M. R. Jambunathan, *Swami Sharddhanand*, p. 73.

the end of the decade. The initial ideological lines of debate set down with the first clashes between Brahmos and Aryas were elaborated in a paper war of tracts, journals, and newspaper articles.[58] Aryas continued to create a place for themselves between orthodoxy and the extreme radicalism—as they saw it—of the Brahmos.

> . . . I beg permission of my Brahmo friends to warn them against a most denationalizing course which they seem to be pursuing. As members of the Indian nation it is their duty to reform the evils which have creeped into our institutions by the tyranny and ignorance of ages, but not to uproot them unless they are found to have been pernicious even in their original states.
>
> It is sufficient that we have been conquered politically, but why undergo a social, moral and religious subjugation by abandoning our own institutions, customs and ideas, which are as good as the foreign ones we can adopt in their stead, if not better. We alone have degenerated, and the remedy lies in bettering ourselves by acting more wisely and honestly on the wise institutions of our forefathers which we have neglected with such woeful results, and not in abolishing those institutions themselves.[59]

Brahmos would abandon the ancient ways and in so doing surrender to the English, creating "social, moral and religious subjugation," in addition to the existing political subordination. The fear of complete surrender, of total cultural abandonment, underlay

58. Lala Radh Kishen Mehta, an aggressive Arya propagandist, provided much of the anti-Brahmo literature of the 1880s. Alone or in cooperation with Lala Manohar Lal, he wrote articles and pamphlet after pamphlet in condemnation of Brahmo ideology and in response to Brahmo tracts. Radh Kishen and Manohar Lal authored *Asrār Brahm Panth* (Mysteries of Brahmoism) (Lahore: Ganesh Prakash, 1886), as the first of a series of pamphlets to "expose" the Brahmo Samaj and to reply to "some of the objections listed against Swami Dayanand." In 1888, Radh Kishen produced another small tract, *Brahm Samāj kī Aslīyat* (The Truth about the Brahmo Samaj) (Lahore: Aror Bans Press, 1888), and also *Ārya Samāj aur Brahm Samāj kī ta'lim* (Teachings of the Arya Samaj and the Brahmo Samaj) (Lahore: Ravi-e-Benazir Press, 1888). Arya criticisms were met primarily by Shiv Narain Agnihotri and Lala Kashi Ram among the Punjabi Brahmos, while visiting Brahmos, such as P. C. Mozomdar, added their voices to the debate. See P. C. Mozomdar, *Words of Advice to Young Panjabis* (Lahore: Tribune Press, 1889), and Lala Kashi Ram, *The Doctrine of Transmigration Refuted* (Lahore: New Lyall Press, 1891). The literature became sufficiently extensive that Salig Ram, the publisher, issued a volume entitled *Sādhāran Brahm Samāj kā Paigambar* (Lahore: Aror Bans Press, 1888) which included a variety of tracts and journal articles on both sides of the debate.

59. *Arya Patrika*, July 4, 1885, p. 7.

Arya attempts to reinterpret their past as well as their condemnation of Brahmo ideology. "We have held it from the very first that Brahmoism was but a perverted or distorted form of Christianity . . . . Pick up any Brahmo paper, and therein you will find the most unmistakable proofs of the fact that the original source of Brahmoism is the religion of Christ. Christianity constitutes, as it were, the vital principle of Brahmoism, it is the source of its life, vigor and strength. Christianity is in short [the] all-in-all of Brahmoism."[60] Keshab Chandar Sen's aggressive eclecticism strengthened Arya feelings that the Brahmo Samaj represented Christianity in disguise.[61]

Arya criticisms of the Brahmo Samaj received a sympathetic hearing among many educated Punjabis, both Hindu and non-Hindu. During the years 1881 through 1886, Punjabis complained of Bengali dominance in occupations calling for education, particularly for English education. Bengalis provided an immediate barrier to the occupational mobility of educated Punjabis. Already entrenched in government service, teaching, law and journalism, their leadership which had been accepted in the 1860s and 1870s came into question in the 1880s.[62] By the following decade this issue no longer seemed crucial. Punjabi Hindus had succeeded in submerging the Bengali elite. While the number of Bengalis and Kayathas from the North-Western Provinces remained nearly stable from 1881 through 1911, the educated Punjabis increased rapidly in numbers and came to dominate the new occupational world of the British Raj.[63] With the rise of Punjabi Hindus to self-confidence, the Brahmo-Arya quarrel subsided. New enemies threatened, new battles erupted; Bengalis retained much of the respect and leadership they had previously exercised but no longer in the areas of religion and social change. Politics would be their sphere of leadership until the end of the century, as new

60. *Arya Patrika,* December 13, 1887, pp. 1–2.

61. Radha Kishen Mehta and Lala Manohar Lal, in *Asrār Brahm Panth,* make an extensive argument linking Keshab Chandar Sen with Christianity. They also saw Pandit Shiv Narain Agnihotri as a Punjabi version of Sen, another cultural traitor.

62. See *Tribune,* October 15, 1881, p. 8; April 16, 1881, p. 8; August 13, 1881, p. 8; and May 29, 1886, p. 8.

63. See Kenneth W. Jones, "The Bengali Elite in Post-Annexation Punjab: An Example of Inter-Regional Influence in 19th Century Punjab," *Indian Economic and Social History Review,* III, No. 4 (December, 1966), pp. 142–143.

ideas of political action and commitment moved up the Gangetic Plain from Bengal.

### THE CULT AS MODERNIZER: ARYAS VERSUS DEV DHARM

Within the Punjabi world Aryas found themselves pitted against a new contender for reform leadership, Pandit Shiv Narayan Agnihotri, and the Dev Samaj. An extension of the older Brahmo-Arya struggle, this contest followed the development of Shiv Narayan as a religious leader. His personal clashes with Dayanand in 1877–1878 permanently embittered him toward both Dayanand and the Arya Samaj. Agnihotri expressed this antagonism from within the Brahmo Samaj through tracts, lectures, and the pages of his monthly, *Birādar-i-Hind.* Yet in time he himself became uneasy with the constraints of Brahmo ideology. He too was greatly disturbed by the Cooch Bihar marriage issue of 1878 and responded by joining the newly-organized Sadharan Brahmo Samaj. Religiously devoted, Agnihotri spent his free time as a Brahmo missionary, becoming one officially in 1879.[64] The following year he founded the Punjab Central Brahmo Samaj in a restless search for a vehicle to express his growing personal religious devotion. The internal tension between religious commitment and the demands of his career led Agnihotri to take *sanyās* and thus to commit himself totally to a religious life. On December 20, 1882, Agnihotri became a Brahmo *sanyāsī* and adopted a new name, Satyanand Agnihotri.[65] Now a professional Brahmo, Agnihotri increasingly sought leadership within the Brahmo movement but failed to find it. He clashed with other Brahmo leaders and in 1887 completely broke with the Brahmo movement.[66] This departure was motivated only in part by personal friction, for Agnihotri possessed a growing sense of religious mission incompatible with Brahmo ideology. He would create a new Hinduism centered around the concept of the *guru,* as Dayanand sought to modernize with the centrality of the Vedas.

On February 16, 1887, Satyanand Agnihotri announced the formation of the Dev Samaj, a new and more perfect Hinduism than either the Brahmos or benighted Aryas. Doctrine in this soci-

64. Anonymous, *Brahmvādī Shrī Satyānand Agnīhōtrī, A Brief Biography Victory to Dev Dharm: Let All Sins be Eliminated* (Lahore: Dev Bidhan Press, 1889), p. 7.

65. *Ibid.*

66. *Ibid.*, p. 301.

ety remained somewhat in flux, although the principles were quite simple. The movement had three classes of members, including *Sahaiks* or sympathizers and *Nāva Jīwan Yāfta* or those who had found a new life. The former joined the Dev Samaj, paid Rs. 10 per year and accepted the leadership of Pandit Agnihotri. The latter members were expected to follow a moral code which stressed honesty, cleanliness, vegetarianism, and temperance. They also had to reject all caste distinctions and all "false" religious symbols, and to donate one-tenth of their income to the Samaj. A third category of members included those who had taken strict religious vows dedicating themselves to the pursuit of Dev Dharm.[67] Agnihotri's Hinduism was essentially puritanical, stressing hard work and honesty. Unlike other reforming bodies, the Dev Samaj depended not on a particular text or texts but on the person of its *guru* who held all doctrinal authority. Essentially a cult, the history of the Dev Samaj tends to be almost totally the history of its prophet.

Initially the Dev Samaj appeared to most Punjabis as an extension of the Brahmo Samaj, more devotional, but in fact possessed of the same ideology and dedicated to the same ends. Ruchi Ram Sahni recalled its inception: "Sometime in 1887 Agnihotri decided to form a new centre for his religious activities. . . . It was to be, so everybody believed, nothing but another place for preaching Brahmoism with even greater zeal and devotion than was found possible in the neutral Brahmo Samaj."[68] Agnihotri's following grew but was still considered a subsection of the Brahmo Samaj. "Before long he had a large pucca built Mandir at his disposal situated a little off the Anarkali Bazar with even a bigger hall than that of the Brahmo Samaj. With a band of enthusiastic and devoted young men to help him in his mission work, Agnihotri carried his message to several other districts. In particular he was able to produce a large volume of propagandist literature." Agnihotri retained his literary skill as well as his main target of criticism, the Arya Samaj.

The establishment of the Dev Samaj heightened the feud be-

67. Quoted in P. V. Kanal, *Bhagwan Dev Atma* (Lahore: Dev Samaj Book Depot, 1942), pp. 317–318.

68. Quotes given below from Ruchi Ram Sahni, "Self-Revelations of an Octogenarian," p. 135.

tween Agnihotri and the followers of Dayanand. The years 1888 through 1892 witnessed an intense pamphlet war between Agnihotri and the Aryas. Agnihotri himself published eighteen tracts during this period in addition to numerous newspaper articles and public speeches, all of which condemned the Arya Samaj and Dayanand. Lala Radh Kishen Mehta, Durga Prasad, Lala Murli Dhar, and Bhai Ram Bhaj Datta led the Arya counterattack. This debate became intensely personal. Agnihotri saw the Arya Samaj as the production of one man, Dayanand. To discredit Dayanand meant to undercut any and all Arya claims for leadership within the Hindu world. For Agnihotri a movement was its *guru*. The destruction of one meant automatically the destruction of the other. His longstanding obsession with Dayanand embittered this controversy. In tract after tract, Agnihotri accused Dayanand of embezzlement, hypocrisy, the teaching of immorality, arrogance, and misrepresentation of the Vedas.[69] Aryas responded in kind, aiming both ridicule and abuse at Agnihotri. The tone of this debate sank steadily and in 1890 produced a libel suit between Agnihotri and his Arya antagonists.[70] The highly personal nature of Arya-Dev Dharm debates stemmed in part from the need to create an identity for each group when little separated the two movements, save personalities and opposing claims to legitimacy.

69. Among the more scurrilous of Agnihotri's writings were *Dayānandī Vēdōn men zinā karī kī ta'līm* (The Adulterous Teachings in Dayanand's Vedas) (Lahore: Brahm Parchar Press, 1888); *Pandit Dayānand kā Sanyās* (Pandit Dayanand's Abandonment of Wordly Ties) (Lahore: Brahm Prachar Press, 1888); *Pandit Dayānand aur unkā nayā panth* (Pandit Dayanand and his New Religion) (Lahore: Brahm Prachar Press, 1888); *Dayānand Kaljugī Dharm* (The Iron Age Religion of Dayanand) (Lahore: 1888); *Vēdic Mahā Pōpe* (The Great Vedic Pope) (Lahore: Dev Vidham Press, 1889); *Mahā Pōpōn kī Samāj* (Society of Great Popes) (Lahore: 1890); *Pandit Dayanand Unveiled* (Lahore: 1891); *Pandit Dayānand kā pakhand Sanyās* (The Sham Abandonment of Pandit Dayanand) (Lahore: Dev Vidhan Press, 1891).

70. See also Azad, *Shiv Narāyan kī shōkhī kā jawāb* (Reply to Narayan's Mischief) (Lahore: Aror Bans Press, 1888); Pandit Murli Dhar, *Sat Asat Prakāsh ya'nī Satyā Nand Agnīhōtrī kē risāla Pandit Sanyās kā Jawāb* (Exposer of Truth and Untruth or Reply to a Pamphlet entitled *Pandit Dayānand kā Sanyās* by S. N. Agnihotri) (Lahore: Ahmadi Press, 1890); Durga Prashad, *A Reply to Mr. Agnihotri's "Pandit Dayanand Unveiled"* (Lahore: 1891); and Ram Bhaj Datta, *Agnihotri Demolished* (Lahore: 1892). Agnihotri won the case with four Aryas receiving sentences for publishing an "indecent" book. Government of India, *Selections from the Vernacular Newspapers Published in the Punjab, 1890*, p. 256, *Dharm Jīwan*, July 6, 1890.

With the 1890s, the gulf between the two societies grew steadily, as Pandit Agnihotri altered and then elaborated on the foundations of Dev Dharm. Agnihotri, who later became known as Bhagwan Dev Atma, announced in 1892 a policy of dual worship—of himself and God. Both Aryas and Brahmos concluded that the Dev Samaj had moved back toward orthodoxy with Agnihotri's claim to the status of near divinity. For Ruchi Ram Sahni, still a staunch Brahmo, Agnihotri became an apostate, a lapsed reformer. In the Dev Samaj hall Ruchi Ram witnessed a ceremony that both repelled him and rejected his passionate belief in rationalism. "After everybody had been seated, from an adjoining room emerged Agnihotri in what appeared to be red silk garments with a golden Mukt over his head. Altogether he did not seem to be very different from the representation of Krishna in Ras Leela performances such as those I myself had seen many a time in the courtyard of [the] Seth Kalyan Dass firm at Dera Ismail Khan. He was appropriately led by some of his followers to his place on the platform just below the canopy." Idolatry appeared to Ruchi Ram reborn in its most repugnant form, the worship of a living *guru*. "Frankly had I not seen it with my own eyes, I would have refused to believe that, of all the men in the world, Agnihotri would allow himself to be worshipped with lights and scents and flowers all in a thal (plate), or that well educated men, including graduates would so far forget themselves as to perform what *I certainly* consider a degrading act of human worship."[71]

Ruchi Ram found himself surrounded by apostate Brahmos who appeared to have voluntarily returned to the worst practices of Hindu orthodoxy. "My anguish was all the keener to see one of my own friends, S. Gurmukh Singh, B.A. leading the party of five worshippers who performed the regular ceremony of the *arti* before Agnihotri in the presence of some five hundred visitors. Involuntary tears flowed down my face. Is this the man, I asked myself again and again, who both by precept and example had brought me into the Brahmo Samaj!" The distance between the Dev Samaj and its fellow Hindu modernizers became such after 1892 that each lost interest in the other. Debates between Aryas and Dev Dharmis declined and nearly disappeared. Under Ag-

71. Quotes given below from Ruchi Ram Sahni, "Self-Revelations of an Octogenarian," pp. 135–136.

nihotri's leadership the Dev Samaj remained essentially a cult centered on the person of its founder with little relevance to the larger issue of the day. In 1895, Agnihotri announced a further development in Dev Dharm ideology—the rejection of God. Now only the *guru,* Bhagwan Dev Atma, would be worshipped. No other spiritual authority remained, neither text nor deity.

Agnihotri dominated the Dev Samaj. Under his leadership it retained the nature of a cult. Small enough to insist on conformity to its creed of loyalty to the *guru,* the Dev Samaj appealed to much the same sections of the Hindu community that supported the Arya Samaj: "graduates, magistrates, doctors, pleaders, moneylenders, landholders and Government servants."[72] It too rejected caste, child marriage, *pardah,* excessive ceremonial expenses, and traditional mourning rites.[73] It too supported female education and more radically coeducational schools. Also, like the Aryas, the Dev Dharmis retained their identification as Hindus,[74] and were considered as such. Puritanical followers of a living prophet, the Dev Dharmis comprised one wing of the reformed Hindu community. A modernized form of the ancient tradition of the *guru* legitimized their neo-Hinduism and at the same time separated them from the textual revisionists, both Brahmo and Arya. Clarification of the Arya position within Hinduism paralleled a similar process between Samajists and the greater world of the Punjab with its multiplicity of religious communities. The search for identity and its resultant ideology transcended the bounds of the parent community, changing the nature of Punjab society and culture.

72. *Census, Punjab Report 1911,* p. 139.

73. *Ibid.,* p. 140.

74. *Ibid.* Confused in the Census returns with followers of the Hindu deity, Devi, it is difficult to ascertain their actual strength. Kaul estimated that the Dev Dharm had approximately 2,300 members by 1911, located largely in Lahore City and the districts of Hoshiarpur, Ferozepore, Simla, Delhi, and Lyallpur, plus the state of Kapurthala.

## Chapter V

# ON DEFENDING THE GROUP: THE ARYA POSITION IN THE PUNJAB

> My view-point is this. All those things which are common to all religions are obviously true and must be accepted. And on this basis should be condemned false things which create differences in different faiths. It is my object to put clearly before the public . . . . all the secret and open things of these religions; so that all and sundry [will] be able to exchange their views and reach some unanimity.
>
> SWAMI DAYANAND SARASWATI

### VED MAT MANDAN: ASAT MAT KHANDAN
Preaching the Vedic Religion, Refuting Untrue Faiths

All sects face two problems: to survive they must maintain their membership; to succeed they must convert. *Mandan* (proving one's case) and *khandan* (refuting other ideologies) are two edges of the same sword—*prachār kā kām,* the work of preaching. One cannot exist without the other. To preach one's own doctrine necessitates condemning alternative beliefs. Aryas' insistance on their own true faith could not be retained within the limits of Hinduism, but inevitably drew them into the wider world of competing religions. Defining the Arya position within the Hindu world led to defending from without. Aryas first realized this in the early 1880s, but only came to grips with the need for extensive preaching and its implications after Dayanand's death, when they could no longer depend on his charismatic leadership for strength and inspiration. They would succeed or fail dependent on their own resources, and would do so in an environment of escalating religious competition, of communities mobilizing for their own survival.

The earliest Arya attempts at systematic dissemination of their beliefs were both fitful and ineffective. Aryas sought to create organizational structures to answer this need, but lacking coordination between the various Samaj branches, they achieved little.[1] The Arya Tract Society of Lahore, founded at the beginning of 1884, became the first successful innovation in support of *prachār*. Sponsored by Lala Ratan Chand Barry, Editor of the *Arya Magazine*, this society was established "for the publication in English of tracts containing Vedic doctrine and Arya religion."[2] R. C. Barry and Lala Salig Ram Vaid, owner of the Arya Press, listed among their periodicals the *Arya Magazine*, the *Regenerator of Arya Varta, Dēsh Upkārak*, and *The Reformer*.

To many Samajists the only hope of effective missionary action depended on the creation of an organizational structure to coordinate the diverse projects of individual Samajes. No single Samaj possessed sufficient resources, either financial or human, to effectively meet the needs of proselytization, of *mandan-khandan*. Efforts to create a central organization for the Samaj began shortly after Dayanand's death. In its first meeting on December 28, 1883, the Paropkarini Sabha, Dayanand's legal heir, resolved "That the Arya Samajes in India should form a representative committee to serve as a channel of communication between the different Arya Samajes."[3] The Paropkarini Sabha sent letters containing its resolution to all Arya Samajes in India, but without immediate result.[4] In spite of the obvious need for a coordinating body, the year passed with scarcely a trace of concrete action. In June 1885, Munshi Lachman Sarup of the Meerut Samaj proposed a meeting of Samaj representatives from the North-Western Provinces for the following year,[5] while in the Punjab, the Amritsar Samaj convened a meeting of representatives at its anniversary celebration. "A great discussion accordingly took place, but it is gratifying to see that the labour and time were not uselessly spent. The rules were passed, and it was resolved in the end that the Lahore Samaj should take the duty of circulating the rules for the information and guidance of different Arya Samajes . . . and making

1. A notice of a "Vedic Mission Fund, Multan" appeared in the *Arya*, November 1882, p. 198, but little is heard of this fund in the years following.

2. *Regenerator of Arya Varta*, February 24, 1884, p. 6.

3. Reported in the *Regenerator of Arya Varta*, February 18, 1884, p. 5.

4. See Indra Vidyavachaspati, *Ārya Samāj kā Itihās*, Vol. I (Delhi: Sarvadeshak Arya Pratinidhi Sabha, 1957), p. 181.

5. *Arya Patrika*, June 27, 1885, p. 5.

arrangements for calling a meeting of representatives of the Arya Samajes of the province on the occasion of its next anniversary."[6]

During the next few months Aryas discussed the proposed representative assembly in their press and in each local Samaj. The Lahore Samaj framed a set of regulations for the proposed representative assembly, circulated them throughout the Punjab, and announced the first meeting: "All the Arya Samajes will be glad to hear that at last the Pratinidhi [representative] Sabha is to be held on 4th and 5th October, 1886."[7] The delegates gathered as scheduled, approved a series of regulations governing the organization of the Sabha, and elected a fifteen-man executive committee. Sixteen representatives from the Punjab attended, along with leaders of the Meerut, Saharanpur, and Prayag Samajes in the North-Western Provinces.[8]

Formation of the Arya Pratinidhi Sabha, Punjab, did not result in a burst of energy and action. Little happened. The new organization had no funds and only a vague concept of its duties. In theory, each Samaj with representation was expected to donate one-tenth of its income to the Pratinidhi Sabha.[9] Yet this amount, even when paid, proved insufficient to carry out even a minimal program. In spite of its impotence, the Arya Pratinidhi Sabha found itself the center of increasing demands for Arya preachers, *updēshaks,* who would proselytize throughout the Punjab. Aryas

6. *Arya Patrika,* November 7, 1885, pp. 7–8.

7. *Arya Patrika,* September 14, 1886, p. 5.

8. Lala Madan Singh, B.A., became secretary of the Executive Committee which included the following Samajists: Pandit Shiv Datt Ram, Amritsar; Lala Umraw Singh, Delhi; one member, Ferozepore City; Lala Ganga Ram, Ferozepore Cantonment; Lala Narayan Das, M. A., Gujranwala; Lala Murli Dhar, Hoshiarpur; Lala Rup Singh, Kohat; Lala Sain Das, Lahore: Lala Jiwan Das, Lahore; Lala Madan Singh, B.A., Lahore; Lala Lal Chand, M.A., Lahore; Lala Tulṣi Ram, Ludhiana; one member, Multan; Lala Mul Chand, Peshawar; Lala Ishwar Das, M.A., Rawalpindi. *Arya Patrika,* October 26, 1886, p. 8. Indra Vidyavachaspati, in *Ārya Samāj kā Itihās,* Vol. I, p. 181, gives a somewhat different listing of representatives which includes Lala Amin Chand in the Lahore delegation and omits Lala Madan Singh. He also states that the first meeting of the Pratinidhi Sabha took place in October 1885 and that the October 1886 meeting was the first formal one of the Sabha. Also see Reid Graham, "The Arya Samaj as a Reformation in Hinduism with Special Reference to Caste," unpublished Ph.D. dissertation, Yale University, 1942, p. 400.

9. *Ārya Patrika,* December 7, 1886, pp. 7–8.

painted a woeful picture of Hindu degeneracy and backwardness that could only be eliminated by the new faith. "Dr. Asanand writes from Alipur, District Muzzafargarh, to the Ferozepore *Arya Gazette* that the people of the place are in a sad state of mental degradation. Their religious ceremonies are disgusting to relate. They invest their sons with the sacred thread and perform the ceremony of their tonsure at the tombs of the Mahomedans, their inveterate foes of religion. As a rule, they are all notorious flesh-eaters, breaking their fast of Shivaratri with the cruel dish of flesh and distributing the same among their friends as offerings of sacrifice. The attention of the Aryan missionaries is invited to this depraved condition of the people."[10]

This letter stirred Aryas to consider methods for *prachār,* "That our missionaries may be able to preach the Vedic religion even in the far distant nooks of the land and save the inhabitants thereof by taking them up, as it were, from the dark abyss of ignorance in which they are struggling."[11] The variety of plans suggested all had one theme: common action by all Samaj branches through a central organization. In practice, Aryas turned to the newly-established Pratinidhi Sabha. "The complaint of the scarcity of Aryan missionaries continues unmodified in Aryan papers. Those Samajes, which can afford to keep Pundits as ordinary chaplains, do not feel the necessity so severely as those which are too poor to employ paid preachers. If a mission be organized by the rich Samajes in several Provinces, infinite good will result to the weak Samajes and accelerate the propagation of Vedaism all over the country."[12] The Arya Pratinidhi Sabha responded to these appeals with great sympathy, but little in the way of concrete assistance.

With few resources at its command, the Pratinidhi Sabha did not succeed in appointing its first Arya *updēshak* until 1887. "In a meeting of the Pratinidhi, held on 27th March 1887, it was decided that an Updeshak [preacher-missionary] should be appointed to meet the demands of the Punjab Samajes. Pandit Muni Ram was, by a unanimous consent, appointed to the post. He has been for some

10. *Arya Patrika,* October 5, 1886, p. 4. See a similar request in *Arya Patrika,* August 17, 1886, pp. 6–7.

11. *Arya Patrika,* August 31, 1886, p. 7.

12. *Arya Patrika,* October 5, 1886, pp. 4–5; see also the letter in the *Arya Patrika,* August 17, 1886, pp. 6–7. Here the appeal for missionaries was directed to the Lahore Arya Samaj.

time past in an indifferent state of health and has therefore been unable to embark on his duties as a preacher. He is now tolerably in good health and has already commenced his rounds."[13] One professional missionary, even in the best of health, could not satisfy the needs of a growing movement. In desperation the Pratinidhi Sabha sought greater funding from its constituents: "It has been, therefore, decided that in addition to this one-tenth income its every first-rate Samaj should contribute, as a donation, Rs. 25 towards the Updeshak fund, every second-rate Samaj Rs. 15 and every third-rate Samaj Rs. 10. We hope the Samajes, represented in the Pratinidhi, in especial, and the rest in general, will generously come to the help of the Pratinidhi, and enable it to carry on its work in this direction with efficiency."[14] In spite of repeated appeals the early years of the Pratinidhi Sabha were plagued by poverty, poor attendance at its executive meetings,[15] and a general lack of visibility. The Pratinidhi Sabha lived in the shadow of the College and the Managing Committee.

The failure of the Pratinidhi Sabha to provide both effective leadership as well as the required manpower for Samaj missions meant that *prachār* would follow the earlier, confused pattern of local initiative. Arya missionaries tended to be either members of the Samaj who preached as part of their overall religious activities or wandering *sādhus* and *sanyāsis.*[16] The latter provided professional missionaries for the Samaj costing little to the organization except their travel and maintenance, which was usually supplied by the local branches. Yet difficulties arose, for these men existed

13. *Arya Patrika,* July 19, 1887, p. 4. In the next few months the *Arya Patrika* carried news of Muni Ram's travels. See issues for July 19, 1887, p. 4; August 23, p. 5; and September 6, p. 5.

14. *Arya Patrika,* July 19, 1887, p. 4.

15. In 1886, only six members of the Executive Committee attended, these from Lahore, Amritsar and one from Multan; see *Arya Patrika,* December 7, 1886, p. 7.

16. Between 1885–1887, Swami Atmanand Saraswati, Swami Sahjanand Saraswati, Swami Ishwaranand Saraswati, Swami Akhayanand and Sanyasi Ala Ram traveled widely throughout the Punjab preaching the Arya doctrine. See: *Arya Patrika,* September 19, 1885, p. 5; September 26, 1885, p. 7; December 5, 1885, p. 7; August 15, 1885, p. 5; April 20, 1886, p. 8; July 27, 1886, p. 6; January 4, 1887, p. 4; for the travels of Ala Ram, see *Arya Patrika,* August 22, 1885, p. 4; August 15, 1885, p. 5; August 1, 1885, p. 7; June 27, 1885, p. 5; June 1, 1886, p. 7; and, October 11, 1887, p. 8.

beyond the control of any Samaj organization. They might indeed be sincere men of faith, as they claimed, or mere opportunists. The *mofussil* Samajes could never be certain when faced with a wandering preacher just who he was, nor could the men at Lahore advise their colleagues, since they themselves were uncertain. "A Sannyasi named Swami Sahjanand Saraswati, we learn from the Arya Gazette Firozpur, is preaching Aryan religion at Dera Ismail Khan. The Sadhu, of whom we have received this notice for the first time, is not to be confounded with the well-known Swami Sahjanand Saraswati, the strenuous preacher of the Vedic Religion. We hope some gentleman from Dera Ismail Khan will kindly supply us with detailed information about this Sadhu."[17] This confusion continued. Both the lack of ideological unity and excessive enthusiasm disturbed Samaj leaders and threatened their public image.

The problem posed by wandering, volunteer holy men, as well as the continued need for missionaries, forced Samajists to search for new sources of reliable manpower. In 1887, the Lahore Samaj announced it would hold examinations on January 15, 1888, for all pandits who wished to serve the Samaj. "It is open to all and comprises as text books Satyarth Prakash, Veda Bhashya Bhumika, Sanskar Vidhi and Aryabhvinai. Besides question papers, set from the above named books, two essays, in Hindi and in Sanskrit shall be required to be written down by the examiners. Oral examinations shall also be held to judge of the pronunciation of the candidates."[18] This announcement commented on the "demand for Pandits who may hold divine service and be competent enough to explain the Veda Bhashya and Veda Bhumika to the Samajists . . . . Such Pundits being altogether unprocurable, the Lahore Arya Samaj was quite unable to comply with the request of the mofussil Samajes to supply them with competent Pundits whom they might take in the service of the Samaj." The examinations produced only one successful candidate, Pundit Sohan Lal.[19] The need for *updēshaks* remained unfilled and the Samaj continued with a mixture of laymen and *swāmīs*, some knowledgeable, others not.[20] No missionary system existed until the mid-1890s.

17. *Arya Patrika,* December 5, 1885, p. 7.
18. Quotes given below from *Arya Patrika,* October 11, 1887, p. 8.
19. *Arya Patrika,* March 27, 1888, p. 3.
20. *Arya Patrika,* April 3, 1888, p. 6.

The functions of preaching and proselytization, which might have become the major preserve of the Pratinidhi Sabha, were developed by local Samaj leadership and resources. Both the centralizing role of the Pratinidhi Sabha and its hoped-for leadership in the field of *prachār* remained a potentiality, while reality moved toward the creation of *mofussil* influence. Growth created centrifugal forces which pulled the Samaj outward from Lahore and redistributed the weight both of members and leadership.

The twin forces of opposition and commitment propelled local Samaj organizations to experiment with new methods of proselytization. Lala Munshi Ram and the Jullundur Samaj led in this innovation. As early as 1886 the Jullundur Samaj announced its intention of establishing a mission "to preach the Vedic religion in the surrounding country."[21] After Munshi Ram settled permanently in Jullundur, he led the local Samaj in an aggressive assertion of their beliefs. The Jullundur Arya Samaj anniversary of 1888 marked a new confidence and with it a new expression of Samaj identity. Munshi Ram described a procession of *Nagar Kīrtan* (city singing) conducted during the anniversary celebrations. "It was usually led to the accompaniment of music by a local rais, carrying an 'Om' flag, followed by Pandit Gurudutt and a number of sanyasis chanting Veda Mantras. They were followed by *grihasthas* [householders] singing the praises of Hari. It was such an impressive sight that the kingdom of peace seemed to have descended into the bazaar and other places."[22]

During the years 1888-1889, the Jullundur Samaj experimented with new forms of *prachār*, while Lala Munshi Ram established the Urdu weekly, *Sat Dharm Prachārak* (Herald of the True Religion)[23] and, in April 1889, began to employ the traditional vehicle of *kathā* (religious stories) in order to reach a nonliterate audience. Rather than turn to the Arya Pratinidhi Sabha in Lahore, the Jullundur Samajists founded their own organization specifically for missionary work, the Doab Updeshak Mandal (The Doab Missionary Circle). B    un toward the end of 1889, the *Mandal* attempted to coordinate Arya proselytization in the towns of

21. *Arya Patrika*, August 10, 1886, p. 7.

22. M. R. Jambunathan, ed., *Swami Sharddhanand* (Bombay: Bharatiya Vidya Bhavan, 1961), pp. 103–104.

23. *Ibid.*, p. 101. Funds for this paper came from the sale of shares at Rs. 25 per share.

Hoshiarpur, Ludhiana, Jullundur, Kapurthala, Phillaur, and in the surrounding countryside. It represented the growing leadership of the Jullundur Samaj and particularly of Lala Munshi Ram, and with that leadership a conceptualization of Aryanism that stressed its religious qualities, demanding in return a militant commitment. A similar center of fervor and proselytization existed in Gurdaspur. By 1890, the Gurdaspur Samaj had appointed its own *updēshak* to tour the towns and villages of that area.[24]

This trend to speak out publicly, to proclaim the truth of Arya doctrines, and criticize all other faiths offended and disturbed members of the Samaj. Proselytization tended to divide the religious from the rationalist, the militant from the moderate. Even the Samaj "Bible," the *Satyārth Prakāsh,* seemed too strong for some Samajists, who would soften its harsh condemnation of other faiths. Yet such proposed tampering verged on heresy to those who saw Dayanand as a *rishi* of old, unalterable in his truth.[25] Many Aryas considered any offense caused by the *Satyārth Prakāsh* unintended and incidental, the result of a dispassionate search for truth. "We are sorry that the book should have set any class of people a grumbling. But it is the fault of these people themselves that they have fallen foul of the book rather than that of the book itself. A little calm reflection will show them that they themselves are to blame and not the book." Militant Aryas rejected suggestions to soften Dayanand's criticisms of other faiths or to change in any way the word of this great *rishi.* "If there is anything in his writings with which you don't agree, you may put your views in print or adopt some other means, more to your convenience, to express your dissent from the Swami. But you cannot make the Swami the mouthpiece of your views." While no tampering or editing of Dayanand occurred, moderate Samajists did worry over the implications of *prachār.*

As early as 1885 the *Arya Patrika* carried a long letter from "an esteemed gentleman" condemning the trend toward public confrontation with other religions. "Of late, I have observed a growing tendency in the local Arya Samaj to join issues on religious questions with Mahomedans, Christians and Brahmos. Whether in the

24. *Tribune,* July 23, 1890, p. 4; and September 6, 1890, p. 4.
25. Quotes given below from *Arya Patrika,* August 9, 1887, p. 6.

papers, or in the Brahmo Mandir, or in the open air evening discussions in the Anarkali Bazar, I have seen and heard the same war cry."[26] Admitting that Aryas were not necessarily the aggressors, the writer still questioned the utility of *prachār*. "But what I ask is, has any good resulted from these fiery discussions, has any Mahommedan been made to believe the doctrine, has any Christian been won over on its side, has any Brahmo been convinced of it? I have seen all parties sticking to the same arguments from day to day a thousand time *ad nauseam*. Not a single new argument has been advanced on any side, since the discussion was first opened in the Brahma Mandir, or even before it. And it could not be otherwise. For the matter is discussed not on its own merits, but on the general consideration of defeat and victory." The "esteemed gentleman" ended with a plea to spend Samajic energy on reforming Hinduism first, to "convince our Hindu brethren that it is repugnant to their religious doctrines and authorities—nay it is a sin—to pay homage at [Muslim] tombs and shrines. There is ample field yet for reformation within, before we employ and entangle ourselves uselessly and unnecessarily in religious discussions with outsiders, and undertake to convert them to our own religious views." Many of the Samaj leaders shared this reluctance to engage in religious debate. Younger, more militant Aryas found themselves criticized and urged to moderation. Older leaders cautioned that "Young Samajists should not initiate any discussion without our approval," and more acidly remarked, "If you are incapable, why beat the drum of discussion?"[27] Those who advised caution and restraint failed both to limit the expansion of *prachār* or to soften its impact. The need to win and retain converts compelled Aryas to continue proselytization.

Religious commitment created an atmosphere of controversy, of *mandan-khandan,* throughout the Punjab. Each religious community and each sect within these communities fought to establish its own claims to truth. By the late 1880s numerous complaints appeared in the press against Arya *updeshaks,* against Islamic, Christian, Sikh and Hindu preachers, and finally against all public preaching regardless of religious affiliation.[28] Lahore became the

26. Quotes given below from *Arya Patrika,* September 5, 1885, pp. 3–5.

27. Jambunathan, *Swami Shraddhanand,* p. 71.

28. See *Waz'ī-ul-Mulk,* July 11, 1888, Government of India, *Selections from the Vernacular Newspapers Published in the Punjab, 1888,* p. 129; *Āshraf-ul-Akhbār,*

center of such street preaching. The *Tribune* complained that "The open air preaching in Anarkali is fast becoming a nuisance. A Maulvi is in the habit of using very insulting language in speaking of the faith of the Hindus and some day a serious breach of peace may occur . . . [for] some Hindu youths had threatened to break his head . . . The Maulvi, it may be mentioned, keeps several roughs around him as his bodyguard."[29] Militant religion marched on, gradually spreading throughout the province. Yet preaching at its worst represented merely the power of the word, and no matter how insulting or vicious the Hindu condemnation of other faiths, it could not threaten them as they threatened Hinduism. For Hindus did not convert and the struggle for adherents by Aryas, Brahmos and Dev Dharmis was limited to the Hindu community, while other religions sought members universally, without restriction of community or creed. Aryas would seek to redress this imbalance and in so doing greatly intensify religious competition to a degree hitherto unknown in the Punjabi past.

### SHUDDHI: THE SWORD OF RECONVERSION

The concept of ritual purification, *shuddhi,* was an integral part of traditional Hinduism. Individuals who had either wittingly or unwittingly broken caste taboos could be restored to purity and the fellowship of Hindu society through one or more ritual acts: bathing in a sacred river, pilgrimage, feeding Brahmans, or *prāyaschitta* (partaking of the five products of the cow). To Samajists, *shuddhi* offered the basis for innovation which would, in time, transform Hinduism into a conversion religion, equal institutionally to its competitors, the prophetic faiths of Islam, Sikhism, and Christianity. This innovative process took time and initially Aryas perceived but dimly the potentialities dormant in the traditional institution of *shuddhi.*

Aryas, including Dayanand, first concerned themselves with purification as a defensive mechanism to win back those lost to conversion religions. During his visit to Amritsar, Dayanand ar-

July 1, 1889, *SPVP 1889,* p. 279; *Dharm Jīwan,* August 11, 1889, *SPVP 1889,* p. 325; *Kōh-i-Nūr,* December 31, 1889, *SPVP 1890,* p. 9; and *Singh Sahāī,* June 18, 1890, *SPVP 1890,* p. 239.

29. *Tribune,* May 12, 1894, p. 4.

ranged for the readmission to Hinduism of a Christian convert.[30] Aryas were not quick to follow Dayanand's example, but by the mid-1880s they began to discuss the problem of conversion and reconversion. "The absence of proselytism in Hindu society is certainly a very important drawback in the way of its reform. No increase can now take place in the number of the Hindus and even persons gone out of their society can not enter it without undergoing a set of ceremonies to submit to which would reflect volumes of discredit upon an educated person."[31] The apathy over conversion exhibited by the Hindu community appalled Aryas, who saw clearly the threat posed by conversion religions.

The transformation of Hinduism into a converting religion meant far more than merely the adoption of the necessary ceremonies; it meant as well the shift from a social world based on birth to one founded on association. Yet few Samajists could conceive of the conversion of non-Hindus, and even the readmission of those recently converted to other faiths posed severe problems of social acceptance. For being a Hindu was not merely a matter of religious belief but also of function, and the question of readmission to caste privileges presented Samajists with an immense obstacle to reconversion, let alone outright conversion of non-Hindus. Still, the potential subjects of reconversion were immense; they included nearly the whole of the Christian and Islamic communities. "Hindus are the ancient sons of the land and so many Mohammedans are mostly the converts from Hinduism to Mohammadanism. If we scrutinize the Mohammedan community we find that only 5 to 10 percent of the so called Mohammedans are the descendants of the original invaders [of] Arya Varta and all the rest are sons and grandsons of those who had changed their religion."[32] The hope for reconversion ran parallel with the fear of further erosion of the Hindu community. Hindus, among others, developed a sensitivity

30. Unfortunately we know little of this event: how the convert was purified, the rituals used, and whether his caste readily accepted him back again or not. Har Bilas Sarda identified this convert as Khada Singh, who was persuaded to abandon Christianity and join the Samaj. He makes no mention of a *shuddhi* ceremony, only that Khada Singh began "to preach Vedic Dharma." Har Bilas Sarda, *Life of Dayanand Saraswati, World Teacher* (Ajmer: Vedic Yantralaya, 1946), pp. 196–197.

31. Quotes given below from *Arya Patrika,* September 14, 1886, pp. 2–3.

32. Quotes given below from *Regenerator of Arya Varta,* May 5, 1884, p. 4.

to the issue of conversion that was heightened and sustained by the decennial census. Unwittingly the British government supplied a tally sheet, a gauge of growth or diminution, of success or failure, in a new numbers game of power and prestige.

Although individual reconversions had scant impact on the general standing of Hindus in relation to other communities, they possessed great symbolic value. They offered hope, lessened the sense of impotence, and signified a new world in which Hindus could fight to maintain themselves and their religion. From mid-1884 onward the Samaj sponsored and gradually came to perform ceremonies of readmission. Individuals and occasionally couples who had converted or otherwise lost their membership in the Hindu community turned to the Samaj for help in regaining their former communal identity. The majority of these cases were recent converts to either Islam or Christianity. Occasionally an element of coercion is mentioned in the reports: "a Kayastha . . . who had been excommunicated and treated as a Muhammadan some time ago on account of his living and eating with Muhammadans," or the case of a Brahman who had fallen ill in Quetta and "had been obliged to eat from a Mahomedan's hand," or again, most pitifully, "a man of Khatri tribe by the name of Badhao, who had become Mahomedan in the state of intoxication."[33] Each turned to the Arya Samaj for assistance in regaining his lost position within the Hindu community, and each succeeded. Samaj papers reported a continual stream of purifications; for Amritsar alone, thirty-nine in 1884 and fifty-five in 1885.[34] Numerically of little importance, these cases marked the development of a new institution which would become a major element in Arya ideology, changing both the Samaj and the religious world around them.

33. Respectively, *Arya Patrika,* August 22, 1885, p. 4; October 31, 1885, pp. 4–5; and, October 5, 1886, p. 4.

34. The figures given above indicate the number of *shuddis* recorded in the *Arya Patrika* and the Lahore *Tribune* as individual reconversions. The *Patrika* for September 12, 1885, p. 6, states that the "Umritsar Arya Samaj has snatched about 40 or 50 persons from the hands of the Mahomedans and Christians conjointly." Reid Graham gives the figures for Amritsar as 39 in 1884, as reported in the pages of the *Arya Magazine,* and 55 for 1885, as reported in the *Arya Patrika.* Graham, "The Arya Samaj," p. 457. Since considerable Samaj data was lost in partition, we have accepted Graham's figures, although our own are far smaller; i.e., 3 in 1884, 6 in 1885, and 10 in 1886.

Reconversion supplied the Hindu community with a defense against Christian and Islamic proselytism. Punjabi Hindus who looked back to the loss of half their community to Islam now possessed a weapon which in theory could end the threat of communal extinction. "Is it not strange that karors [tens of millions] of Hindus were made Mahomedans by force and yet those who remained behind took no steps to open the door and readmit them in their society when the age of terror was gone. Millions of our brethren, in whose veins runs the same blood as in ours, and who would have co-operated with us as friends and kinsmen, have turned into deadly foes, and that simply for the mistake alluded to above. Thanks to the All-preserving God that in this age when different religions were eating away the remnant of the Hindu society some steps are being taken to save what can yet be saved."[35] Yet reconversion remained more a potential than an actual weapon. In the decade between 1884 and 1894 at least eighteen local Arya Samajes sponsored reconversions, but only four—Amritsar, Gujranwala, Lahore, and Rawalpindi—showed any consistent interest in the problem. For many Samajes a single reconversion sufficed as a symbolic act. But as early as 1884 the Amritsar Arya Samaj, in cooperation with a leading pundit, began a sustained drive to purify those who wished to reenter Hinduism. "[The] Amritsar Arya Samaj has taken the lead in this matter [*shuddhi*] and the Hindu Society must be grateful to that Samaj. Very much is due, in this direction, to Pundit Tulsi Ram of Amritsar. . . . Up to this time the Hindu Society alone has been the store-house on which all other religions used to feed themselves, but the Hindus also have been forced by circumstances to feel that if they take no steps to recover their lost brethren they may one day, one by one, be engulfed wholly by other religions."[36]

The cooperation of Pandit Tulsi Ram aided in muting objections by the orthodox community. Also the Amritsar Samaj did not seek in this issue to oppose existing Hindu practices and rituals. Instead, they utilized the traditional purification ceremonies. Candidates for reconversion were sent to Hardwar for a bath in the sacred Ganges River, followed by the ritual of *prāyaschitta,* all under the supervision of orthodox Brahmans. Gradually Aryas

35. *Arya Patrika,* October 31, 1885, pp. 4–5.
36. *Arya Patrika,* August 22, 1885, p. 4.

developed their own set of ceremonies consisting of tonsure, the fire or Hom sacrifice, investment of a sacred thread, and instruction in the *Gayātrī Mantra.*[37] The Sāmaj employed both their own ceremonies and a trip to Hardwar for orthodox purification. This still left the major problem of social acceptance. Ceremonies which might satisfy a Pandit in Hardwar or the local Arya Samaj did not mean automatic readmission to caste privileges. The Samaj met this problem through a combination of persuasion and public ceremonies. Whenever possible, they sponsored a meeting of reconciliation in which the newly purified distributed food and all ate, signifying his readmission to society. The story of Ganga Pershad, a young Kayastha, who had converted to Islam, illustrates the method of reacceptance.

On the 26th ultimo, some of the relatives of Ganga Pershad gave a dinner party to which they invited about 60 representatives of the various communities. The proceedings were opened by Swami Ishwra Nand Saraswati who recited a good many mantras from the Vedas and performed the ceremony of Hōm. After this meals were served (Ganga Pershad took a special part in this) to all present, and Ganga Pershad [was] sanctified and blessed. The dinner being over Swami Ishwara Nand and others made very eloquent speeches and impressed upon the minds of their audience the supreme importance of doing away with the baneful custom of not allowing our "wandering away friends" to rejoin our fold and they no doubt succeeded in proving to the satisfaction of all that this custom was undermining our social strength. With usual thanks to the President the party dispersed leaving the priest to cry in the wilderness.[38]

This *shuddhi* succeeded, but serious opposition did exist and caused many local Samaj chapters to hesitate before performing a reconversion. Even in Amritsar, with its ties to the orthodox community, the Samaj debated the advisibility of an occasional *shuddhi.*[39] More serious than opposition from without the Samaj was the reluctance of many Aryas to enter into daily social relations with the newly purified. "The Arya Samaj converts Mohamma-

37. The *gāyatrī mantra* is a prayer recited by all Hindus in their daily worship. Drawn from the *Rig Veda,* it could be learned and used only by members of the three upper *varnas,* the Brahmans, Vaishyas, and Kshatriyas. Under no circumstances should it or any other section of the sacred Vedas be taught to Sudras, outcastes, or non-Hindus.

38. *Arya Patrika,* July 26, 1887, p. 4; also see the *Patrika,* August 10, 1886, p. 8.

39. *Qaumi Akhbar,* September 5, 1889, *SPVP 1889,* p. 380.

dans and Christians but most of the Arya Samajists are not willing to mix socially. This is really shutting the doors of the Arya Samaj practically if not [in] theory . . . members of the Samaj are afraid the Hindu Biradri will expel them."[40] This fear of social ostracism helped to limit *shuddhi* to individual cases performed by only the most confident and daring Samajes.

Even though most Aryas accepted the necessity of *shuddhi*, many became vocally critical of the employment of Brahmans with their traditional ceremonies. "Do Aryas hold the *Praschit* ceremony of Hindus? Do they insist on the eating of cow-dung, paying of visits to the Ganges, and feeding of the Brahmans? Such *Praschit* is degrading and a true Arya would never bow down to such unmeaning ceremonies and their selfish advocates the Brahmans."[41] As in other rituals, Aryas sought to break with Brahmanical Hinduism to legitimize their own religious innovations. "The Arya Samaj is strong enough to get Hindu converts back to Hinduism, but owing to its weakness it has had to compromise with Hinduism and accept the process of *Praschit*. This state of things has continued and I am sorry the Arya Samaj has not been able to wield so much influence as to transform even Hindu converts without asking help from Hindus by way of *Praschit*."[42] Confidence and criticism moved the Samaj toward replacing the traditional rituals with its own ceremonies. In 1890, the Montgomery Arya Samaj purified a Muslim convert and in so doing performed the *prāyaschitta*, but eliminated the long and costly trip to Hardwar.[43] Within a few years the Samaj would abandon all cooperation with orthodoxy and perform *shuddhi* ceremonies solely on their own authority, using purely Samajic rituals. The need for orthodox allies lessened as the Samaj grew in strength and also with the appearance of new allies, reformers like themselves, educated men of the Sikh community.

As early as 1885 the Rawalpindi Arya Samaj received public assistance from the local Singh Sabha in its attempt to purify a Muslim convert.[44] In the early nineties the Singh Sabhas began their own program of *shuddhi* to win back Sikhs from Islam and Christ-

40. Quotes given below from Reid Graham, "The Arya Samaj," p. 463.
41. Quotes given below from *Ibid.*, p. 464.
42. Jambunathan, *Swami Shraddhanand*, p. 111.
43. *Tribune*, May 28, 1890, p. 5.
44. *Arya Patrika*, August 22, 1885, p. 4.

ianity. They possessed what Hindus did not, a tradition of conversion complete with initiation ceremony. For Sikhs, both conversion and reconversion had an air of the traditional, although they also faced problems of caste acceptance. During the years 1893-1894, the reform Sikhs of Gujranwala joined with the local Arya Samaj to sponsor *shuddhis*. Together they succeeded in purifying numerous "lost Sikhs and Hindus in Gujranwala and the surrounding area."[45] Sikh-Arya cooperation in the sponsoring of *shuddhi* was only a single strand of the tangled and contradictory relations between reformed Sikhs and Aryas, a relationship contained within the generally ambiguous interaction between the evolving identities of Sikh and Hindu. No single institution would have a greater impact on Sikh-Hindu identities as they related to each other than *shuddhi*. Still in an early stage of development, from 1884 through 1894, *shuddhi* would in the next decade seriously alter existing intercommunal relations between Hindus and Sikhs. By 1894, *shuddhi* had added a new weapon of defense and even offense to Hinduism. *Prachār* and *shuddhi*, the word and the act, awaited their full impact on society, an impact to be born of militancy and fear.

### ĀRYA-SIKH BHĀĪ BHĀĪ (Aryas and Sikhs, Brothers! Brothers!)

From the beginning, Aryas related ambiguously to Sikhs and Sikhism. For Dayanand, Sikhism was one of the innumerable cults of Hinduism, to be noted, refuted, and then forgotten. "*Nānakjī* had noble aims, but he had no learning. He knew the language of the villages of his country. He had no knowledge of Vedic scriptures or Sanskrta."[46] Without Sanskrit Nanak could have no understanding of the Vedas and without such understanding could accomplish nothing of permanence. His followers lost what little of value existed within Nanak's teachings, becoming mere idolators, one in degeneracy with Puranic Hindus. "They do not worship idols, but they worship the *Grantha Saheb* which is as good as idolatry. Just as idol-worshippers have set up their shop in order to

45. The first instance of cooperation between the Gujranwala Arya Samaj and the Singh Sabha was noted in the *Tribune*, February 18, 1893, p. 4. See also Lahore *Tribune*, April 8, 1893, p. 4; January 24, 1894, p. 4; February 7, 1894, p. 4; March 14, 1894, p. 3; and August 18, 1894, p. 4.

46. Ganga Prasad Upadhyaya, *The Light of Truth, English Translation of Swami Dayananda's Satyarth Prakasha* (Atlahabad: The Kala Press, 1956), p. 522.

get their livelihood, so have these people. Just as the priests of temples ask their devotees to see the goddess and offer presents to her, similarly the Sikhs worship the book and present gifts to it."[47] Aryas of the Punjab could not dismiss the Sikhs as Dayanand did, in three and a half pages of the *Satyārth Prakāsh,* nor did they choose initially to condemn the Sikhs as degenerate idolators.

The earliest response was one of identification with Sikhism as a movement which, like the Samaj, sought to establish a pure Hinduism devoid of idolatry, caste, and the evils of priestly dominance. Aryas would capture the Sikh past and make it their own. Young Sikhs reacted to the Samaj with sympathy, interest and, for a few, enthusiastic commitment. Bhai Jawahir Singh worked closely with Swami Dayanand during his tour of the Punjab, served as vice-president of the Paropkarini Sabha (1878-1883), as secretary of the Lahore Arya Samaj from its inception, and as secretary of the Dayanand Anglo-Vedic College fund collection committee.[48] Jawahir Singh's leadership in the Samaj brought other Sikhs into the movement, including Bhai Ditt Singh Gyani and Bhai Maya Singh. Others, such as Bhagat Lakshman Singh, joined the Samaj, finding in it similar ideological answers at Punjabi Hindus.[49] Through the early 1880s, educated Sikhs worked in the Samaj with little noticeable strain, but by 1885, Aryas began to condemn contemporary Sikhism for the same ills they found in popular Hinduism. If Sikhs were simply a part of Hinduism, then Aryas should attack the evils of Sikh orthodoxy, as they did Brahmanical priests. As with Hinduism, the past was glorious, the present dark. "That sublime and pure faith founded on the Vedas, which was taught by Guru Nanak and his worthy successors, has since greatly degenerated. Idolatry has again been introduced, and priest craft in another form has become rampant."[50] The Sikh community had fallen from the high moral standard of Guru Nanak in both practice and belief, even to the point of deifying the great Guru himself. "The superstitious Sikhs do believe him to be an incarnation of the Deity and would be uncommonly wrath if

47. *Ibid.*, p. 525.

48. Bhagat Lakshman Singh, *Autobiography* (Calcutta: Sikh Cultural Centre, 1965), p. 135.

49. See *Ibid.*, pp. 23–28.

50. *Arya Patrika,* December 12, 1885, p. 6.

any body dared to hint that *Granth Sahib* is not *absolutely* true."[51] Guru Nanak's ignorance of Sanskrit and Vedic scripture severely limited his ability to see truth and to understand the proper nature of Hinduism. "All we can say about him is that he made less mistakes than could be expected from a man who had received no education worthy the name and who had entirely to depend on the resources of his own uncultivated mind." Aryas through faint praise attempted to place Guru Nanak in his historical role as "an intelligent and good man" who because of his lack of education was clearly less in every way than Swami Dayanand. Few Sikhs agreed and many found this interpretation infuriating.

Arya criticism of contemporary Sikhs grew more shrill with the passage of time. In a lengthy article entitled "Sikhism Past and Present," the Arya critique of Sikhism appears fully articulated in derogatory, if not inflammatory, terms. After a brief complimentary note on the "Sikh of the past" as an "uncompromising theist," the writer noted that unlike the progressive Hindus, Sikhs remained sunk in degeneracy. "The intellectual forces brought into play by the spread of English education are slowly and imperceptibly infusing a spirit of liberalism into the Hindu mind, but it is our individual opinion, and we think we have good grounds to come to such a conclusion, that the Sikh is as much a bigoted and narrow-minded being now as he was thirty years back."[52] Beyond the reach of "progressive" thought, Sikhs drifted into the practice of idolatry, a belief in magic, and polytheism. "By and by they [the Sikhs] became to be what they at present are—a body of people under the special care of the goddess of ignorance and superstition." Similar attacks on Sikhism appeared in the Arya press throughout 1887 and 1888. The culmination of Arya criticism of Sikhism took place at the Lahore anniversary celebration on November 25, 1888. Lala Guru Datta in a speech to the assembly sharply criticized Sikhism. ". . . the lecturer (Lala Guru Datta) trampled under foot the honour of the Khalsa community, and in the course of his speech he said that the fact is that Keshab Chander and Guru Govind Singh were not even a hundredth part like our Maharishi Swami Dayanand Saraswati and it is difficult to say whether the Sikhs have any religion or not, but surely they have no

51. Quotes given below from *Arya Patrika,* May 25, 1886, p. 3.

52. Quotes given below from *Arya Patrika,* September 13, 1887, pp. 1–4.

knowledge of any kind." Not only were the Sikh *gurus* inferior to Dayanand, contemporary Sikhs had no grounds for criticizing the great *rishi*. ". . . 'If Swami Dayanand Saraswati Maharaj called Guru Nanak a great fraud, what did it matter? He held the sum of the Vedas in his hands, so if he wanted to compare this light with anything, what was that?'"[53]

Other Arya leaders, specifically Pandit Lekh Ram and Lala Murli Dhar, rose to second Guru Datta's comments, adding their own words of condemnation.[54] The reaction was immediate. Bhai Jawahir Singh, Bhai Ditt Singh Gyani, and Bhai Maya Singh resigned their Samaj membership and joined the Lahore Singh Sabha. This defection meant more than the loss of three members of the Samaj, as each became a staunch defender of reformed Sikhism. Within a few days of the anniversary celebrations the Sikhs held a large protest meeting and condemned all Aryas but specifically Pandit Guru Datta.[55] The Sikh-Arya controversy quickly moved from the platform to the press. Sikh and non-Sikh papers denounced the Samaj for its aggressive stance, its habit of condemning other religious leaders and doctrines. Throughout 1889, the debate remained active and virulent.[56] In the process of argument and debate, reforming Sikhs increasingly concerned themselves with defining their own identities within Sikhism, and for Sikhism within the broader world of Punjab. Clearly, Aryas they would not be, but if they could not identify with the newly-purified Hinduism, then where did they belong? This quest lay dormant, implicit in the search of young Sikhs for self and for community. It

53. Bhai Amar Singh, *Ārya Samāj aur uskē bānī kī taraf sē dunyā kē mukhtalif hādīyān-i-Mazhab kē be'Īzzati* (Disrespect of the Leaders of Various Religions in the World by the Arya Samaj and its Founder) (Lahore: Dev Bidhan Press, 1890), pp. 23–24.

54. *Ibid.*, pp. 24–26.

55. An account of this meeting and of more Sikh charges against the Arya Samaj appeared in the tract *'Amal-i-Ārya* (The Actions of the Aryas) by Bhai Jawahir Singh (Lahore: Islamia Press, 1889); additional mention of this meeting can be found in Amar Singh, *Ārya Samāj aur uskē bānī . . .*, pp. 23–28.

56. See *Aftāb-i-Punjāb*, December 14, 1888, *SPVP 1888*, p. 340; *Aftāb-i-Punjāb*, January 28, 1889, *SPVP 1889*, pp. 40–41; *Akhbār-i-'Ām*, February 23, 1889, *SPVP 1889*, p. 93; *Rāvī*, August 7, 1889, *SPVP 1889*, p. 324; *Kōh-i-Nūr*, September 17, 1889, *SPVP 1889*, p. 302; *Nānak Parkāsh*, August 25, 1889, *SPVP 1889*, p. 366; and *Singh Sahāī*, January 17, 1891, *SPVP 1891*, p. 230.

would become explicit with the close of the century, and with a second confrontation between Aryas and Sikhs.[57]

CHRISTIAN MAT KHANDAN (Refuting the Christian Religion)

Unlike Sikhism, Christianity provided Arya Samajists with a clearly defined enemy, the white man's *mat.* While Dayanand spent little time speaking against Christianity, his writings show great concern for refuting Christian claims of superiority. Seventy-seven pages of the *Satyārth Prakāsh* are devoted to a discussion of Christianity based on the Bible, which Dayanand had read in both its Hindi and Sanskritic translations.[58] Almost all later Arya criticism of Christian ideology was rooted in Dayanand's own arguments. He attacked Christianity on two levels: first, for its belief and practice of customs repugnant to Hindus and, second, for a theology based on superstition and irrationality. Christianity taught not only sacrifice in the Old Testament, but cannabalism in the New. Examples of animal sacrifice produced deep feelings of revulsion. "Now see. Are these not things of uneducated persons? How wild and savage-like it is for God to receive the sacrifice of oxen, and sprinkle blood on the altar. When the God of the Christians accepts the sacrifice of oxen, why should not his devotees fill their bellies with beef and do harm to the world?"[59]

Dayanand emphasized the brutality and ruthlessness of Christians. He saw a parallel between the ancient Israelites who slew and conquered their enemies and British colonialism. Identification for Dayanand was not with the "chosen people" but with their historic enemies. Commenting on the story of the Israelites in Egypt, Dayanand reacted with: "Horrible. This God of the Christians goes at mid-night like a robber and mercilessly kills children, old men and even cattle; shows no kindness; there is a great bewailing

57. See N. G. Barrier, *The Sikhs and their Literature* (Delhi: Manohar Book Service, 1970), pp. xvii-xlv. In his introduction, "The Sikh Resurgence: The Period and its Literature," Professor Barrier has given an excellent short summary of the Sikh search for self and the Arya contribution to that search. Also see Ganda Singh, "The Origins of the Hindu-Sikh Tension in the Punjab," *Journal of Indian History,* XXIX (April 1961), pp. 119–123, and Bhagat Lakshman Singh, *Autobiography,* pp. 58–60.

58. Ganga Prasad Upadhyaya, *The Light of Truth,* p. 683.

59. *Ibid.,* p. 715.

in Egypt, but his cruelty knows no abatement."[60] Cruel, aggressive, given to a flesh diet, Christians and their ancestors conquered and slew whenever it suited their needs. The New Testament added the final Christian abomination in the form of communion. "No civilized man will do such things except an uneducated and wild savage—to tell his disciples that their bread is his body and their drink his blood. And this thing the Christians of these days call 'Lord's supper,' i.e. on whatever they eat and drink, they impose the idealism that it is the flesh and blood of Jesus Christ. How awful? How can those men leave others alone, who could not spare the flesh and blood of even their own preceptors from conceiving it as food and drink?"[61] Dayanand's carefully chosen Biblical examples created a demonic Christianity, particularly as he addressed an elite moving toward strict vegetarianism and militant cow protection.

Not only did Christianity utilize rituals and customs unacceptable to a civilized man, but no one with an education could possibly believe in the various miracles attributed to Christ and to other Biblical figures. Christianity, like Puranic Hinduism, was a tissue of superstition fit only for the ignorant. If Christianity however was mere superstition, why was it still followed in the West by educated and modernized people? The answer was "political considerations and obstinacy." In one paragraph which examines Matthew 24:29, Dayanand responded with a capsule history of Christianity.

Hullo Jesus! What science told you that stars will fall? What powers of heavens are there that will shake? Had Jesus a little education he would have known that the stars are worlds and cannot fall down. It shows that Jesus was born in a carpenter's family. His familiar objects were the sawing of the wood, and peeling, cutting or joining the pieces. All of a sudden a wave rose in his mind that he should also pose as a prophet in that uncivilized country. . . . He said many good things but many more bad. The savages of that country believed them. Had Europe been as enlightened in those days as it is now, his super human claims would have produced no effect. Now they are educated to a great extent, but political considerations and obstinacy do not allow them to forsake this hollow religion and incline towards the Vedic faith. It is a great defect in them.[62]

60. *Ibid.*, p. 712.
61. *Ibid.*, p. 736.
62. *Ibid.*, p. 734.

Naive and at times inconsistent, Dayanand's logic was not dissimilar from arguments utilized by Christian missionaries in attacking orthodox Hinduism and the Arya Samaj. Both sides tended to be literalistic and dogmatic, appealing sometimes to reason, sometimes to traditional values and, on occasion, to modern science.[63] Dayanand's arguments were effective partly due to their own weight, but also to the relative lack of sophistication found among his opponents.

Christian ideology ran counter to many of the basic assumptions of philosophic Hinduism. Its rejection of transmigration, its creator deity and concern for sin provided Dayanand with ample opportunity for refutation. In commenting on the entire creation myth of Genesis, Dayanand rejected it with a flat statement. "This description of the creation of the world does not tally with the scientific process." Reason, the laws of nature and science were invoked by Dayanand and later Samaj writers, along with Vedic Scriptures, as counters to other beliefs. The Arya Samaj acceptance of *karma*—justice according to one's deeds—precluded salvation by faith and also made immoral the Christian concept of original sin. ". . .is it not horrible to say that all men from their birth are sinners; that the sin of father produces a sin in and give[s] a punishment to his poor son? When shall reason and experience guide all the world and bias be universally relinquished?"[64]

During the late 1880s Aryas looked forward to a new era when "reason and experience," knowledge in its true and Vedic sense, would dominate. Still fearful of Christian missionaries, engaged in a continual ideological struggle, Aryas prided themselves on hav-

63. Dayanand's rejection of the supernatural, his concern for truth, reason, and knowledge have enabled later Samaj writers to claim that their form of Hinduism is "scientific." In his translation of the *Satyārth Prakāsh,* Ganga Prasad Upadhyaya consistently translated *vidya* as "science!" Dayanand did not employ the modern Hindi word for science, *vigyān,* and it is doubtful that he saw any difference between the traditional concept of knowledge and Western science. His naturalism and rationalism stemmed from traditional Hindu concepts with some additions of Western knowledge, but it is unlikely that he conceived of scientific knowledge as an alternative truth arrived at through verification. That science might produce a truth superior to Vedic revelation remained unthinkable to Dayanand as to many of his followers. The entire thrust of Dayanand's reaction to Western science and technology was to capture and incorporate it, not to refute it. In this he was largely successful.

64. Quotes given below from *Arya Patrika,* July 6, 1886, p. 3.

ing blunted the Christian threat to convert the whole of Hindudom. "The Arya Samaj has dealt a most fatal blow to the interests of the Missionaries, by disabusing the native mind of those wrong and pernicious ideas, which it has been the constant endeavour of the Missionaries, to instill into it, ever since they set their foot upon Indian soil."[65] A new aggressiveness matched this sense of hope.

Aryas not only experimented with *shuddhi* but challenged missionaries in the streets, at religious fairs and in print. Lala Munshi Ram could report with satisfaction having met the missionaries in public for the first time as a body of Samajists.

> Dassara at Jullunder was a grand success. . . . Near the Ram Leela Tank (the present Gandhi Mandap) we had pitched our tents. It was strange to see Bhakta Ram Headmaster of the local Mission High School, who was then the Vice-President of the Arya Samaj, driving one of the pegs of the tent into the ground and holding in his hand an "OM" flag. Intense propaganda was carried on there on behalf of the Arya Samaj. . . . Even the sons of Zamindars and Sowcars who were wasting their lives in vice were moved by our lectures. The two or three Hindu boys who were attending Christian lectures also came of their own accord to our camp. That year's Christian propaganda was a distinct failure.[66]

Similar attempts to meet the missionaries in the field occurred as tests of strength between contending ideologies. At a fair near Pind Dadan Khan, Jhelum District, Aryas from Peshawar, Jhelum and Ferozepur gathered to combat Christian proselytization. "They formed themselves into different parties and vigorously preached the Vedic faith throughout the fair. The Christian missionaries could not give the 'joyful tidings' to the benighted heathens to their hearts' content, for no sooner would any minister of the Gospel commence his discourse in a loud key, than a party of Aryan preachers would come into view, determined to contest the ground with him. The mere sight of the party however, would soon determine the missionary of what course to adopt. A word with the offensive party and he would soon clear out of the fair."[67] The growth of the Samaj in both numbers and confidence made it possible to provide teams of propagandists for fairs as well as for

65. *Arya Patrika,* July 26, 1887, pp. 1–2.

66. M. R. Jambunathan, *Swami Shraddhanand,* p. 78.

67. *Arya Patrika,* May 15, 1888, p. 5. See also the *Arya Patrika,* September 7, 1886, p. 6, for an account of a similar clash between Aryas and Christian missionaries in Ambala Cantonment.

street preaching, public lectures, and occasional missionary work. The Samaj published a continual stream of anti-Christian tracts both in condemnation of Christianity generally and in response to specific statements, either written or oral. Christian missionaries in turn were avid propagandists, producing literally hundreds of tracts and pamphlets.[68] Aryas responded in kind in a debate that ranged from the philosophic to the most trivial level of name-calling.[69] Religious debate often sank to the level of insult and insinuation intended not to refute an opponent's ideology so much as to destroy his personal reputation. The village tradition of contest through insults had like many customs found an elaborated, modernized form of existence.

Throughout the 1880s, Christian-Arya competition continued with reports of conversions and reconversions, of debates, pamphlet wars, street preaching, and tours by rival missionaries. The dilemma posed by Western education, which offered such great economic rewards at the possible cost of one's religion, had eased. Success by the Dayanand Anglo-Vedic School promised deliver-

68. Some missionaries specialized in anti-Arya literature, particularly Pandit Kharak Singh, a converted Sikh, Dr. Henry Martyn Clark, and Padri T. Williams of Rewari. In 1886, Kharak Singh published the anti-Arya tract, *Usūl wa Ta'līm Ārya Samāj, Likchār No. 2* (Principles and Teachings of the Arya Samaj, Lecture No. 2) (Amritsar: Chashma-i-Nur Press, 1886). The next year Kharak Singh and Dr. Clark followed with an English tract entitled *The Principles and Teachings of the Arya Samaj* (Lahore: New Imperial Press, 1887).

69. See Lekh Ram, *Risāla-i-Sadāqat-i-Usūl-o-ta'līm Ārya Samāj, ya'ni muta'-ssib Pādīryōn kī nā fahmī kā qarār wāqa'-i-'ilāj nambar ēk* (a Pamphlet on the Truth of the Principles and Teachings of the Arya Samaj, i.e., a Suitable Remedy for the Ignorance of the Bigoted Clergymen, No. 1) (Ferozepore Cantonment: Gouldsbury Press, 1888). Of all the missionary writers, the Reverend T. Williams had by far the sharpest and most bitter pen. He produced a steady stream of polemical tracts. Two of his earliest were *Exposure of Dayananda Saraswati* (Delhi: 1889) and *A Farce: A Religion professedly based on a book which as translated for that Religion has no existence* (Rewari: 1892). Pandit Lekh Ram replied to the Reverend Williams in his *Risāla-i-Niyōg par Pādrī T. Williams kē I'tirāzāt kā Jawab* (A reply to the Criticisms by Reverend T. Williams on the Doctrine of Widow Marriage) (Jullundur: Parcharak Press, 1893). Various Aryas wrote against the Christian missionaries, with Durga Prasad the most active. He translated a debate between Dayanand and the Reverend T.G. Scott into Hindi in the Gurmukhi script—*Satyāsatya vivēk* (The Distinction between Truth and Untruth) (Lahore: Virajanand Press, 1889), and published two of his own tracts, *A Triumph of Truth* (Lahore: Virajanand Press, 1889), and *A Defence of Manu against the Calumny of the Christian Priests* (Lahore: 1891). The above tracts were typical of Arya and Christian propaganda.

ance from a painful choice, and the growing Hindu elite saw in its future a period of economic expansion with a degree of cultural security. "There was a time when the faith of all educated Hindus in their own religion had been shaken. Many through ignorance embraced Christianity and many others were ready to follow them. But thanks to God that the tide has now turned, and in these days it is a very rare occurrence to see an educated Hindu embracing Christianity or Muhammadanism. The educated Hindus have now learned that the religion of their forefathers is founded on solid rock of truth."[70]

This Arya sense of hope was rudely shocked by the census report for 1891. In the years 1881–1891, Christian missionaries managed to increase the number of Indian Christians in the Punjab by over fourfold, and in Sialkot District the Christian convert community literally exploded from 253 in 1881 to 9,711 in 1891, an increase of over 3,000 percent.[71] The Arya view of the mission movement was partially correct. Few young upper caste Hindus had converted. But the missions found great success during this decade, as they had before, among the lowest castes, the "ignorant and uneducated brothers" of the Samaj. Missionary tactics tended to shift from individual to group conversions, leaving many Samajists dismayed by a reinvigorated Christian threat. "Few people have any idea of the rapidity with which the number of the Indian Christian community is being swollen by the conversion of the people of the lowest castes. In fact if conversions go on at this rate there will no longer remain any 'low castes' at a not very distant date and the 'higher castes' will have to exert all their energies in protecting themselves from being pushed to the wall by aggressive *mehters* and *chamars* elevated from their degraded position to the religious level of their rulers."[72] The Samaj and other Hindu leaders found themselves faced with the possible loss of all Hindu outcastes. This threat they readily accepted. The past had already shown deep inroads into the lowest castes by both Islam and Sikhism. Yet Aryas were slow to react. This external

70. *Arya Patrika,* April 13, 1886, p. 5. Also see the *Arya Patrika,* August 17, 1886, p. 4, an account of saving a young man from conversion to Christianity. "This is one of the many examples wherein the Arya Samaj has saved the Hindu lads from going to the Devil, the most prominent feature of Christianity."

71. *Census, Punjab Report 1891*, pp. xxxliv; 97.

72. Quotes given below from *Tribune,* October 19, 1892, p. 4.

threat coincided with deepening internal problems and was as well over-shadowed by increasing tensions between the Samaj and an older Hindu enemy, Islam. The Christian threat would await both internal developments and the greater struggle—Arya versus Muslim.

### ARYAS, LEKH RAM, AND ISLAM

As with Christianity, Dayanand provided the basic anti-Islamic arguments in the *Satyārth Prakāsh*. He devoted more space to a refutation of Islam than to any other religion, using in the process many of the same arguments and points of criticism levelled against Christianity. Islam, too, possessed a creator God, sin, judgment, salvation, and miracles attributed to Mohammad, a superstitious faith unfit for the rational, modernized man.[73] As with all religions, Dayanand felt it necessary to equate Islam with Puranic Hinduism. His attempt to paint Islam as idolatrous proved difficult, but exemplified the need to discredit that religion in terms relevant to his overall critique.[74]

The main thrust of Dayanand's attack centered on Islam's division of the world into the faithful and the infidel, plus the twin themes of brutality and sensuality. Dayanand saw Islam as a religion of slaughter, both of animals and men.[75] Beneath the sanctioned brutality of holy war lay the concept of an "infidel," a person beyond the realm of the faithful who could and should be exterminated. "Now look at this bigotry—those who are not within the fold of the Moslem religion are declared as heretics and even those among them who are good are not regarded worthy of friendship, and even evil-doers among the Moslems are to be befriended. Such teachings tend to make God ungodlike. This shows that the Quoran, the Quoranic God and the Moslems are full of bigotry and ignorance."[76] Dayanand repeatedly linked this exclusiveness to Muslim willingness to destroy an infidel. "Now see what a great fanaticism it is. Who is not a Moslem, kill him wherever you get him, but do not kill a Muslim! . . . Moslems say that

73. Ganga Prasad Upadhyaya, *The Light of Truth,* pp. 767, 798, 802, 804–805, and 810.

74. *Ibid.*, pp. 777, 812.

75. *Ibid.*, p. 797.

76. *Ibid.*, p. 785. For sections critical of animal sacrifice and the Islamic method of slaughtering animals for food, see pp. 763–764.

the murder of a Moslem would result in hell, the followers of other faiths say that the killing of Moslems win[s] paradise. Now which of these two should be accepted and which abandoned? It is proper for all men to forsake such foolish religions and accept Vedic faith, because it enjoins that it is always best to follow the path of Aryas or good persons and shun the path of *Dāsyus* or evil doers."[77] Islam, which promoted violence, the slaughter of animals, and meat eating, was as well sexually degenerate. Dayanand criticized Qu'rānic statements on the role of women and on relations between men and women.[78] But by far his sharpest remarks centered on the Islamic concept of paradise. His rejection of paradise as such was coupled with indignation over its refinements. "What a humbug is this paradise of the Quoran having gardens, ornaments, raiment, pillows, beddings for enjoyment. Well, think a little."[79] "Is this a paradise or a grove of prostitutes? Shall we call Him God or a woman hunter? Can any wise man call such a book God's?"[80]

Dayanand's attacks on Islam made no mention of the historic clash between Islam and Hinduism, nor did he emphasize contemporary points of conflict between the two religious communities. Typically he limited himself to scriptural exegesis. Yet implicit in his comments lay a consciousness of Islamic political domination. Later Samaj writers would make explicit the tie between Islamic doctrine and historical conflict, finally relating both to communal tensions of nineteenth-century Punjab. Unlike Arya-Christian competition, the struggle between Samajists and Islam quickly became identified with two champions—Pandit Lekh Ram for the Samaj, and Mirza Ghulam Ahmad, the leader of an aggressive Islamic sect, the Ahmadīyahs. Once more religious controversy became a highly personal matter, ending with the assassination of Pandit Lekh Ram in 1897.

Born in the village of Saiydpur, District Jhelum, in 1858, Pandit Lekh Ram did not participate in the Lahore culture of his contemporaries. A Saraswat Brahman, he received his first education in the village *madrasa,* where he studied Urdu. At the age of eleven

77. *Ibid.,* p. 789; for other references to the killing of infidels, see pp. 780, 789, 800, 801.

78. See *Ibid.,* p. 821 on *pardah,* and p. 835.

79. *Ibid.,* p. 809.

80. *Ibid.,* p. 784.

Lekh Ram left the village for Peshawar where his uncle had been posted in the local police. Under the guidance of Muslim tutors he studied both Urdu and Persian. Lekh Ram reacted to his Muslim teachers as other young Hindus reacted to their Christian instructors. He developed a heightened sense of his own religious identity and a growing animosity to Islam. At the age of fourteen he returned to his village, this time to work under a Hindu tutor. Three years later in December 1875, he finished his education, returned to Peshawar, and joined the local police. His career in the Peshawar police lasted only four years and was brought to a close by two sets of interlinked circumstances. First, he served under Muslim superiors and increasingly clashed with them on personal and religious grounds. Second, his problem in the police service coincided with a personal search for religious answers that led him eventually to a career within the Arya Samaj.

His first religious mentor was a Sikh soldier with whom he studied Gurmukhi and the *Bhāgawad Gītā*. A more lasting influence appeared in the person of Kanhya Lal Alakhdhari, who lent the young Pandit books on religious reform including Arya Samaj literature. After the Peshawar Arya Samaj opened its doors in 1880, Pandit Lekh Ram began using its library. Finally, impressed with Samajic doctrine, he traveled to Ajmer to meet Dayanand. From this time onward Lekh Ram became increasingly committed to the Arya Samaj as an organization and to Dayanand as his personal *guru*.[81] In the years following, Lekh Ram retained this sense of a personal tie to the departed prophet, a feeling shared by Guru Datta who had been at the Swami's death bed, and Lala Munshi Ram who had heard Dayanand on his speaking tours of the North-Western Provinces. Each could remember Dayanand the man, the great *rishi,* a remembrance calling for greater loyalty and self-sacrifice than commitment merely to the written word.

After joining the Peshawar Arya Samaj in 1880, Lekh Ram began to take an active part in local Samaj affairs. In addition to propagating Samaj doctrine, he spoke out against cow slaughter, and called for the use of Hindi as a medium of instruction in government schools.[82] Devotion to the Samaj cause and tensions in the

81. M. R. Jambunathan, *Swami Shraddhanand,* pp. 17–18.

82. Rām Chandra Jāved, *Ārya Samāj kē Mahā Purush* (Jullundur: Yunivarsitī Publisharz, n.d.), p. 66.

police service led him to resign in September 1884.[83] After this, Lekh Ram devoted his life to the Samaj. He spent much of his time touring as a Samaj missionary. Munshi Ram intensified his attacks on the Ahmadīyah movement and its leader Mirza Ghulam Ahmad. He even carried his message to Kadian (Gurdaspur District), the headquarters of the Ahmadīyah sect where he publicly denounced the Mirza. Adding insult to injury, Lekh Ram founded an Arya Samaj in Kadian which continued to attack the doctrines of the Ahmadīyahs.[84] From 1887–1890, Lekh Ram moved to Ferozepore to become editor of the *Arya Gazette*, an Urdu monthly owned and published by the Ferozepore Arya Samaj. During these years he wrote extensively both as a journalist and a pamphleteer. Although he covered a wide variety of subjects, Lekh Ram focused on Islam, both reformed and orthodox. He elaborated on many of Dayanand's criticisms and added his own view of the past. He soon led a group of Samajists at least partly knowledgeable in Islamic philosophy and literature and fanatically opposed to it.[85]

Among the various factions and groups within the Islamic community the Ahmadīyahs provided the Samaj one of its most aggressive opponents. The Ahmadīyah movement paralleled the Arya Samaj. It too was concerned with modernizing and reinterpreting a religious tradition, and it too became involved in a many-sided competition both within the Islamic community and without. Its founder, Mirza Ghulam Ahmad, proclaimed himself the Madhi of Islam, the Christian Messiah, and the final *avatār* or incarnation of Vishnu. Born in Kadian, in 1838, Ghulam Ahmad descended from an aristocratic family and looked back to a past far more glorious than the present.[86] The Mirza would through his religious genius re-establish the fame of Islam and his once-illustrious family. Ghulam Ahmad began to preach his doctrine of revitalized Islam in 1879, but did not achieve prominence until the later 1880s after the controversy following his first book, *Burāhīn*

83. *Ibid.*, p. 65.

84. *Ibid.*, pp. 66–67.

85. Pandit Vishnu Lal Sharma, *Hand Book of the Arya Samaj* (Allahabad: The Indian Press, 1912), p. 117. Among this group were Dharmpal, Bhoj Dutt, Murarilal and Yogindrapal.

86. Mirza Ghulam Ahmad, *The Kashf-ul-Gita* (Lahore: The Victoria Press, 1898), pp. 1–2.

*Ahmadīyah* (Faultless Ahmadīyah).[87] Mirza Ghulam Ahmad wrote, using a "logical method of discussion" designed to appease and quiet the "excited passions" of Punjabi Muslims. "And although the *Burahin Ahmadiyah* was only defensive and written in reply to Christians and Aryas who had overstepped all bounds in abusing our Holy Prophet (peace and blessing of God be with him), yet it was couched in soft and polite language and did not contain any harsh words with the exception of a few proper attacks that suited the occasion and such as are necessary for every controvertialist to silence his opponents."[88] The Mirza neither calmed his own community nor silenced his opponents. His message inaugurated a multi-sided controversy within the Islamic community and the religious world of Punjab. Aryas, led by Lekh Ram, soon became embroiled in rejecting the Mirza's claims to prophecy as part of their general critique of Islam.

Arya reaction to Mirza Ghulam Ahmad grew in volume with the establishment of Lekh Ram's career as a Samaj leader. Beginning in 1886, the *Arya Patrika* took note of this "so-called prophet of Qadian," who "encouraged by the success of the Mahdi in Soudan . . . declared himself a prophet sent by God to convert the people of Islam."[89] In 1887, Pandit Lekh Ram published his first tract specifically against the Mirza, *Takzīb-i-Burāhīn-i-Ahmadīyah* (Refutation of Ahmadīyah Arguments), Volume I subtitled, "A Gunfire to break the flanks and tyranny of Mohammad's Islam." Thus opened a war of words between Lekh Ram and Ghulam Ahmad.[90] Each tract incited a counter-blast of criticism and condemnation,

87. In 1880, Mirza Ghulam Ahmad began publishing his statement of belief, the *Burāhīn-i-Ahmadīyāh,* which appeared finally in four volumes. The last volume was completed in 1884. Also see Spencer Lavan, *The Ahmadiyah Movement: A History and Perspective* (Delhi: Manohar Book Service, 1974).

88. Mirza Ghulam Ahmad, *The Message or a Cry of Pain, an Extract from Al-Balach* (Lahore: Victoria Press, 1896), pp. 18–19.

89. *Arya Patrika,* April 27, 1886, p. 6; see also the *Patrika* for August 24, 1886, p. 3; and October 4, 1887, pp. 5–6.

90. Ghulam Ahmad responded to Lekh Ram's attacks in 1887 with *Surma-i-Chashma-i-Ārya* (Antimony to open the Eyes of the Aryas). Lekh Ram replied in *Nuskha-i-Khabt-i-Ahmadīyah* (A Prescription for the Madness of the Ahmadiyas) (Amritsar: Chashma-i-Nur Press, 1888). He followed this with *Radd-i-Khil'āt-i-Islām* (Rejection of the Islamic Robe of Honor) and *Ibtāl-i-Bashārāt Ahmadīyah* (Refutation of Ahmadiya Statements).

culminating in Lekh Ram's infamous pamphlet, *Risālā-i-Jihād ya'ni Dīn-i-Muhammadī kī Bunyād* (A treatise on holy war, or the basis of the Muhammadan Religion).[91] In *Jihād* Lekh Ram drew on the sections of the *Satyārth Prakāsh* which charged Islam with violence, slaughter, and a love of loot. He also turned to history for his ammunition.

Beginning with the earliest struggles of Mohammad, Lekh Ram surveyed the history of Islamic conquest in Africa, the Mid-East, and South Asia to support his argument that Islam grew through war and the desire for wealth. In *Jihād* he also answered the writings of Sir Sayyid Ahmad Khan and his rationalist followers who sought to reinterpret the Islamic doctrine of holy war. Sir Sayyid wished to allay British suspicions of possible Muslim disloyalty stemming from the revolt of 1857–1858 and the holy war of Sayyid Ahmad Shahid. Lekh Ram would have it otherwise. "All educated people started looking down upon the forcible conversions and even started objecting to their very basis. Since then some naturalist Mohammadis [Muslims] are trying, rather than opposing falsehood and accepting the truth, to prove unnecessarily and wrongly that Islam never indulged in Jihad and the people were never converted to Islam forcibly. Neither any temples were demolished nor were ever cows slaughtered in the temples. Women and children belonging to other religious sects were never forcibly converted to Islam nor did they ever commit any sexual acts with them as could have been done with the slaves—males and females both."[92] According to Lekh Ram, Islam was born of violence and would always remain tied to religious warfare. Such an indictment of Islam not only fitted well into Hindu prejudice and conformed to their own dim memory of past conflicts but threatened the British as well, for clearly such a people could never be considered loyal to any but an Islamic government. Religious *khandan* now impinged on the political world of ruler and ruled.

Lekh Ram proceeded to review chapter by chapter the expansion of Islam, using Islamic histories written by and for Muslims. He cited instances of slaughter, forced conversion, enslavement,

91. Lahore: Aror Bans Press, 1892.

92. Lekh Ram, *Risāla-i-Jihād ya'ni Dīn-i-Muhammadī kī Bunyād* (A Treatise on waging War, or the Foundation of Muhammadan Religion) (Lahore: Aror Bans Press, 1892), p. 1.

and the destruction of non-Muslim religious buildings. The Islamic invasion of South Asia offered the best examples of Muslim ruthlessness, the most frightening to his audience. The historical figures of Mahmud of Ghazni, Timur, 'Ala-ud-din Khalji, and, of course, Aurangzeb, march through *Jihād* in a procession of horror. "Ala-ud-Din Khalji looted a lot of wealth during his invasion. Twenty thousand beautiful women were enslaved. The number of the boys and girls was also much great and beyond the description of the pen. This King had not even the slightest hesitation in killing and burning the people alive."[93] Running through his accounts is the theme of forced conversion and its corollary that the Muslims of today were the Hindus of the past.[94] Given this historical "truth" and a knowledge of the Vedic religion, they should return willingly to the faith of their ancestors. Lekh Ram pleaded with them to do so in the last paragraph of *Jihād*. "Dear Brethren! Let us remove hatred and jealousy from our hearts, sit in an atmosphere of love and unity and worship the one God. Let us purify our hearts through the Vedic way of worship. The doors of penance of your return to the fold of your former real faith are wide open to let you in. Shed the burden put on your necks by force and under compulsion. Befriend the truth and help us in spreading the truth, because God helps those who help themselves."[95]

The publication of *Jihād* exacerbated already existing tensions between Aryas and their Muslim opponents. Tract and countertract followed closely upon each other during the closing years of the 1880s, growing in volume with the new decade. Lekh Ram's leadership in this refutation of Islam caused Muslim anger to focus on him. He stood for all they despised and feared. Repeatedly at-

93. *Ibid.*, p. 55.

94. Lekh Ram even claimed that the peoples of the Mid-east, including the Arabs, were actually Aryans. "The word 'Arab' has Sanskrit origin (i.e., Āryabah or the path of the Aryans). The path of the Aryans leading to Egypt. This is more evident from the form of the English name of that land i.e. Arabia (Ārēbaya). Thus in fact the Arabian people are the descendants of Saam, the son of Shri Krishna." *Jihād*, p. 50.

95. *Ibid.*, p. 64. For examples of the response to *Jihād*, see Hakim Nur-ud-din Maulawi, *Tasdīq-i-Barāhīn-i-Ahmadīyah* (Affirmation of Arguments of Ahmad) (Sialkot: Punjab Press, 1890); Abu Said Muhammad Husain, *Treatise on Jihad* (Lahore: Islamia Press, 1893); and Nawab Munshi-ul-Mulk, *Likchār Ishā'at-i-Islām Par* (Lecture on the Diffusion of Muhammadanism) (Lahore: Islamia Press, 1893).

tacked both in print and on the platform, he could not be silenced. In 1890, a group of Bombay Maulvis threatened Lekh Ram with court action if he did not "make over to them all copies of a work in which the Pandit has wounded the religious feelings of the Muhammadans by using disrespectful language in criticising their religion and its founder." The editor of the *Akmal-ul-Akhbār* of Delhi commented on this with a nostalgic note that "Formerly respectable people used to give a sound thrashing, and in some cases even went so far as to kill those who abused them on their religion, but British liberty has made people indifferent in religious matters."[96] Frustration and anger mounted among Muslims as Lekh Ram continued to condemn Islam in all its forms. Threats of both civil and criminal action failed to deter the Pandit or to moderate his statements.[97] Lekh Ram and his fellow Aryas continued their condemnation of untrue faiths, while each religious group "sounded the drum of debate" in their own defense.[98]

The early nineties saw a rapid escalation in tensions between Aryas and Muslims corresponding to a general worsening of relations between Hindus and Sikhs. Religious competition and conflict had long been a part of Punjabi society. The points of conflict between Muslims and Hindus varied, although none remained as inflammatory as the slaughter of cattle for meat and on Muslim religious festivals. Even though the Arya Samaj did not officially join in efforts to protect cattle, many individual Aryas followed the example of Swami Dayanand who had been active in founding the *Gaurakshā Sabhā* (Society for the Protection of Cows).

96. *Akmal-ul-Ākhbar,* March 21, 1890, *SPVP 1890,* p. 123; also see *Tribune,* May 3, 1890.

97. *Singh Sahāī,* September 7, 1892, *SPVP 1892,* p. 317; *Bhārat Sudhār,* August 27, 1892, *SPVP 1892,* p. 296; *Paisā Ākhbar,* July 11, 1892, *SPVP 1892,* p. 219; and *Tribune,* August 24, 1892, p. 4. The *Tribune* reported that a group of Lahore Muslims served notice on Lekh Ram to "burn his books, retract publicly all that he had stated about Islam and to apologize to the Islamic community, if not, they would haul him into court."

98. For further examples of anti-Arya literature, see Hafiz Muhammad Abdul-Majid, *Sadaqa-i-Jārīya bārā-i-Firqa-i-Ārya* (Everlasting Kindness toward the Arya Sect) (Delhi: Ansari Press, 1892); Muhammad Khalil, *'Adam Najāt-i-Ārya* (Ludhiana: Indian Army Press, 1893); and Shah Muhammad Sharf-ul-Haqq, *Ibtāl-i-Qadāmat-i-Vēd ma'rūf ba Munāzara-i-Kālka* (The Falsity of the Claims of the Vedas to Eternity, or the Kalka Discussion) (Delhi: Akmal-ul-Matabi Press, 1893).

Dayanand, in his *Gōrakunānidhi,*[99] laid down the basic arguments for cow protection used by both Punjabi Aryas and non-Aryas. The resulting tension over the kine question periodically broke into open violence and rioting. Commenting on the severe riots in Rohtak, the *Punjābī Akhbār* for September 14, 1889, noted "that kine-slaughter has been practised in India ever since the Muhammadan conquest, and that the present agitation in favour of the preservation of kine is due to the preachings of the Aryas, who go about exciting the feelings of the Hindus."[100]

The 1890s opened with a deepening of ill will between Hindus and Muslims paralleled by a communal mobilization on the part of all religious groups. Arya attempts to defend themselves from external criticism and to maintain and enlarge their own group had succeeded, but increasingly at the cost of conflict within the Punjab and among themselves. *Mandan-khandan* without produced disagreement within, leading by 1894 to a struggle between Arya and Arya over power, commitment, and meaning.

99. Dayanand's *Gōkarunānidhi* was first published in 1880 and then widely reprinted. See Yudhishtar Mimansak, *Rishi Dayānand kē Granthōn kā Itihās* (Ajmer: Mira Karyyalaya, 1941), pp. 135–136. For the impact of these societies, see N. G. Barrier, "The Punjab Government and Communal Politics, 1870–1908," *Journal of Asian Stories,* XXVII, No. 3 (May 1968), pp. 528–529.

100. *Punjābī Akhbār,* September 14, 1889, *SPVP 1889,* p. 370.

## Chapter VI

# TRANSITIONS: TOWARD THE 20TH CENTURY

> Such, then, should be our Vedic scholars, thorough adepts in science and philosophy, unprejudiced and impartial judges and seekers after truth. But if impartiality be supplanted by prejudice, science and philosophy by quasi-knowledge and superstition, and integrity by motive, whereas predetermination takes the place of honest inquiry, truth is either disguised or altogether suppressed.
>
> PANDIT GURU DATTA

In the decade after Dayanand's death Aryas adjusted to both internal dynamics and external demands. As the major voice of the Punjabi Hindu elite, the Samaj was altered by success as it spread throughout the province, winning converts, creating new institutions, and establishing a lifestyle for its members. Initially the Samaj rested on the commitment of individuals to a charismatic leader, to Swami Dayanand. With his death, Dayanand's individual vision, the product of his own search for identity, passed into the hands of his followers. They would make of his identity an ideology, a systematic conceptualization of the past and present. Shared perception of contemporary needs supported agreement as to meeting those needs and produced individual commitment to the expressed goals of the Samaj. Conversely, disagreements over meaning, terminology, and Samajic symbols threatened both the Arya's newly-won identity, his "Aryanness," and Samaj unity. Two processes, the setting of priorities in a real world and the rapid growth of the Samaj, produced increasing stress on the underlying ideological agreement which retained all Aryas within a single movement. Arya attempts to maintain organizational cohesion failed in the face of disagreement over meaning, priorities, and the clash of strong personalities. Growth and its accompanying diversity proved stronger than cohesion and shared commitment. Success for the Samaj created centrifugal forces both organizationally and ideologically which finally broke the initial unity of Punjabi Aryas.

### IN THE MOFUSSIL

Expansion of the Arya Samaj with the addition of new members and local societies flowed along existing lines of communication as Aryanism spread throughout the province. The Samaj grew slowly at first. By October 1886, the initial eleven Samajes became nineteen scattered throughout seventeen districts. At the end of the following year Samaj branches numbered thirty-one in twenty-three districts.[1] The Samaj continued to grow rapidly. In 1890, fifty-five Samajes located in thirty-three districts and princely states supported the Dayanand Anglo-Vedic College movement.[2] From the original group of Samajes, the movement spread into the southeastern Punjab, from Multan outward, down along the western border tracts, and finally into the Punjab hills. The Arya Samaj came late to princely India. As of 1890, Samaj branches existed in only two of the thirty-four princely states, Bahawalpur and Chamba. Yet at least one Samaj could be found in every district of British Punjab with the exception of Montgomery. The distribution of Samajes can be seen on p. 157, showing financial support for the Dayanand Anglo-Vedic College. Samajic activity and wealth followed population density and urban concentration, although not perfectly. Local leadership and the dedication by a small group occasionally produced sizable donations to the College Fund from an extremely limited base.

In addition to the pivotal districts of Lahore and Amritsar, Samaj expansion created four centers of subprovincial strength:

1. There is no comprehensive record of early Samaj growth and this picture has to be pieced together from various sources which are not necessarily complete. Thirteen Samajes sent letters or representatives to the initial Dayanand Anglo-Vedic College Trust and Management Society meetings in January and February 1886, while the organizational meetings of October drew responses from nineteen local societies. Two of the original Samajes did not respond, namely, Gurdaspur and Jullundur, but later information shows that they continued to exist throughout this period. The *College Report, 1886–87* lists twenty-eight Samajes which donated to their fund. Three others, Delhi, Hoshiarpur, and Wazirabad, were not listed but are known to have been in existence at this time. *College Report, 1886–87*, p. 21.

2. *College Report, 1889–90*, Appendix H, pp. 50–53.

(1) the Peshawar–Rawalpindi axis which dominated the northwest, (2) Multan to the southwest, (3) the Jullundur Doab, and (4) the Rohtak–Hissar–Delhi tracts to the southeast. In each of these sub-regions young Aryas joined with locally prominent Hindus to form the nucleus of an effective Arya Samaj, winning converts and establishing societies in the surrounding territory. In time these centers became bases of personal and factional power. Local Samajes often led in introducing new techniques or ideas within the movement, and at other times they challenged the leadership of the Lahore Samaj. As Aryanism became more firmly rooted in the Punjab, it responded to and merged with the local life of the province, reflecting the variety of this life and suffering tensions in part from this variety.

In the northwest, Kanhya Lal Alakhdhari founded the Peshawar Samaj in 1880. From 1880 to 1887, Pandit Lekh Ram was an active member of the Samaj and imparted to it something of his militancy. The character of the area contributed as well to a strong sense of Hindu identity. Here Muslims were in an overwhelming majority. Hindus lived mainly in the towns and in Peshawar City. Peshawar's key position astride the routes to the border areas of Kohat, Bannu and Dera Ghazi Khan, plus its proximity to Abbotabad, Attock and Hazara, led it to strongly influence these surrounding Hindu communities. Its leadership, however, was surpassed by the rise of an extremely active Samaj in Rawalpindi. A group of Arya lawyers, led by Bakshi Jaishi Ram and later by Lala Lajpat Rai Sawahney, became a significant faction in the Samaj and eventually in Punjab politics. Their prominence culminated in the disturbances of 1907, when the government arrested and tried nearly all well-known Aryas of Rawalpindi City.

In the south, Multan played a similar and even more decisive role than either Peshawar or Rawalpindi. The only city in the southwestern Punjab, Multan sat at the center of both new and old communications, linking Rajasthan and Delhi to the east with the caravan routes into southern Afghanistan. It also commanded the north–south route from Lahore down the Sutlej to Sind. Here the initial enthusiasm for the Samaj drew on a combination of Pandit Guru Datta's intellectual and ideological leadership plus the powerful family of Lala Jawala Sahai, a wealthy contractor. The support of Jawala Sahai and later leadership of Rai Bahadur Hari Chand helped to create an energetic Samaj which assisted in

# Financial Support for the Dayanand Anglo-Vedic College Fund Drive by Leading Local Samajes as of March, 1890

**Districts by Number**

1. Mandi *
2. Suket *
3. Hoshiarpur
4. Kapurthala *
5. Faridkot *
6. Nabha *
7. Patiala *
8. Jind *
9. Delhi
10. Simla
11. Chamba *
12. Kangra
13. Simla Hill States *
14. Ambala
15. Karnal
16. Rohtak
17. Gurgaon
18. Jullundur
19. Ludhiana
20. Patiala *
21. Hissar

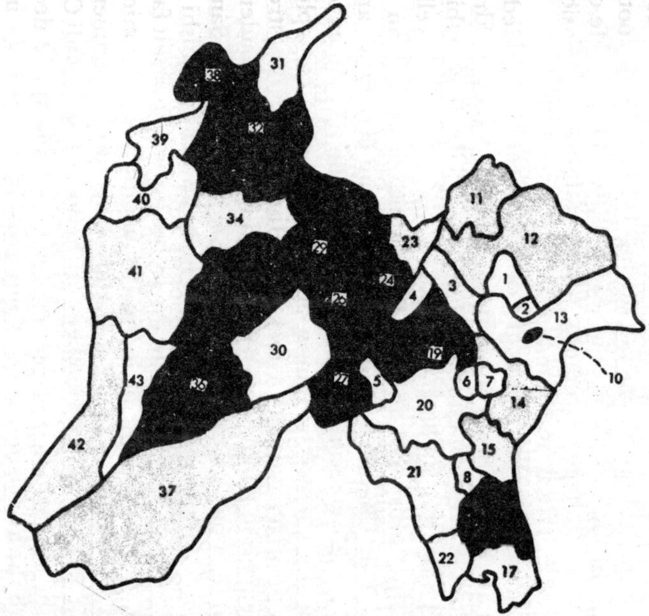


**Districts by Number**

22. Princely States *
23. Gurdaspur
24. Amritsar
25. Sialkot
26. Lahore
27. Ferozepore
28. Gujrat
29. Gujranwala
30. Montgomery
31. Hazara
32. Rawalpindi
33. Jhelum
34. Shahpur
35. Jhang
36. Multan
37. Bahawalpur *
38. Peshawar
39. Kohat
40. Bannu
41. Dera Ismail Khan
42. Dera Ghazi Khan
43. Muzaffargarh

Rs. 1 - 1,000

Rs. 1,000 - 3,000

Rs. 3,000 and up

* Princely State or States

Adapted from the Census, Punjab Report 1891.

Maurice Schwanke

spreading Aryanism to Bahawalpur, Musaffargarh and Dera Ghazi Khan. Multan City dominated the southwestern Punjab, a hub of religious, social, and later political creativity.

The most well-documented development of a subregional Samaj occurred in the southeast, in Rohtak and Hissar. Once again the combination of a young Samaj leader, Lala Lajpat Rai, and a locally prominent family provided the basis for Samaj penetration into the entire area. In 1884, Lajpat Rai moved from his home in Jagraon to Rohtak to continue his career as a *mukhtār*. He became secretary of the Rohtak Samaj and during 1884–1886 made numerous trips throughout the area in search of funds for the Dayanand Anglo-Vedic College movement. After obtaining his *vakīl's* license he moved to Hissar and remained there from 1886 to 1892. His arrival marked the beginning of a close involvement with the family of Lala Ramji Das, a prominent, wealthy Aggarwal Baniya.[3] Suspicious of Western-educated youth, Ramji Das made an exception of Lajpat Rai, a fellow Aggarwal.

As Lajpat prospered, the Samaj grew with direct familial sponsorship. Lala Chandu Lal, grandson of Ramji Das, became president of the Hissar Samaj, Lajpat Rai its secretary.[4] Lajpat Rai, describing the character of Lala Chandu Lal, pictured a man of wealth, prestige, and high status within the local community. "He was an expert in Hindi book-keeping and was regarded an authority in indigenous commercial usage of *hundis* (bills of exchange), etc. He has a reputation in ability to manage an estate and landed property . . . . He was aristocratic by birth and temperament and had an expensive style of living."[5] Chandu Lal, "the most respected and the most forceful leader of his own region," Pandit Lakhpat Rai and other members of the local Hindu community joined the new Samaj. It prospered and soon took on a new dimension with the association of Dr. Ramji Lal. One of the few English-educated Jats, Ramji Lal was both a friend of Lajpat Rai and a prominent member of the Jat *birādarī*. His influence helped popularize the Samaj among the Jats of Hissar, Rohtak, and Delhi districts. Influence with the Jat castes brought to the Samaj in this area

3. Lajpat Rai, *Autobiographical Writings*, ed. V. C. Joshi (Delhi: University Publishers, 1965), p. 36.

4. Lajpat Rai, *Ibid.*

5. Lajpat Rai, *Ibid.*, p. 37; for a description of Lala Ramji Das and his reputation, see p. 35.

a unique strength, merging Baniya leadership with the greater mass of Jat peasants. Lajpat Rai gave direction to this union and even after his return to Lahore maintained his ties to the Aryas of Hissar and Rohtak.[6]

The last subprovincial center of importance was the Jullundur Doab dominated by Jullundur City. Jullundur, like Peshawar and Multan, was located on a series of important lines of communication. It sat astride the Grand Trunk Road between Ludhiana and Amritsar. Southwest was Ferozepore, west the state of Kapurthala, northwest the road to Pathankot, directly north Hoshiarpur, and east the small town of Phillaur, home of Pandit Shraddha Ram. From its very beginning the Jullundur Arya Samaj was associated with Lala Munshi Ram. While still a student in Lahore, Munshi Ram became friends with Raizada Bhagat Ram, later a prominent barrister of Jullundur. On the invitation of Lala Dev Raj and with the urging of Bhagat Ram, Munshi Ram accepted the presidency of the Jullundur Samaj, while Lala Dev Raj took the post of secreary. Munshi Ram settled in Jullundur beginning his law practice and quickly established local ties, particularly with the prominent and wealthy family of Lala Salig Ram, father of Lala Dev Raj. In time Munshi Ram provided leadership for Samajists in the surrounding districts. After 1887, he had the support of Pandit Lekh Ram, then editor of the *Arya Gazette* of Ferozepore. Munshi Ram and Lekh Ram came to lead a large section of the Samaj movement with Jullundur one center of strength. In the ensuing struggle and division of the Arya Samaj, Munshi Ram was able to maintain his position partly through his base of power in the Jullundur area and partly through support from other subregional centers of the Samaj.

The Arya Samaj spread throughout Punjab and beyond by a combination of forces, a mixture of missionary zeal and official policy. As the subregional centers gained strength, they penetrated the surrounding countryside, sending their members, as well as paid missionaries, into the nearby villages and towns. In addition, the social position of most Aryas, as teachers, lawyers, and doctors, brought a steady stream of people to them who were

6. The different focus of the Samaj in the southeast may have in part resulted from the altered social structure of this area. Few Khatris are to be found below Karnal. Their place is in part taken by Baniyas along with the Brahman castes, while the Jats dominate at the peasant level.

often influenced favorably toward Samaj doctrines.[7] Often Arya social prestige aided their missionary efforts, especially in villages and small towns. The Arya press carried numerous accounts of Samajes founded by volunteers carrying their gospel of reform Hinduism throughout the province.[8] Aryas traveled as well to areas beyond Punjab, organizing Samajes in Sind, Baluchistan, along the northwestern border, and eventually into the native states including Kashmir. Yet the forces that brought the Samaj into Sind and other outlying areas were more economic and bureaucratic than religious. The spread of British business and administration carried Punjabis and the Arya Samaj to the west and south. "Some of your readers may be aware that it was in December 1882 that the headquarters of the Indus Vally State Railway were removed from Multan to Sukkur. Consequently a number of Arya brothers who belonged to the Multan Samaj having changed their abode felt want of an Arya Samaj which was accordingly established here on the 4th February 1883 through the exertions of Lala Munghoo Ram and other zealous members."[9] The Sukkur Samaj would become an active and successful center for dissemination of Arya ideology in Sind and Baluchistan. Punjabis flowed into these areas through much the same process which introduced Bengalis into the Punjab. Just as Bengalis brought Brahmoism with them, Punjabi Hindus carried Aryanism as their primary ideological innovation. In time they would take their Arya ideals to the Caribbean, Africa, and Southeast Asia, following lines of commerce and the British empire.

The most immediate impact of Arya success lay in the realm of ideology and internal cohesion. From a handful of Samajes dominated almost totally by Aryas of Lahore, the movement grew into a sprawling rather anarchical set of organizations led by men in search of ideological answers which could be applied to the real world surrounding them. Various levels of commitment, differing perceptions of needs, and a variety of interpretations of both Dayanand and his message led to internal struggles for meaning

7. Lajpat Rai, *Autobiographical Writings*, p. 40; for other comments on the spread of Aryanism in Hissar and Rohtak, Sri Ram Sharma, *Mahatma Hans Raj, Maker of The Modern Punjab* (Jullundur: Arya Pradeshik Pratinidhi Sabha, 1941), pp. 255–256.

8. *Arya Patrika*, October 17, 1885, p. 5.

9. *Regenerator of Arya Varta*, November 10, 1884, p. 6.

and power. With rapid growth and increased internal complexity Aryas would come to disagree, to struggle, and to divide.

## GURU DATTA AND IDEOLOGICAL ELABORATION

Arya ideology evolved through a variety of pressures, both external and internal, and according to the genius of its leadership. No one man controlled or totally shaped its development. Yet more than anyone else Pandit Guru Datta gave direction to Samajic thinking in the years 1885–1890. His speeches and writings followed closely the arguments utilized by Dayanand, extending them and making them more relevant to young Punjabis. Guru Datta erected a more sophisticated and elaborate ideological structure on the base of Dayanand's thought, but in doing so he carried only part of the Samaj with him. Others could not or would not follow. Elaboration of meaning required increased commitment as implications became explicit, and thought followed its inner logic. Guru Datta would have his "Aryanness" be all, an identity requiring total dedication. Few followed this path of religious commitment, while others came to reject it and with their disagreement ended Samaj unity.

After receiving his Bachelor's Degree, Guru Datta threw himself into the college movement. He succeeded in becoming an extremely effective fund raiser. "His learning, his noble bearing, his spotless character, his child-like simplicity drew large audiences everywhere and his pathetic and vigorous appeals so charming and eloquent had a marvelous effect in moving the people to open their purses in the interest of the College."[10] Guru Datta's pen proved equally effective. In a series of newspaper articles and pamphlets, Guru Datta began to publicize and elaborate his ideas.[11] In 1886, he received his Masters Degree, becoming an assistant professor of science at the Government College in Lahore, while the following year, when J. C. Oman went on leave, Guru Datta acted in his place as professor of science. His position at the Government College enhanced his leadership within the Samaj.

10. Pandit Guru Datta, *The Works of Pandit Guru Datta Vidyarthi,* ed. Lala Jivan Das (Lahore: The Punjab Printing Works, 1902), p. 25.

11. The *Arya Patrika* established by the Lahore Arya Samaj in June 1885 provided Guru Datta with an additional outlet for his writings. Lajpat Rai, *Life of Pandit Guru Datta Vidyarty, M.A.* (Lahore: Virjanand Press, 1891), p. 36.

He spoke with an authority rarely possessed by other young Punjabis. Moreover, his authority lay in two crucial areas of knowledge: Sanskritic studies and Western science.

Pandit Guru Datta's thinking evolved from an essentially religious base. In the Samaj, its writings and its *guru,* he found emotional and spiritual satisfaction. Yet he could not turn his back on science and Western knowledge without in some way incorporating them into an all-encompassing ideology. The few years of his post-college life saw Guru Datta create just such a world view, with considerable success for himself and the Samaj. Guru Datta saw two worlds, the inner and outer, or spiritual and material, which must be reconciled. He did so by considering the two spheres as "but a sign of the Unknown Reality which underlies both."[12] Reality in turn found its final expression in only one source, the Vedas. Vedic knowledge and science complemented each other in a hierarchical arrangement with Vedic truth superior to all other forms of knowledge. "Modern science, especially, as far as chemistry was concerned, was extremely defective, when judged by the different tests of a true science. The methods on which it was pursued, differed widely from those on which the ancients pursued it, and the methods of those ancients, when considered in the light of calm reason, were undoubtedly the only ones on which the structure of science could be raised on a sound basis. The ancient methods were simple, certain and unerring, and hence it was that the researches and conclusions of the ancients were beyond question."[13]

Guru Datta elaborated on the theme of Vedic knowledge as ultimate, beyond question and all-embracing, while scientific knowledge—useful as it might be—remained limited in its capacity to establish truth. "The modern scientist might dissect every nerve and bone, subject every drop to a most searching examination, under the most powerful microscope he could possibly have, but he was as hopelessly lost over his question as ever. He could not undo the mystery of life. . . . That question could not be solved but by the aid of the Vedas. They alone could unravel that grand mystery, and to them the scientist must ultimately turn."[14] Science

12. *Arya Patrika,* August 9, 1887, p. 5.

13. Lajpat Rai, *Life of Pandit Guru Datta,* p. 67.

14. *Arya Patrika,* December 4, 1888, quoted in Lajpat Rai, *Life of Pandit Guru Datta,* pp. 65–66.

then was the art of the material—useful but mundane. "For, how can God be thus known: Geology, Natural History, Physiology, Anatomy, Phrenology, Mathematics, Chemistry, Astronomy, and all are but grosser developments, the outer kernel. They deal only with the tangible, the tactual, the optical, audible, the edible, the olfactory and the palatal."[15] Guru Datta went to great lengths to establish the scientific nature of the Vedas, using the scheme of reinterpretation laid down by Dayanand. Technology as well as science and the ultimate answers to all questions were contained in the Vedas and their allied commentaries. Pandit Guru Datta's discovery of science within the ancient texts followed Dayanand's insistance that steamships, telegraphy and cannons existed within the Vedas. The ancient Aryas had known about and invented all the gadgetry of the contemporary world.

Guru Datta's preoccupation with science was not an individual phenomenon. Science and even more technology began to attract the attention of young educated Punjabis in the later 1880s. By April 1884, Aryas had established their Arya Samaj Science Institution with the assistance of J. C. Oman, professor of science at the Government College.[16] This was followed with the more successful Punjab Science Institute, a creation of Professor Oman and Lala Ruchi Ram Sahni of the Punjab Meteorological Service.[17] The Institute received wide support both in Lahore and in the outlying towns. Ruchi Ram traveled throughout the province, delivering illustrated lectures on science and technology. "I find it difficult to describe the interest and, in fact, the enthusiasm which the popular lectures of the Punjab Science Institute excited over the length and breadth of the province, including some of the Native States as well as at Quetta."[18] The acceptance of science and its allied technology rested on functionalism; it worked. The "valid conclusions of science, the sphere of the empirically demonstrable, finally enforced their claims of acceptance, regardless of their cultural origins."[19] Psychological acceptance of science, in turn, rested on

15. Pandit Guru Datta, *The Works of Pandit Guru Datta,* pp. 215–216.

16. *Regenerator of Arya Varta,* April 14, 1884, p. 5.

17. Ruchi Ram Sahni, "Self-Revelations of an Octogenarian," unpublished manuscript in the possession of V. C. Joshi, Nehru Memorial Museum, pp. 141–142.

18. Ruchi Ram Sahni, *Ibid.*, p. 144.

19. Joseph R. Levenson, *Confucian China and Its Modern Fate, The Problem of Intellectual Continuity* (Berkeley: Univ. of Calif. Press, 1958), pp. 60–61.

belief in the Arya view of the past, in the Hindu origin of science. A new mythology of antiquity legitimized adaptation of modern technology and scientific knowledge. No longer the possession of the white imperialist, science became a part of Hindu tradition, rediscovered and newly reapplied to contemporary problems. Conversely, anything that threatened the reinterpreted past also threatened to de-legitimize the future. Western scholarship of the Vedas and of Sanskritic texts appeared to undercut and destroy the Arya conceptualization of a golden age, and in so doing made Europeans the sole possessors of modernity.

With the growth of Sanskrit scholarship both in Europe and British India, the Arya conception of an ancient Vedic civilization came increasingly under attack. Swami Dayanand felt little pressure from European scholarship and could dismiss it with a disdainful shrug.[20] Dayanand's followers found themselves far less able to simply reject or ignore scholarly opinion. They lived in a world dominated by European ideas and were themselves partial products of Western scholarship. Throughout the 1880s and 1890s newspapers and journals gave increasing attention to Europe's discovery of the ancient Indian past. Literate Punjabis reacted with mixed emotions, complimented and thrilled by European attention, yet uneasy about the implications of this scholarship and the uses put to it in their own world. For supposedly disinterested academic writings provided ammunition for existing polemical struggles. Christian missionaries found the works of Monier-Williams, Max Muller and Indian Sanskritologists who agreed with them extremely useful in deriding Arya claims to Vedic civilization.[21]

Pandit Guru Datta made the discrediting of Western Sanskritic scholarship his special mission. His position as a professor of science placed Guru Datta intellectually in the midst of European thought, in daily contact with the enemy, while his growing emotional commitment to Vedic truth and Sanskritic studies gave him much to defend. In 1888 he established the *Vedic Magazine* to publicize his own concepts of the ancient Arya past. In speeches, in the

20. Ganga Prasad Upadhyaya, *The Light of Truth, English Translation of Swami Dayananda's Satyarth Prakasha* (Allahabad: The Kala Press, 1956), p. 391.

21. For a typical Christian tract using Western scholarship to undercut revived Hinduism, see Anonymous, *Papers on Indian Reform. Religious Reform. Part III. Vedic Hinduism* (Madras: The Christian Vernacular Education Society, S.P.C.K Press, 1888).

pages of the *Vedic Magazine,* and in tracts, Guru Datta rejected European scholarship as of poor quality and prejudicial. Either the Arya view must prevail or the European. "For, if the Vedic philosophy be true, the interpretation of the Vedas, as given at present by Professor Max Muller and other European scholars must not only be regarded as imperfect, defective and incomplete, but as altogether false."[22] To substantiate his arguments, Guru Datta turned to his own Western authority. "We are not alone in the opinion we hold. Says Schopenhauer. I add to this the impression which the translations of Sanskrita words by European scholars, with very few exceptions, produce on my mind. I cannot resist a certain suspicion that our Sanskrita scholars do not understand their text much better than the higher class of school boys their Greek or Latin."

The need to discredit European interpretations of the Vedas stemmed from the general acceptance of their views by educated Punjabis. "We are, indeed, so often authoritatively told by our fellow-brethren who have received the highest English education but are themselves entirely ignorant of Sanskrita, that the Vedas are books that teach idol-worship or element-worship, they contain no philosophical, moral or scientific truths of any great consequence, unless they be the commonest truisms of the kitchen."[23] Employing both the system of Vedic interpretation laid down by Swami Dayanand and his own scientific background, Guru Datta proceeded to illustrate the ignorance of European scholars.

Few Punjabis could understand or in any way enter into this debate. The educated Hindu community had its roots in Persian and English culture. They applauded and stood in awe of anyone who seemed to know Sanskrit, who dared to explain the sacred Vedas, and to debate the "Pandits" of the West. Guru Datta, who did all three, possessed the coveted M.A., and spoke with both eloquence and authority, managed to still the doubts raised by foreign Sanskritists.

Our learned brother Pandit Guru Datta Vidhyarthi, M.A., is conferring a real boon upon the educated community of Lahore in particular and the learned world in general, by his lectures on "Monier Williams and Indian

22. Quotes given below from Pandit Guru Datta, *The Works of Pandit Guru Datta,* p. 26, from the opening statement of his article, "The Terminology of the Vedas and European Scholars."

23. Pandit Guru Datta, *Ibid.*, p. 28.

Wisdom." What makes the lectures sought after and appreciated by the people is the method in which they are delivered. Every passage quoted from the "Indian Wisdom" is read twice and slowly, and then analysed into the propositions asserted therein. Each proposition is then most ably refuted with sound arguments, supported and back[ed] up with quotations from the Vedas, the Upanishads and other authoritative Aryan Shastras.[24]

Reassured by this message, Aryas retained full faith in their vision of the past.

Guru Datta's successful defense against Western scholarship opened the way to an elaboration of the Arya past. With the Vedas as truth revealed by God rather than the religious expression of a primitive people, the Aryas stood forth both as civilized and civilizer.

The English derived the rudiments of their civilization from Romans, and the Romans from Greeks, and the Greeks from Egyptians, and the Egyptians from Hindus, or more properly speaking, Aryas . . .

Now as we have arrived at the home of all civilization, let us enquire who was their civilizer. There being no nation previously civilized to the Aryan, who could impart them the rudiments of civilization? Were the Vedas held as "outpourings of savages in the age of sensation," in which view our Brahmo brethren seem to hold them? No, certainly not, they esteemed them as a revelation from God, and held them as the fountainhead of all civilization, inasmuch as they inculcate wisdom and religious truth, and have been the great civilizer of human beings.[25]

Guru Datta, by capturing science and placing Western civilization in a derivative position clearly inferior to the Vedic Aryas, established, for those who believed as he did in this vision of the past, the path to future greatness. It lay in Sanskrit and the Vedic scriptures. Guru Datta's drive to change the Dayanand Anglo-Vedic schools, to include in them a greater emphasis on Sanskrit and scriptural studies, grew from and exemplified his emphasis on the Vedas.

Gradually Guru Datta drew around him a circle of disciples dedicated both to the Samaj and to his person. By 1888, Guru Datta's disciples included a group of traditional *sanyāsīs* who accepted him as their *guru*. Together they studied the Vedas, Vedic commentaries, Sanskritic grammars, and Western science.[26] Guru

24. Quotes given below from Lajpat Rai, *Life of Pandit Guru Datta*, p. 63, quoting the *Arya Patrika*, July 24, 1888.

25. Pandit Guru Datta, *The Works of Pandit Guru Datta*, pp. 315–316.

26. Lajpat Rai, *Life of Pandit Guru Datta*, p. 71.

Datta organized classes in the *Mahābhāshya* of Patanjali and Pannini's *Ashtādhyāyī* for members of the Samaj and an *Updēshak* class to train Arya missionaries.[27] He showed a passionate drive toward religious commitment and spiritual satisfaction. He inspired in those who followed him an ardent belief in his own leadership as well as a religious and deeply emotional commitment to the Samaj. Guru Datta's acceptance of Vedic truth paralleled a growing belief in the infallibility of Dayanand and his writings. In the last years of his life he could bear no criticism of the great *rishi* or his works. His religiosity pulled Guru Datta away from the mainstream of the Samaj and in particular from those who retained a moderate or rationalistic conceptualization of the movement and its purposes.

Guru Datta in turn had only contempt for men of moderation.[28] Only those who would dedicate themselves totally to a life of religious or social work earned Guru Datta's respect. His passion had brought him into opposition with the new elite's desire for success. Writing to Lajpat Rai, he taunted him for pursuing a legal career in the *mofussil.*

What are you doing at Hissar or Rohtak? Life is not worth living in the way you seem to lead it. Have you any warm friends to enjoy there? (Be happy and blessed, if such be the case.) Have you any prospect of bettering your country there? (I must not be too perverse in my mind, if I could think of it.) Have you any chance of obeying the impulse of your nature, of cultivating your gifts, your once charming oratory, now crest-fallen, feminine unmanly voice to supplant the former? . . . fame is a wonderful impetus. But my dear sir, don't pant after fame. Do solid good to your country without shaming yourself more than you deserve. Work silently and then the fame of posterity shall be your reward.[29]

Not only had individuals fallen from their promising beginnings but Arya institutions as well failed to live up to their initial promise and sought unworthy goals. The school and college movement provided a prime example of mistaken effort. It was not founded, in Guru Datta's opinion, "with the object of supplying clerks, judicial officers, engineers, or other lower strata of the machinery of Government."[30] Such professions fell far short of Dayanand's noble concepts as envisioned by Guru Datta. By the time of his death on March 19, 1890, Guru Datta had succeeded in defending

27. Lajpat Rai, *Ibid.*, pp. 90–91.
28. Pandit Guru Datta, *The Works of Pandit Guru Datta,* pp. 281–282.
29. Quoted by Lajpat Rai in his *Life of Pandit Guru Datta,* pp. 51–52.
30. Lajpat Rai, *Ibid.*, p. 85.

and elaborating Dayanand's thought and, in so doing, he added an ideological base for increasing religious commitment to the Samaj. Many young men drawn into the movement found in it a focus for their passion and belief. The explanation of meaning and its defense from external criticism polarized the Samaj between a militant section who saw the movement primarily in religious terms and a moderate wing, more rational and secular in its conceptualization of Samaj goals.

### THE DYNAMICS OF DISAGREEMENT

The deaths in 1890 of Pandit Guru Datta and Lala Das Sain slowed briefly the drift toward division. External issues became interwoven with internal debates, hardening and embittering Samaj differences. Prime among such external issues was the question of vegetarianism, and its associated cause—cow protection. Initially, the Samaj did not concern itself with either. The Ten Principles ignore both issues and the founders of the Punjab Samaj included both meat eaters and vegetarians. Swami Dayanand, however, organized Goraksha Sabhas, cow-protection societies, wrote on the need to protect kine and upheld the moral superiority of vegetarianism. Many Aryas followed his lead, giving support and leadership to both movements. Arya publications called for the protection of cattle, cited Dayanand's arguments in tract, *Gōkarunā Nidhi,* and elaborated on them.[31] The arguments of Western vegetarians supplied additional ammunition and legitimization, indicating that even in a meat-eating, virile and progressive society, vegetarianism had a growing acceptance.[32]

By 1885, the protection of cattle had broadened in many minds to include the protection of all animals from slaughter. Thus the issue of kine became fused with the question of meat eating. "We are ready to concede that the cow renders more important and substantial services than other animals, but that is no reason why we should surrender the latter on the principle of this relativity. . . . how can we accord our sanction to the killing of sheep, goat, and withhold it in the case of cow?"[33] The logical progression

31. See *Arya,* August 1882, pp. 131–132; *Regenerator of Arya Varta,* June 30, 1884, pp. 1–2; July 21, 1884, pp. 1–2; *Arya Patrika,* July 18, 1885, p. 4.

32. See *Regenerator of Arya Varta,* April 7, 1884, pp. 1–2.

33. *Arya Patrika,* September 26, 1885, pp. 3–4.

was clear: all eating of meat caused cruelty to animals and produced the habit of cruelty in man. "A man, who from his very infancy has been harangued on the spiritual merits of sacrificing animal life at the altar of the carnivorous God, has by degrees his soul hardened to a degree that the destruction of animal life to him becomes a sort of pastime. . . . He is ready to cut the throats of his fellow creatures, when placed in circumstances when starvation is staring [him] in the face and the icy hand of death is already felt. He will kill them and eat them up for his food, or when he is thirsty, drink their blood, while manliness requires quite the reverse."[34]

After 1887, the advocacy of cow protection and vegetarianism by Samaj members and Arya journals raised the question of whether the Samaj as an organization supported these causes. The Samaj was officially separate from the cow-protection movement, but many Aryas passionately advocated it and came to believe that vegetarianism was the mark of a moral man. Led by Durga Prasad, Lala Atma Ram, and Lala Munshi Ram, the defenders of vegetarianism produced a steady stream of tracts and pamphlets attacking meat eating as immoral.[35] Concerned Aryas joined the Vegetarian Society founded in Lahore in 1889 and later led by Lala Durga Prasad.[36]

By 1890, the existing policy within the Samaj acquired the further dimension of vegetarian versus non-vegetarian. Under the influence of Munshi Ram, Guru Datta, and Lala Durga Prasad, the militants' definition of Aryanism came to include veg-

34. *Arya Patrika,* October 24, 1885, pp. 5–6.

35. See Durga Prasad, ed., *Physical Evils of Flesh Eating and Spiritual Awakening of Vegetarianism by Dr. L. Salzer, M.D.* (1887); Durga Parshad, *Spiritual Advantage of Vegetarianism* (Lahore: Virajanand Press, 1889); and his *Reason and Instinct* (Lahore: Virajanand Press, 1889); Lala Atma Ram, *Kyā Māns Bhakshan Ārya Dharm anukūl hai* (Is Flesh Eating in accordance with the Aryan Religion?) (Lahore: Aror Bans Press, 1890); Durga Prasad, *Manu and Vegetarianism* (Lahore: Virajanand Press, 1891); Durga Prasad, *Vegetarianism* (Lahore: Virajanand Press, 1892); Munshi Ram Kishen, *Sangit Mānas varjan* (Verses Prohibiting Flesh Eating) (Amritsar: Chashma-i-Nur Press, 1892); Pandit Khuni Lal Shastri, *Māns Bhakshan Nishēdh* (Prohibition of Meat-Eating) (Lahore: Virajanand Press, 1892); Lala Atma Ram, *Māns Bhakshan Nishēdh* (Prohibition of Meat-Eating) (Jullundur: 1892).

36. *Tribune,* September 14, 1889, p. 5. Also *Bhārat Sudhār,* February 8, 1890, Government of India, *Selections from the Vernacular Newspapers Published in the Punjab, 1890,* p. 57.

etarianism. In the March 15, 1890, issue of the *Sat Dharm Prachārak,* Munshi Ram noted with great satisfaction that "The Antaranga Sabha of the Quetta Arya Samaj had passed a resolution that no flesh-eater should be admitted as a member of the Arya Samaj. . . . This act is most commendable. Other Arya Samajists would do well to copy and follow this policy."[37] Others did. The Peshawar Samaj tightened its policy of admissions as did the Jullundur Samaj.[38] These steps toward an Arya orthodoxy in the *mofussil* Samajes followed the failure of similar moves in Lahore. On July 30, 1889, a resolution was placed before the Executive Committee of the Lahore Samaj which prohibited any member from becoming an *Ārya Sabhāsad* (exalted member) if he used either meat or liquor unless on a doctor's orders. The motion was successfully amended by Lala Hans Raj to require merely an adherence to the Ten Principles and as amended won by a vote of eight to five.[39] With this motion, vegetarianism became an integral part of the growing division between Aryas, symbolizing for many the existing polarity of opinion.

The Samaj moved quickly toward internal strife and division. Lala Mul Raj set off the final round of quarrelling and struggle in 1892 at the anniversary celebrations of the Lahore Arya Samaj. Once again the spark was vegetarianism. Mul Raj, in a lecture to the assembled Aryas, aggressively insisted that a non-vegetarian diet was acceptable and that vegetarianism had nothing to do with Aryanism. He followed this with an anti-vegetarian tract, *Mās Prachār kā Silsila* (The Continued Advocacy of Meat Eating).[40] Before this few Hindu voices had been raised in support of meat eating and almost none within the Samaj. Mul Raj's open rejection of vegetarianism produced a furious reaction by the vegetarian-militant faction.[41] A struggle for purity and power broke out within the Lahore Samaj and the Arya Pratinidhi Sabha.

37. M. R. Jambunathan, ed., *Swami Shraddhanand* (Bombay: Bharatiya Vidya Bhāvan, 1961), p. 121.

38. The Jullundur Samaj insisted on a ten months' probationary period for all new applicants. Jambunathan, *Ibid.*

39. Sharma, *Mahatma Hans Raj*, p. 60.

40. Lala Mul Raj, *Mās Prachār kā Sisila* (Lahore: Gulzar-i-Muhammadi Press, 1893).

41. See the tracts Laia Narayan Das, *Ham Hamārē Karya aur Bakrē* (We, Our Rites and Goats) (Amritsar: Chashma-i-Nur Press, 1893); Shri Jhamb Dev, *Shabd Tardīd-i-Gōsht Khuwārī* (A Word in Refutation of Flesh Eating) (Amritsar: Anand

In March 1893, Lala Munshi Ram led an attempt to restrict membership in the Pratinidhi Sabha to vegetarians. He lost, but in August he tried again with a resolution of censure against Lala Mul Raj. Again he lost, but the voting showed the vegetarian party's growing strength. The nonvegetarians then made a tactical error. Following the August resolution, Hans Raj on the advice of a close friend, Lala Radha Kishen, resigned his position as president of the Lahore Arya Samaj, an office he had accepted and held since the death of Lala Sain Das. Lala Lajpat Rai, who had now returned to live in Lahore, was nominated for the vacant office of president. Lajpat Rai was at this time a strict vegetarian, as well as secretary of the Dayanand Anglo-Vedic College Society. Hans Raj apparently put Lajpat Rai forward as a compromise candidate, perhaps because he could no longer be certain of a majority on the committee. The result would bear this out, since Lajpat Rai was successfully opposed by Lala Durga Prasad, the foremost exponent of vegetarianism. In September this struggle for control of the Lahore Samaj ended with the defeat of Hans Raj and the College Party. The two factions possessed equal votes within the Antarang Sabha. In order to gain the needed majority the Hans Raj–Lajpat Rai group had one of its supporters elected to the Executive Committee, but Lala Durga Prasad as president declared this election invalid and refused to allow the new member to take his seat on the Committee. With this defeat, the non-vegetarians withdrew from the Antarang Sabha and the Lahore Arya Samaj.[42]

Immediately following their withdrawal the dissidents founded a rival Samaj in Anarkali, a suburb of Lahore. Meeting at the house of Lala Ishar Dass, M.A., they elected Lajpat Rai as president and Lala Sangam Lal as vice-president.[43] There were now two Samajes in Lahore—one in Wachhowali in the old city (the original Samaj now in the hands of the vegetarian militants), and the other in Anarkali (the moderate non-vegetarian college faction). Following

---

Parkash Press, 1893); Lala Jawala Das, *Binatī* (Petition) (Lahore: Koh-i-Nur Press, 1893); and Pandit Lekh Ram, *Ārya Samāj Men Shāntī Phailānē kē Aslī Upāō* (The Real Means of Spreading Peace throughout the Arya Samaj) (Jullundur: Sat Dharam Pracharak Press, 1893). One of the few attempts to view this issue rationally and without passion was Lieutenant-Surgeon Bhola Nath's *Ham Ghōsht Khāēn yā Ghāns Phūns* (Shall We Eat Meat or Grass?) (Amritsar: Rast Guftar, 1894).

42. Sharma, *Mahatma Hans Raj*, p. 65.

43. *Tribune*, November 15, 1893, p. 4. Lala Budha Mal became secretary.

the election of officers the Anarkali Samaj began weekly meetings in the house of Ishar Das. The original buildings and the *mandir* (temple) passed into the hands of the militants, who quickly established control over the Punjab Arya Pratinidhi Sabha.[44]

Public opinion reacted strongly to the news of this division. Aryas now seemed doomed to fruitless bickering—itself a disturbing prospect—but what caused far greater alarm was the possible effect this internal strife might have upon the college. Lala Harkishen Lal, in a letter to the *Tribune* of November 18, 1893, expressed the fears of many: "Cannot you, gentlemen of the Arya Samaj divide your property amiably and peacefully and without resorting to law or what is mightier than law, might itself? Let you divide everything that you have but do not for God's sake divide the College which has been established not for the good of your own children but for all who will come to it."[45] Concern for the fate of the Dayanand Anglo-Vedic College paralleled public disillusion with the Samaj. Both friends and enemies were shocked by the bitter fighting among Aryas. The image of the Samaj grew more tarnished as Aryas squabbled publicly throughout the province. During 1893–1894, they fought for control of each individual Samaj and each Arya organization.

The most immediate problem posed by the division of the Lahore Samaj lay within the Dayanand Anglo-Vedic College Managing Committee. Which of the two Lahore Samajes possessed the right to send representatives to the Committee? Lala Munshi Ram's dramatic departure from the Managing Committee meeting of May 27, 1893, had left power in the hands of Hans Raj and his associates. But after the founding of the Anarkali Samaj in September 1893, Hans Raj and many of his key supporters could be challenged as no longer representing "the Lahore Arya Samaj." The Munshi Ram faction returned in strength to the next Managing Committee meeting held on February 25, 1894. After initial sparring, Munshi Ram proposed that members of the Lahore Arya Samaj, either branch, be excluded from participating in the discussion. This proposal, if passed, would have cut drastically into the strength of the Hans Raj group which was heavily represented in the Lahore delegation. The Committee rejected this proposal by

44. Sharma, *Mahatma Hans Raj*, p. 65.

45. *Tribune*, November 18, 1893, p. 5. For similar statements, see *Tribune*, November 15, 1893, p. 4.

a vote of 18 to 6. Lala Mul Raj responded with a resolution declaring the Anarkali Samaj the only legitimate Samaj in Lahore with the sole right to send representatives to the Managing Committee. At this point Lala Munshi Ram left the meeting with his supporters in order to break the quorum and make passage of the Mul Raj resolution impossible. The meeting adjourned.

The Committee resumed its deliberations at 7 p.m. the same day, after persuading Rai Labdha Ram, who had left with Munshi Ram, to return, thus establishing the needed quorum. They immediately passed a resolution recognizing the Anarkali Samaj as legitimate with the sole right to representation on the Committee.[46] The remaining members of the opposition who were still on the Committee attempted to have the evening session declared illegal, since it was held after the original adjournment, but the Managing Committee met on March 22 and upheld the February decisions.[47] The Hans Raj faction consolidated its hold over the Managing Committee in a regular meeting held on April 8 and a special meeting on April 9. Two issues faced the Committee: first, refuting the continual challenges to its legality by the Munshi Ram group, and establishing the legitimacy of representatives from the various Samajes. The final round of contention took place at the annual meeting of the Dayanand Anglo-Vedic College Society, on May 24 and 25, 1894. All strangers were excluded from the meeting and only those delegates with certificates attesting to their legitimate status were allowed to enter. The opposition tried to first disrupt this meeting and then to censure the officers of the Managing Committee for their "misconduct." They failed, leaving the college firmly and permanently in the hands of Hans Raj, Lajpat Rai and their allies.[48]

The termination of this struggle in the Dayanand Anglo-Vedic College Society marked the division of the Samaj into two separate wings. The militant-vegetarians, descendants of Guru Datta's Sanskritists, dominated the original Lahore Samaj, the Arya

46. Sri Ram Sharma gives an excellent account of this struggle in *Mahatma Hans Raj*, pp. 65–66. His account closely parallels the *Proceedings of the Managing Committee* for February 24, 1894. The proceedings for the 24th are recorded separately for the adjourned session and the evening meeting.

47. *Proceedings of the Dayanand Anglo-Vedic College Managing Committee*, March 22, 1894.

48. Sharma, *Mahatma Hans Raj*, pp. 67–68. Meeting also discussed in *Proceedings of the Dayanand Anglo-Vedic College Managing Committee*, June 26, 1894.

Pratinidhi Sabha of the Punjab, and controlled the *Arya Patrika*, while the moderates retained their hold over the college. Civil war spread from Lahore to every local Arya Samaj where rival factions fought again and again, with the militants winning control in a majority of the local bodies. The Hans Raj–Lajpat Rai faction found itself in possession of the schools but without the organizational structure responsible for past financial support. The militants, with control over most of the organizational structure, lacked a popular cause, education, which had appealed successfully to the wider Hindu community.

## THE EDUCATED HINDU: FROM TRIUMPH TO ANXIETY

The divided Aryas would face a rapidly evolving world as the implications of British rule cut deeper into Punjabi life. Some forms of change accelerated; others slowed. The optimism of the 1880s gradually faded to be replaced by economic stagnation and heightened competition between the educated elites of each religious community. By the end of the century British law drove a wedge between urban and rural society weakening the urban classes, and British policy introduced religious discrimination in governmental hiring. This action helped to further communal competition on both the economic and ideological levels. Punjabis organized, quarrelled, and struggled while the British sought stasis and stability. British colonial rule, so often the instigator of change, attempted to halt change. The survival of the British Raj demanded tranquillity, not the shifting sands of modernization. The British failed to find their dreams of stability, for they, like all Punjabis, were caught up in a dynamic world demanding continual adjustment. Amidst this kaleidoscope of change Aryas too sought to defend their ideology, to maintain their class status, and to relate to an emerging political world.

Forces of modernity created initially by British rule continued to feed the expansion of the educated classes who, in turn, sought to exploit opportunities in the professions, government service, trade, and industry. Yet rates of change and development proved markedly different. Economic advance fell behind the pace of education, and by the close of the century, the educated classes experienced declining opportunities. Growing anxiety and concomitant competition for increasingly scarce economic resources replaced the optimism of the eighties. By 1900, educated Hindus, who dominated the provincial economy, faced expanding Muslim and Sikh elites. The first decade of the new century would see the inherent contradictions of a colonial regime manifest themselves in social and political unrest, as the forces of change and the proponents of stasis clashed, as new elites challenged the old.

The educated classes grew steadily beyond the control of government and unrelated to economic development. Government, missionary, and private schools continued to expand unchecked by opportunity or regulations. By 1911, the literate community reached 899,195 in spite of a rigid definition of literacy. At the apex of the literates stood those who possessed a higher education and were proficient in English. In 1911, 86,106 Punjabis could read and write English.[49] Still the number of students in such colleges rose, from 468 in 1891 to 2,270 in 1911.[50] This student community remained heavily Hindu, as the commercial and Brahmanical castes continued to dominate in all forms of literacy and education. By 1891, they accounted for 89 percent of those literate and 82 percent of English literates among Punjabi Hindus. Within the general population of male literates, they accounted for 57 percent and 55 percent, respectively.[51] The Khatris, Baniyas, Aroras, and Brahmans led in all forms of literacy, being far ahead of any other caste, either Muslim or Hindu. Yet the relative position of literates and students, between Hindus and Muslims, began to change as more Muslims entered schools. Muslim literacy began to grow faster than literacy among the relatively advanced Hindus. Competition between an expanding Muslim educated elite and the entrenched Hindus became a bitter issue during the last years of the century, fueled as it was both by Muslim competence and governmental employment policies. Muslims still faced the reality of educated Hindus already in control of much of the Punjab's wealth and many of its economic opportunities.

By 1911, the educated Hindus of the Punjab formed a class of people sharing similar economic interests, communal orientation, and common frustrations. Three great caste clusters—the Khatris,

49. *Census, Punjab Report 1911,* p. 326. This figure includes Europeans and Anglo-Indians.

50. *Ibid.*, p. 323.

51. N. G. Barrier, "Punjab Politics and the Disturbances of 1907," Ph.D. dissertation Duke University, 1966, pp. 16–17.

Baniyas, and Aroras—controlled over half of the non-agricultural wealth of the province. The Khatris stood foremost in professional and industrial occupations, while the Baniyas dominated their traditional field of trade.[52] By the mid-1880s, the Hindu commercial and priestly castes stood supreme in occupations demanding education, particularly English education. They accounted for over 80 percent of the "superior appointments" in government service and dominated as well the professions of Western medicine, engineering, and law. The number of Muslims by contrast fell far below their communal strength and in some categories they were totally unrepresented. Yet within two decades this situation changed dramatically as the spread of education brought new elites into the professional, commercial, and governmental classes.

Education by 1911 expanded into the agricultural and warrior classes, mainly Rajputs and Jats, and in the Islamic community among the Sheikhs, Kalals, and Sayyids. Although the older Hindu elite still retained its position of superiority, they were increasingly challenged by the newly educated. This process can be clearly seen in the areas of government service and law. Of a total of 1,032 gazetted officers, 589 were held by Europeans and other Christians. The Khatris occupied 21 percent of the remaining 488 posts, by far the largest share held by any single caste cluster. Second came the all-Muslim Sheikhs who were in turn followed by Brahmans, Aroras, Baniyas, Pathans, Rajputs, and Sayyids. Khatris still retained primacy and the Hindu elite continued numerically dominant, but they did so in a more complex world with new competitors advancing rapidly up the economic and social scale. The law profession also shows a similar developmental pattern. In 1885, out of 48 first-class pleaders, Hindus accounted for 29, Muslims 4, and Bengalis 7, with Khatris the most numerous among the Hindus; within the 160 second-class pleaders, 129 were Hindus, 20 Muslims, and 4 Bengalis.[53] By 1911, Khatris still led among lawyers with 412 members of the bar, but the Sheikhs now stood second with 333. Among lawyers' clerks, the pattern was similar, with Khatris first, then Brahmans, Aroras and Sheikhs fourth. Punjabi Muslims were moving rapidly into the law profession at its higher levels. This was emphasized by the "gradual disappearance

52. *Census, Punjab Report 1911*, p. 527.

53. Barrier, "Punjab Politics and the Disturbances of 1907," pp. 17–18.

of the Kāzī as a referee of religious and legal questions."[54] Muslims in the law now tended to be English-educated men entering what had been almost solely a Hindu preserve.

The economic forces set in motion by British annexation of the Punjab led quickly to the monetization of trade and agriculture. The creation of an efficient system of communications tied the Punjab to the outer world, encouraged trade and the expansion of the commercial classes. By 1911, the number of people earning a living from banking and moneylending had grown steadily. In turn, this group founded modern banking institutions to utilize their expanding financial resources. Communal mobilization led to the mobilization of capital which, in turn, was invested in land, trade or industry. Patterns of industrial development, of ownership, and enterprise illustrate the relative strength of the Hindu and Islamic elites. A listing of individual factory owners shows Khatris leading with 78 factories, followed by Aroras (52), and Sheikhs (34), all three groups in advance of the Europeans and Anglo-Indians. In the field of industrial management Khatris stood second after the Christians, but in advance of the Aroras, Sheikhs and Brahmans.[55] The social pattern for industrial ownership and management showed nearly an identical configuration to the pattern of professional and governmental employment: domination by the urban, educated Hindu with competition from an emerging Muslim elite and a new class of educated Rajputs and Jats.

The educated elite among Punjabi Hindus had a strong commercial bias. They came heavily from the traditional Vaishya castes and maintained this orientation regardless of preoccupations in education, government service, and religious reform. In the 1890s, Punjabis began to open their own modernized commercial establishments. Arya and Brahmo entrepreneurs, in association with Sardar Dyal Singh Majithia, the Sikh millionaire,

54. *Census, Punjab Report 1911*, p. 518; for occupational statistics in law, see p. 524.

55. Other castes listed included: Aggarwal (31), Jat (20), Rajput (15), Brahman (12), and Kalal (12). *Census, Punjab Report 1911*, p. 525. The caste groups managing more than ten factories were Christians (98), Khatris (80), Arora (52), Sheikh (35), Brahmans (35), Aggarwal (Baniyas) (32), Rajput (16), and Jat (10). *Census, Punjab Report 1911*, p. 526.

founded the Punjab Material Improvement Society in 1891.[56] A year later the Punjab Banking Corporation appeared, as Punjabis emphasized and articulated a doctrine of self-help. Aryas first discussed the need for *swadēshī,* indigenous industry, during the 1880s, following the government's imposition of an excise tax on Indian cotton goods.[57] Concern for *swadēshī* enterprise contributed in 1895 to the organization of the Punjab National Bank.[58] Brahmos and Aryas cooperated in this enterprise. Lala Lal Chand, Lala Mul Raj, Kali Prosanna Roy, Sardar Dyal Singh Majithia and his protégé, Lala Harkishen Lal, joined together to establish this bank, choosing Lajpat Rai's brother, Lala Dalpat Rai, as Manager.[59] The next year this same group formed the equally successful Bharat Insurance Company.[60] Within the decade Punjabis founded a variety of commercial and industrial enterprises.

Two distinct factions formed among these Hindu entrepreneurs, one composed of Aryas, the other centered around Lala Harkishen Lal and his supporters, many of whom were Brahmos or members of the orthodox community. This factional pattern reached back into the struggle between Brahmos and Aryas, and forward toward future political competition. Harkishen Lal was a brilliant young Punjabi, one of the very few who had received advanced education in England. Born in Leiah, Muzzafargarh District, he grew up in Dera Ismail Khan, and attended Lahore Government College where he won a scholarship in mathematics to Trinity College, Cambridge. After an honors career at Cambridge, he studied law and economics. Returning to Lahore in 1890, he

56. Barrier, "Punjab Politics and the Disturbances of 1907," p. 73.

57. In a series of articles entitled "The Poverty of India," Aryas placed the burden of poverty heavily on the lack of local enterprise. See *Arya Patrika,* January 3, 10, 17 and 24, 1888, pp. 1–3 of each issue.

58. During the mid-1890s, *Swadēshī* had become a favorite topic in the schools, particularly the Dayanand Anglo-Vedic College in Lahore. See Ajit Singh, "Autobiography," unpublished ms. in the possession of V. C. Joshi, Nehru Memorial Museum, pp. 10–11, and the Lahore *Tribune,* June 8, 1895, p. 5; February 29, 1896, p. 4; March 11, 1896, p. 4; and, May 27, 1896, p. 4.

59. K. L. Gauba, *The Rebel Minister: The Rise and Fall of Lala Harkishen Lal* (Lahore: Allied Indian Publishers, 1938), p. 27; Lajpat Rai, *Autobiographical Writings,* pp. 96 and xxv-xxvi. Joshi mentions that Lajpat Rai was one of the original promoters of the Punjab National Bank, while Lajpat Rai himself stated that Harkishen Lal worked with both Dyal Singh Majithia and Nagendra Nath Gupta, then editor of the *Tribune.*

60. K. L. Gauba, *The Rebel Minister,* p. 28.

began his law career, but soon became involved in a series of commercial ventures. Harkishen Lal came to distrust and then to despise Aryas who he felt possessed a reactionary ideology and who as well provided active competition for his businesses.[61] By 1902 dissention appeared among the directors of the Punjab National Bank,[62] and the following year Harkishen Lal opened his own competing institution, the People's Banking and Commercial Association. Between 1902 and 1906, he founded a series of firms in banking, flour milling, soap, brick, ice, and lumber production, plus a laundry or two.[63] Harkishen Lal stood supreme among Hindu entrepreneurs but others soon followed his example.

This industrialization was, however, extremely limited. By far the largest number of factories processed agricultural or mineral resources for local consumption. Brick kilns, tile works, and a lime factory contributed to the construction industry. Factories processed agricultural products including cotton, wheat, rice, tea, leather, wool, and silk, and in a few instances manufactured finished consumer goods such as buttons, hosiery, rope, tents and carpets. In addition, the province could boast of two coal mines, a glass factory, a brewery or two, several printing presses, and a few scattered iron foundries.[64] Industrial development was characterized by small units with relatively limited capitalization. The agricultural nature of the Punjab had not been altered significantly by British rule, merely commercialized.[65]

Punjab officialdom had invested in economic development almost solely in the realm of agriculture. Vast irrigation works turned waste land into rich, productive farming tracts filled, so the government hoped, with contented peasants. As population increased in the densest tracts of the submontaine, the districts of Jullundur, Hoshiarpur, Sialkot, and Amritsar, it flowed into these

61. See Barrier, "Punjab Politics and the Disturbances of 1907," pp. 74–75.

62. See *Shamin-i-Hind,* March 2, 1902, *SPVP 1902,* pp. 156–157; *Tribune,* March 4, 1902, p. 5.

63. Lala Harkishen Lal's enterprises included The Punjab Cotton Press, the Amritsar Bank, Ltd., the Cawnpore Flour Mills, Ltd., and "various Soap Factories, Brick Kilns, Saw Mills, Ice Factories and Laundries." N. B. Sen, ed., *Punjab's Eminent Hindus* (Lahore: New Book Society, 1944), p. 157.

64. *Census, Punjab Report 1911,* p. 526.

65. By 1911, 9 percent of the total population lived by trade and about 20 percent by industry. This is industry in its very widest and loosest definition. *Census, Punjab Report 1911,* p. 9.

newly-watered areas. The relatively empty lands of the southeast, the southwest and west slowly filled with the extension of tube-wells and canal irrigation.[66] Irrigation from the lower Chenab River created a huge canal colony which included the whole of the Lyallpur and Jhang districts, plus two *tahsīls* of Gujranwala. Government-sponsored colonization began in 1892 and by 1911 approximately 608,000 immigrants had settled in the colony. They came overwhelmingly from the crowded central districts of the province, relieving in part the intense pressure on the land created over the past years. These much-heralded irrigation schemes did little to change the nature of Punjabi life. Instead, rural society spread more evenly throughout the province as population grew to fill empty lands.

The limited nature of colonial modernization is even more evident in the slow growth of Punjab cities and towns. Maclagan could write in the Census of 1891 "The urban population . . . has increased 8.7 per cent in the last ten years whereas the remaining population has increased 11 per cent."[67] A decade later urbanization had progressed little. "The proportion which the rural population bears to the whole remains remarkably constant, the slight tendency of the urban to increase faster than the general population, observable in 1891, having virtually disappeared. There is no trace in these provinces of that general movement of the population to the towns which is so marked in Western Europe, though there is perceptible movement towards the cities."[68] The source of this "perceptible movement" is clear. By far the most crucial force propelling people into the larger towns was the railway. Towns by-passed by the road and rail nets declined and slowly died, their populations moving to the larger and more favored units.[69] The Punjab, like mid-twentieth-century rural America, was dotted with small decaying towns which had ceased to function as local trade and business centers. By 1911, the number of towns under 10,000 dropped from 228 to 122 as people moved into the larger urban centers.[70] Yet even with this migration, the largest cities did

66. *Census, Punjab Report 1891*, pp. 62, 90–94.
67. *Ibid.*, p. 91.
68. *Census, Punjab Report 1901*, p. 14.
69. By 1911, the Punjab rail net had reached an impressive figure of 5,369 miles of track. *Census, Punjab Report 1911*, p. 54.
70. *Ibid.*, p. 17.

not grow dramatically.[71] Plague and influenza all but halted Amritsar's growth, while urbanization in large part often stemmed from the transfer of British troops rather than migration of Punjabis to the major cities.[72]

Punjabi cities then were more marked for their continuity of population than for a rapid rural-to-urban migration. As cities they could not be characterized by the smoke and clang of industry, but by the quieter forces of intellectual and commercial activity. Living in Delhi, Lahore or Rawalpindi would mark a man, and give him memories more akin to Paris than Pittsburgh.

> When I went there as a boy of ten, Lahore was to me the centre of all that is lovely and attractive. The notice-board, the incessant noise of wheels and machinery, the loud-voiced preachers, the cheating hawkers, the narrow streets and long roads, the Museum, the Botanical Gardens, the ancient buildings seen here and there struggling against the onslaught of Time, the scavenger, the Anarkali with its busy hum of human life, and above all the Fort with its sloping massive walls, made Lahore appear to me a place than which there could be nothing grander or more beautiful.[73]

In later years other dimensions of Lahore were evident. "Lahore became in course of time the centre of intellectual and religious life, and to live there was to be in touch with men and institutions that could make one 'sadder and wiser.' Lahore was now the Lahore of books and newspapers, of Public Library and Reading Rooms, of schools, and Colleges, of Clubs and Associations, of Samajes and Sabhas." The commercial base of this intellectual and religious life in urban Punjab stemmed from British rule and by 1900 had come to threaten the stability of that rule

71. The three most populated cities in Punjab show the following pattern of growth: Delhi in 1881 was 173,393 and in 1911 was 232,837; Lahore went from 157,287 to 228,687; and Amritsar grew from 151,893 to 152,756 in the same period. *Ibid.*, p. 15.

72. Amritsar suffered drastically from both plague and malaria. From 1881 to 1891, the population of Amritsar fell by 10 percent, regained its lost ground by 1901, and then suffered another loss during the decade prior to the 1911 census. Other cities, such as Delhi, grew but mainly from natural increase of the city's population and local migration from within the Delhi district. A similar pattern was evident in Amritsar. Only Lahore and Rawalpindi had a larger number of strangers, of men from without the district and beyond. See *Census, Punjab Report 1911*, pp. 23–25.

73. Quotes given below from *Tribune*, February 5, 1903, p. 5.

The advent of British administration and particularly British law introduced into the Punjab a new conceptualization of land-ownership. Land became private property to be sold or mortgaged as its owner saw fit. The alienability of land, plus the monetization of agriculture, modernized communications, and large-scale irrigation created a rapid rise in land values which in turn provided landowners with vastly improved access to credit. A peasant could pledge his land, not merely his crop as in the pre-British days. Also this pledge could be effectively enforced in the new courts. British administration stood behind legal contracts and thus became the ally of the commercial classes, of the traditional moneylenders who prospered under these new rules.

Land began to move into the hands of the Hindu commercial classes as the forces of financial change penetrated rural Punjab.[74] The rapid and accelerating transfer of land from peasant proprietors to a largely Hindu and urban monied class undermined the very foundation of Punjab society and the British state. Officials envisioned a world of sullen, dispossessed peasants living on their land as tenants to absentee landlords. Not only did this development threaten the stability and peace of the Punjab, it also struck at the British self-image of benevolent and paternalistic protectors of the lowly peasant. Concern among Punjabi officialdom turned to an active debate during the 1890s over possible measures to halt the transfer of land. The doctrine of laissez-faire government was abandoned when, on September 27, 1899, the Lieutenant-Governor, Charles Rivaz, presented the Punjab Alienation of Land Bill to the Imperial Legislative Council. The fruit of long bureaucratic debate, this bill sought to protect landowners from the evil moneylender. The Punjab Land Alienation Act divided Punjabis into "agriculturalists" and "non-agriculturalists," and strictly controlled the sale of land from one group to the other. This bill struck at the aspirations of the Hindu trading castes. They could no longer hope to acquire land and the traditional status attached to it, nor could they invest their money as freely and profitably as before. It was as well a radical departure from the concept of unhindered rights to private property. Ideology could not in-

74. N. G. Barrier, *The Punjab Alienation of land Bill of 1900* (Durham, North Carolina: Duke University, 1966), Monograph and Occasional Paper Series, Program in Comparative Studies on Southern Asia, Commonwealth Studies Center, p. 103.

hibit the desire for political stability among British officialdom and was justified by a paternalistic appeal for the protection of the peasant.

Educated Punjabi Hindus reacted to the proposed Land Alienation Act with anger and fear. They saw it both as an attempt to discriminate against them as a class and as part of an overall anti-Hindu policy already apparent in the realm of governmental hiring. Government service provided Hindus with prestigious careers, yet such positions grew more difficult to obtain. From the 1880s onward, three forces converged to heighten competition for government jobs: (1) the steady growth in the numbers of educated Punjabis searching for such employment, (2) the tendency for government servants to discriminate in favor of their own coreligionists and fellow caste members, and (3) the abandonment by Punjab officials of their earlier neutral hiring policy. Each force acted upon the others, as together they created an increasingly ugly environment of competition, anxiety, and anger over the threat posed by each community against all others. Fear of other elites and the belief that men of other religions could not be trusted fed favoritism which, in turn, justified the original apprehensions.

In 1886, the Aitchison Commission visited Punjab to examine the question of "native employment in the public services," setting off an extended debate over the issue of Hindu dominance both existent and potential. While Muslims charged Hindus with bigotry and nepotism, government officials argued over possible action within the area of official employment.[75] Under Lieutenant-Governor James Lyall (1887–1892), the government decided to favor recruitment of Muslims over Hindus. This would, they hoped, curb abuses of power by lower level servants and check the growing dominance of educated Hindus in government service. The government would try for a balance between the two religious communities, but would do so tactfully and gently. This decision was to be kept secret, known only to European officials. Yet complaints over discrimination against educated Hindus appeared within two years of Lyall's retirement as Lieutenant-Gov-

75. This is very well documented in Barrier, "Punjab Politics and the Disturbances of 1907," pp. 32–39 and also Barrier, "The Punjab Government and Communal Politics, 1870–1908," *Journal of Asian Studies*, XXVII, No. 3 (May 1968), pp. 533–535.

ernor. "The secret policy now being followed in every department is to favour the appointment of Mahamodans and to reduce the number of Hindus. . . . Any protest against this unfairness is promptly interpreted as an attempt to befriend the Hindus and to oppose the interests of the Mahomedans."[76] This move against laissez-faire recruitment later merged with the policy of limiting influence of the Hindu literate class.[77] Meanwhile, tales of discrimination by officials, British and Punjabi, as well as charges of governmental bias, appeared in the pages of the press.[78] Communal loyalty was deprecated, but was also the overriding principle upon which people acted.

In 1904, the government disclosed its policy of "balance" and thus intensified communal competition over employment. Each community now appealed to the government for protection of its "rights" and for redress of its economic grievances.[79] Hindus demanded open examinations and an end to the policy of discrimination which favored non-Hindus. But the government easily found reasons to retain the vitality of the aristocrats, and thus office by appointment, against pressure from a newly-formed educated class. Punjabi officials sought the dream of social stasis through an expanding but traditional agriculture. They faced instead growing communal competition and bitterness, particularly within the Hindu elite.[80] The struggle over jobs spread into the princely states both within and beyond Punjab. There local officials stood condemned of bias rather than the British, but the pattern of complaints was strikingly similar. In Kashmir local elites found themselves faced with competition from Punjabis, and Punjabis spoke

76. *Tribune,* May 30, 1894, p. 3, quoting the *Sindh Official Gazette.*

77. John R. McLane, "The Development of Nationalist Ideas and Tactics and the Policies of the Government of India, 1897–1905," unpublished Ph.D. dissertation, University of London, School of Oriental and African Studies, 1961, p. 22.

78. The number of such items runs into the hundreds and would be impossible to cite. Even a cursory examination of the *Selections of the Vernacular Press, Punjab* or of any of the existing newspapers and periodicals published between 1890 and 1914 would provide numerous examples of this literature.

79. Barrier, "The Punjab Government and Communal Politics, 1870–1908," p. 539.

80. 1904 provides ample evidence of the increasing communal competition over jobs and disillusionment with governmental policies. See the *Vakīl,* March 21, 1904, *SPVP 1904,* pp. 93–94; *Tribune,* October 1, 1904, p. 3; October 8, p. 3; *Panjabee,* October 10, 1904, p. 1; October 17, p. 1.

bitterly of Bengalis who held many of the highest positions in the state and discriminated against their Punjabi competitors.[81]

By the first decade of the twentieth century, communal competition became institutionalized partly through the dynamics of ideology and group identification, but also from social and economic pressures which tended to separate and place in opposition elites of the same class. The similarities of class aspirations and frustrations which might have placed all educated Punjabis in opposition to British rule could not overcome communal loyalties. Educated Hindus saw the new Muslim elite more as competitors than members of the same class. British attempts to maintain a status quo succeeded in making themselves increasingly evil in the eyes of educated Hindus who, in turn, became a threat in British minds. Aryas led in these new developments, first toward communal mobilization and second toward an articulation of a Hindu political consciousness.

81. On the native states in general, see *Rafīq-i-Hind,* September 27, 1902, *SPVP 1902,* p. 523; *Tribune,* February 12, 1903, p. 5; April 2, 1904, p. 4; April 21, 1904, p. 5; and June 17, 1905, p. 3. For complaints on Kashmir, see *Chaudhwin Sadī,* March 23, 1896, *SPVP 1896,* p. 183; *Ibid.,* April 15, 1896, p. 241; *Watan,* September 26, 1902, *SPVP 1902,* p. 532; *Tribune,* September 1, 1904, p. 5; *Panjabee,* November 14, 1904, pp. 4–5; *Tribune,* January 7, 1905, p. 5; January 14, 1905, p. 5; and January 19, 1905, p. 5.

## Chapter VII

# MATURITY OF AN IDEOLOGY: IMPLICATIONS OF CONSCIOUSNESS

> Time's revolution has reached this point, and ignorance has brought us to this day, when the people have lost the ability to recognize their own name. Our brothers have come to love and be infatuated with an obscure, fictitious, uncivilized and inappropriate disgrace. And being far from the acquaintance with and dignity of their true and authentic name, they are also separated from knowing and believing in it. And to this extent, they roost in ignorance. They begin to call themselves and to be called Hindus instead of Aryas and to use Hindustan instead of Aryavarta. Alas, a hundred thousand regrets!
>
> Pandit Lekh Ram

### MILITANCY UNLEASHED

The division of the Samaj into two bitterly opposed camps did more to invigorate the movement than to exhaust it. Although bickering and intra-Aryan competition disillusioned many outside of the Samaj, the same dynamics unleashed a new flood of energy and organizational innovation. Militant Samajists no longer felt the restraining hand of the moderates, nor were they committed to that major Samaj preoccupation, the Dayanand Anglo-Vedic College. The militants, in control of the Arya Pratinidhi Sabha and most of the branch Samajes, now sought goals and programs to exploit this organizational strength. With the leadership of Lala Munshi Ram and Pandit Lekh Ram, the militants also searched for concrete expression of an Arya identity as sketched by Dayanand and Pandit Guru Datta. Within a decade they would succeed in this quest, both institutionally and ideologically. Belief in and commitment to a religious ideal provided for militant Aryas a driving force for their attacks on existent traditions and customs; it legitimized their modernity, their desire to change deeply and pervasively the nature of their social and religious world. Militant Aryas completed Dayanand's personal vision, the Arya as a religious man, a modernized, committed Hindu. But in the months immediately following the division, they faced the primary task of consolidating their victories.

In November 1895, at the first meeting of the Arya Pratinidhi Sabha following the split, militants approved new rules of procedure designed to forestall challenges to their own leadership. In December, they registered the Sabha with the government under Act XXI of 1860, transforming it into a legally recognized body claiming title to all funds and property owned by the old organization.[1] Simultaneously, with the question of legal right to Sabha resources, they faced the problem of representation within the Pratinidhi Sabha. They had learned from the contest within the Dayanand Anglo-Vedic College Managing Committee. New Arya Samajes were carefully screened before they could join the Sabha and acquire representation. After its reorganization the Pratinidhi Sabha contained representatives from forty-eight Samaj branches, with applications from another seventy.[2] By 1897, only thirty-five of these applicants succeeded in gaining admission to the Pratinidhi Sabha. Clearly those in power would remain so.

With the Arya Pratinidhi Sabha reorganized and representing a militant consensus, the Sabha soon found agreement on goals. *Vēd Prachār,* the preaching of the Vedas, would be the major focus of the Pratinidhi Sabha. Demands for leadership and assistance so long neglected by the Sabha now would be fulfilled. The Sabha officially abandoned its support of the Dayanand Anglo-Vedic schools and turned instead to the creation of an elaborate missionary system so that the "flag of Om" might fly throughout the land. The Sabha divided the entire province, plus Sind and Baluchistan, into *mandals* (circles). Each *mandal* would have its officer-in-charge plus paid *updēshaks* (missionaries). The system detailed the extensive duties of both the *mandal* officer and the Samaj missionaries. Each would tour his *mandal,* visiting all towns, cities, and local Arya Samajes. Circle officers were required to submit yearly reports to the Pratinidhi Sabha and to supervise Arya missionaries under their charge. The duties of these missionaries fell roughly into four categories: (1) *mandan-khandan,* the presentation of public

1. Arya Pratinidhi Sabha, Punjab, *Report of the Arya Pratinidhi Sabha, Punjab, for the Year 1895–96,* pp. 41–43.

2. *Ibid.,* p. 4.

lectures expounding Samaj doctrine and attacking false ideologies—both religious and social; (2) the promotion of *shuddhi;* (3) the encouragement of social reform activities, such as widow remarriages or the use of reformed Samaj rituals; and (4) general encouragement and assistance to local Samaj branches, particularly the newer, smaller and weaker organizations. *Mandal* officers shared in these goals with the additional responsibilities of supervising and reporting to the Sabha.

This system demanded manpower and money far beyond the resources of the Pratinidhi Sabha. It required thirty full time missionaries and extensive funding. This *mandal* system remained an ideal rather than reality. Yet the Sabha did partially implement this scheme. By November 1895, they had hired six full time *updēshaks* who were assisted by various Samaj members acting as honorary missionaries.[3] Volunteers and professionals claimed to have visited 1,175 places and reached over 400,000 people during the year 1895–1896.[4] The *mandal* system remained underdeveloped but did alter the Samaj missionary program. *Updēshaks* provided a small body of professionals who comprised the core of Samajic proselytization and were aided by enthusiastic members.[5] Arya missionaries toured branch societies, appeared at religious fairs, participated in public debates, preached in bazaars and in the streets; they provided an expertise and presence that greatly strengthened the entire sphere of Arya activities.[6]

The missionary system soon forced other changes. The Pratinidhi Sabha established a central tract and publishing department to supply polemical literature to its *updēshaks* and member Samajes. Aryas admittedly followed the example of their enemies, the Christian missionaries, while complaining bitterly of their inability to successfully compete with the Christians whose literature flowed in "Lakhs and crores."[7] As the leader of militant Aryanism the Pratinidhi Sabha acquired the *Arya Patrika* from the Lahore Samaj. The *Patrika* became the official voice of the Sabha,

3. *Ibid.*, p. 7.
4. *Ibid.*, p. 12.
5. In 1896–1897, the number of paid *updēshaks* rose to thirteen and were supported by up to thirty part-time missionaries; see *Report of the Arya Pratinidhi Sabha, Punjab, for the Year 1896–97*, pp. 11–12.
6. *Report of the Arya Pratinidhi Sabha, Punjab, for the Year 1895–96*, pp. 7–12.
7. *Report of the Arya Pratinidhi Sabha, Punjab, for the Year 1896–97*, p. 32.

sharing the militant world with the *Sat Dharm Prachārak* of Jullundur, then under the control of Lala Munshi Ram. The *Patrika* provided an excellent vehicle for communication between the Sabha, its missionaries, and supporters. It also proved a financial burden. With only 566 subscribers in 1896, the paper lost money as the Sabha urged its missionaries to sell subscriptions along with their proselytization.[8] The problem of money continually plagued the Sabha. After ceasing its support of the college movement, the Pratinidhi Sabha organized a *Vēd Prachār* fund to finance its missionary activities. Militants now applied their experience and techniques of past fund raising to the cause of *prachār*. The Jullundur Samaj, led by Munshi Ram and Lala Dev Raj, collected "Atta" for *prachār*. A Char (four) Anna Fund was opened to channel small amounts from the local Samajes, and anniversary celebrations within the militant wing donated their greatest amounts for Vedic missions.[9] *Vēd Prachār*, however, only appealed to dedicated Aryas. The general Hindu community was uninvolved. Proselytization served no immediate need among Punjabi Hindus. Many no doubt sympathized with the *prachār* movement, and may even have enjoyed the spectacle of Arya missionaries tilting with Muslim or Christian preachers; but they felt little desire to dedicate their rupees. *Vēd Prachār* progressed but haltingly, limited and dependent solely on a base of militant Aryanism. Although College Aryas too employed their own missionaries and tracts for proselytization, the militants led the way as defenders of a true faith.

The placing of proselytization on an organized basis did not alter patterns of conflict between the Samaj and its opponents. Aryas now competed more effectively with Christian missionaries, Sanatanists, Muslims, Sikhs, Brahmos, and Dev Dharmis, but with the exception of relations between Aryas and Sikhs, the period of dramatic change lay in the past. Specific events occasionally created an outburst of animosity followed by a return to the norm of bickering. Arya relations with the orthodox community best illustrates this ebb and flow of tensions.

During the years 1894–1904, Arya-Sanatanist animosity peaked three times, each stemming from a particular issue. In spring 1898, a girl proclaiming to be an incarnation of the goddess Durga

8. *Report of the Arya Pratinidhi Sabha, Punjab, for the Year 1895–96*, pp. 35–37.
9. *Ibid.*, p. 46, and the Lahore *Tribune*, November 6, 1895, p. 4.

toured the Punjab. Her appearance in various towns produced outbursts of religious fervor among believers and outrage among reformers. The worshippers of "Devi," the female goddess, stood for all that appeared repellent to educated Aryas.[10] While hoping for a more rational future, educated Hindus witnessed the continuation of superstition, magic, and bloody rituals. "It is an open secret that several persons who cut off their tongues and offered them to the 'Devis' have lost their power of speech, and that the tongues of not a single person has been made whole." During the spring and summer other incarnations of the goddess appeared throughout the Punjab, as a wave of religious passion swept the province. Sanatanists applauded this revival of faith and the miracles that accompanied it.[11] Aryas fumed and joined the widespread condemnation: " . . . cardsharpers, gamblers, *gundas* and the like have hit upon a new plan of earning money and living in comfort, viz., mounting their grown-up daughters, sisters and female friends on their shoulders and visiting every town and village where tongue-cutting tricks are performed and simple people relieved of their money."[12] By fall, the excitement subsided, and with it this round of controversy.

Relations between Aryas and Sanatanists returned to their previous pattern of grumbling antagonism, only to erupt anew in December 1900, when Pandit Bhim Sain of Attawa, a prominent Arya and Sanskrit scholar, left the Samaj. The Pandit not only returned to orthodoxy but began "touring in the country, with the object of laying the true Vedic religion before the Hindus and preventing them from being imposed upon [by] the Dayanandis."[13] Pandit Bhim Sain's defection embarrassed the Samaj and cheered the orthodox.[14] The acrimony which resulted was soon lost in a

10. Quote given below from *Arya Gazette*, April 14, 1898, Government of India, *Selections from the Vernacular Newspapers Published in the Punjab*, 1898, p. 256; also see *Sarāj-ul-Akhbār*, April 18, 1898, *SPVP 1898;* and *Nūr Afshān*, April 15, 1898.

11. *Sanātan Dharm Gazette*, April 1898, *SPVP 1898*, p. 318.

12. *Hamadard-i-Hind*, June 4, 1898, *SPVP 1898*, p. 381; for similar opinions, see *Sarāj-ul-Akhbār* (Jhelum), April 18, 1898, *SPVP 1898*, p. 256; *Nūr Afshān*, April 15, 1898, *SPVP 1898*, p. 256; *Sat Dharm Prachārak*, July 1898, *SPVP 1898*, pp. 428–429; *Sat Dharm Prachārdk*, September 16, 1898, *SPVP 1898*, p. 629.

13. *Akhbār-i-'Am*, April 25, 1901, *SPVP 1901*.

14. Some claimed that he did not quit the Samaj but was expelled from it; see *Sanātan Dharm Gazette*, February 14, 1901, *SPVP 1901*, p. 151.

more sensational and bitter confrontation between Lala Munshi Ram and the Sanatanist, Pandit Gopi Nath. The two leaders not only forcefully argued their respective ideologies but also engaged in a vicious personal quarrel. Finally, Gopi Nath charged Munshi Ram and his associates on the *Sat Dharm Prachārak* with defamation. The resulting law suit went to court in April 1901.[15] As this case dragged on through the summer, Punjabi newspapers reported each argument, each telling point, as the contestants struggled to prove their purity of motive and to blacken the name of their opponent.[16] The trial ended in Pandit Gopi Nath's bitter humiliation, for the magistrate labelled him an "imposter. . . . who has persistently played on the Hindu public for the sake of his own aggrandizement." The Sanatanists were acutely embarrassed.[17] Their chagrin in turn led them to even more vigorous denouncement of the Samaj and its evil influences. The years 1901 and 1902 witnessed a rekindling of conflict between Aryas and orthodoxy. This continued into the future yet with an undertone of cooperation and at times grudging respect.

As with the Sanatanists, so with the Christian missionaries; relations followed well-established patterns. Charges and countercharges followed one upon the other with monotonous regularity. Aryas continued to condemn Christianity for its insistence on miracles and its blood-thirstiness. In spite of Arya success in founding schools, conversion of students still occurred and such incidents reinforced the elite's fear of missionary alienation of the young.[18] Missionaries were accused of "mesmerizing boys, of kid-

15. *Tribune,* April 27, 1901.

16. See *Tribune,* August 29, 1901, a special supplement covering the trial and the issue for September 3, p. 5, which contains the judgment; also the special supplement of September 12.

17. *Tribune,* September 3, 1901, p. 5; also comments on the trial in *Punjāb Samāchār,* September 7, 1901, *SPVP 1901,* p. 574; *Sat Dharm Prachārak,* September 6, 1901, *SPVP 1901,* p. 596; *Vakīl,* September 13, 1901, *SPVP 1901,* p. 599; *Sanātan Dharm Gazette,* August-September 1901, *SPVP 1901,* p. 640; *Public Gazette,* September 24, 1901, *SPVP 1901,* p. 640; *Paisā Akhbār,* September 24, 1901, *SPVP 1901,* p. 640; *Sat Dharm Prachārak,* November 15, 1901, *SPVP 1901,* pp. 733–34; and *Tribune,* October 3, 1901, p. 5.

18. See *Sanātan Dharm Gazette* for June 1897, *SPVP 1897,* p. 576. The Sanatanists admitted Arya effectiveness in education. The *Tribune,* August 28, 1897, p. 4, carried an account of a Christian conversion of a young boy, raising the spectre of mission influence in the schools.

napping prospective converts and of luring young girls away from their homes."[19] During the years 1894–1895, the Zanāna missions aroused particularly strong response to their tactics in securing female converts.[20] Anti-missionary critics utilized well-established arguments and increasingly widened these to include a condemnation of Western culture and mores. Not only did missionaries practice unfair and unethical modes of conversion, not only was their theology in error, but the civilization from which they came was decadent, immoral, and violent. ". . . the propagators of Christianity having failed on every side hit upon the device of dressing themselves like the Hindu Sadhus . . . . The Gazette observes that it is the duty of every Arya to unmask these Christian Sadhus. Murder, dacoity, theft and such like vices are not unknown either in Europe or America. As a matter of fact heinous crimes prevail there to a greater extent than in India."[21] Pointing to the "sahib" lifestyle of the missionaries, Aryas found a compelling motive for their efforts in India. "Perhaps the Missionaries are attracted to India because they can live here far more comfortably than they can in their own country, otherwise there is sufficient room for religious reform in Europe and America." The Western world more often than not was characterized as "sinful," "atheistic," full of drink, divorce, and illegitimate children.[22] Although the West provided models for modernity and progress, increasingly these were coupled with negative images both real and fancied. The fate of Christianity as a competing religion was inevitably interwoven

19. *Nūr Afshān* for February 10, 1893, *SPVP 1893,* p. 104, writing in reply to charges by the *Arya Gazette; Arya Gazette,* January 1, 1893, *SPVP 1893,* p. 115; and *Tribune,* November 9, 1895, p. 3.

20. The *Tribune* for October 23, 1895, p. 4, reported an anti-missionary protest meeting in Taran Taran which spelled out Hindu and Muslim complaints in a series of resolutions: "(1) that as there are two other girls' schools at Taran Taran, no Hindu or Mussulman should send his girl to the Mission Girls' School. (2) No Hindu or Mussulman should send his daughter, sister or wife or any other female relation to the Mission Zenana Hospital. (3) The Municipality be asked to withdraw its support from the Zenana Mission Hospital. (4) That Christian preachers be not allowed to enter the blind lanes *(band galis)* in the town to villify the faith of the Hindus and Mussulmans. (5) Missionary ladies be requested not to enter private houses uninvited."

21. Quotes given below from *Arya Gazette,* December 17, 1896, *SPVP 1897, p. 9.*

22. *Arya Gazette,* February 1, 1893, *SPVP 1893,* p. 76; *Arya Magazine,* May 1898, *SPVP 1898,* pp. 588–589.

with the broader question of Western civilization and its status in the minds of educated Punjabis. No such ambiguity existed with Islam which possessed all the evils of Christianity and none of its advantages. Here the road was straight and unambiguous, a clear path of antagonism.

### THE MARTYRDOM OF PANDIT LEKH RAM

Arya struggles against Islam also followed well-established patterns. The years immediately prior to the split witnessed an intensification of mutual animosity between Aryas and the followers of Islam, led by the continued crusade of Pandit Lekh Ram. For many Muslims of the northwest, Lekh Ram symbolized resurgent Hinduism. To Muslims he was a fanatic, an implacable opponent determined to discredit and if possible destroy all that they held precious. Lekh Ram continued in his speeches to denounce Islam, while his writings drew constant criticism from the Muslim press. "Takzib-i-Burahin-i-Ahmadiya . . . is calculated to cause great mischief. The book purports to be a refutation of Mirza Ghulam Ahmad's 'Burahin-i-Ahmadya,' but the Pandit, in utter disregard of the cannons of strict criticism has used the most offensive and insulting language towards Islam, its leaders, its followers, including the Prophets, and things held sacred by the Muhammadan "[23] So complained the *Paisā Akhbār,* calling at the same time for a government ban of this offensive book. Other Muslim papers joined in the lament, decrying both Muslim apathy and the continuation of Lekh Ram's notorious career.[24] The Muslims of Delhi decided to act rather than merely complain and filed a law suit against Lekh Ram in the hope of persuading the government to suppress his publications.[25] The suit failed. The court dismissed the case and Muslim frustrations continued to mount. During the last months of 1896 and early 1897, Punjabis witnessed a steady flow of charges and countercharges, of insults and provocations, as relations between Aryas and Muslims drifted inevitably toward violence.

On March 3, 1897, the *Tribune* reported an assault on Lala Ralla Ram, a prominent Arya leader of Peshawar. The attacker was a Muslim, perhaps a member of an organized anti-Arya plot. Great

23. *Paisā Akhbār,* August 29, 1896, *SPVP 1896,* p. 517.
24. *Chaudhwin Sadī,* September 1, 1896, *SPVP 1896,* p. 530.
25. *Punjāb Samāchār,* September 15, 1896, *SPVP 1896,* p. 560.

tension existed between Hindus and Muslims in the town.[26] Three days later, the *Punjāb Samāchār* stunned the province—Pandit Lekh Ram had been murdered, assassinated by "a Muhammadan who was living with Lekh Ram under [the] pretension of becoming a Hindu again."[27] The assassination sent shock waves throughout the province. Rumor dominated reality. By March 10, the assassination grew into a fearful plot. " . . . it is general knowledge that the murderer of Lekh Ram also wanted to kill Lala Hans Raj, Principal DAV College, and Lala Lal Chand. . . . More rumors to the effect that [a] party of 25 Muhammadans is out to murder all the leading Hindus of Punjab. . . . Four people killed at Lahore. Also Lala Ralla Ram, founder of the National High School was murdered at Peshawar."[28] The story of the assassination grew with the telling. The *Tribune* reported that the "murder was deliberately planned and carried out by a Muslim who was a stranger to Lahore who had gotten himself into Lekh Ram's confidence; murderer shadowed Lekh Ram for three weeks . . . pretended he wanted to become a Hindu. Deed committed on March 6 (Saturday) evening in front of wife and mother, and murderer got away."[29] The rumors multiplied as police searched in vain for the assassin.

This murder stirred Aryas as no other event since the death of Dayanand. Lajpat Rai called for all Hindus to unite against all attacks on Vedic religion, while Lala Munshi Ram swore he would stop working for the Samaj if the two factions failed to unite and become immediately reconciled.[30] The Pandit's funeral drew an estimated crowd of 20,000 people to the burning *ghat*. "At the funeral grounds the leaders of the Samaj vowed to end all their petty differences and to work together for Vedic dharm. At 7 P.M. the same day a meeting was held at the D.A.V. College grounds where speeches full of sorrow and indignation at the 'bigoted conspiracy' were made." Aryas praised Lekh Ram and confidently predicted the arrest of his assassin.[31] But he was not caught and in the weeks

26. *Tribune*, March 3, 1897, p. 3.
27. *Punjāb Samāchār*, March 6, 1897, *SPVP 1897*, p. 169.
28. *Bhārat Sēwak*, March 10, 1897, *SPVP 1897*, p. 182; also see *Tribune*, March 10, 1897, p. 4.
29. *Tribune*, March 10, 1897, p. 3.
30. *Bhārat Sudhār*, March 10, 1897, *SPVP 1897*, pp. 181–182.
31. *Tribune*, March 10, 1897, p. 4.

which followed rumors and violence spread throughout the towns and cities of the Punjab, fed by suspicion and communal hatred.

Aryas met to mourn their fallen hero. In town after town Aryas, often with the support of the Hindu and Sikh community, held meetings and demonstrations of grief and solidarity.[32] Spurred by shock, Aryas quickly moved to reunite the Samaj. By March 17, "The *Pratinidhi Sabha* (The Central Council of the Church) as well as the various *Antarang Sabhas* (local executive committees) now stand practically in the same position as they did before the dissensions broke out."[33] Schools, opened in opposition to the D.A.V. College system, were brought under its jurisdiction and a new era of Samajic unity seemed at hand. On March 14, the two Lahore Samajes met with great ceremony and elected Lala Hans Raj as President of the united Aryas. Lala Munshi Ram rose and in a speech to the assembly praised his old opponent while giving his blessing to the reunion.[34] Throughout the province feuding Aryas joined together, propelled by their fears and an accelerated loyalty to the Samaj. Reunited, Aryas gazed upon a province swept by fear and communal antagonism partly of their own creation. Eulogies for the *shahīd*, the martyred Lekh Ram, dwelt on the need for Hindu solidarity in the face of present Muslim animosity and on remembrances of past atrocities. Both communities lived in fear, and both saw themselves as persecuted minorities.

Tensions did not ease, but deepened throughout March and April, as each day brought a new crop of reported threats, plots, provocations, and violence. Hindus reacted first. On March 13, the *Tribune* reported "something like panic" among Lahore's Hindu

32. *Tribune*, March 13, 1897, p. 5. Also see the *Tribune* for March 17, p. 5, which carries a listing of such memorial meetings held throughout the province. These meetings did much to enflame passions. At Dinanagar a riot resulted when "a Muhammadan called Sikander came in and asked whether there were any Mussalman there because the Muhammadan faith was being insulted and right on his heels a group of Muhammadans charged the meeting—led by the police sergeant. Rioters had heavy sticks and used very abusive language. Police Sergeant egged rioters on instead of trying to stop them, and said that he would arrest the Hindus. At this point the Hindus went home." *Punjāb Samāchār*, March 27, 1897, *SPVP 1897*, p. 276. For a less dramatic retelling of this incident, see *Tribune*, March 27, 1897, p. 4.

33. *Tribune*, March 17, 1897, p. 5.

34. *Ibid.*

population.[35] Sinister stories circulated of a secret organization which planned to murder Hindu leaders, particularly those involved in the *shuddhi* movement. Reports of suspicious Muslims seen in Lahore supposedly making inquiries about Arya Samajists appeared in the press.[36] Lahore remained the center of such tales but others began to filter in from various Punjab cities and towns. By the end of March, the *Bhārat Sudhār* gloomily noted that "the bigotry of the Muhammadans has ever led them to oppress and massacre the Hindus. They were kept in check by a powerful force for a time, but the spirit of fanaticism is again abroad in the Muhammadan world, as the murders committed in Lahore, Sialkot, Peshawar, Kohat, Nur Mahal and other places clearly show."[37]

By April, posters and pamphlets added fuel to the existing communal fire. Mirza Ghulam Ahmad published a tract in which he thanked God for the fulfillment of his prophecy that Lekh Ram would die a violent death. Rumor had it that prayers of thanksgiving were said for the death of Islam's arch enemy.[38] Individuals reported receiving threatening letters,[39] and mysterious notices appeared on walls throughout the province. "All Hindus are warned to remember the Islamic prophets and believe in them; otherwise they will be murdered like Lekh Ram. The members of the Shuddhi Sabha and the Arya Samaj should consider themselves dead men. (sd.) A well wisher of the nation."[40] The editor of the *Punjāb Samāchār* warned that "the publication of such notices, the assassination of several Hindus by the Muhammadans in different cities in the Punjab, the conduct of the Muhammadan papers in inciting their co-religionists against their Hindu fellow subjects, the publication by the Amir of Kabul of a treatise on 'Jehad' and its dissemination in India tends to show that a religious war will soon be waged in this country." In its apprehension, the paper appealed to the government while indirectly threatening it as well. ". . . the policy of the Government in main-

35. *Tribune,* March 13, 1897, p. 4.

36. *Tribune,* March 13, 1897, p. 5; and *Aftāb-i-Punjāb,* March 15, 1897, *SPVP 1897*, p. 191.

37. *Bhārat Sudhār,* March 30, 1897, *SPVP 1897*, p. 280.

38. *Tribune,* March 24, 1897, p. 5 and April 7, 1897, p. 4.

39. *Tribune,* April 7, 1897, p. 4.

40. *Quotes given below from Punjāb Samāchar,* April 10, 1897, *SPVP 1897, p. 301.*

taining silence at such a critical time is utterly unintelligible. . . . It should be remembered that the Hindus have hitherto refrained from taking the law into their own hands, as they have a firm belief in the justice of the British Government; otherwise they are not in any respect inferior to any other race inhabiting India." Hindus would stand united in their opposition to revived Muslim aggression and in loyalty to the Raj.

Muslims too suffered from paranoia and panic. Lekh Ram's aggressiveness had not died with him, and who could tell what might be the purpose and goals of militant Hinduism? The *Akhbār-i-'Ām* warned Punjabi Muslims that "Hindus declared . . . some years ago that Muhammadans must either quit India or consent to live in it as their slaves." The paper then published rumors of Hindu determination to murder both Mirza Ghulam Ahmad and Sayyid Ahmad Khan. They ended with a call to expel all Aryas from India, since Aryas were the enemies alike of Christians, orthodox Hindus, Sikhs, and Muslims.[41] Threats against the Muslim community appeared throughout the press. The *Sādah-i-Hind* warned that "According to the *Paisā Akhbār* a Hindu speaker is said to have advised his co-religionists to avenge themselves on Muhammadans by abusing the founders of their religion and assassinating their chief men. It is things like these that lead to most undesirable results. . . . The circulation of hand-bills and the taking of oaths of vengeance against the Muhammadans will not tend to promote the welfare of the country."[42] In the face of such a threat from the majority community, Muslims must unite, for "Hindus hate us worse than sweepers . . . [and] if we do not return hate for hate, with interest, we should be shameless and chicken-livered indeed."[43]

Communal bitterness moved to a more basic level with economic separatism. The *Nāzim-ul-Hind* declared on March 27 that the Hindu community wanted to sever all relations with Muhammadans. They raised the spectre of 19 crore (190 million) Hindus combining to push all Muslims from the land of Arya Varta.[44] Ear-

41. *Akbār-i-'Ām,* March 15, 1897, *SPVP 1897,* pp. 190–91; and *Rahbar-i-Hind,* March 15, 1897, *SPVP 1897,* pp. 189–90.

42. *Sādah-i-Hind,* March 15, 1897, *SPVP 1897,* p. 209.

43. Quoted in the *Tribune,* April 7, 1897, p. 5 and from an article in the *Subdat-ul-Akhbār.*

44. *Nāzim-ul-Hind,* March 27, 1897, *SPVP 1897,* p. 340.

lier reports claimed Hindu moneylenders had been instructed to "bring their Muhammadan debtors into disgrace."[45] On March 27, the *Akhbār-i-'Ām* reported "The Muhammadans of Lahore are trying their best to stop all dealings with Hindus." They intended to open shops in trades hitherto monopolized by Hindus. Both sides called for a boycott of the opposing communities.[46] By early April, the boycotts were reported as "getting worse," and were accompanied by attacks in the streets, as rival groups appeared in the bazaars carrying *lāthīs* to enforce their new economic policy.[47] Efforts to end this by the People's Confidence Committee, a joint Hindu and Muslim group, got nowhere. Their call to close all shops opened after Lekh Ram's death had little or no effect.[48]

By the second week of April, a new dimension to this economic struggle erupted, with the first of a series of "poisoning stories." The *Sādah-i-Hind* reported that the number of poisoning cases was on the rise, and further that Hindus planned to poison 1,000 Muslims in retaliation for Lekh Ram's assassination.[49] Hindu papers quickly struck back, claiming that the stories of poisoning incidents were pure fabrication. "It is amusing to see how the Paisa Akhbar publishes false reports of poisoning cases having taken place in different parts of the Punjab, and how it tries to prove from this that the Hindus have hatched a plot to exterminate their Muhammadan fellow-countrymen. The authorities should, however, know that these stories have been invented by the Akhbar itself with the object of diverting their attention from the conspiracy to which Pandit Lekh Ram has fallen a victim, and inducing the Muhammadans to take to trade more largely."[50] Furthermore, Hindus would take measures in self-defense if necessary. "That paper may rest satisfied that the Hindus cannot be starved in this way, and that if a portion of their trade passes into the hands of the Muhammadans, they will be obliged to resort to the occupations which have hitherto been monopolised by the community represented by the Paisa Akhbar."

45. *Paisā Akhbār,* March 17, 1897, *SPVP 1897,* p. 203.

46. *Akhbār-i-'Ām,* March 27, 1897, *SPVP 1897,* pp. 279–280.

47. *Tribune,* April 7, 1897, p. 3.

48. See *Paisā Akhbār,* April 12, 1897, *SPVP 1897,* p. 296; *Kōh-i-Nūr,* April 20, 1897, *SPVP 1897,* p. 321; and *Tribune,* April 17, 1897, p. 4.

49. *Sādah-i-Hind,* April 12, 1897, *SPVP 1897,* p. 295.

50. Quotes given below from *Bhārat Sudhār,* April 19, 1897, *SPVP 1897,* pp. 325–326.

Threat followed threat, as reports of poisonings continued.[51] Hindus accused Muslims of holding meetings to collect funds for new shops. Muslims condemned, and on one occasion punished, those who traded with Hindus.[52] As May progressed, stories persisted of poisonings and continued efforts to create communal separatism.[53] The *Tribune* concluded that "The Moslem leaders have done a thorough job of severing connections from the Hindus; not even the poorest Moslem buys from a Hindu shop, but he buys at his *'Dini Dukhan'* as he calls it. The 'labours' of the reconciliation committee have evidently done no good. Numerous shops have been opened to manufacture and sell all those articles formerly sold only by Hindus."[54] Attempts by various peace committees failed to persuade the Islamic community to close their newly-opened shops and to return to the traditional patterns of economic relations.[55] Instead, communal quarrelling turned once more to supposed job discrimination by government policy and informally by government servants.

Muslims charged Hindus with exclusiveness which denied economic advance to all but their own community. "Take for instance the case of Lala Hansraj, principal of the D.A.V. College, who suggested, at a meeting held at Anarkali on the 12th December 1896, that the Hindus should write the addresses of all letters in the Devanagri character and thus compel the Government to employ Hindu peons. It is apparent that these men are bent on depriving the Muhammadans of all means of livelihood."[56] Although Muslim leaders castigated their own community for lack

51. *Paisā Akhbār,* April 19, 1897, *SPVP 1897,* p. 317; and *Tribune,* April 24, 1897, p. 4.

52. See *Bhārat Sudhār,* April 28, 1897, *SPVP 1897,* p. 340 and *Tribune,* May 1, 1897, p. 4.

53. See *Punjāb Samāchār,* May 8, 1897, *SPVP 1897,* p. 370 and *Khālsā Bahādur,* May 3, 1897, *SPVP 1897,* p. 367.

54. *Tribune,* May 12, 1897, p. 4. The paper then goes on to print a poster from one of the new Muslim shops. "SUGAR-CANDY STORE FOR MUSSALMANS AT LAHORE—Praised be to the Lord that after years of effort and exertions we have got together a number of men skilled in the preparation of candies and loaf sugar. They have begun work and a very superior quality of the commodities are now selling at our shop. The Islamic community should take note that they should never use sugar, etc. which only appears white prepared by impure (uijas) hands, they should come to our shop, etc."

55. See *Tribune,* April 24, 1897, p. 5.

56. *Paisā Akhbār,* April 19, 1897, *SPVP 1897,* pp. 316–317.

of energy, for falling from the true faith, for squabbling among themselves, and a host of similar failings, they inevitably lashed out against the Hindus who stood, or at least appeared to stand, between them and economic advance.[57] Communal anxieties might be expressed in a variety of symbols, religious and linguistic, but economic competition lay beneath, intensifying the struggles of competing identities.

With the arrival of the monsoons, passions cooled and life slowly returned to a surface normality. Yet after-shocks ran through the province during the late summer and fall months, as incidents or rumors revived the controversy with its accompanying fears. Failure to capture Lekh Ram's assassin meant a continued speculation. Muslim spokesmen charged that the crime was one of "illicit intrigue" and raised the spectre of an unknown mistress, plus an outraged avenger of virtue.[58] Periodically newspapers reported his capture. In November, such a rumor once more stirred the province. By the end of the year quiet returned,[59] but with one major difference. The Arya Samaj, particularly the militant wing, had a new martyr. Lekh Ram's anti-Muslim legacy would be maintained. He would not have died in vain. This the Aryas pledged and Muslims feared.

Aryas moved to institutionalize the memory of Lekh Ram as well as his life's work. Out of the memorial meetings came the Lekh Ram Memorial Fund with the dual purposes of supporting the Pandit's family and continuing his work. The Fund quickly received support from Samajists still impassioned over the murder,[60] and as quickly became a point of contention both within and beyond the Samaj. Muslims plus orthodox Hindus and Sikhs attacked the Fund as they had previously attacked Lekh Ram.[61] Within the Samaj quarrels erupted as early as January 1898, and by June, the Memorial Fund became a bone of contention between

57. See *Nāzim-ul-Hind,* May 22, 1897, for a catalog of Muslim shortcomings in the race for place and privilege with the Hindu community.

58. See *Punjāb Samāchār,* March 20, 1897, *SPVP 1897,* p. 211; *Akhbār-i-'Ām,* March 26, 1897, *SPVP 1897,* pp. 245–246.

59. See *Tribune,* November 17, 1897, p. 4 and November 27, p. 4. An earlier report appeared in the *Tribune,* March 27, 1897, p. 5.

60. See *Tribune,* March 24, 1897, pp. 4–5.

61. See *Khālsā Gazette,* April 22, 1897, *SPVP 1897,* p. 347; *Sanātan Dharm Gazette,* May 15, 1897, *SPVP 1897,* pp. 519–520; and pp. 441 and 443.

the two Samaj groups. Lekh Ram's widow charged that she had received nothing from the Fund then under control of the militant Samajists. Members of the College Party supported her charges, as the Samaj moved toward redivision and internecine war.[62] All the original unresolved issues which divided Aryas in 1893–1894 returned to haunt the Samaj, and the resulting clash between opposing factions again divided the movement, this time more bitterly than before. Quarrelling turned to a struggle for control with each side retaining roughly the same assets as they had possessed in the period after the original division. This time, however, violence erupted. In contests over control of schools and temples, near riots and the use of *lāthīs*, long sticks favored by the Punjabi peasants, characterized this round of internal fighting. By the end of 1898, the Samaj was once more divided, although some of the *mofussil* Samajes continued to fight over local issues until as late as 1902.[63] The Fund itself, after an initial burst of enthusiasm, found little support. It appealed only to the dedicated amongst Samajic militants. The initial goal of Rs. 50,000 seemed unobtainable in September 1897, and equally so the following year.[64] Still, with the Rs. 25,000 collected, the Memorial Fund provided additional support for proselytization, for the work of *mandan-khandan*.

Proselytization was legitimized by faith, by need, and by the twin martyrs, Dayanand and Lekh Ram. In October 1898, the militant Aryas inaugurated a new journal, the *Ārya Musāfir*, in memoriam to their fallen leader. This Urdu monthly proclaimed its goals as "the same burden of spreading the greatness of the Vedic Religion throughout the entire Universe and of fortifying the Vedic Religion against the opponents' attacks, as was taken by Pandit Lekh

62. Lajpat Rai accused Lala Munshi Ram of failing to pay the widow her agreed-upon allowance and of making a profit off reprints of the Pandit's works. See *Arya Gazette*, June 19, 1898, *SPVP 1898*, p. 414; *Arya Gazette*, July 7, 1898, *SPVP 1898*, pp. 445–446; *Arya Gazette*, July 21, 1898, *SPVP 1898*, pp. 469–470; and *Arya Gazette*, July 28, 1898, *SPVP 1898*, p. 506.

63. See *Arya Gazette*, February 17, 1898, *SPVP 1898*, pp. 130–31; *Akhbār-i-'Ām*, February 19, 1898, *SPVP 1898*, p. 132; *Sat Dharm Prachārak*, March 4, 1898, *SPVP 1898*, pp. 158–159; *Bhārat Sēwak*, February 7, 1898, *SPVP 1898*, p. 115; *Akhbār-i-Ām*, August 26, 1898, *SPVP 1898*, p. 555; *Aftāb-i-Punjāb*, September 5, 1898, *SPVP 1898*, p. 628; *Tribune*, July 1, 1899, p. 4; *Sanātan Dharm Gazette*, January 15, 1901, *SPVP 1901*, p. 134; and *Tribune*, June 26, 1901, p. 4.

64. *Sat Dharm Prachārak*, September 24, 1897, *SPVP 1897*, p. 878; *Sat Dharm Prachārak*, November 25, 1898, *SPVP 1898*, p. 756.

Ram on his shoulders."[65] Published and printed under the supervision of Lala Munshi Ram, the *Musāfir* became the voice of the militants in matters of theology and polemics. In its pages, Aryas found answers to their doubts and even more importantly answers to the criticisms of their many opponents.[66] Even though both the *Ārya Musāfir* and the Memorial Fund remained under-subscribed, the magazine survived, continuing the martyred Pandit's struggle with the enemies of Aryanism. Readers found it a rich source of intellectual support, a mine of arguments against those who would question their faith in Dayanand and his message.

### SHUDDHI: FROM INDIVIDUAL TO MASS CONVERSION

In the wake of Lekh Ram's death and its ensuing communal struggle, Arya attention, particularly among the militants, turned once more toward defending their community from conversion. In the last years of the century, this threat came not so much from defection by educated youths but from the possible loss of the lowest levels of Hindu society, the outcastes. The 1891 Census dramatically underscored Christian successes in reaching Punjabi outcastes. With a 410 percent increase in "native" Christians during the last decade, even the most sanguine Arya felt a renewal of the "Christian threat." Yet the division of the Samaj produced a parallel division among advocates of *shuddhi.*[67] The Shuddhi Sabhas under the leadership of militant Sikhs instituted a "pork test" for

65. *Ārya Musāfir,* October 1898, p. 2.

66. The magazine was divided into four sections: "Vidyā Prakāsh (The Light of Knowledge). In this section, apart from publishing the proper and authentic translation of the Vedas, the truth about the Vedic principles and their greatness will be discussed. *Vēd Mārtand* (The Vedic Sun). This section will contain replies to the objections and criticism of the Vedic Principles, now and then made by people, who do not believe in the Vedas. *Avidyā kā Nāsh* (Destruction of Ignorance). In this section efforts will be made to offer arguments and comments against the unnecessary customs and beliefs which are being followed and practised in the name of the religion, and for ending such customs and beliefs. *Historical and Educational Notes.* Every possible subject will be discussed in this section with seriousness and politeness. This magazine would not do anything in connection with personal wranglings or religious mud-throwing." *Ārya Musāfir,* October 1898, pp. 2–3.

67. For an example of Arya reaction to this conversion, see *Sat Dharm Prachārak,* August 20, 1897, *SPVP 1897,* p. 766; and Lala Jai Chandra's *Īsāiōn kē Hāth sē Bhāiōn kō Bachāō* (Save your Brethren from the Hands of the Christian Missionaries) (Lahore: Kishan Chand Press, 1898).

converts from Islam. If the eating of beef could transform a Hindu into a Muslim, then by similar logic the eating of pork would signify the return of a Muslim to Hinduism or Sikhism.[68] Militant Aryas with their rigid insistence on vegetarianism withdrew all support from the Shuddhi Sabhas and condemned them for their "degenerate Hinduism."[69] Similar criticisms came from the Muslim community, from orthodox Hindus, and orthodox Sikhs,[70] leaving the College Aryas as the only effective allies of the Shuddhi Sabhas. During the years 1895 and 1896, reconversions continued to be sponsored by the two competing groups, the Shuddhi Sabhas with their Arya supporters and the militant Samajists. Both concerned themselves largely with returning individuals lost to other conversion religions. As a result, the practice of shuddhi became a normal part of Punjabi life and as such contributed to communal discord.

On March 31, 1896, the Shuddhi Sabha reconverted a group of five people and on April 5, another group of six.[71] *Shuddhi* began to move from its focus on individual toward mass purifications. In August, the Lahore Shuddhi Sabha broke through past restraints. "They 'purified' according to Sikh rites a family of over two hundred outcaste Sikhs—men, women and children—dwelling in a village by themselves. Their common great-great-grandfather had been excommunicated for taking unto himself a Mussulmani woman."[72] This step not only represented the largest group purified at one time but marked a new goal for the movement: the transformation of outcastes into clean caste Hindus and Sikhs. Although this change of direction clearly stemmed from Christian missionary successes among outcastes, its most immediate impact lay elsewhere: in the realm of Sikh-Hindu relations and in the difficulties of adjusting the newly purified to his regained social order.

Militant Aryas, having broken with the Shuddhi Sabhas, continued to perform reconversions, but also turned their attention to

68. Reid Graham, "The Arya Samaj as a Reformation in Hinduism with Special Reference to Caste," unpublished Ph.D. dissertation, Yale University, 1942, p. 466.

69. *Sat Dharm Prachārak,* January 8, 1897, *SPVP 1897*, p. 40.

70. *Singh Sahāī,* March 12, 1895, *SPVP 1895*, p. 162.

71. *Tribune,* April 8, 1896, p. 4.

72. *Tribune,* September 2, 1896, p. 4.

the fundamental question of social relations between themselves and the Hindu community. Dayanand's ideas of *varna vyavasthā*, a four-class system based on merit, not birth, held great attraction for Aryas frustrated by the conservatism of the Hindu world and of a majority of their fellow Samajists. *Varna vyavasthā*, an essentially open but still hierarchical social system, would solve the dilemma faced by successful *shuddhi*, namely, what to do with the newly purified. It also promised supreme status to the educated elite since position in this system would be based on individual achievement rather than birth. Aryas knew of Dayanand's scheme but had done little to implement it.

By 1895, some Aryas began to call for a new social order, one that would require a complete break with Hindu society. "It is time that we cut the orthodox caste connection and form a living connection between Aryas. We think alike, but fear the excommunication of the biradri, and consequently fear to perform our Sanskars. Beyond *namaste* and meeting together for an hour or so on Sundays there is hardly any living connection between us. Our standard of honour at the present time is not the Arya Samaj but the orthodox biradri."[73] The nightmare of extinction transcended the fear of social ostracism for a growing band of militant Aryas. "We are in danger of being swallowed by Hinduism. The Arya Samaj will become null and void if it does not act. Let the Aryas form a biradri to effect caste reform and make the Arya Samaj more successful." The removal of birth as the decisive factor in social stratification necessitated the development of a new methodology for placing individuals in their proper social class, their *varnāshrama.* Various methods of assigning *varna* rank were discussed but none proved widely acceptable.[74] This vision of a bureaucratized social order met with little approval from Samaj members, although young militants repeatedly attempted to found a new social order throughout the closing years of the decade. "There is need of a Vedic Society called by any name: Arya Biradri, Arya Jati, Arya Bhratri Sabha, Aryan Dharma Sabha."[75] An Arya Bhratri Sabha was formed but failed to attract sufficient

73. Quotes given below from *Arya Patrika,* January 16, 1897, p. 6, quoted in Graham, "The Arya Samaj," p. 477.

74. Graham, "The Arya Samaj," pp. 478–479.

75. *Arya Patrika,* May 5, 1900, p. 8, quoted in Graham, "The Arya Samaj," p. 481.

Aryas to sustain itself. Once again Samajists would not break with the Hindu world. The same constraints which prohibited commitment to the Brahmo Samaj in the 1870s and 1880s still existed to doom similar militancy within the Arya Samaj of the 1890s.

The drive for a separate Arya brotherhood brought forth another of Dayanand's schemes, the Gurukul, a revival of the ancient Hindu College, which would prepare students to enter into this new casteless world.

> Following an education in this Gurukula, isolated from the caste feelings of ordinary society, the graduate is to be classified according to abilities and character in the proper class of the varna vyavastha society; he is to set up a home in which the Vedic Sanskars of Dayanand's *Sanskar Vidhi* will be observed. . . . Such was the dream of the leaders of the Arya Bratri Sabha, a dream that was almost directly inspired by the teachings of the founder of the Arya Samaj.[76]

This dream remained unfulfilled and the dilemma created by *shuddhi,* determining the social position of the reconverted, continued to haunt the Samaj. By 1902, the drive to establish an Arya Samaj *birādarī* disappeared, as the impossibility of creating a new social system was recognized by even the most visionary Samajist. Yet the dilemma did not disappear but remained a chronic problem arising from the *shuddhi* movement.[77] In the meantime, *shuddhi* had driven a wedge between the Hindu and Sikh communities, and propelled the Sikhs onward toward a separate Sikh consciousness.

Young educated Sikhs found themselves caught up in a historical process like that of their Hindu compatriots. After becoming disillusioned with the Arya Samaj in the later 1880s, they sought to define a place for themselves within a distinctly Sikh world, yet in opposition to Sikh orthodoxy. During the 1890s, the question of Sikh identity was posed with increasing frequency. Were Sikhs simply another branch of Hinduism, or a separate faith and a separate people? In part, British writers were blamed for raising this question, another example of their "divide and rule" tactics.

76. *Arya Patrika,* March 14, 1896, p. 5, in Graham, "The Arya Samaj," p. 484. For an example of the Arya arguments on caste, see Lala Hazari Lal's *Awāza Chhūt Shikan* (A Shout to Break the Caste System) (Lahore: Khatri Samachar Press, 1899).

77. See Graham, "The Arya Samaj," pp. 483–485.

"English writers, even Anglo-Indian editors, who might know better, always make a grave mistake when speaking of the Sikhs. They seem to think that Sikhs are a people totally different from the Hindus, with whom they have very little in common. While the fact is that practically what differentiates a Sikh from a Hindu is his long hair and unclipped beard. In many families one brother may be a Hindu and the other Sikh. As to religious belief, there is very little difference between the average Hindu and the Sikh *in the Punjab,* the Guru and the Granth being held in equal reverence by both."[78] Events at the close of the decade forced this question to the forefront of Sikh and Hindu minds, surrounding it with increasingly bitter controversy.

The redivision of the Samaj brought the College Party to publicly assist the embattled Sikhs, much to the horror of the militants. Lala Paira Ram, Extra-Assistant Commissioner at Lahore and a leading member of the militant faction, charged that the "Editor of the *Arya Gazette* in his anxiety to please the Sikhs observes in the issue of the 15th July that Swami Dayanand had an imperfect knowledge of Gurmukhi, and that the remarks made by him regarding Guru Nanak in the '*Satyarth Prakash*' are based on second-hand information and were not endorsed by the Arya Samaj."[79] The question of Sikhs' identity had now become tangled in internal Samaj bickering. Militant Aryas, in order to uphold the sanctity of Dayanand, attacked Guru Nanak and the Sikh faith, while the moderates stayed with their allies in the Shuddhi Sabhas.

In 1898, the question of Sikh separatism became both a legal as well as a public issue. Sardar Dyal Singh Majithia died in September of that year, leaving his vast wealth to the Dyal Singh Trust. His widow, Sardarni Dyal Singh, and her cousin contested the will, claiming that the Hindu law of inheritance under which he had given his property in trust did not apply in that he was a Sikh and not a Hindu. Thus the Punjab High Court found itself forced to declare whether Sikhs were or were not Hindus. Their decision that the Sardar was, in fact, a Hindu set off a great debate. Throughout 1898, 1899, and 1900, the issue was argued in public meetings, in the press, and through pamphlets. Bhai Jagat Singh, a

78. *Tribune*, August 27, 1892, p. 4.

79. *Sat Dharm Prachārak*, August 13, 1897, *SPVP 1897*, p. 765; and *Khālsā Bahādur*, August 30, 1897, *SPVP 1897*, p. 800.

Sikh member of the Arya Samaj, in his tract, *Risāla sat Prakāsh,* attempted to prove that Sikhism was merely an earlier version of the Arya Samaj.[80] Lala Thakar Das and Bawa Narain Singh agreed in their tracts entitled *Sikh Hindū Hain* (Sikhs are Hindus).[81] Sardar Kahan Singh, in his famous polemic *Ham Hindū Nahīn* (We are not Hindus), argued the Sikh case for separatism.[82] This debate continued with undiminished vigor, creating considerable confusion within the Sikh community. The search for identity within the Sikh community and between Sikhs and Hindus became suddenly embroiled in the Samaj campaign to purify and thus save outcastes from Christian conversion.

From time to time Aryas had spoken out against the treatment of outcaste Hindus. The census reports showed clearly what danger lay among this group. Muslims had already converted from the lowest segments of Hindu society; now Christians followed their example. The Sikh community contained as well similar targets for conversion. As early as 1886, Samajists discussed this issue but did nothing.[83] By 1900, however, the idea of transforming outcastes into pure castes began to find adherents. Aryas, who joined the *Birādarī* movement and who had witnessed the purification of outcastes by the Shuddhi Sabha, decided to act, a decision hastened by pressure from one outcaste group, the Rahtias of the Jullundur Doab. By tradition weavers, the Rahtias had their own educated leaders who now wanted to raise the status of the whole caste. They turned first to leaders of the Sikh community but found little encouragement, and so approached the Arya Samaj. Militant Aryas welcomed them and began plans for their entrance into pure caste society, thus setting the stage for a communal conflict of impressive proportions. The Rahtias were outcaste Sikhs and once purified would become good Aryas and "pure" Hindus.

80. See *Tribune,* February 7, 1899, pp. 3–4.

81. Lala Thakar Das, *Sikh Hindū Hain* (Sikhs are Hindus) (Hoshiarpur: Khatri Press, 1899); and Bawa Narain Singh, *Sikh Hindū Hain* (Sikhs are Hindus) (Amritsar: Mat-Bakarnuni Press, 1899). Also see the account in B. L. Singh, *Autobiography,* ed. Ganda Singh (Calcutta: Sikh Cultural Centre, 1965), pp. 154, and 133–134 and 137–138.

82. Sardar Kahan Singh, *Ham Hindū Nahīn* (Amritsar: Khalsa Press, 1899).

83. *Arya Patrika,* April 27, 1886, pp. 4–5, from a lecture by Lala Kunja Behari Thaper.

On June 2, the day before the actual ceremony, Bhagat Singh joined in a futile attempt to dissuade the Rahtias from their announced plans. "Bhai Kanhaiya Singh addressed them a few words of advice. Their leader, Nagina Singh, accosted him with the reply that if we could assure them that the Sikhs would intermarry and inter-dine with them they would not even dream of going out of the Sikh fold. The demand was only in keeping with the promise made at the time of *Pahul* (baptismal) ceremony which was honoured more by its breach than by observance."[84] Unable to meet the demands of the Rahtias, Bhagat Singh could only counsel retreat. The Khalsa Sikhs were trapped. They could promise little, for they did not speak as leaders of the entire Sikh community. Nevertheless, they returned the next morning for one more attempt to argue with the Rahtia leaders and failed a second time; Bhagat Singh and his companions could only watch with growing horror as the ceremony progressed. Sikh anger focused as much on the methods of *shuddhi* as the fact of it, for the ceremony itself was in their eyes an insult to their faith.[85]

Sikhs of all sects were outraged at a public shaving and haircutting, while orthodoxy, both Hindu and Sikh, found the investiture of the sacred thread and inter-dining an affront to all they held sacred and proper. ". . . . when the time of initiation of the Rahtia Sikhs came, they were seated on a pulpit and their heads were shaved by half a dozen barbers before hundreds of the multitude that had assembled to witness the performance. A sprinkling of Sikhs was also present but insult done to their feelings in such public fashion drove them mad and they withdrew from the scene. By 12 A.M., however, the whole Sikh [community of] Lahore was mad with rage and ran to and fro in a helpless manner."[86] In the aftermath of the *shuddhi,* Sikhs held meetings of protest,

84. B. L. Singh, *Autobiography,* pp. 161–162. For further details on Arya-Sikh conflict, see Kenneth W. Jones, "Ham Hindu Nahīn: Arya-Sikh Relations, 1877–1905," *Journal of Asian Studies,* XXXII, No. 3 (May 1973), pp. 457–475.

85. "The principal feature of the Parvesh ceremony (of shuddhi) was the investment of the person desiring admission with the *Yajnopavit Sanskar.* First there was the *Mundan* Ceremony or shaving the head; then all put on new *dhotis* (clothing). *Havan* was performed. The *Gayatri* was performed. They were told their five daily duties and the sixteen Sanskars they were to perform. A copy of Dayanand's Mahayajnavidhi was given each. They were then declared to be in the Samaj. Almost all the people present took *Sherbat* at their hands." Graham, "The Arya Samaj," p. 465.

86. *Khālsā,* June 6, 1900, pp. 3–4.

passed resolutions condemning both the Samaj and the Rahtias. In the swirl of frustration, fear, and anger, the educated Sikh community struck out against the Aryas and even more their orthodox brothers. Inevitably they, as did all injured communities, raised the spectre of unrest and violence, invoking the God government who always hung in the background ready to swoop down and trample the instigators of dissension.

In the months that followed this purification, other Rahtias came forward for *shuddhi* by the Samaj. The Lahore Samaj continued its drive to uplift the Rahtias and was joined by Samajes in Rupur and as far west as Lyallpur.[87] With the widening campaign, the Rahtia dispute spread far beyond Lahore. Rahtias returning to their villages met determined opposition to their claim to pure caste status. Attempts by Rahtias to use village wells, hitherto barred to them, were defeated at times violently by their fellow villagers.[88] Each incident further justified the *Khālsā's* position that the Samaj was bent on destroying the tranquillity of the British Raj. "Should a great riot take place, of which there is not the least hope, we would then show to the officers of the Government what result there is in *yielding to any particular race of men* or showing them any particular favours. The Arya Samajists will bear whatever lot is in store for them; but it is the Government of the day that will suffer *whose administration* will be disturbed."[89] In the weeks that followed, each side continued to invoke the government on his own side and to discredit his opponents in the eyes of officialdom.

The Rahtia purification and the resulting furor added new vigor and passion to the debate over Sikhs as Hindus. Books, newspapers, articles, tracts, and speeches passionately argued for one position or the other.[90] By 1904, the College Aryas, who had been

87. *Khālsā,* June 13, 1900, p. 2; July 25, 1900, p. 2; and *Arya Patrika,* December 8, 1900, p. 7, quoted in Graham, "The Arya Samaj," p. 492.

88. *Khālsā,* July 4, 1900, p. 3; and *Tribune,* June 28, 1900, p. 3.

89. *Khālsā,* August 8, 1900, pp. 3–4.

90. See *Akhbār-i-'Ām,* March 13, 1901, *SPVP 1901,* p. 168 and March 25, 1901, *SPVP 1901,* p. 202; April 2, 1901, *SPVP 1901,* p. 220; *Sat Dharm Prachārak,* March 21, 1902, *SPVP 1902,* pp. 217–218; *Khālsā Akhbār,* July 18, 1902, *SPVP 1902,* pp. 475–476; *Tribune,* October 30, 1902, p. 5; Mahan Singh Omkari, *Sāhib Diyāl kē Parāgrandah Khayalōn kī Partāl* (A Repayment for the Dirty Tricks of Sahib Diyal) (Amritsar: Wazir Hind Press, 1904); Bhai Ganda Singh, *Nuskha-i-Khabt-i-Dyanāndiyān* (Prescriptions for the Insanity of the Followers of Dayanand) (Amritsar: Amar Press, 1904); and Bawa Chhajju Singh, *The Ten Gurus and their Teachings* (Lahore: Punjab Printing Works, 1903).

longest and most closely allied to the reformist Sikhs, joined the ranks of the enemy. In *The Sikhs and Sikhism* for November 1904, this old alliance was proclaimed dead.

In the recent two issues of the "Arya Gazette" Lahore, there have appeared two articles headed "*Sikhon ka Ruhani Doctor*" in which the impudent writer has in a manner insulted the Sikhs and their sacred religion. The language of the articles is decidedly harsher than that of the *Sat Dharam Pracharak* even which is considered a scurrilous reviler of the Sikhs. Now it is gratifying to let it be known to our readers that the cultured [College] Hindus have openly commenced to oppose the Khalsa.[91]

With this rejection of Arya support came as well the rejection of *shuddhi* as a concept that was essentially Hindu. Sikhs turned back to their own traditional baptism as a truly Sikh form of conversion.

Having abandoned cooperation in the area of *shuddhi,* educated Sikh leaders sought to define their community around the symbols of the Sikh past including that most powerful determinant of separatism, linguistic identity. As Hindi in the Devanagri script defined the revived Hindu, so Punjabi in the Gurmukhi script came to symbolize the demands for a separate Sikh identity.

Now whether Punjabi or Hindi should replace Urdu has again become a burning topic of the day. Those who for bigotry's sake, wanted Hindi to become the Court language, which is nonetheless a foreign language like Persian and Urdu, finding that they will meet with utter failure in this attempt, have now commenced to argue that for the Punjab there should be no language other than Punjabi, but it should be written in Hindi characters instead of in the Gurmukhi characters. On our part we are confident that such noises as have been made against the Punjabi being written in Gurmukhi characters are doomed to go effectless.[92]

Throughout the years 1901 through 1903, Sikhs debated with Aryas on the meaning of Sikhism, on Sikh separateness from the Hindu community and on alleged job discrimination by the government. Economic competition between educated Sikhs and Hindus added fuel to this communal competition.[93]

91. Quotes given below from the periodical *The Sikhs and Sikhism,* November 8, 1904, p. 5.

92. *The Sikhs and Sikhism,* May 16, 1904, p. 7; also see *Tribune,* September 1, 1900, p. 4; September 27, 1900, p. 5; and October 13, 1900, p. 5.

93. *Khālsā Bahādur,* January 24, 1901, *SPVP 1901,* p. 15; *Sat Dharm Prachārak,* February 1, 1901, *SPVP 1901,* p. 123; *Sanātan Dharm Gazette,* January 31, 1901,

In 1905, attempts by Sikh reformers to purge their religion of idolatry produced a direct confrontation with Hindu orthodoxy over the most sacred of all Sikh institutions, the Golden Temple at Amritsar. The customary performance of Hindu rituals in the temple compound offended the reformers who saw this both as contrary to Sikh beliefs and as an intrusion of a decadent faith. The Manager of the Temple ordered that all Hindu idols should be excluded from the Temple precincts, thus ending the performance of Hindu rituals in that area. Hindus reacted with outrage at this attack on their traditional privileges.[94] Brahman priests and their idols had been associated with the Golden Temple for at least a century and had over these years received the patronage of pious Hindus and Sikhs. In the 1890s these practices came under increasing attack by reformist Sikhs. Finally, "the Manager of the Temple, Sirdar Arur Singh, turned them out of the precincts of the temple a few days ago on the ground, it is said, that they were idol-worshipping intruders on the sanctity of a monotheistic Temple." In the ensuing melee of protest meetings, tracts, newspaper articles, and letters to the press, reformed Sikhs fought against their own religious establishment, against claims that they were weakening their community from within, and setting Hindu against Sikh. Some blamed the British for "apparently the doctrine of 'divide and rule,' which has had more or less acceptance at headquarters during all these years, has at last succeeded in making its entrance into the Golden Temple at Amritsar."[95]

In the years following this controversy Sikhs would come increasingly to struggle over issues of power and leadership within their community, and in defense of Sikhism as a separate entity. The days of even limited cooperation between Hindu and Sikh reformers had ended and been replaced by a world of communal mobilization. The parallel searching for identity by both Aryas and educated Sikhs now ran in separate channels. With the old alliance of reformers dead, educated Sikhs turned toward a struggle for control within their own community, a struggle which would

---

*SPVP 1901*, p. 153; *Akhbār-i-'Ām*, April 17, 1901, *SPVP 1901*, p. 266; *Ahluwālia Gazette*, August 1, 1902, *SPVP 1902*, p. 436; *Ahluwālia Gazette*, August 16, 1902, *SPVP 1902*, p. 467; *Public Gazette*, November 24, 1902, *SPVP 1902*, p. 583.

94. Quotes given below from *Tribune*, May 11, 1905, p. 3.

95. *Panjabee*, May 15, 1905, p. 1.

dominate the Sikh community throughout the next two decades. Increasingly, Aryas and Hindus in general lay beyond the world of Sikhism, and urgent calls to unity or exclamations of lament could not reverse this process of division into separate communities.

The reaction of the Sikh community to the purification of the Rahtias did not intimidate or deflect the militant Aryas from their drive to uplift and thus save the outcaste community from Christian conversion. On the contrary, they moved forward rapidly to utilize mass *shuddhi* and did so under pressure from other depressed caste groups. Leaders of the Ode community located in the districts of Multan and Muzzafarnagar requested that the Samaj purify them. Aryas responded by organizing a public *shuddhi* and gathered support throughout both the reformed and orthodox community. In 1901–1902, the Multan Samaj successfully purified several hundred families of Odes,[96] and within the decade, Aryas reclaimed 23,000 Odes in the southwestern Punjab.[97]

Success with both the Rahtias and Odes led militant Samajists to a much more massive campaign among the Meghs of Sialkot and the surrounding districts. The Sialkot Arya Samaj decided on March 14, 1903, to "lend its strong shoulder in lifting this car of social reform so far as it concerned the Meghs of the Punjab from the slough and mire of ignorance and misery, and placing it on the highroad of progress."[98] During the next six years the Samaj mounted an effective campaign, purifying more than 36,000 Meghs from the districts of Sialkot, Gujrat, and Gurdaspur.

The Sialkot Samaj next moved to found a school for the "Arya Bhagats" as the newly purified were called. On June 25, 1903, they resolved to open a Central Industrial School for Megh boys who would receive technical, literary, and religious education. The Sialkot Samaj followed this with the founding of elementary schools.[99] The education offered Megh youths differed sharply from the Dayanand Anglo-Vedic College system. It was mainly technical education, teaching "Weaving, Tailoring, Carpentry,

96. Graham, "The Arya Samaj," p. 493.

97. Specifically in the districts of Multan, Muzaffargarh, Lyallpur, Jhang, and Montgomery, *Census, Punjab Report 1911*, p. 150.

98. Ganga Ram and Charu Das, *The Uplift Movement at Sialkot Punjab: A Brief Report of the Working of the Arya Megh Uddhar Sabha (Aryan Mission for the Uplift of the Megh Untouchables), Sialkot, Punjab* (Calcutta: A. C. Sarkar, 1915), p. 8.

99. *Ibid.*, p. 24.

Smithy and Drawing . . ."—an education for the lower classes, pure but lowly.[100] In this the Samaj paralleled social reality, for the Meghs were by tradition a weaving community.[101] Aryas, as upper class, educated and from among the community of the "pure," would lead the Meghs to a better life, but under no circumstances toward an immediate social equality. "In spite of being poor the habits of those who have come under our influence so far as cleanliness and decency go, have vastly improved and the day is not far off when they will compare favourably with the average Hindu."[102]

Arya paternalism fitted with the self-image of the educated elite and with traditional Hindu concepts of social hierarchy. It was, as well, accepted by members of the depressed classes, but only reluctantly after their suspicion of strangers and the higher castes had been neutralized. Pandit Ram Bhaj Datta, one of the Arya leaders in caste purification, described the difficulties in approaching outcaste groups, in this case the Dhommas of the Himalayan foothills. "At the principal meeting at which he was to have opened his campaign not a single Dhomma attended. But the Pundit was equal to the occasion. Instead of delivering his address, he at once betook himself to the quarters of the town in which the untouchable dwelt, and was able to induce many of them to follow him to the place of meeting. He assured them that he had no intention of demanding money from them or of taking away their women, but that his sole object was to have their rights accepted by the higher castes."[103] After lengthy discussion with members of the pure castes, Ram Bhaj Datta proceeded with the *shuddhi* ceremony. "In the presence of thousands of Hindu men and women the great work of Shuddhi or purification was performed on thousands of untouchables. 'For two days,' writes the Pundit, 'we went on shaving and purifying crowds of men, women and children. More than 1,400 were admitted into the Arya or Hindu community.'"

The dramatic culmination of this *shuddhi* came when the ex-outcastes performed their first acts as members of "pure" caste society.

100. *Ibid.*, p. 30.

101. *Ibid.*, p. 3.

102. *Ibid.*, pp. 22–23.

103. Quotes given below from an account which originally appeared in the *Times of India* during 1912, quoted by Graham in "The Arya Samaj," p. 496.

Thousands of Hindus stood round the well when the Pundit called upon one of the Dhomma leaders to draw water from it. . . . 'It was too much for him. He took off his shoes, and with folded hands trembling with emotion he asked the biradri if he could really go up to the well. They cheerfully assented. I helped him up the stairs, and told him to ask their permission three times. He did so thrice, each time the permission was granted, the brotherhood becoming more and more enthusiastic and full of feeling in their sympathetic reply to his petition. On this I asked the man to fall at the feet of the brotherhood who had raised him. He obeyed and drew water from the well amidst cheers.'

Not all attempts to raise the oppressed met with enthusiasm or even acceptance of the local community, and when it did such emotional fervor could hardly be maintained. More often than not attempts to move up the social scale ran directly into the existing power structure, producing in response social boycotts and occasional violence.

The story of one such conflict between the newly purified and the dominant caste illustrates intercaste rivalry stimulated by the Arya *shuddhi* campaign. "The Meghs of the village Pattansen in the Sialkot Tahsil were purified. The Rajputs took it very ill. They attacked the poor Bhagats in their houses, armed with 'lathies,' beat them severely and ordered them to leave either the Aryan religion or the village." Clearly, Arya attempts to elevate the lower end of the Hindu social spectrum threatened the traditional system of hierarchical social status. For urban Aryas such change mattered little, but in the villages radical caste reform challenged the total social order. In spite of this, caste uplift continued bringing thousands of ex-outcastes into the Samaj, altering its social composition. The educated elite, the urban vaishya and brahmanical castes became a minority within the movement, although they maintained their leadership, if not unchallenged, at least undiminished. In the years after 1905, Hindu leaders saw *shuddhi* for caste reform as a major weapon in maintaining communal strength and solidarity. "The need felt by them for the safeguarding of Hindu communal interests in the struggle already begun for political rights and privileges and their growing knowledge of the progressive decline of the numerical strength of the Hindus in comparison with Christian and Muhammadan population—due to conversion to Christianity or Muhammadanism, all these several factors have combined to stimulate and strengthen the movement in favour of the Depressed Classes."[104] Fear and a growing political consciousness proved stronger than social mores in the years following this first round of caste uplift.

### THE ARYA COMPLETED: MILITANT EXPERIMENTS IN EDUCATION

As militants followed the dream of a reconstructed social order through the Bratri Sabha movement and *shuddhi,* they followed as well the search for a new man, the Arya of Dayanand's vision. Less motivated by fear than the purification campaigns, this drive for a modernized Vedic man represented the culmination of an ideology, the working out of concepts brought by Dayanand and modified by later militant thinkers. In the years immediately following the division of the Samaj, Munshi Ram and his allies in Jullundur concentrated on the quest for a new woman. Begun in the early 1890s, the drive to provide opportunities for women's education gathered strength in 1895, as the Jullundur Samajists expanded their successful girls' school, the Arya Kanya Path Shala. In March, they opened a boarding house for girls, the Kanya Ashram,[105] which soon had residents from the Punjab, the North-Western Provinces, and as far away as Poona.[106] This act in itself marked a daring departure as the school now took on the additional responsibility of guarding the morality of its students. Success of the Path Shala encouraged its supporters to increase their efforts to establish a Kanya Mahavidyalaya, a girls' high school. During 1895, the Jullundur Samaj promised Rs. 5,000 to the high school fund, while Lala Dev Raj pledged a personal donation of Rs. 1,010.[107] Advocates of female education used techniques pioneered in the Dayanand Anglo-Vedic College movement, but failed to find the same widespread support as exhibited for the education of young men.[108] Female education did not entail the same dynamics as the earlier dilemma created by the need for a safe education for males. As a consequence the institutions created to educate girls remained on a far smaller scale than the

104. Ganga Ram and Charu Das, *The Uplift Movement at Sialkot Punjab,* p. 1.
105. *Tribune,* March 16, 1895, p. 4.
106. *Kanya Mahavidyalaya Reports - Digest, 1895.*
107. *Tribune,* January 12, 1895, p. 4.
108. *Tribune,* February 29, 1896, p. 4; and April 8, 1896, p. 4.

Dayanand Anglo-Vedic College system and taught to a much lower educational standard.

After completing the necessary organizational innovations, Lalas Dev Raj and Munshi Ram opened the Kanya Mahavidyalaya on June 14, 1896.[109] Initially, the Kanya Mahavidyalaya was little more than an extension of the older Path Shala, more a statement of intention than a reality. It grew slowly but steadily over the next decade. By 1906, the school contained 203 students in all grades and the Ashram provided for 105 girls.[110] The Ashram housed married, unmarried, and widowed girls from throughout British India.[111] Expansion in the number of students led to the founding of a second school two miles outside of Jullundur City. By 1913–1914, the City school served 175 students and the new school held 214. Housing arrangements had also been enlarged with the opening in 1906 of a Vidhva Bhavan, a widows' hostel. By 1913–1914, the original Ashram hosted 254 girls and the Vidhva Bhavan another 22.[112] The growth of this school—slow but steady—exemplified the limited but increasing demand for the education of girls. Girls would be educated, although not many and not well. The slow growth of the Kanya Mahavidyalaya resulted in part from a limited financial base. The first year's report showed an income of Rs. 6,511 and expenditures of Rs. 5,007. By 1904, the figures were Rs. 4,307 and Rs. 2,275. Funded capital stood at Rs. 25,984 for the same year. The Kanya Mahavidyalaya did not lose money, closing each year with a slight profit, yet it did not attract large donations, increasing both its annual expenditures and funded capital only gradually.[113]

The curriculum of the Kanya Path Shala and its descendant, the Kanya Mahavidyalaya, was circumscribed, functional, and safe. In addition to basic literacy, the girls learned sewing, embroidery,

109. *Kanya Mahavidyalaya Annual Report for 1898*, p. 3.

110. Satyadev Vidyalankar, *Lālā Dēv Rāj* (Jālandar Shahar: Mukhya Sabhā Kanyā Mahavidyālaya, 1937), pp. 153–154.

111. In 1904–1905 girls came from Berar, Rajputana, United Provinces, Punjab, Sindh, the North-West Frontier Province, and Baluchistan. In the years 1908–1910, other provinces and areas were represented, namely: Hyderabad, Deccan, Bombay, Assam, Bengal, and Burma. Satyadev Vidyalankar, *Lālā Dēv Rāj*, pp. 254–255.

112. *Ibid.*, pp. 154–155.

113. See *Annual Reports Kanya Mahavidyalaya for 1896–97 through 1902–03* and the *Panjabee*, October 31, 1904, p. 2.

drawing, cooking, some music, poetry, games, arithmetic, hygiene, and the religious literature of the Samaj.[114] It was, in effect, a reformed Hindu finishing school, teaching first up to the seventh year and later to the eighth. The school found it very difficult to insure regular attendance and, of even greater importance, the continuation of students past the most elementary grades. The number of students dropped off from the first through the fifth year classes and then diminished dramatically for the sixth through eighth years. Few students finished the entire course of study, particularly among the married girls.[115] Those who did complete their education often became teachers in other girls' schools. The staff of the Kanya Mahavidyalaya urged their graduates to open schools in their own homes if necessary in order to spread the work of female education.[116] The shortage of educated women who would or could enter into teaching greatly hindered the spread of schools. Even when such schools managed to open they faced a further problem in the lack of books and teaching materials.

The Kanya Mahavidyalaya's first attempt to meet this literacy gulf came with the founding of the *Panchāl Panditā* in 1898, a Hindi monthly designed to "preach and propagate about female education."[117] The Mahavidyalaya also began to publish a series of readers, instructional texts, and morally uplifting books for use in their own and other girls' schools.[118] With the steady production of educated girls as potential teachers, of propaganda for women's education, and of literature needed to open and maintain a girls'

114. See *Annual Report, 1896–97,* pp. 8–10; *Annual Report, Kanya Mahavidyalaya for 1898,* pp. 7, 10.

115. *Annual Report, Kanya Mahavidyalaya, 1898,* p. 7; *Annual Report Kanya Mahavidyalaya, 1899–1900,* p. 14; and *Annual Report, Kanya Mahavidyalaya, 1902–03,* p. 7. They were plagued as well by poor attendance, see *Annual Report, Kanya Mahavidyalaya, 1896–97,* p. 5; *Annual Report, Kanya Mahavidyalaya, 1898,* p. 7; and *Tribune,* December 1, 1904, p. 3.

116. *Annual Report, Kanya Mahavidyalaya, 1896–97,* p. 7.

117. Originally this magazine was written in both English and Hindi, but by 1903 it had shifted completely to Hindi. See, *Annual Report, Kanya Mahavidyalaya, 1898,* p. 19, and *Annual Report, Kanya Mahavidyalaya, 1902–03,* p. 18.

118. Published by the year 1902–1903 were the following books: (1) *The Kanyā Mahāvidyālaya First Reader, Pāth Shālā kī Kanyā,* (2) *The Life of Christopher Columbus,* (3) *The Kanyā Mahāvidyālaya Akshar Dīpaka,* (4) *The Kanyā Mahāvidyālaya Vāran Mālā,* (5) *The Kathā Vidhi,* (6) *The Subōdh Kanyā,* (7) *The Nārī Prāthana,* (8)

school, the Kanya Mahavidyalaya became both a model to copy and the provider of the necessary parts to construct that model. In a developmental process paralleling the Dayanand Anglo-Vedic College movement, the Kanya Mahavidyalaya stimulated the growth of female schools which in time became tied to it through both formal and informal relations.[119] The Kanya Mahavidyalaya, with its students, its teachers, and publications, made the educated young girl a reality, clearly visible throughout the province. Anniversary ceremonies and fund drives now might have a group of girls from the school to add to their festivities.[120] Neat, clean, educated, and Aryanized, they stood for the new female, as the school itself symbolized the drive to change permanently the traditional role of women.

Paralleling the Arya search for an educated woman was their campaign to promote widow marriage. The remarriage of widowed girls slowly grew in acceptance throughout the latter half of the decade, as families of distinction and high social status led in legitimizing this break with tradition. In 1895, Diwan Sant Ram Chopra celebrated the marriage of his widowed daughter. The Diwan's family could boast of a distinguished heritage, for his grandfather was the famous Governor of Multan, Diwan Sawan Mal, who had served under Ranjit Singh and later revolted against the British. Sant Ram himself annually hosted the Khatri Conference and was one of the foremost leaders of his caste. Wedding guests included distinguished Aryas, Brahmos, and Sanatanists, as well as prominent Sikhs and Muslims. This marriage not only attracted widespread attention throughout the province but was used, as well, to launch a widow remarriage society, the Adhikarı Bidhva Beva Sahayak Sabha of Lahore. Lala Hans Raj became president of this society and the Diwan provided initial funding.[121]

---

*The Bālā Vināya*, (9) *The Patra Kaumadī*, and (10) *The Sāvitrī Nātak*. The Kanya Mahavidyalaya had also started a Literary Fund to encourage the writing, translation, and publishing of books on female education. *Annual Report, Kanya Mahavidyalaya, 1902–03*, p. 12.

119. The Kanya Mahavidyalaya Managing Committee took over the Mai Bhagvati Putri Pathshala of Hariana, which, in 1901, had a total of sixty-four students. *Tribune,* May 14, 1901, p. 5.

120. *Annual Report, Kanya Mahavidyalaya, 1896–97*, p. 8; *Annual Report, Kanya Mahavidyalaya, 1898*, p. 15; and, *Tribune,* September 6, 1904, p. 5.

121. *Tribune* (Lahore), Supplement, December 11, 1895, p. 1.

Within the next decade the acceptance of widow remarriage spread steadily among the educated community. Khatris led the way, followed by Aroras, Suds, Kayasthas, Baniyas, Ahluwalias, and even Brahmans.[122] Over the next ten years Bhattias and Jains joined in those willing to marry widows, although both groups had not previously encouraged social reform.[123] Aryas openly promoted widow marriage and found allies among educated Hindus of varying ideological backgrounds. In 1896, a remarriage performed by Sanatanist Pundits took place in Phagwara,[124] and the following year, the Orthodox Widow Remarriage Society of Lahore sponsored three marriages.[125] Societies and associations dedicated to the cause of widow marriage were active in Lahore (1896), Jullundur (1903), Rawalpindi (1905), Sialkot (1905), Shahjahanpur, United Province (1902), and Delhi (1906).[126] The spread of such organizations added to those groups already willing to publicly assist widow remarriages. Yet a sharp line was drawn between virgin and non-virgin widows. Remarriage of the former found considerable public approval, for the latter strong opposition.[127] The issue of virgin widow remarriage would gradually fade in the early twentieth century, both from acceptance by the educated sections of society and by the fact of female education. With the growth of girls' schools and the trend toward educating young women, marriage came later, lessening the instances of widowhood among the very young. For older women, those who had actually lived with their husband and who might have children as well, social acceptance of remarriage remained an unsettled question.

The militant Aryas' search for a new man and a new woman grew from their earlier rejection of the Dayanand Anglo-Vedic

122. *Tribune*, December 11, 1895, p. 4; March 18, 1896, p. 4; May 6, 1896, p. 4; May 9, 1896, p. 4; July 8, 1896, p. 4; November 18, 1896, p. 4; December 19, 1896, p. 4; January 11, 1900, p. 4; June 15, 1901, p. 5; February 3, 1903, p. 5; January 27, 1903, p. 4.

123. *Panjabee*, July 11, 1906, p. 4; *Tribune*, December 14, 1906, p. 3; February 6, 1907, p. 5.

124. *Tribune*, May 30, 1896, p. 4.

125. *Tribune*, September 29, 1897, p. 4.

126. *Tribune*, November 18, 1896, p. 4; August 1, 1903, p. 4; *Panjabee*, March 20, 1905, p. 3; March 21, 1905, p. 5; July 25, 1905, p. 4; September 23, 1905, p. 4; February 17, 1906, p. 5; and *Tribune*, July 24, 1906, p. 3.

127. *Tribune*, June 6, 1896, p. 4 and June 17, 1896, p. 4.

College and its education. "It began to turn out not Gautamas and Kanads, but babus, with the result that the Samaj was compelled to throw it over-board and start a Veda Prachar Fund with the object of carrying out the dying behest of Swami Daya Nand."[128] To replace the Dayanand Anglo-Vedic College, militants dreamed of a school patterned after the ancient Hindu universities. "Something more, however, is needed to ensure the preservation of this religion and enable the Aryas to bring up their children in the faith of the old Rishis. The writer feels confident that the proposed establishment of a Guru Kul (an educational institution maintaining resident teachers, who look after the education, morals and health of the pupils) in the Punjab would supply this need and achieve what the Daya Nand Anglo-Vedic College failed to do." Not "babus" but "Gautamas" echoed Guru Datta's contempt for the worldly Aryas enmeshed in money-making and the search for government jobs. Militant Aryas wanted a religious man purified from the corrupt past and decadent present.

During the years 1897, 1898, and 1899, Lala Munshi Ram and his allies moved from discussing the Gurukul concept and defending it from critics to collecting funds and creating the concrete plans to found an institution. They spelled out their unhappiness with the existing schools, both governmental and Arya. Contemporary education had "put an end to the spiritual relation which existed between a teacher and his pupil."[129] Students no longer practiced Brahmacharya (celibacy) necessary for a proper Vedic education. The "education imparted in the public schools and college . . . not only encourages cramming, but makes its recipients lead a sort of artificial life, and increases their wants. Its worst feature, however, is that it has a tendency to undermine both religion and morality."[130] Progress could only be maintained by founding a new type of school which would break completely with established educational patterns.[131] In 1898, the Arya Pratinidhi Sabha of the Punjab voted to open just such a school.[132] This decision set off an intense effort to raise the necessary capital as well as increased

128. Quotes given below from *Sat Dharm Prachārak,* February 24, 1899, *SPVP 1899*, p. 142.

129. *Sat Dharm Prachārak,* December 9, 1898, *SPVP 1898*, p. 805.

130. *Sat Dharm Prachārak,* August 11, 1899, *SPVP 1899*, p. 459.

131. *Sat Dharm Prachārak,* August 27, 1897, *SPVP 1897*, p. 801.

132. *Sat Dharm Prachārak,* December 9, 1898, *SPVP 1898*, p. 105

criticism of the proposed school. Opponents saw it as idealistic, impractical, or more mundanely, an attempt to undercut support for the Dayanand Anglo-Vedic College.[133] Lack of sufficient funding created a genuine bar to fulfilling this dream. During 1899 and 1900, Lala Munshi Ram led an intensive drive to raise Rs. 30,000.[134] By 1900, he had collected Rs. 17,000 in cash. He traveled continuously, and in desperation vowed not to enter his house again until the full Rs. 30,000 was in hand.[135] The school finally became possible in 1901, when Chaudri Aman Singh donated a large tract of land three miles south of Hardwar City.[136] With this gift in hand, the Pratinidhi Sabha announced the opening of the Gurukul on the auspicious day of Holi in 1902.[137]

While the search for funds continued, proponents of the Gurukul gradually completed their plans for the new school and explained them to the Punjabi public. The *Tribune* carried a statement describing the aims of this new institution in its issue of January 18, 1900. The Gurukul would teach:

(A) Physical improvement, by enforcing *Brahmacharya* (celibacy), active habits and well regulated daily life.

(B) Intellectual improvement, by instructing them in our satya shastras (true scriptures), sciences and philosophy and English language and literature.

(C) Religious and ethical improvement, by teaching the Theistic religion of the Holy Vedas, the Ethics and other ancient Rishis, from Brahma to Jaimini, and of other devotees at the temple of Truth.

(D) Social or Samajic improvement, by placing before them elevating ideals, such as the ideas of showing due respect to age and learning, altruistic notions of *Paropkara* (charity or benevolence) and self-abnegation, and the regulation of conduct in life accordingly. It also aims at the improvement of national character, by placing the local or national ideas on a sounder basis, by giving to their education the colouring of Indian

133. See *Arya Gazette,* September 28, 1899, *SPVP 1899,* p. 590; *Sanātan Dharm Gazette,* October 31, 1899, *SPVP 1899,* p. 669; *Tribune,* January 23, 1900, p. 3; *Sat Dharm Prachārak,* February 28, 1902, *SPVP 1902,* p. 154; and Rama Deva and Munshi Ram, *Gurūkul aur us kē Mukhālif* (The Gurukul and its Adversaries) (Jullundur: Sat Dharm Pracharak Press, 1899).

134. *Sat Dharm Prachārak,* September 29, 1899, *SPVP 1899,* p. 590.

135. N. B. Sen, *Punjab's Eminent Hindus,* pp. 302–303.

136. *Sat Dharm Prachārak,* November 8, 1901, *SFVP 1901,* p. 738.

137. *Sat Dharm Prachārak,* January 3, 1902, *SPVP 1902.* pp. 26–27.

tradition and the vitality inborn of the genius of the people of Hinduism.[138]

The Pratinidhi Sabha published a full statement of the rules, organization, and educational philosophy for the new school. It repeated with considerable detail previous complaints against "denationalizing" education, and called instead for learning based on morality, on a revival of the *guru* who would teach by example and personal piety, on education through the vernacular languages with a substructure of Sanskritic learning, and on the removal of students from the influence of their homes and the surrounding society. It proclaimed as well complete educational equality between boys and girls. Education would be free, total, beyond distinction of caste, and "truly national."[139] Popular nationalism was false and un-Indian, the outgrowth of an English plot. "A plan was devised which would virtually convert into Englishmen those Indians who would cherish the ambition to rule over their country. The plan was simply this, that they should be brought over and educated in England. It has admirably served the purpose; whether the civilian, who really governs the country, is an Englishman or an Indian, English ideas, English thoughts and English sentiments rule over the country."[140] The orientalism of Leitner now returned in a new form, identification with a Hindu past and a partial rejection of westernization. The Gurukul would teach both English and science, but as secondary knowledge subordinate to Vedic truth and viewed through the lenses of Sanskrit and Hindi.

On March 22, 1902, the Gurukul opened with pomp and ceremony. Three days of meetings and processions marked the occasion. The organizers collected Rs. 3,000 and the initial band of twenty students soon grew to nearly sixty.[141] Lala Munshi Ram di-

138. *Tribune*, January 18, 1900, p. 4; a similar statement appeared five days later, see *Tribune*, January 23, 1900, p. 4. The *Ārya Musāfir* also carried several long articles on the Gurukul and on the educational ideas of Dayanand. See *Ārya Musāfir*, January 1901, pp. 1–16; and February 1901, pp. 1–16.

139. Lala Ralla Ram, *The Rules and Scheme of Studies of the Gurukuls* (Lahore: Punjab Printing Works, 1902), p. 5. A Hindi version appeared at the same time under the title *Gurūkula kē Niyam aur Pathan Pathan vidhi kī Paddhati.*

140. *Ibid.*, p. 5.

141. *Punjāb Samāchār*, March 29, 1902, *SPVP 1902*, p. 220; *Sat Dharm Prachārak*, April 4, 1902, *SPVP 1902*, p. 237; and *Tribune*, April 26, 1902, p. 5.

rected the new school. He had become increasingly enmeshed in this project, to the point of abandoning his law career and devoting himself totally to the new Gurukul. He became its manager, its chief proponent, and its moral guide. In 1903, Munshi Ram moved the Sat Dharm Pracharak press to the Gurukul where it remained under his control.[142] During the next five years Munshi Ram would succeed in creating in concrete terms a school patterned after the ideals of Dayanand and Guru Datta. Here militant hopes focused for the creation of the truly Aryan man. With the success of the Gurukul, the Bratri Sabha movement declined. A new world, when it was born, would come from the graduates of the Gurukul Kangri and schools similar to it. With the founding of this school, militant ideology had achieved a concrete expression of its ideals. The Gurukul, along with *shuddhi* and the Kanya Mahavidyalaya, while giving expression to militant Arya ideology, also marked a turning away from institutional innovation to a concern for the preservation and defense of these institutions. Like the moderate College faction, they too would need to maintain their organizational creations in a rapidly changing world of politics and government suppression. The Arya once created now needed to survive.

142. *Tribune*, November 21, 1902, p. 5.

## Chapter VIII

# THE MATURITY OF AN ELITE: MODERATES IN THE HINDU COMMUNITY

> I am too old now to continue to believe that the name Hindu was for the first time given to us as one involving abuse, contempt, and reproach by our Mohammedan invaders. Rather, I believe that our fall and degradation helped the fall of the word also, and perhaps a peep into the philosophical history of the word might prove that all bad meanings that are now assigned to the word in the Persian lexicon were of a comparatively later origin, and an outcome of the fall of the Hindu nation.
>
> LALA LAJPAT RAI

### THE DAYANAND ANGLO-VEDIC COLLEGE: FROM SCHOOL TO SYSTEM

In the wake of the division and redivision of the Samaj, moderate Aryas returned to their concentration on education. Prime among non-governmental education in the province, the Dayanand Anglo-Vedic College continued through its success and growth to provide a model of "native" enterprise. Its students repeatedly achieved distinction in the state examinations and dispersed throughout the province, forming a distinct element among educated Hindus, the "old boys" of the Dayanand Anglo-Vedic College. Yet leaders of the college found themselves faced with severe problems as a result of the division of 1893–1894. While they retained control of the Managing Committee and with that the property and assets of the college, they lost the allegiance of many local Samajes. If the militants possessed a structure without a cause, the moderates had a cause without a structure. First, the College Aryas would insure their continued control of the educational movement and then return to an endless search for funds.

The Managing Committee meeting in February 1895 represented only twenty-eight Samajes scattered through the Punjab, Sind, the Northwest Frontier and the United Provinces.[1] With a

1. The list of Samajes with the number of their representatives from each district is as follows: Lahore (10); Rawalpindi (3); Gurdaspur (1); Hissar (3); Feroze-

quorum reduced to ten members out of fifty-two, the Committee remained in the hands of Lala Lal Chand and a few Lahore colleagues.[2] Those in power carefully protected their position. They continued the policy of issuing certificates to each representative and requiring him to present it before attending any meeting of the Managing Committee.[3] Representatives were carefully screened and those Samajes which no longer supported the college had their representatives removed.[4] The Managing Committee grew slowly over the years, as new "College" Samajes were opened in competition with the original organizations now allied to the militant wing of Aryanism. Fortunately for the college, its strength lay beyond the Samaj in the general Hindu community. It appealed widely to Hindus of the commercial and Brahmanical castes who sought a safe education for their sons.

During the years following the division, leaders of the college managed to find sufficient funds to maintain and then expand the Lahore school and college. By 1900, the college enrolled 355 students. The years prior to 1914 witnessed an impressive sustained growth, as the college increased to 961 students in 1914, and the school section rose to 1,737.[5] This growth did not entail any seri-

---

pore (3); Peshawar (2); Gujrat (1); Sialkot (1); Jhelum (1); Dharmshala (1); Abbotabad (1); Hoshiarpur (1); Multan (3); Jullundur City (2); Quetta (1); Hirokh (1); Sibi (1); Sukkur (1); Dera Ismail Khan (1); Simla (1); Lucknow (1); Muradabad (1); Delhi (1); Ludhiana (1); Gujranwala (1); Pind Dadan Khan (1); and Jhang Majhiana (1). *Proceedings, Dayanand Anglo-Vedic College Managing Committee,* February 22, 1895.

2. *Proceedings, Dayanand Anglo-Vedic College managing Committee,* March 28, 1895. His closest associates included Lala Hans Raj, Lala Lajpat Rai, Lala Ishwar Das, Lala Sukh Dayal, Lala Amir Chand, Lala Sohan Lal, and Lala Sangam Lal; all attended meetings regularly.

3. *Proceedings, Dayanand Anglo-Vedic College Managing Committee.* May 12, 1895.

4. The Abbotabad Samaj lost its representative when it ended collection of funds for the college at its anniversary celebrations and through its *atta* fund. *Proceedings, Dayanand Anglo-Vedic College Managing Committee,* October 18, 1895. Similar questions arose over the representatives from Jhang and Quetta, see *Proceedings, Dayanand Anglo-Vedic College Managing Committee,* October 18, 1895, and May 30, 1896. Jhang, Abbotabad, and Quetta remained unrepresented on the new Managing Committee formed in 1898 in spite of attempts to gain such representation. See *Proceedings, Dayanand Anglo-Vedic College Managing Committee,* February 26, 1898.

5. *Dayanand Anglo-Vedic College Report, 1901–02,* p. 18; for the college enrollments, see *Ibid.,* p. 17, and *Report of the Dayanand Anglo-Vedic College, 1914,* p. 4.

ous deviation from the form and substance of the institution as it had been initially created. The student body was overwhelmingly Hindu and remained so.[6] The Dayanand Anglo-Vedic College steadily solidified its Hindu character. In 1896, the Managing Committee decided that it was unnecessary to publish an Urdu edition of the annual reports, but would merely publish an Urdu summary for the year 1895–1896.[7] Three years later Sanskrit replaced Persian. It became a compulsory language required of all students in the ninth class.[8] In 1914, Sanskrit received a further emphasis: all students from the high school were compelled to know it for the college entrance examinations.[9] Few Muslims found the atmosphere of the Dayanand Anglo-Vedic College congenial nor were they encouraged to do so. When one Ahmad Hassan applied for admission to the boarding house, his application was denied, ". . . the College Boarding House Sub-Committee . . . resolved that the Managing Committee can not allow any Mahommedan students to reside in the College Boarding House, as the Committee can not make proper and efficient arrangements for their residence."[10] Although the school did not refuse admission to Muslims, its general atmosphere of Aryanism and revived Hindu culture grew with both institutional and informal developments.

The creation of a system of boarding houses constructed and run by the Managing Committee produced a degree of communal life among the students. By 1914, 687 students lived in the College Boarding Houses under the guidance of Arya morality.[11] Many of these students, as well as others from the college and from other colleges in Lahore, joined the Young Men's Samaj. Founded in 1896 by Lala Hans Raj, the Young Men's Samaj offered students their own organization for service and social life.[12] Students par-

6. *Dayanand Anglo-Vedic College Report, 1901–02*, p. 18.

7. *Proceedings, Dayanand Anglo-Vedic College Managing Committee*, March 28, 1896.

8. *Proceedings, Dayanand Anglo-Vedic College Managing Committee*, March 19, 1899.

9. *Proceedings, Dayanand Anglo-Vedic College, 1911–1915*, June 7, 1914.

10. *Proceedings, Dayanand Anglo-Vedic College Managing Committee, 1909–10*, meeting of April 9, 1909, p. 2.

11. *Dayanand Anglo-Vedic College Report of the Managing Committee, 1914*, p. 10.

12. Sri Ram Sharma, *Mahatma Hans Raj, Maker of the Modern Punjab* (Jullundur: Arya Pradeshik Pratinidhi Sabha, 1941), p. 78.

ticipated in the Samaj, raised funds for Arya organizations and causes, attended lectures, and held meetings in similar fashion to the regular Arya Samaj. Students would provide much of the manpower for Arya efforts in orphan relief, disaster assistance, and later political action. By the twentieth century, the Dayanand Anglo-Vedic College student was a visible factor in the life of Lahore, a new social and political force to be reckoned with and at times feared by the authorities.

The college strengthened its Hindu character by subsidizing the study of Ayurvedic medicine, the medical science of traditional Hinduism. In 1901–1902, the Managing Committee began sending Rs. 20 to the Punjab University College to finance their Ayurvedic class.[13] Left over from the orientalist enthusiasm of Dr. Leitner, Ayurvedic studies became an increasing anomaly in the Government College. In 1904, the Government College transferred Ayurvedic studies to the Dayanand Anglo-Vedic College. The Managing Committee hoped to revive and make respectable this ancient art of healing, but this new department remained small with only thirty to forty students.[14]

The college also turned its attention to research in the Vedas and to the addition of a Theological Department. In 1910, the Managing Committee founded a research fellowship for "a critical study of ancient Aryan scriptures, for writing a treatise on the Vedic sanskars."[15] The institution could also boast of a Theological Department which by 1911 had thirty-four students and a Vedic Studies Department of thirty-seven students in 1914.[16] Descendants of Guru Datta's short-lived *updēshak* class, these programs sought to provide modernized trained missionaries and preachers for the Samaj. The efforts of the college, however, were overshadowed by the Gurukul Kangri's program to train men for the new Hindu world.

Concern among moderates for *swadēshī* led them in 1895 to open a class for engineers. The engineering department proved

13. *Dayanand Anglo-Vedic College Report, 1901–02*, p. 15.

14. A few enrollment figures will indicate the popularity of this course: 1911, forty-five students; 1913–14 and 1914, thirty-eight. See *Dayanand Anglo-Vedic College Reports, 1910–11*, p. 12; *Dayanand Anglo-Vedic College Report, 1912*, p. 10, and above mentioned *Report for 1914*.

15. *Dayanand Anglo-Vedic College Report, 1910–11*, p. 13.

16. *Ibid.*, p. 12, and *Dayanand Anglo-Vedic College Report, 1914*, p. 22.

successful and in 1903, the Mayo College of Arts proposed to move their engineering course to the Dayanand Anglo-Vedic College. From 1903 to 1914, the engineering course continued with government assistance as part of the transfer agreement.[17] This experiment in technical education ended in 1914, when the government school of engineering was moved from Lahore to Rasul. The Managing Committee decided to close this class which had up to then provided over 500 engineers for the province.[18] A more modest endeavor in tailoring continued, but by 1914 only contained six students.[19] No matter how one might preach the need for technical training and the patriotic duty to support industrial enterprise, those seeking education within the Punjabi Hindu community wanted that education in the standard arts subjects. Technical training had relatively low status and rarely appealed to the sons of the commercial and brahmanical castes.

Expansion in education meant a recreating of the Dayanand Anglo-Vedic College experience in school throughout the province. Local elites in town after town built their own institutions, sometimes with the aid and advice of the Managing Committee, at other times solely on their own initiative and resources. The National High School of Peshawar opened on June 5, 1895, to teach Hindu children under Hindu influence. Begun independently, the school faced financial difficulty until it accepted a government subsidy in 1913.[20] Problems of financing and management beset a similar school opened in Multan on May 12, 1896. Its founders soon turned to the Managing Committee for assistance, adding one more institution to the expanding Dayanand Anglo-Vedic system.[21] The Managing Committee continually gained schools. Occasionally they established new institutions themselves or in partnership with local Arya Samajes. Schools sprang up throughout the entire province: in Jullundur (1896), Simla (1896), Ambala City (1897), Jalalpur Jattan, Gujrat District (1897), Ferozepore

17. *Report, Dayanand Anglo-Vedic College Managing Committee, 1903–1907*, p. 6.

18. *Report, Dayanand Anglo-Vedic College Managing Committee, 1914*, p. 20.

19. *Dayanand Anglo-Vedic College Report, 1914*, p. 23.

20. Sri Ram Sharma, ed., *Our Education Mission. An Account of the Educational Work of the Samajes under the Arya Pradeshak Prati Nidhi Sabha, The Dayanand Anglo-Vedic College, Lahore* (Lahore: The Arya Pradeshik Pratinidhi Sabha, 1925), pp. 128–130.

21. Sharma, *Ibid.*, p. 105; and, *Tribune,* May 13, 1896, p. 4.

(1898), Karor (1898), Rawalpindi (1899), Kangra (1899), Hissar (1899), and Mubarkur, Kalsia State (1902). By 1910, the Managing Committee faced the need to frame rules for the affiliation of local schools.[22] Expansion continued, creating a variety of relationships ranging from direct control by the Managing Committee or by a special subcommittee to informal cooperation and discussion.[23]

The Managing Committee not only gave direction, expertise, and control for the educational activities of the moderate Samajists but was as well the only central institution for the Samaj branches allied to the college. The work of *prachār*, other than that carried out by individual Samajes, came under the direction of the Managing Committee. From 1894 through 1914, *updēshaks* were hired, fired, and supported by the Committee.[24] The number of *updēshaks* on the payroll varied from year to year but seldom exceeded a half a dozen.[25] In 1905, the college dispatched its most

22. *Tribune,* March 18, 1896, p. 4 and December 30, 1896, pp. 4–5; Sharma, *Our Education Mission,* pp. 85–86, 111–112.

23. The Dayanand Anglo-Vedic College Managing Committee discussed the opening of the Behrampur School in its meeting of June 19, 1910. On December 18, they considered applications of affilation from eight schools: (1) A. S. School, Hoshiarpur, (2) A. S. School, Multan, (3) A. S. School, Ambala, (4) A. S. School, Jullundur, (5) A.V.A.S. School, Abbotabad, (6) D.A.V. School, Rawalpindi, (7) H. M. School, Ferozepore, and (8) the D.A.V. School, Kangra. The Committee entered into a variety of relationships with these and other schools. On March 22, 1913, they drafted rules for control of a new school at Hafizabad in Gujranwala District. In this instance a special subcommittee was established to control the school in the same way that the Managing Committee supervised the Lahore school and college. See *Report of the Dayanand Anglo-Vedic College, 1909–10,* p. 16; *Proceedings, Dayanand Anglo-Vedic College Managing Committee, 1909–1910,* p. 29; *Report of the Dayanand Anglo-Vedic College, 1913,* p. 27; and *Proceedings, Dayanand Anglo-Vedic College Managing Committee, 1911–15,* pp. 35–36.

24. See *Proceedings, Dayanand Anglo-Vedic College Managing Committee,* Vol. IV, for meeting of November 20, 1898; *Dayanand Anglo-Vedic College Report, 1901–02,* p. 11; *Proceedings, Dayanand Anglo-Vedic College Managing Committee, 1909–10,* p. 26, for meeting of May 15, 1910; *Ibid.,* p. 59, for December 18, 1910; *Report, Dayanand Anglo-Vedic College Managing Committee, 1912,* p. 11; *Proceedings, Dayanand Anglo-Vedic College Managing Committee, 1911–15,* p. 2, for meeting of January 14, 1912; and *Ibid., Proceedings, Dayanand Anglo-Vedic College Managing Committee, 1911–15,* p. 23, for meeting of May 10, 1914.

25. The college *updēshaks* accepted various tasks as can be seen from the *Dayanand Anglo-Vedic College Report, 1901–02.* "In this year they had eight updeshaks working for the school. They attended anniversary ceremonies, worked on the Hindu Orphan Relief Movement, one worked as superintendent of the Boarding

famous missionary, Lala (later Bhai) Parma Nand, M.A. He traveled to Africa to popularize the work of the Samaj among Indian residents in the British Colonies.[26] After his tour of Africa Parma Nand returned to his professorship at the college and fame as one of the defendants in the Lahore Conspiracy Case.

In addition to its work with missionaries, the Managing Committee became prime publisher for the moderate Aryas. It supervised and supported the *Arya Gazette,* the leading voice of the "College" party. From 1897 to 1899, Lala Hans Raj and Lala Lajpat Rai jointly edited the *Gazette.*[27] In 1898, the Committee agreed in addition to provide a subsidy for the *Arya Messenger*[28] and also started the *Dayanand Anglo-Vedic College Magazine.* The Committee accepted the task of providing textbooks for its own use and for the growing number of Hindu-sponsored schools. By 1910, the Managing Committee had organized a group of its members to evaluate the entire curriculum of Hindi readers and to prepare new texts for the primary grades.[29] The lack of texts, particularly those with a proper, that is Arya, moral tone, posed a problem from the beginning and was only slowly met as Aryas produced their own educational literature.

The Managing Committee provided de facto leadership and coordination for its related Samajes. In 1903, leaders of this wing decided to establish a formal representative body, the Arya Pradeshak Pratinidhi Sabha (The Aryan Provincial Representative Society). This new organization, patterned after the older Arya Pratinidhi Sabha,[30] did not replace the Managing Commit-

House—at the end of the year one had quit, two had been lent by Hissar and Ft. Sandeman Samajes respectively. The updesh work suffered from lack of qualified men and from lack of money." *Report, Dayanand Anglo-Vedic College, 1901–02,* p. 11.

26. *Proceedings, Dayanand Anglo-Vedic College Managing Committee, 1903–07,* pp. 12–13.

27. Sharma, *Mahatma Hans Raj,* pp. 249–250; and *Tribune,* April 28, 1897, p. 4.

28. *Proceedings, Dayanand Anglo-Vedic College Managing Committee,* Vol. IV, for the meeting of December 17, 1898.

29. *Proceedings, Dayanand Anglo-Vedic College Managing Committee, 1909–10,* pp. 50–51, for meeting of October 23, 1910.

30. Indra Vidyavachaspati, *Ārya Samāj kā Itihās,* Vol. II (Delhi: Sarvadeshak Arya Pratinidhi Sabha, 1957), p. 112. Among the founding members were: Lala Lal Chand, Mahatma Hans Raj, Lala Lajpat Rai, and Rai Sahab Mul Raj.

tee but lived in its shadow and was, in fact, a creature of that committee. Leadership and power remained in the hands of the college trustees. Even though the Pratinidhi Sabha was charged with the task of *prachār*, the Managing Committee did not transfer their *updēshaks* to the Sabha until 1914.[31] The power of the Managing Committee remained and rested largely on its control of an ever-growing pool of capital, patronage, and its physical resources.

The total assets of the College Society stood at Rs. 396,410 by March 31, 1902.[32] During the next decade these assets grew rapidly to Rs. 1,138,272 by the end of 1914.[33] Income for the school and college still depended heavily on donations by the local Samaj branches, particularly the Lahore Samaj in Anarkali which in 1910–1911 raised three-fourths of the total funds donated from this source.[34] School fees and interest both from individual loans and bank deposits provided a rising income for the school. The very size of their capital funds worried Dayanand Anglo-Vedic officials who anticipated a decline in individual donations by those who were "lulled into the fond belief that the long sought-for millenium has been reached."[35] While not a millenium, the school rested on a sound economic basis, sufficient to maintain its policy of not accepting government grants.[36]

The economic strength of the Dayanand Anglo-Vedic movement insured continued independence and expansion; it also tied the Managing Committee to the world of the educated Hindu. Through donations the Committee became a shareholder in various Punjabi enterprises. Representatives of the Managing Committee attended meetings as stockholders of companies which

31. *Report, Dayanand Anglo-Vedic College Managing Committee, 1914*, p. 25.

32. *Report, Dayanand Anglo-Vedic College, 1901–02*, p. 1.

33. These figures include assets in land, buildings, stock in various companies, fixed bank deposits, monies held for affiliated schools, donations to special funds, and cash on hand. Sharma, *Mahatma Hans Raj*, p. 115, and *Report, Dayanand Anglo-Vedic College, 1914*, p. 26.

34. *Report, Dayanand Anglo-Vedic College, 1910–11*, p. 28. The Lahore Samaj, Anarkali, sent in Rs. 33,672-14-1 out of a total for that year of Rs. 41,923-3-7, while the Wacchowali Samaj donated a mere Rs. 12.

35. *Report, Dayanand Anglo-Vedic College, 1914*, p. 26.

36. *Proceedings, Dayanand Anglo-Vedic College Managing Committee, 1911–15*, p. 55, for November 20, 1912.

often were controlled by other College Aryas.[37] Although its stockholdings were small and scattered throughout several companies, the Managing Committee did become heavily involved in one financial institution, the Punjab National Bank. Initially, college funds were deposited in various banks for short periods, often three or six months, at fixed interest rates. School officials gradually consolidated these accounts so that by 1911 they had Rs. 299,403 in one fixed deposit with the Punjab National Bank.[38] The college not only held the majority of its funds in the Punjab National Bank but also did most of its business through the bank. The Punjab National Bank became the "college" bank tied by mutual interest and overlapping personnel to the educational movement and to moderate Aryas.

The Managing Committee also acted as a private banker, issuing loans to Samaj organizations and individuals. The Committee provided loans to Arya Samaj branches in Quetta, Rawalpindi, Simla, and Dera Ismail Khan for the purchase of land and the construction of Samaj temples.[39] Individuals applying to the Committee received amounts as high as Rs. 30,000, though private loans of this size were rare.[40] No communal pattern appeared in the Committee loans. Sikh aristocrats, specifically Sardar Dyal Singh

37. The D. A.-V. Society held stock in a number of enterprises including the Delhi Cloth Mills, the Lahore Spinning and Weaving Mills, the Punjab Cooperative Bank, the Cooperative Assurance Company, the General Mills Company of Amritsar, the Delhi Flour and General Mills, and the Punjab National Bank. See *Proceedings, Dayanand Anglo-Vedic College Managing Committee,* Vol. IV, special meeting of April 25, 1896; *Proceedings, Dayanand Anglo-Vedic College Managing Committee, 1906–1908,* pp. 58–59, November 8, 1908; *Proceedings, Investment Sub-Committee,* Vol. II, February 23, 1909; *Proceedings, Dayanand Anglo-Vedic College Managing Committee, 1909–10,* p. 31, for June 19, 1910; *Proceedings, Investment Sub-Committee,* Vol. II, April 9, 1911; and *Proceedings, Dayanand Anglo-Vedic College Managing Committee, 1911–15,* August 11, 1912.

38. See *Report, Dayanand Anglo-Vedic College, 1910–11,* pp. 29, 30, 31, Appendix E, containing a full account of all balances and investments of the Committee.

39. *Proceedings, Investment Sub-Committee,* Vol. I, for December 3, 1897; *Proceedings, Dayanand Anglo-Vedic College Managing Committee* for January 25, 1896; *Proceedings, Investment Sub-Committee,* Vol. I for June 18, 1896; *Ibid.,* for December 3, 1897; *Proceedings, Dayanand Anglo-Vedic College Managing Committee,* Vol. IV, for October 29, 1898; *Ibid.,* for June 26, 1899; *Proceedings, Investment Sub-Committee,* Vol. II, for March 20, 1908; *Ibid.,* for April 9, 1911; and *Ibid.,* October 1, 1913.

40. *Proceedings, Investment Sub-Committee,* Vol. II, meeting of December 22, 1913.

Majithia and Sardar Kirpal Singh, received the largest share of such loans.[41] Muslims and Hindus also applied for and were granted private loans. The Investment Sub-Committee was far more interested in collateral than community. The college then acted both as a bank and in support of banking institutions founded by members of the Hindu elite. Close ties between college Aryas and various enterprises angered non-Aryas such as Lala Harkishen Lal, yet typified the linkages of interest undergirding the Dayanand Anglo-Vedic College system. These links also illustrate the power centralized in the Managing Committee, power and influence far beyond its avowed educational role.

The Managing Committee sat at the center of the educational movement, of the college Aryas and their allies among educated Punjabi Hindus. During the years 1895 to 1900, this committee remained in the hands of Lala Lal Chand and those closely associated with him. After the split between militants and moderates, no group existed within the Managing Committee which could or cared to contest the leadership of Lala Lal Chand, Lala Hans Raj, Lajpat Rai, Lala Sukh Dyal, and Lala Ishwar Das.[42] With the new century a gradual change took place in the leadership of the college party. After 1900, Lal Chand played a diminishing role in decision making, attending meetings of the Managing Committee and its subcommittees less frequently. The years between 1900 and 1906 marked a transition period, as Ishwar Das, Lajpat Rai, and Lala Sukh Dyal, along with Lal Chand, gradually reduced their participation in college affairs. A new generation of men entered the college staff and acquired greater power within the movement. During the last five years of the nineteenth century, several young men followed the example of Hans Raj and offered to serve the college in an honorary capacity.[43] By 1900, Lala Hans

41. See *Proceedings, Investment Sub-Committee,* Vol. I, meetings of January 11, 1895, and January 13, 1896; also, *Ibid.,* Vol. II, meeting of April 6, 1909; *Ibid.,* August 18, 1909; and *Ibid.,* February 8, 1911.

42. Lala Lal Chand served as president of the Managing Committee from 1886–1895, 1896–1900, and 1902–1903. He also chaired the investment subcommittee and the school and college subcommittee.

43. Lala Jaswant Rai, M.A., and Lala Balmokand, B.A., first served the college as honorary staff. They were followed by Lala Ishwar Das Sahni, M.A., and Bakshi Tek Chand, son of Bakhshi Jaishi Ram. Sharma, *Mahatma Hans Raj,* pp. 104–105.

Raj decided to inaugurate an order of Life Members who would agree to teach in the Dayanand Anglo-Vedic schools for a basic stipend of Rs. 75 per month. First to join the college under these terms was Lala Gokal Chand Narang.[44] In this manner the school received at a minimal cost the services of distinguished, highly educated young men who later became leaders within the college movement. They would soon share power with the older generation.

By 1906, three young men, Lala Durga Das, Lala Dwarka Das, and Bakhshi Tek Chand, had joined the Managing Committee and moved into positions of considerable authority.[45] Beginning in spring 1906, the Managing Committee opened a long debate over the question of constructing a college building on the Committee's land at Ichhra, outside of Lahore City. This debate set allies of Lal Chand against supporters of Lala Hans Raj. In a series of votes the majority sided repeatedly with Lala Hans Raj and decided finally to purchase land within the city.[46] A debate next ensued over the question of timing and once again Lal Chand lost.[47] In January 1908, factional strife reached its height in a struggle over the presidency. The Managing Committee meeting degenerated into name calling between the two factions, with Lajpat Rai facing Mul Raj in a verbal duel. Finally, Lala Dwarka Das was elected president, following which Lal Chand left the meeting ac-

44. After Gokal Chand Narang, next to join the Life Members was Lala Sain Das, M.A., then Lala Diwan Chand, M.A., Lala Paramanand, M.A., Pandit Mehr Chand, B.A., and Lala Devi Chand, M.A. Sharma, *Mahatma Hans Raj,* pp. 105–106.

45. Durga Das had first joined the Managing Committee in 1900. For the next decade he served on the Committee faithfully, attending with a regularity matched only by Bahkshi Tek Chand. Together they formed the nucleus of a new core within the Committee. Dwarka Das joined with them during the years 1907–1909. All three men remained personally close to Lala Hans Raj and on occations voted against Lala Lal Chand and his diminishing band of allies.

46. See *Proceedings, Dayanand Anglo-Vedic College Managing Committee, 1903–07,* p. 12, meeting of April 14, 1906; *Ibid.,* p. 14, meeting of April 15, 1906; *Ibid.,* pp. 13–14, meeting of February 17, 1907; *Ibid.,* pp. 16–17, meeting of March 3, 1907; and *Ibid.,* p. 24, meeting of March 30, 1907.

47. *Proceedings, Dayanand Anglo-Vedic College Managing Committee, 1903–07,* p. 29, meeting of April 5, 1907; *Ibid.,* p. 41, meeting of August 11, 1907; *Ibid.,* pp. 56–59, meeting of December 8, 1907; *Proceedings, Dayanand Anglo-Vedic College Managing Committee, 1906–08,* pp. 4–5, meeting of January 25, 1908.

companied by several of his allies.[48] He would serve only one more year, 1910–1911, as president of the Managing Committee before his death in 1912.

Drawn into the world of Hindu politics, Lal Chand's influence and participation in the college faded as power rested with three men, Lala Hans Raj, Bakshi Tek Chand, and Lala Durga Das. Together they controlled the Managing Committee and its subcommittees. The resignation in 1911 of Lala Hans Raj as principal of the college did not see any diminution of his influence, since he replaced Lal Chand as president from 1911 to 1918.

The Dayanand Anglo-Vedic school system stood in 1914 as a monument to the abilities and dedication of two men, Lala Lal Chand and Lala Hans Raj, plus a host of able Aryas. It was as well a concrete expression of the Punjabi Hindu elite's dream of achieving economic and social status, of educating their sons in a safe Hindu environment. Hindus throughout northwestern India also sought a "safe" education. As a result, the Dayanand Anglo-Vedic school system expanded far beyond Punjab and also beyond the limits of the Samaj. It taught Hindu youths of all sects and persuasions, producing a growing class of young men who shared similar educational backgrounds, expectations, and frustrations.

### TOWARD A WIDER COMMUNITY: THE HINDU ORPHAN RELIEF MOVEMENT

From its inception the Samaj contained the concept of service to the general Hindu community. It would revive, enlighten, and care for all Hindus who accepted its truth and even for those who did not. The first institution of Arya service opened in 1877, when Rai Mathura Das established the Ferozepore Orphanage.[49] For many years this was the only orphanage under Arya control, and it grew but slowly. By the end of 1882, the Ferozepore Orphanage housed nineteen orphans, with an average attendance during the

48. *Proceedings, Dayanand Anglo-Vedic College Managing Committee, 1906–08,* pp. 22–23; Sharma, *Mahatma Hans Raj,* p. 107.

49. The government donated the land and Lalas Shankar Das and Banka Mal Rs. 20,000 each for its beginning. Others contributed generously, including the Maharana of Udaipur, Lala Ram Sukh Das, Mr. Din Shaw, and the Maharaja of Faridkot. See Pandit Vishnu Lal Sharma, *Handbook of the Arya Samaj* (Allahabad: The Indian Press, 1912), p. 99, and the *Regenerator of Arya Varta,* Vol. I, No. 7, March 19, 1883, p. 5.

following year of only seventeen. The number fluctuated as children moved in and out of the institution. During the remainder of the decade the orphanage averaged between twenty to thirty children.[50] A girls' school originally intended to educate the orphans proved far more successful and grew steadily, as it admitted students from the wider Hindu community. The success of this school tended to divert resources from the orphanage itself, limiting its expansion.[51] Funded primarily by the people of Ferozepore, the orphanage appealed to all communities. It accepted orphans regardless of caste or religion. Muslim children accounted for approximately one-third of its orphans.[52] By 1892, the orphanage managed to purchase land just outside of the cantonment and a year later began construction of a permanent building.[53] As a charity of the Samaj, somewhat outside of its main developmental stream, the orphanage stood more for an ideal of service than a reality of commitment.

As the year 1896 drew to a close, the stable world of orphan relief was disrupted by famine. Reports of starving peasants, of homeless children, and of Christian missionary efforts at relief reached Samajists in the Punjab. The Ferozepore Orphanage responded with an incredible offer: "The Committee are prepared to take charge of *any orphan child,* male or female, sent to them *from any part of the country*. Many a Hindu waif should thus be saved from being brought up in a Christian asylum."[54] Brave words, far beyond the ability of the orphanage itself. Lala Lajpat Rai and his associates in the Lahore Samaj led the ensuing campaign of orphan relief. In February 1897, Lajpat addressed a meeting in Anarkali to raise money for what became the Hindu Orphan Relief Movement.[55] During the spring Lajpat Rai continued to publicize his new cause, to gather followers, and to collect funds. In May he called for Punjabi Hindus to accept 50,000 children from

50. *Regenerator of Arya Varta,* September 24, 1884, p. 2; also see *Arya Patrika,* August 17, 1886, pp. 1–2; October 11, 1887, pp. 5–6; and *Tribune,* April 3, 1889, p. 4.

51. *Arya Patrika,* January 23, 1886, pp. 3–5.

52. *Arya Patrika,* November 7, 1885, pp. 4–5; May 18, 1886, p. 8; and *Tribune,* April 3, 1899, p. 4.

53. *Tribune,* February 6, 1892, p. 3; September 27, 1893, p. 4.

54. *Tribune,* December 5, 1896, p. 4. [Italics mine.]

55. *Tribune,* February 3, 1897, p. 4. For his own account, see Lajpat Rai, *The Arya Samaj* (London: Longmans, Green and Co., 1915), pp. 212–213.

the Central Provinces so that they might not fall into the hands of the missionaries.[56] His campaign was helped immeasurably by stories of suffering, of destitute peasants and homeless children, and bitter tales of missionary exploitation. The famine and the missionaries became interlinked in the minds of many Punjabis. ". . . it is an open secret that the Christian Missionaries in India have taken advantage of the famine to swell the number of their converts by taking over the children of the famine-stricken Hindus and Muhammadans."[57] Although missionaries defended their actions on humanitarian grounds, no such argument convinced the educated Punjabi.

By June, the *Tribune* could report with obvious joy that all sections of the Hindu community, Aryas, Sanatanists, and Sikhs, had taken up the work of orphan relief.[58] Individual organizations now applied for governmental permission to care for groups of orphans. Meanwhile, Pandit Shiv Dutt Ram of Amritsar traveled to the Central Provinces to arrange for the dispatch of orphans to the Punjab. He also founded a temporary orphanage at Jabbulpore as a collection point in the famine-affected area. The need for official approval brought Hindu relief workers into direct confrontation with the government. A three-way struggle developed between the missionaries, Hindu relief workers, and the government over who should be allowed to take charge of destitute and orphaned children. Stories of official obstinacy soon appeared, as time passed and the government failed to approve applications by Hindu organizations.[59] While still awaiting government permission, the first group of orphans arrived from Jabbulpore, fifty children in the care of Lala Bisheshar Das. They were met with due celebration and the Lahore Committee opened its orphanage amidst an atmosphere of Hindu solidarity.[60]

56. *Arya Gazette*, May 17, 1897, *SPVP 1897*, p. 410.

57. Quotes given below from *Tāj-ul-Akhbār*, April 3, 1897, Government of India, *Selections from the Vernacular Newspapers Published in the Punjab, 1897*, pp. 254–255. Also see the anti-missionary comments in *Punjāb Samāchār*, June 9, 1897 *SPVP 1897*, p. 56, and *Bhārat Sudhār*, June 9, 1897, p. 497. An earlier tussle over the guardianship of an orphan is recorded in the *Tribune*, July 1, 1896, p. 4.

58. The *Tribune* included Singh Sabhas among the Hindu organizations active in their movement, *Tribune*, June 16, 1897, pp. 3–4.

59. *Tribune*, July 3, 1897, p. 3.

60. *Tribune*, July 14, 1897, p. 4; also July 17, 1897, p. 4; and, August 4, 1897, p 2.

In August, the government finally permitted the Hindu Orphan Relief Association to accept 200 orphans.[61] Official approval of other applications came only slowly and grudgingly. In fact, for many applicants it did not come at all. By 1898, the Hindu Orphan Relief Movement had rescued approximately 250 orphans who were brought to the Punjab and dispersed throughout the province.[62] In addition to the Ferozepore and Lahore orphanages, the Kanya Mahavidyalaya in cooperation with the Jullundur Samaj opened its Kanya Ananthalaya, or orphanage for girls. Their own agent traveled to the Central Provinces and returned with fifty-two orphans, nineteen of whom remained at the Kanya Ananthalaya. These orphans joined the students at the Mahavidyalaya.[63] By mid-1898, this first round of the orphan movement ended with its modest achievement. Yet it provided a useful lesson in communal cooperation and a practical exercise in the problems associated with orphan relief.

Hardly had the first crisis subsided when news of a second and more extensive famine began to reach the Punjab. In November 1899, Lajpat Rai once again called for funds to save the destitute, and the Ferozepore Orphanage reiterated its willingness to accept orphans from the stricken areas. This time crop failure extended throughout Gujarat and Rajasthan as well as the Central Provinces.[64] Experience gained in 1897–1898 enabled Hindus to mobilize quickly, expand their orphanage facilities, and send agents into the affected areas.[65] Within November, Aryas found 175 orphans and sent some of them to the Ferozepore Orphanage.[66] The movement to save the destitute spread with the famine

61. *Tribune,* August 7, 1897, p. 4.

62. The total figures for this first round of orphan relief are not available. Lajpat Rai states that "About 250 Hindu children were rescued by agents deputed by the movement and were brought into the Punjab . . . ," while Sharma, in the *Handbook of the Arya Samaj,* gives the number as about 1,000. Lajpat Rai's estimate is in all probability the more accurate. See Lajpat Rai, *The Arya Samaj,* pp. 212–213, and Sharma, *Handbook of the Arya Samaj,* p. 93.

63. *Annual Report, Kanya Mahavidyalaya,* April 11, 1898, p. 14; and Lahore *Tribune,* February 11, 1899, p. 5.

64. *Tribune,* November 2, 1899, p. 5.

65. *Tribune,* November 23, 1899, notes donors to the revived Orphan Relief Movement.

66. *Tribune,* December 9, 1899, p. 3. By this time the Bhiwani Orphanage had seventy-three children under its care.

into southeastern Punjab. Through the remainder of 1899 and the spring of 1900, Aryas continued to extend their program.[67] Additional funds were acquired and soon a growing stream of orphans reached the Punjab. By April, the newly-established Bhiwani Orphanage had accepted 349 children and by September the Ferozepore Orphanage contained 1,135 orphans. Many of those admitted to various orphanages remained only a short while until they were reunited with family or relatives; nevertheless, those remaining strained existing resources to the breaking point.[68] Hindus founded additional institutions to handle this growing tide of refugees.[69] Throughout this campaign students and faculty at the Dayanand Anglo-Vedic College participated both in the collection of funds and in the search for destitute children. With practice mobilization of college students proved relatively easy, creating a pool of talent and energy that could be used to support a variety of causes.[70]

Fear of Christian missionary successes during famine periods drove Hindu leaders to sustain and whenever possible extend their orphanage systems and associated relief work. Stories of missionary cunning, of their vast resources and dedication heightened this fear, as speeches and journals stressed the unequal nature of the contest. "Our ruin is the prosperity of the Christians. Our woes are their blessings. When our crops fail, theirs are the richest. The famine of Rajputana makes a heyday for them. They are always on the watch for such opportunities and the visitation of heavenly wrath upon the poor people of India affords them golden opportunities to add hundreds and thousands of the starving Indians to their fold."[71] Writers repeatedly blamed the Hindu community for its apathy, callousness, and internal divisiveness which allowed Christian missionaries to prey upon the miseries of

67. See *Tribune*, December 12, 1899, p. 6; January 9, 1900, p. 4; March 22, 1900, p. 5; June 16, 1900, p. 3.

68. See *Tribune*, April 19, 1900, pp. 4–5; May 29, 1900, p. 4; and, September 20, 1900, p. 4.

69. *Tribune*, May 10, 1900, p. 5.

70. *Tribune*, December 12, 1899, p. 4; Lajpat Rai, *The Arya Samaj*, pp. 213–214; Sharma, *Mahatma Hans Raj*, pp. 183 and 192.

71. Quotes given below from *Arya Messenger*, March 7, 1902, *SPVP 1902*, pp. 141–142. For similar comments, see *Public Gazette*, February 16, 1902, *SPVP 1902*, p. 128; and *Arya Gazette*, August 28, 1902, *SPVP 1902*, p. 474.

the Hindu community.[72] "When one thinks of the cruel indifference and neglect of which Hindus are guilty towards their own orphans, one has to blush for his community and hang down his head in shame and mortification. Even savages like the Zulus and Hottentots are wont to stand up for their kind at a pinch, and strike a blow in defence of their faith."

Hindus faced as well the power of the government in an apparent alliance with the missionaries. The government's position, however, did change. In October 1901, Lala Mela Ram, president of the Simla Arya Samaj, was arrested in a custody case between the Samaj and a Christian missionary. In April 1902, after months of hearings, the suit was settled in favor of the Samaj. This case established the principle that "relief from physical distress of a minor during famine does not make the relieving organization or any one of its nominees the lawful guardian of the minor."[73] Christian missionaries could not then claim or bestow guardianship over children in their care. In 1901, Lajpat Rai helped persuade the Famine Commission to accept the principle that children "should not be made over to persons or institutions of different religions until all efforts to find persons or institutions, of their own religion willing to take charge of them have failed."[74] This principle was reaffirmed by the courts in 1904.[75] The weight of law had moved to assist non-Christians in orphan relief, although local officials might still act to aid the missionaries and impede Hindu relief efforts.[76] Changed governmental policy, as well as increased efficiency of the Hindu Orphan Relief Movement, increased to 1,700 the number of orphans brought to the Punjab by 1904.

Plague reached the Punjab during 1901 and spread into the most densely populated districts. During the years 1901–1907, plague ravaged the province, turning public concern to its special horrors as the threat of famine eased. Bubonic plague did not produce in its wake the same organized response as had famine.

72. *Panjabee*, November 7, 1904, pp. 4–5.

73. Sharma, *Mahatma Hans Raj*, pp. 185–186; also see, Lajpat Rai, *The Arya Samaj*, p. 273; and Madan Mohan Seth, *The Arya Samaj, A Political Body, An Open Letter to Viscount Morley* (Gurukul Kangri: n.d.), pp. 44–45.

74. Lajpat Rai, *Writings and Speeches, Vol. I, 1888–1919*, ed. V. C. Joshi (Delhi: University Publishers, 1966), p. xxv.

75. *Panjabee*, October 10, 1904, p. 3; also see October 3, 1904; and for a discussion of a similar case in Madras, August 28, 1907, p. 5.

76. Lajpat Rai, *The Arya Samaj*, pp. 215–217.

Aryas called for the proper use of *havans* to cleanse the air and end the disease; occasionally local Aryas dispensed medicine or other assistance to plague victims.[77] Plague lasted throughout the decade, but public attention was diverted by a massive earthquake in the Kangra Hills on April 4, 1905. The swift response of the Arya Samaj to this disaster marked the opening of a new campaign of social service. By 1906, the Kangra Relief Fund held Rs. 1,351,749, almost all of which was spent on direct assistance in the disaster area.[78] As in the Orphan Relief Movement, all elements of the Hindu community participated, but leadership and manpower rested heavily with the college section of the Samaj, particularly with Lala Lajpat Raj.[79] Experience in the orphan movement and in the various Samajic campaigns enabled Aryas to organize, fund, and execute relief operations on a growing scale and with increased efficiency. In addition, Aryas furnished leadership for the broader Hindu community of Punjab in areas beyond Arya ideology where all Hindus could stand together. Lajpat Rai, Lala Lal Chand, and members of the college faction began to move out of the specific world of the Samaj into the wider Hindu community. In this they pointed to a future of increasing political consciousness, a world transitional between the nineteenth and twentieth centuries.

## ARYAS, HINDUS, AND THE INDIAN NATIONAL CONGRESS

At all times a colonial milieu possesses forms of political action, arenas in which power is sought, decisions made, and privileges granted. These forms, however, do not necessarily coincide with democracy or even modern totalitarian structures. Using a Weberian definition of politics as "striving to share power or striving to influence the distribution of power, either among states or among groups within a state,"[80] one can identify two types of overt politics in the Punjab of the 1880s, with the beginning of a third. First and

77. See *Arya Gazette,* April 4, 1901, *SPVP 1901,* pp. 233–234; *Arya Gazette,* February 6, 1902, *SPVP 1902,* p. 106; *Sat Dharm Prachārak,* April 18, 1902, *SPVP 1902,* p. 291; *Sat Dharm Prachārak,* June 28, 1902, *SPVP 1902,* pp. 374–375; *Tribune,* November 27, 1902, p. 4; May 21, 1904, p. 4; and May 28, 1904, p. 3.

78. *Panjabee,* January 17, 1906, p. 3.

79. This pattern is evident from a list of donors given in the *Panjabee,* April 17, 1905, p. 3. Also, see Sharma, *Mahatma Hans Raj,* pp. 186–187.

80. Max Weber, *From Max Weber: Essays in Sociology,* trans. and ed. H. H. Gerth and C. Wright Mills (New York: Oxford Univ. Press, 1958), p. 78.

most clearly political were the elected boards created by Lord Ripon's Local Self-Government Act of 1881. Under this legislation municipal boards with limited powers and even more limited electorates introduced the principle of political competition, as it is commonly understood in democratic countries. This legislation stirred educated Punjabis, coming as it did in a vacuum of formal politics, and quickly led to the mobilization of public opinion. Ruchi Ram Sahni recalled that "We read the discussions in the *C. & M. Gazette* on the one side and the *Tribune* on the other. We also attended the public meetings in support of the resolution. We also held our own meeting in the Boarding House at which we resolved to go round to the nearby towns and villages and address public meetings explaining the objects and importance of the reforms."[81] After returning home, Ruchi Ram Sahni attempted to politicize his fellow Hindus. "During vacation when I went to my native town, Behra, I got together three or four meetings, mostly of shopkeepers along with a few school teachers, and set out to them as well as I could, the aims and objects of the new reforms, and what good it was going to do to the people. I also went round to some of the villages in the neighborhood and addressed similar meetings." The techniques of public agitation learned by Ruchi Ram while still a student in the Government College in Lahore would be used in electioneering for local office. Punjabi response to this opportunity for political action took the form of communal competition. The Municipal Committees "soon became foci of religious antagonism. Hindus, Sikhs, and Muslims fought for control of the new structures. Victory meant prestige and patronage, defeat, loss of influence and 'face.'"[82] Communal rather than regional or national orientations determined loyalty in the first openly political arena. As in the competition for jobs, the Hindu commercial castes succeeded while Muslims, in spite of their numerical superiority, failed to gain either power or prestige.

A more pervasive and earlier form of politics stemmed from the nature of bureaucratic decision making within the British Raj. As a colonial bureaucracy, the British-Indian government utilized

81. Quotes given below from Ruchi Ram Sahni, "Self-Revelations of an Octogenarian," unpublished manuscript in the possession of V. C. Joshi, Nehru Memorial Museum, pp. 117–118.

82. N. G. Barrier, "The Punjab Government and Communal Politics, 1870–1908," *Journal of Asian Studies*, XXVII, No. 3, (May 1968), p. 529.

commissions as a link between itself and those whom it governed. In issues of policy where officialdom wished to gather evidence and consult "public opinion," the government created a commission which held hearings and issued a final report as the basis for future legislation. Commissions became, in fact, invitations to public agitation. Once the government declared its intention to consider a particular issue, interested groups would organize their followers through meetings, press statements, and delegations in the hope of influencing the commission's final decision and thus governmental action. Repeatedly these commissions stirred Punjabis to communal mobilization. The Hunter Commission on Education produced an intense struggle over the use of Hindi versus Urdu in the schools. The Aitchison Commission created similar controversy, when it investigated the question of communal "balance" in government employment. The commission approach to decision making produced two fundamental attitudes: first, that those who made the most noise might succeed in determining government policy to their own profit, and, second, that nothing was ever considered final. There always existed the hope that another commission, with another round of public pressure, might reverse an earlier decision. Issues did not die, they merely oscillated between active and dormant states.

Not all commissions or governmental actions stirred communal passions. Occasionally issues tended to unite all against the British. The Ilbert Bill, which threatened the privileges of the white ruling class, united all "natives" in a common front against the bill's opponents. Similarly, the imprisonment of Surendra Nath Banerjea and the Idol Contempt Case proved to be "national" questions transcending regional and religious differences. The growing class of English speakers with similar educational experiences and common frustrations in relation to the colonial regime, plus modernized communications, created the beginnings of a public consciousness and a new politics that encompassed the whole of British India. In fact, much of this consciousness rested on the Bengali communities spread throughout northern India. Bengali Brahmos and their allies played a crucial role in Punjab. Their leadership established an awareness of the greater world that was stronger in the Punjab of the 1880s than it was in the mid-1890s.

Surendra Nath Banerjea's trip to Punjab in 1877 and his later tour of 1884 brought a new "national" politics to the attention of educated Punjabis. He helped as well to create in Lahore a small nucleus of politically conscious leaders. During his first trip he met and became friends with Sardar Dyal Singh Majithia. Out of this friendship came the *Tribune* and its Bengali staff. Also Dyal Singh furnished much of the financial support for the newly-organized Lahore Indian Association, while Bengalis, such as Kali Prosanna Roy, P. C. Chatterjee, and Novin Chandra Rai, supplied leadership in public causes. Among Punjabi Hindus, Bakshi Jaishi Ram, Lala Lajpat Rai, Lala Murli Dhar, and later Lala Harkishen Lal became active in purely political associations. Their participation, with the exception of Jaishi Ram, was rather sporadic. Provincial issues and the Arya Samaj remained far more attractive than either the Indian Association, the Lahore Students Association, or the newly-organized Indian National Congress.

Punjabis showed little enthusiasm for the Congress. Only two delegates attended the first Congress session in Bombay, Pandit Murli Dhar, a pleader from Ambala, and the Brahmo militant, Shiv Narayan Agnihotri. The following year, 1886, the Lahore Indian Association chose a delegation of fourteen in a last minute effort to insure Punjabi representation.[83] The 1887 delegation consisted of only nine men, "two Arya pleaders from western towns, two Hindu pleaders, an erratic editor known for his libelous articles [Pandit Gopi Nath], and the two perennial delegates, Murli Dhar and Agnihotri." The year 1888 marked the first upsurge of Punjab interest in the Congress. Their delegation numbered eighty, a dramatic increase over the previous year, although still small in comparison with other provincial delegations.[84] Punjabi Hindu leaders became involved in the Congress following the anti-Congress statements of Sayyid Ahmad Khan in 1887. Congress politics took on the characteristic of communal competition, of an issue between Hindus and Muslims, and as such appealed particularly to Arya Samajists.[85] Also during the years 1887 and 1888 the British-Indian government became increasingly uneasy about the Congress. It moved from a posture of be-

83. N. G. Barrier, "Punjab Politics and the Disturbances of 1907," Ph.D. dissertation, Duke University, 1966, p. 42.

84. Annie Besant, *How India Wrought for Freedom: The Story of the National Congress Told from Official Records* (Adyar, Madras: The Theosophical Publishing House, 1915), p. 58.

85. Barrier, "Punjab Politics and the Disturbances of 1907," p. 50.

nevolent tolerance to active opposition. Public controversy over the Congress helped to popularize it, to make it a "cause." Punjabis attended the Congress in the hope that they could persuade it to accept their own methods of national revival, namely, "swadeshi and self-help."[86] Lala Lajpat Rai joined the Congress at this time and attended as a delegate, beginning a long but uneven involvement in that organization.[87] Lajpat's oscillating participation typified Punjabi Hindu reaction to the Congress.

Punjabi interest in the National Congress dropped off over the next three years. Issues within the province dominated the educated elite, while the Congress, in the opinion of many Punjabis, remained a tool of politicians from Bengal and Bombay.[88] Punjabis sent smaller and smaller delegations: sixty-two in 1889; eighteen in 1890; and five in 1891.[89] Aryas were often critical or indifferent to the Congress, while many Bengalis held positions with the Punjab Government and thus could not openly support it.[90] Political activity such as it was tended to center around the *Tribune*, Majithia, and his allies.[91] The emergence of the Congress, a clearly political association, posed problems for Aryas. What should be the official position of the Samaj toward the Congress and generally toward the world of political action? As early as 1886, the Samaj attempted to separate its organizational role from the acts of individual members. The *Arya Patrika* for March 8, 1886, commented "The object for the realization of which the movement of the Arya Sasmaj has been started is mainly religious and social. . . . If energetic patriotic Arya Samajists do take an active part in the political regeneration of Aryavarta, it should be distinctly understood that they *do so* as patriotic *citizens*, and not at all as *members* of the Arya Samaj."[92] The Samaj reiterated this position both officially and unofficially throughout the next decade.

Arya reluctance to openly support political organizations and

86. Barrier, "The Arya Samaj and Congress Politics in the Punjab, 1894–1908," *Journal of Asian Studies,* XXVI, No. 3 (May 1967), p. 368.

87. Barrier, "Punjab Politics and the Disturbances of 1907," pp. 90–91; and Besant, *How India Wrought for Freedom,* p. 62.

88. Barrier, "Punjab Politics and the Disturbances of 1907," p. 53.

89. See Besant, *How India Wrought for Freedom,* pp. 76, 104, and 122.

90. Barrier, "Punjab Politics and the Disturbances of 1907," p. 49.

91. Narendra Nath Gupta, *Reflections and Reminiscences* (Bombay: Hind Kitabs. 1947), p. 145.

92. *Arya Patrika,* March 8, 1886, pp. 1–3.

causes brought criticism from those who wished for greater political activism. ". . . it is a matter of great regret that Aryas as a body should not take up the cause of the National Congress. They are under the impression that they have hitherto acted as a religious body, and that by taking up political questions they might rouse the suspicions of Government."[93] Even when local Samajes did elect representatives to the Congress, the government in its public utterances accepted the non-political stance of the Samaj. The census of 1891 noted that: "In its desire to advance the self-governing institutions of the country, it was generally found ranged on the side of the Congress agitation . . . but the Samaj as such is not a political but a purely religious body."[94] Even though the government publicly absolved the Samaj of political aspirations, it could not help but wonder, as Aryas grew to dominate the educated Hindu elite which in turn furnished the base for political awareness within the Punjab.

Advocates of political action and particularly supporters of the Indian National Congress held high hopes for the year 1893. The Congress would hold its annual session in Lahore. If Punjabis would not come to the Congress, it would go to them and end their indifference to its cause. Punjabis did flock to the Congress meetings, 481 delegates out of a total of 867.[95] Sardar Dyal Singh Majithia acted as chairman of the reception committee and was assisted by Bakshi Jaishi Ram as secretary.[96] Hindus and Aryas, including Lala Lajpat Rai, Lala Harkishen Lal, and Ruchi Ram Sahni, participated in the meetings amid an atmosphere of great excitement and enthusiasm.[97] But this enthusiasm proved short lived. Punjabis found little willingness on the part of the Congress establishment to accept their program of educational and indus-

93. *Āftāb-i-'Ālamtāb*, October 23, 1888, *SPVP 1888*, p. 262; also see the *Tribune*, June 16, 1888, p. 5, for similar comments on the position of the Samaj in relation to politics.

94. *Census, Punjab Report 1891*, p. 177. For criticisms of the Samaj and claims that it was indeed a political body, see the *Tribune*, September 7, 1887, p. 5, and *Dōst-i-Hind*, December 20, 1888, *SPVP 1888*, p. 350.

95. Besant, *How India Wrought for Freedom*, p. 162.

96. Besant, *Ibid.*, p. 162, and Munshi Ram, *Inside Congress* (Bombay: Phoenix Publications, 1946), p. 21.

97. See Ruchi Ram Sahni, "Self-Revelations of an Octogenarian," pp. 110–111, and Besant, *How India Wrought for Freedom*, pp. 172–173.

trial "self-help," and the meetings ended in bitterness between the provincial and national leaders.[98] In the years following, Punjabi delegations to the Congress fell to four in 1894, then three in 1895, seven in 1896, and one in both 1897 and 1898.[99] The Congress seemed irrelevant to many Punjabis. Aryas were engrossed in the intra-organizational struggles and their economic enterprises, preoccupations which they shared with other Punjabi Hindus. Also pressure from the Punjab Government kept many officials and other employees of the state from attending the Congress sessions.[100] For the more militant Aryas the Congress appeared pro-Muslim in its search for a transcendant nationalism.[101] Clearly, provincial issues and goals took precedence over the Congress in the minds of leading Punjabi Hindus. During the years prior to 1899, no forces brought the Congress and the Punjab together.

The nadir of political action came in the fall of 1898. Sardar Dyal Singh Majithia died in September, removing the lynch pin of the Punjab Indian Association and the provincial Congress. Dyal Singh had led and more often financed a variety of public causes. He was respected by Brahmos, Aryas, and Sanatanists, and could bridge divisions between contending Hindu factions. Without him the Indian Association became comatose, as Punjabis remained involved in their economic and communal affairs. Only Jaishi Ram carried on as a perennial delegate to the annual Congress meetings.[102] Within one year, however, the urban Hindu elite of Punjab returned openly to politics, to both the Indian Association and the Congress. Growing apprehension among educated Hindus focused on the proposed Land Alienation Act. The threat of this legislation stimulated political action. Aryas and Brahmos joined a revived Indian Association utilizing it to organize a campaign of petitions, protest meetings, and propaganda aimed at deflecting this threat to the economic interests of urban Hindus. Punjabis

98. Barrier, "Punjab Politics and the Disturbances of 1907," p. 59.

99. Besant, *How India Wrought for Freedom*, pp. 182, 206, 229, 251, and 170.

100. Barrier, "Punjab Politics and the Disturbances of 1907," pp. 44 and 63–64.

101. Munshi Ram writes with bitterness about Congress efforts to persuade Muslims to attend the meetings. See *Inside Congress*, pp. 24–25; also see Lajpat Rai, *Writings and Speeches*, Vol. I, p. xxi; and, Barrier, "Punjab Politics and the Disturbances of 1907," p. 56.

102. Barrier, "Punjab Politics and the Disturbances of 1907," pp. 79–80.

turned to the Congress as well for aid. In place of the single delegate sent in 1898, twenty-six Punjabis journeyed to Lucknow for the 1899 Congress session. Lala Murli Dhar's resolution which condemned the proposed Land Alienation Act was carried by the assembled delegates.[103] For the first time the Congress stood together with Punjabi Hindus in a common cause, but not one with national nor even regional appeal. This victory of the urban commercial class placed the Congress in opposition to both Punjabi Muslims and peasants of all communities.[104]

In the wake of this success newly-enthusiastic supporters of the Congress began plans for the 1900 meetings scheduled for Lahore. The work of preparation fell to two men, Lala Harkishen Lal and Bakshi Jaishi Ram. Harkishen Lal turned to his friends, business associates, and the remnants of the older Dyal Singh faction, while Jaishi Ram appealed to his fellow Aryas. Both men found allies who joined the reception committee.[105] Kali Prosanna Roy became head of this committee, one of the last Bengalis to exercise effective leadership in the Punjab.[106] At the request of Jaishi Ram, Surendra Nath Banerjea toured the Punjab. He visited Delhi, Amritsar, Lahore, and Rawalpindi in order to publicize the forthcoming Congress meetings.[107] In the middle of Banerjea's tour Jaishi Ram died. His death removed one of the most consistent al-

103. Besant, *How India Wrought for Freedom*, p. 195.

104. John R. McLane, "The Development of Nationalist Ideas and Tactics and the Policies of the Government of India, 1897–1905," unpublished Ph.D. dissertation, University of London, School of Oriental and African Studies, 1961, p. 188.

105. Barrier, "Punjab Politics and the Disturbances of 1907," p. 90.

106. Kali Prosanna Roy typified the leadership provided by the Bengali community of Punjab. Nagendra Nath Gupta described Kali Prosanna in his memoirs. "When I went to Lahore Kali Prosanna Roy, a graduate in Arts and Law of Calcutta University, was the acknowledged leader of the Indian Bar while Sir William Rattigan was the leader of the other section. . . . We became very intimate friends at Lahore and the family intimacy was maintained even after K. P. Roy's death in 1904. Kali Prosanna was not a scholarly man, but he was an accomplished advocate, brimming over with wit and humour. He was a man of independence of character and marked dignity of bearing. Kali Prosanna was among the early Bengali settlers in the Punjab. He was greatly respected and was elected Chairman of the Lahore Congress Reception Committee in 1900." Gupta, *Reflections and Reminiscences*, p. 173.

107. Surendra Nath Banerjea, *A Nation in the Making* (Bombay: Oxford Univ. Press, 1963), p. 153.

lies of the Congress cause and a link between Aryas and the Harkishen Lal-Brahmo faction.[108]

The Lahore Congress session opened amid scenes of jubilation and political enthusiasm. Punjabis swarmed to the meetings, 421 delegates out of a total of 567. While the 1900 Congress appeared to Punjabis as a high point in their political activism and a grand illustration of political unity throughout the subcontinent, it was in fact the smallest, most poorly attended Congress session since 1886.[109] Optimism and enthusiasm overrode reality as the meetings seemed to symbolize Punjab's final acceptance of the Congress cause.[110] Aryas returned to the Congress in the hope of gaining acceptance for their favorite goal of self-help in economic and educational enterprise.[111] The Congress establishment seemed to respond, as Punjabis found places on various crucial Congress committees and received a sympathetic hearing for their special appeals. For a few days educated Punjabis could rub shoulders with national figures of prominence and feel that a genuine enthusiasm would heal existing divisions.[112] Yet this glow of enthusiasm and political euphoria soon evaporated to be replaced by quarreling within the ranks of the Punjab Congress and apathy without.

Educated Hindus who joined together in the Congress brought with them animosities and factional strife generated in economic and religious competition. Rival factions, Arya and Brahmo, struggled for control of the Congress. Competition between the Lal Chand-Lajpat Rai faction and the Harkishen Lal-Brahmo group extended from the board rooms of the Punjab National Bank to Congress committees.[113] In the wake of the 1900 meetings, the Aryas contested Lala Harkishen Lal's position of leadership, and a bitter controversy developed over the handling of Congress funds. Sufficient evidence existed to discredit Harkishen Lal and to paralyze the Congress program within the province. Only the mediation of Kali Prosanna Roy prevented a complete

108. Banerjea, *Ibid.*, p. 153; and Barrier, "Punjab Politics and the Disturbances of 1907," pp. 93, 97–98.

109. Besant, *How India Wrought for Freedom*, p. 311.

110. Barrier, "Punjab Politics and the Disturbances of 1907," p. 101.

111. Lajpat Rai, *Writings and Speeches*, Vol. I, p. xxvii.

112. *Tribune*, January 5, 1901, *SPVP 1901*, p. 43.

113. Barrier, "Punjab Politics and the Disturbances of 1907," p. 75.

break between the two groups and the defection of Aryas from the Congress.[114] Disillusionment with the Congress quickly set in as earlier enthusiasts turned back to older and more permanent interests. The lack of concrete action on the part of the Congress revived the charge that it was a "do-nothing" movement, all talk and no action. The *Sat Dharm Prachārak* remarked in its issue of October 25, 1901, that "when Mr. Hume and certain other Englishmen were among the supporters of the National Congress the movement was a living force. In the hands of Natives, however, it has degenerated into a tame affair, and educated Indians now attend its annual gatherings merely to enjoy themselves."[115] A proposed political association which would "popularize the aims and objects of the National Congress and safeguard the political rights of Punjabis" failed for lack of interest.[116] Aryas left the Congress to return to religion, social reform, and communal solidarity.

In the aftermath of the Congress, Aryas again faced charges of being political and seditious. In 1898, Swami Alaram, a Sanatanist missionary, revived the question of Arya sedition.[117] During the following three years, similar accusations appeared throughout the vernacular press and in wake of the Lahore Congress, open quarrels broke out between the Samaj and the government.[118] In March 1901, Aryas in Abbotabad publicly complained of government discrimination by Sir Frederick Cunningham, the District Commissioner. For the next four months newspapers carried the story of this feud between aggressive yet fearful Aryas and local officialdom. Aryas accused the local commissioner of "open hostility bordering on maligned hatred" which led him to "refuse to promote clerks of that denomination."[119] Aryas appealed to the Viceroy, while government reports characterized them as a

114. See Barrier, *Ibid.*, pp. 102–103, 108–109 and 110. Also see Lajpat Rai, *Autobiographical Writings*, ed. V. C. Joshi (Delhi: University Publishers, 1965), p. 91.

115. *Sat Dharm Prachārak*, October 25, 1901, *SPVP 1901*, p. 718.

116. See *Tribune*, October 26, 1901, *SPVP 1901*, p. 692, and December 10, 1901, pp. 779–781.

117. *Tribune*, December 1, 1897, p. 4, and Sharma, *Handbook of the Arya Samaj*, p. 114.

118. See *Rafīq-i-Hind*, November 11, 1899, *SPVP 1899*, p. 679; and *Arya Gazette*, December 14, 1899, *SPVP 1899*, pp. 733–734.

119. *Tribune*, June 1, 1901, p. 5.

"notorious party of Hindus . . . headed by a disreputable clique of dismissed clerks and others of doubtful character."[120] This dispute subsided by mid-summer, but marked a new low in relations between the Samaj and government. Such incidents would return as official suspicion of the Samaj deepened and intensified.

In spite of the Congress, of "national" issues, politics remained for the Punjab a matter of communal loyalty. Lajpat Rai, the weathercock of Punjabi politics, led a post-Congress move toward an overtly Hindu politics. In speeches both in Lahore and Calcutta, he turned back to the struggle of Hindu against Muslim for examples of unity and patriotism. Not only did he resurrect a sense of honor for his community, but as early as 1902, Lajpat attempted to revive the term "Hindu" and to find in it a basis for religious nationalism. In doing so, he broke with the more religious Aryas by abandoning the attempt to replace "Hindu" with "Arya." The need for communal solidarity as the base for future political action necessitated saving this all-powerful symbol.[121] Lajput Rai's use of "Hindu" rather than "Arya" brought sharp criticism from militant Samajists but fitted with the growing politicization among some moderate Aryas whose primary loyalty shifted from sect to community. This paralleled an expanding consciousness of Hindu symbols and Hindu heroes both within and beyond Punjab. During 1903 Punjabis, led by Bengali residents, took up the cult of Shivaji, seeing in him the hero par excellence of past communal Hindu struggles against Muslim aggression. Shivaji—not Akbar, a hero to those who wished for secular unity— commanded the loyalty and sympathy of Punjabi Hindus.[122] Communal competition dominated Punjabis as they drifted toward a future of political action and government suppression.

During the first two decades of its existence the Arya Samaj along with other educated, urban Hindus, acted within the framework of the British Raj, but not in direct confrontation with

120. *Tribune*, June 15, 1901, p. 3. Earlier reports of this quarrel are carried in the *Tribune*, March 2, 1901, *SPVP 1901*, p. 149; *Tribune*, May 14, 1901, pp. 5–6; and May 9, 1901, p. 5.

121. Lajpat Rai, *Writings and Speeches*, Vol. I, p. 39.

122. See *Tribune*, June 2, 1903, p. 5; July 28, 1903, p. 1; and, McLane, "The Development of Nationalist Ideas and Tactics and the Policies of the Government of India, 1897–1905," p. 11.

it. British administration provided the rules of the game, but the game was more with other communities and within the Hindu community than directly with the government. Issues of identity formation, ideological elaboration, the reformation of traditions, relations with reformers, with orthodoxy, and with other religious communities dominated. Educated Hindus struggled with problems created by the British Raj, but government itself was seldom a point of issue. The decade of the 1890s saw a gradual change as government moved to the forefront of the stage to be directly encountered, to be both feared and challenged. The question of job discrimination and then the Land Alienation Act created a new situation. The British appeared increasingly hostile, actively so, and as a result Hindu leaders began to search for ways to counter what they perceived as a growing threat to their elite position.

# Chapter IX

# ON THE DEFENSIVE: THE EDUCATED HINDU IN FEAR

**Speaking for myself I am an out-and-out Swadeshist and have been so for the last twenty-five years, in fact ever since I learnt for the first time the true meaning of the word patriotism. For me the words Swadeshi and patriotism are synonymous. . . . I look upon it as remedy upon the right and on continued use of which depends the alleviation of the sufferings of our country. I regard it as the salvation of my country. The Swadeshi ought to make us self-respecting, self-reliant, self-supporting, self-sacrificing, and last, but not least, manly.**

LALA LAJPAT RAI

### APATHY AND APPREHENSION: 1904–1906

The decade before World War I witnessed the establishment of a new set of relationships between the British Raj and its subjects. The British sense of confidence typical of the nineteenth century gave way to increasing insecurity, and as a result they began to tinker with constitutional reforms in an effort to contain unrest and change largely of their own creation. They expanded the sphere of overt politics, but also arranged the dynamics of that political sphere in order to divide community from community. They did not by their own actions create communal competition nor institutionalize it, but after 1906 they manipulated communal animosity and opened new arenas for such competition. The British "channeled" overt politics much as they had channeled previous forms of economic and social action.

Within this new world educated Hindus found themselves directly confronting the British government who in turn seemed determined to limit and frustrate their interests. Urban, Westernized Hindus as a minority of a minority were well aware of their weaknesses. As a result, they sought allies and institutions for self-defense. They experimented with new tactics and when existing institutions failed them created new ones of their own. Effective political action demanded unity, but factional and sectarian loyalties, old feuds, and past struggles could not be easily forgotten. The heritage of Arya struggles with reformers and orthodoxy remained, as did internal divisions within the Samaj. Class interests of the urbanites clashed with emerging peasant leadership, while communal competition precluded class solidarity. Punjabis remained divided by their fundamental patterns of identity and their resultant ideological loyalty. Individuals functioned amidst a diversity of loyalties which sometimes conflicted and at other times converged. The process of increasing politicization, a growing awareness of "national" issues and changes in the wider world forced individuals to rethink their relations to existent forms of identity with the concomitant loyalty that each entailed. To be an Arya, a Hindu, an Indian, what did this mean and how did each identity relate to all the others? Where did one's fundamental loyalty lie and how could conflicting loyalties be reconciled? Individuals and groups would forge their own answers in response to new situations and changed circumstances. Aryas who had established their relations within the Hindu community and beyond now had to adjust to the process of politicization. Driven to protect themselves and the institutions they had created, Aryas attempted to come to terms with the Hindu community, other religions, the government, and "Indian" nationalism. They needed to clarify the connection between Arya Dharm and Hindu consciousness. Were they the same or one part of the other, and above all else how did they relate to the concept of "nation"? A complex world of shifting loyalties and new pressures demanded continual adjustment by Aryas who were both in and of this world.

The ten years prior to World War I opened amidst political fragmentation and lassitude. Following the Lahore Congress, Punjabis again abandoned national politics. The delegations to annual Congress meetings reflected provincial attitudes: thirty in 1901, zero in 1902, and five in 1903.[1] Punjabis still dreamed of a provincial political organization, but in reality few individuals remained loyal to the Congress cause. Lala Harkishen Lal served as secretary for the Congress in Punjab, and Lala Murli Dhar con-

1. Annie Besant, *How India Wrought for Freedom: The Story of the National Congress Told from Official Records* (Adyar, Madras: The Theosophical Publishing House, 1915), pp. 333, 345, 352, 372, 374, and 392.

tinued his role as spokesman for the Congress.[2] Educated Punjabis remained preoccupied with local issues, their own organizations, and older quarrels of community and faction. This provincial world appeared far more real and relevant than the wider sphere of the Congress and national issues. Instead of national politics, factional struggles and communal competition commanded the attention of Punjabi Hindus.

Anxiety over the government's educational policy had grown steadily since the beginning of 1904. Reports appeared of school closures, of new stringent rules governing education, and of hostility among officials toward educational enterprise. By October, the government's apparent hostility to education appeared as part of Lord Curzon's grand strategy. "In fact men of light and leading in the Panjab instinctively feel that their interests and specially those of the coming generations are indissolubly bound up with the University, and the action they, or rather the local Government, now take (for they themselves are helpless in the matter) will influence for weal or woe the destinies of the future generations of Panjabees."[3] The reforms justified earlier fears, for they brought "greater officialization and careful exclusion of independent elements."[4] Growing evidence of governmental hostility intensified criticism of officialdom, of British rule, and beyond that, of Western civilization.

By the middle of 1904, Punjabis found they could view the West from a perspective hitherto impossible. Western omnipotence had met its first successful challenger, Japan. The impending conflict between Japan and Russia fascinated educated Punjabis.[5] By July, Japanese victories amazed and stirred the "natives" as no other event. Suppositions of white supremacy, long held as uncontestable, now came into disrepute.

For a long time ever I had one question before me: What it was that made them masters of the world? From the time I arrived here I made it a point

2. *Tribune,* January 23, 1904, p. 1.

3. *Panjabee,* October 3, 1904, p. 1.

4. *Tribune,* November 24, 1904, p. 3. This was in reference to the reconstitution of the Senate of the University of Calcutta. For comments on the Fellows chosen for the Punjab University, see the *Panjabee,* October 10, 1904, p. 3; October 24, 1904, p. 1; November 14, 1904, p. 1; and November 21, 1904, p. 2.

5. See *Paisā Akhbār,* January 22, 1904, Government of India, *Selections from the Vernacular Newspapers Published in the Punjab, 1904,* p. 27.

to find out an answer to this. The first thing that struck my simple mind was the colour. It is not so ridiculous as it appears to be. Colour is made much of in politics of the modern world. Their idea is that superiority lies in colour. Even a thinker like Montesque had argued in its favour.

I for my person would have been quite satisfied with this fact alone but for the newly risen Japs. Their rise practically gives a turn to my question and makes it rather a more serious object of consideration.

I give credit to Japan for the . . . devotion and sacrifice of her sons and for this also that she has disillusioned me of the idea of supremacy of colour.[6]

Japan—small, virtuous, successful, and Asiatic—provided a new model of modernity beyond the world of the white man.[7]

British rule and its accompanying introduction of Western culture, no longer the sole possessor of the future, could now be viewed with open scorn. The earlier comparisons of the British Raj with Muslim rule, comparisons in favor of the British, were reversed. Whatever immorality and evil existed, it stemmed from the British, from the introduction of a decadent culture. "Who is to blame for that extensive litigation which distinguishes the Hindus of to-day from the Aryas of yore? Who is to blame for that prevalence among the Indian people of the use of the poisonous weed which is so injurious to the moral, physical and intellectual welfare of the community? And lastly, who is to blame for that habit of drinking which so largely characterises the average Indian of to-day? The answer to all these questions consisted of two words—the West."[8] With the diminution of prestige held by European civilization and increasing anxiety on the part of educated Hindus, the way was opened for a renewal of political activity as well as a revival of Punjabi efforts at "self-help."[9]

Rising discontent among Hindu leaders turned them back toward established channels of agitation, both provincial and national. Above all sat the Indian National Congress, a symbol of what might be, but a bitter disappointment to educated Punjabi

6. *Panjabee,* July 21, 1906, p. 1.

7. See also *Panjabee,* October 3, 1904, p. 1.

8. *Arya Messenger,* April 14, 1905, *SPVP 1905,* p. 130. Also see *Sat Dharm Pracharak,* July 26, 1905, *SPVP 1905,* p. 286.

9. Barrier discusses this revival of patriotism in "The Arya Samaj and Congress Politics in the Punjab, 1894–1908," *Journal of Asian Studies,* XXVI, No. 3 (May 1967), pp. 369–370.

Hindus. Its disinterest in "self-help," in industrialization, and national education, repeatedly frustrated Punjabis. In April, the *Vakīl* urged the Congress "to leave off politics and 'nationalism' and to try to improve the financial condition of the people; . . . and devise means to develop trade and industry."[10] Yet no matter how Punjabis might wish the Congress were different or desire it to accept their program of national improvement, they met with little response from Congress leaders. Throughout the months of spring and summer, Congress, its problems, the lack of communal unity, and need for local political committees remained topics of extensive discussion.[11] Lack of hope of reviving political action within the province paralleled continual disillusionment with the Congress described most bitterly as "a paper horse which is trotted out annually for eight days of Christmas."[12]

In October a group of Aryas, led by Lala Lajpat Rai, founded a new newspaper, the *Panjabee,* as a voice of the politically-conscious Punjabi Hindu. It would, they hoped, revive politics in this all too quiet province. The *Panjabee* quickly became a recognized advocate of political activism, to the left of the more conservative *Tribune.* It did not succeed, however, in resurrecting enthusiasm for the Congress. As the annual meetings loomed ahead, criticism of the Congress intensified to the point where the Lahore Indian Association declared a boycott of the Bombay session. The Congress had turned its back on the creation of Punjabi politicians, the Indian Congress Committee, and now Punjabis would respond in kind. "The Indian Congress Committee was an executive or working body called into being by a resolution of the Lucknow Session of the Congress, which was, moreover, confirmed and ratified by the next gathering of the Congress at Lahore, and yet the Calcutta leaders chose to practically abolish it as it were behind the back of the whole Congress."[13] The abolishing of the Indian Congress Committee removed Punjabi leadership from an effective role in the Congress and appeared to restrict the Congress to its role of a "paper horse." A week later the Indian Association changed its

10. *Vakīl,* April 6, 1904, *SPVP 1904,* p. 112.

11. See *Vakīl,* May 4, 1904, *SPVP 1904,* p. 151; *Curzon Gazette,* July 1, 1904, *SPVP 1904,* pp. 233–234; and *Tribune,* August 4, 1904, *SPVP 1904,* p. 254.

12. *Sat Dharm Prachārak,* October 7, 1904, *SPVP 1904,* p. 330.

13. *Panjabee,* December 12, 1904, p. 1.

position and decided to send delegates to Bombay.[14] The decision created little enthusiasm for the Congress meetings, and the Punjabi delegation accounted for only 28 representatives out of a total of 1,010.[15]

Once at the Congress meetings, Punjabi delegates protested the removal of the Indian Congress Committee before a special meeting of the Subject Committee. After describing the campaign begun in 1889 to reorganize the Congress, Lajpat Rai summarized Punjabi goals: "an executive committee to supervise and be responsible for all political work in the country; and that the control and guidance of the Indian National Congress should vest in a properly constituted body rather than in individuals, however able, high minded or self-sacrificing they may be."[16] Lajpat Rai and his fellow Punjabis envisioned an Indian National Congress structured for continuous political action along much the same lines as their own institutions, a Congress with its "Managing Committee," and annual society meetings. Their efforts to remake the Congress failed, and were realized only with M. K. Gandhi's reorganization in 1920.

In March 1905, the Indian Association of Lahore appealed to the public for Rs. 5,000, the necessary funds to send a representative of the province to England as part of a Congress deputation. Both the *Tribune* and the *Panjabee* enthusiastically supported this plan with the hope of reviving political activism, but revival did not come easily. The Indian Association scheme produced enthusiasm but soon generated, in addition, a bitter personal struggle between Lajpat Rai and Lala Harkishen Lal. The *Panjabee* immediately assumed that Lajpat Rai would lead this new political crusade.[17] His nomination by the press became official at a meeting of the Indian Association held on March 23.[18] But on April 1, Lala Harkishen Lal challenged both the representative and the method of his selection.[19] The resulting controversy sputtered on through April,

14. *Panjabee,* December 19, 1904, p. 1.

15. Besant, *How India Wrought for Freedom,* p. 393. For the selection of delegates, see *Panjabee,* December 20, 1904, p. 4.

16. *Panjabee,* March 6, 1905, p. 2.

17. *Panjabee,* March 20, 1905, p. 7.

18. *Tribune,* March 28, 1904, p. 4.

19. *Tribune,* April 1, 1905, p. 5.

but the final outcome remained clearly evident. Lajpat Rai would be the delegate. He commanded the allegiance of the largest group of politically-active educated Hindus, those who in turn provided the necessary funds for his trip. On May 10 he left for England and quiet returned to the Punjab political scene.

A summer's peacefulness ended on the last day of August, as news of the proposed partition of Bengal reached the Punjab. The resulting agitation excited Punjabis, though not so much as an issue in itself; instead, they were stirred and gratified by Bengalis' enthusiasm for *swadēshī*. "The example of Punjab should be very encouraging at this crisis. It is more than twenty years ago that a few educated Punjabi gentlemen at Lahore, mostly connected with the Arya Samaj, resolved to eschew cloths and other necessaries of foreign manufacture."[20] Following the great *rishi*, Punjabis campaigned for *swadēshī* decades before the more "progressive" Bengalis. "The little Swadeshi Movement in Lahore in the early eighties was one of the fruits of his exertions. At first the Swadeshi band had to make the best of the coarse country fabrics available, and to bear at the same time the jeers of the 'common sense' critics. But their numbers grew faster and faster, and the quality of the country cloths also improved *pari passu*, till Ludhiana and Gujarat weavers produced pieces which were scarcely inferior in appearance and superior in durability to those imported from Europe."

Punjābis looked out on a resurgent nationalist movement which had finally come to them by accepting Punjabi goals as its own. They revived their long established institution, the Swadeshi Vastu Pracharni Sabha (Society for the encouragement of indigenous products), as a vehicle for agitation. Nearly every town and city throughout the province soon had its Swadeshi Sabha which now awoke to renewed activism. In the wake of the partition news, Punjabis held meeting after meeting to proclaim their rededication to *swadēshī*. Led by urban Hindus, these gatherings emphasized practicality and self-help. Hindu businessmen, prominent college Aryas, industrialists, and shopkeepers planned and founded new economic enterprises.[21]

20. Quotes given below from *Tribune*, August 31, 1905, p. 5.

21. See *Panjabee*, September 4, 1905, p. 3; September 25, 1905, p. 3; *Tribune*, September 5, 1905, p. 5; and September 14, 1905, p. 4.

The educated community, represented by teachers at various schools and colleges and by organized groups of students, provided both leadership and manpower to the *swadēshī* campaign. Students, as a definite and obvious group, now entered into the arena of politics, mainly as followers, but occasionally even in the role of leaders.[22] Lajpat Rai, after his return from England, provided direction for the *swadēshī* movement and particularly for college Aryas. For many Punjabis *swadēshī* remained a matter of commerce and industry. Increasingly, meetings concentrated on popularizing *swadēshī* products and persuading individuals to take the pledge to use no foreign-made products.[23] The tendency to separate *swadēshī* from politics was for some a conscious policy. "Nothing could certainly be more suicidal to the best interests of the movement than to identify it with politics. This will not only debar thousands of our countrymen in Government service from taking active part in a movement to whose service their patriotism commands them to stand pledged, but will alienate the sympathies of an important body of cautious persons who are adverse to the policy of remaining always at daggers drawn with our rulers."[24]

While some Punjabi leaders could view *swadēshī* and politics as separate issues, many did not. The partition revived interest in politics in general and specifically in the National Congress. Once more Punjabis turned to the Congress, expecting it to provide for them a national platform receptive to their ideas and goals. Led by Lala Lajpat Rai, Lala Murli Dhar, and Pandit Ram Bhaj Datta, the Punjab sent its strongest delegation, 104 men, to the Congress session in Benares.[25] The year 1905 closed on the crest of a wave of political enthusiasm. The Punjab had returned to the Congress and the Congress, with its emphasis on *swadēshī*, had finally come to the Punjab.

22. See meetings described in the following newspaper accounts: *Panjabee*, September 18, 1905, p. 3; September 25, 1905, p. 3; October 2, 1905, pp. 2, 3; November 6, 1905, p. 3; November 11, 1905, p. 3; *Arya Gazette*, September 21, 1905, *SPVP 1905*, p. 341; *Tribune*, September 21, 1905, p. 5; September 28, 1905, p. 4; September 26, 1905, p. 4; October 10, 1905, p. 5; October 12, 1905, p. 5; October 14, 1905, p. 3.

23. See accounts for the *swadēshī* meetings in the *Panjabee*, November 13, 1905, p. 5; November 20, 1905, p. 3; December 11, 1905, p. 3; December 25, 1905, p. 3; *Tribune*, November 23, 1905, p. 3; November 25, 1905, p. 4; December 5, 1905, p. 4.

24. *Tribune*, October 17, 1905, p. 5.

25. Besant, *How India Wrought for Freedom*, p. 416.

### THE RESURGENCE OF POLITICS: 1906

In the wake of the annual Congress meeting, 1906 began with a characteristic upsurge of political enthusiasm. As the Punjab's largest delegation returned home, old plans for political action were revived and a new note of aggressiveness appeared in the local press, echoing the drift within Congress toward more extreme policies. The established Congress policy of petitioning and passing resolutions at their annual meeting never appealed to Punjabis who preferred the activism of self-help. Now this policy came under attack within the Congress itself by a new, radical wing demanding aggressive action against the British Raj. Even the *Tribune,* with its relative political conservatism, could envision a more radical Congress in part because moderate Punjabis also felt frustrated and suppressed by officialdom, by a government grown hostile to the aspirations of the educated classes.[26] Having catalogued present and past grievances, the editor looked expectantly for a future of escalating political activism. "And if all these measures did not increase discontent and rouse the ire of the public against a form of administration under which they have become possible, well may we abandon all hope of our emancipation."

Within an atmosphere of political activism Punjabi leaders strove to achieve unity of purpose between factions and communities. Lala Lajpat Rai and Lala Harkishen Lal served together in the Indian Association, both as vice-presidents.[27] *Swadēshī,* which remained the overriding cause to Punjabis, would be intensified. The *Panjabee* boldly called for the use of power in *swadēshī,* beyond its existing focus on the expansion of indigenous industry and commerce: "Boycott, strike, or *Hartal,* call it whatever you like it is the same thing, and truly it is the weapon *par excellence* of the weak against the strong."[28] Punjab would, it was hoped, follow Bengal in its use of this new methodology. Yet as spring advanced the cause of aggressive *swadēshī* faded. Punjabis returned to their preoccupation with new businesses and existing enterprise.[29] Public meetings grew less frequent as the political momentum of mid-winter slackened.[30]

26. Quotes given below from *Tribune,* February 24, 1906, p. 2.
27. *Panjabee,* February 14, 1906, p. 4.
28. *Panjabee,* January 24, 1906, p. 1.
29. See *Panjabee,* February 28, 1906, p. 4; *Tribune,* April 3, 1906, p. 2.
30. *Panjabee,* April 7, 1906, p. 4.

In April, the arrest of Surendra Nath Banerjea revived political passions as Punjabis gathered to denounce this new evidence of governmental tyranny.[31] In a mass meeting at Bradlaugh Hall in Lahore, Punjabis declared their solidarity with Bengal and condemned Banerjea's arrest and government repression in general.[32] While the Banerjea affair created an opportunity for public castigation of the government, this response proved transitory; only suppression within Punjab could provide stimulus to sustained activity. In June, the Punjab Government generated just such a *cause celebre* with the arrest of four teachers at Lyallpur Government High School "[who] . . . were dismissed on the supposition that the said teachers had privately preached the Swadeshi doctrine to their pupils with the result that the latter refused to accept sweets made of foreign sugar at the last Prize distribution of the school."[33] The "Lyallpur Swadeshi Case" disturbed and threatened Punjabis. In July, two incidents of government suppression occurred when Swami Yogendra Pal, an Arya *updēshak,* was forbidden to preach by the Batala police superintendent, and the Aryas of Dinanagar were refused a license for their traditional street procession, a *nagar kīrten.*[34] Small and insignificant events in themselves, for the extremely sensitive they were straws in the wind, indicative of a new trend toward increased official hostility. Fear engendered new life into Punjab politics, but not new unity. By mid-summer, factions once more struggled over progress and leadership.

The first hints of renewed factional strife among educated Punjabi Hindus came in the arena of economics. In April, a consortium of "cultured" Aryas from the Anarkali Samaj discussed the organization of a new insurance company. Members of the Harkishen Lal-Brahmo faction publicly condemned them for creating unnecessary competition against *swadēshī* companies already in existence.[35] Acute business competition between Lala Harkishen

31. *Tribune,* April 18, 1906, p. 3.

32. *Panjabee,* April 18, 1906, p. 3.

33. *Panjabee,* June 2, 1906, p. 3. The four teachers were all Hindus of the commercial castes: Lala Devi Chand, Lala Nanak Chand, Lala Tirath Das, and Lala Bagh Mall.

34. See *Panjabee,* July 25, 1906, p. 4; August 4, 1906, p. 3; *Hindustān,* August 3, 1906, *SPVP 1906,* p. 202.

35. Squabbles broke out in June over the Lahore Bank, Ltd., which once again pitted Aryas against Harkishen Lal; see *Tribune,* June 9, 1906, p. 5.

Lal and Aryas, particularly of the college party, led to further strife within the Hindu community. In January 1906, the *Tribune* became a daily paper with a new editor, Alfred Nundy. He was an Indian Christian, a fact that initially caused little comment. By June, however, Aryas charged that Nundy came "to the Punjab with the avowed object of running down and boycotting the Arya Samaj . . . and that he had begun by purging the Arya Samajic element out of the Tribune itself."[36] Throughout the summer months an acrimonious debate continued in the pages of the *Tribune* and the *Panjabee*. Old animosities (commercial, personal, and political) burst forth as Lajpat Rai and Harkishen Lal listed their grievances both past and present.[37] This factional strife paralleled a renewal of controversy between the college and Gurukul wings of the Samaj. Lala Munshi Ram summed up the political conditions within the leadership of the educated Hindus when he stated that the "Punjab is split up into four political parties under the respective leaderships of Lala Lajpat Rai, Harkishen Lal, Ram Bhaj Dutt and Rai Sahib Murli Dhar."[38] Munshi Ram was not far from wrong, and this divisiveness, this factional and personal strife, presented an extremely difficult hurdle for anyone who would attempt to mobilize educated Hindus for political action.

While the *Tribune-Panjabee* controversy and its allied factional debates continued, attention shifted to possible renewal of formal political action. In August, a letter appeared in the *Tribune* calling for a meeting of the Punjab Provincial Conference. Its author shared Lala Munshi Ram's perception of existent political apathy and factional strife:

> While all other provinces have been holding their Conferences, the practical Punjabees are all asleep in this matter. Lala Harkishen Lal, the premier leader of the Punjab is immersed in his banking business, Lala Lajpat Rai who has raised more hopes than anyone else is busy with his College Education Scheme and College Party propaganda. Lala Munshi Ram is engaged in finding fault with everyone who does not fall in with

36. *Panjabee*, June 9, 1906, pp. 1–2

37. *Tribune*, June 13, 1906, p. 3; July 18, 1906, p. 3; *Panjabee*, June 20, 1902, p. 3; *Tribune*, June 27, 1906, p. 3; July ', 1906. p. 3; July 4, 1906, p. 3; July 11, 1906, p. 3; July 12, 1906, p. 3; July 14, 1906, p. 3; *Panjabee*, June 30, 1906, p. 4; July 4, 1906, p. 4; July 4, 1906, pp. 4–5; July 7, 1906, p. 3; July 14, 1906, p. 2. Also see both papers during August and September 1906.

38. *Panjabee*, November 3, 1906, p. 4.

> his stereotyped views and Pandit Ram Bhaj Datt Choudhry with his noble Chowdharain has embarked in forming a Hindu Sahayak Sabha throughout India. All are moving in their own restricted grooves and none for the greater cause of the country at large, forgetting for the moment that herein lies salvation for all.[39]

The divisiveness of Punjabi leaders threatened them with a complete loss of influence in the national Congress. If they failed to act, they "would have no face to present themselves before the next Conference with any hope of securing a constitution for the Congress for which they have been fighting for such a long time."[40] Five days after this letter appeared, Lala Murli Dhar invited the Conference to Ambala.[41] During August and September, both the *Tribune* and the *Panjabee* gave strong, consistent support to the proposed Conference,[42] while with Lala Murli Dhar as president of the reception committee, plans moved steadily ahead gaining support from provincial political leaders.[43]

The Conference, when it opened on September 29, with seventy delegates, only partially fulfilled the expectations of its organizers. Hailed as a great success, as such conferences inevitably were, it was in reality a meeting of political leaders among the educated Punjabi Hindus. Aryas, particularly from the college faction, dominated the meeting, while a handful of Sikhs and Bengalis also attended. Only two Muslims participated—Syed Hyder Raza, an educated *zamīndār* from Delhi, and the highly controversial editor from Lahore, Moharram Ali Chishti.[44] Delegates to the Conference came largely from the fields of law, commerce, and journalism.[45] Also most cities of the Punjab were represented, with the

39. *Tribune,* August 17, 1906, p. 3. This letter was signed "H.M."

40. *Ibid.*

41. *Panjabee,* August 22, 1906, p. 3; for a similar letter, by Murli Dhar, see the *Tribune,* August 22, 1906, p. 2.

42. See *Tribune,* August 29, 1906, p. 3, and the bitter complaint of political apathy in the *Tribune,* August 30, 1906, p. 3.

43. See *Tribune,* September 11, 1906, p. 3: September 13, 1906, p. 2; *Panjabee,* September 12, 1906, p. 3.

44. Moharram Ali had served as editor of both the *Kōh-i-Nūr* and the *Rafīq-i-Hind.* See N. G. Barrier and Paul Wallace, *The Punjab Press, 1880–1905* (East Lansing: Asia Studies Center, Michigan State Univ., and Research Committee on the Punjab, 1970), pp. 78, 115.

45. The *Panjabee* printed a list of delegates giving a slightly larger group—eighty-eight—than other reports. Since the name, occupation and city represented was given for most of the delegates, it provides a basis for analysis of the

exception of Multan, Gujranwala, Gurdaspur, and Hoshiarpur.[46] The Conference followed well-established political issues, passing resolutions on government policy in the courts, education, temperance, the salaries of government clerks, administration in the North-Western Frontier Province, local government, and the perennial problem of Congress organizational structure.[47] Delegates discussed at length the scheme for District Congress Associations and a constitution for the Indian National Congress.[48] The Punjab delegation to the National Congress, 139 strong, traveled to Calcutta determined to revive the issue of a Congress constitution. For Punjabis political action meant political organization. They could conceive of an effective Congress only in terms of their own successful and highly structured institutions.

In the wake of the 1906 Congress, Punjabis returned to establish political associations at the district level. This time political organization achieved some limited success, as local groups formed in Rawalpindi, Sialkot, Jullundur, and Delhi during the month of January.[49] The creation of a permanent Provincial Congress Committee proved more difficult. At the provincial level political organization remained chaotic, unformed, and divided. The proposal for a Congress constitution and a "Central Standing Committee" was revived, but did not get beyond the stage of preparatory discussion. Punjabis could not persuade the Congress to accept their views on the need for a new organizational structure.[50] While Hindu politicians sought to inject new life into the Congress,

---

overall group. Professions when given provide the following picture: law (including pleaders, advocates and holders of an LL.B.), 39; commerce (including merchants, contractors and business managers), 19; bankers, 3; journalists, 7; doctors (and one chemist), 4; others (including one teacher, one woman, two reis and two zamindars), 6. Geographic distribution was heavily from Ambala (31), and Lahore (24), and Delhi (10), with scattered representatives from Rawalpindi, Amritsar, Ferozepore, Ludhiana, Jullundur, Kasur, and Sialkot. Communally, when it is possible to ascertain through the name patterns, were: Hindus, 71; Muslims, 2; Sikhs, 7; and Bengalis, 8. See *Panjabee,* October 10, 1906, p. 4.

46. *Panjabee,* October 6, 1906, p. 11.

47. For a complete list of the resolutions passed at this conference, see the *Panjabee,* October 2, 1906, p. 2.

48. *Panjabee,* October 10, 1906, p. 4.

49. *Panjabee,* January 8, 1907, p. 5; January 12, 1907, p. 2; January 16, 1907, p. 3; January 19, 1907, p. 4; January 30, 1907, p. 4; *Tribune,* January 10, 1907, p. 2; January 30, 1907, p. 2.

50. *Panjabee,* January 2, 1907, p. 3.

both locally and nationally, events turned toward an intensification of communal consciousness, of communal mobilization, and the politicization of the older Hindu-Muslim struggle.

In April, news had already reached the Punjab of a proposed Muslim political organization, a parallel to the Congress. A meeting of Muslim leaders held in Lahore on May 30 declared "That we members present, form ourselves into an Association to be called the 'Indian Moslem League' the object of which will be to develop a political instinct among the Indian Mussulmans, inculcating the true spirit of loyalty to the British Government, to enable them to grasp accurately their political situation and to review with calm, deliberate and studied vigilance the different phases which our political life may present at various times, thus safe-guarding the public interests of the Mahomedan community."[51]

Hindus expressed mixed feelings of hope, frustration, and fear in reaction to a proposed Muslim deputation to the Viceroy. Discussions of possible constitutional changes that finally led to the Minto-Morley reforms spurred Muslim leaders to approach the government directly with a plea for special consideration of their community. Muslim leaders met with the Viceroy, Lord Minto, on October 1, 1906, and presented their case for governmental protection from the majority Hindu community. Skillfully written, this plea, with its air of abject humility, both begged and threatened the British Government. It stressed the size of the Muslim community, with two opposing themes: its minority status in relation to the Hindus, and its position as "a community itself more numerous than the entire population of any first class European Power except Russia . . . ."[52] Thus the delegation laid claim to separate treatment of Muslims in future constitutional reforms.

"Still, it cannot be denied that we, Muhammadans, are a distinct community, with additional interests of our own, which are now shared by other communities, and these have hitherto suffered from the fact that they have not been adequately represented." Punjab newspapers commented on the deputation, with the *Panjabee* taking a hostile stance, as they chided Muslims for their

51. *Tribune*, April 24, 1906, p. 5.

52. Quotes given below from the "Great Muhammadan Deputation to the Viceroy" in the *Panjabee*, October 6, 1906, p. 2. which carried a complete text of this address.

sycophantic posture.[53] The Muhammadan deputation and reaction to it illustrated an underlying point of tension; for one community to succeed, all others must fail. Muhammadan preferential treatment meant discrimination against Hindus. "While we [the Panjabee] think it is perfectly legitimate on the part of our Muhammadan brethren to try their best to get a due share of Government patronage in the employment of officials, we think it is highly objectionable on their part to press their claims for a larger share on grounds which touch the susceptibilities of other communities."[54] During the months of November and December, Muslims spoke increasingly of new organizations to defend the Islamic community. Even the *Tribune,* with its optimism and relatively secular outlook, became uneasy with the stress on loyalty by such Muslim leaders as Nawab Salimulla of Bengal. "In fact, the gist of his address was that at this critical time, it should be the duty of the Mahomedans to gird up their loins and buckle their armour for they may be called on to fight perhaps against the Hindu rebels at any moment."[55] Muslim insistence on their own loyalty and disloyalty of all others stirred Punjabi Hindus into another round of communal mobilization.[56]

The general climate of political organization, plus the new stirrings among Muslims, posed the question of who spoke for the Hindus. In August, Ram Bhaj Datta called for the formation of a Hindu organization which would protect Hindu interests amidst a world of expanding political activism. "The Hindustan of the

53. "Stand up on your Legs, Brethren! Our Muhammadan countrymen do a great injustice to themselves when they advance such absurd claims for preference in the service of the Government. Claims like these are unworthy of their past greatness and are not likely to infuse much enthusiasm in the future generations of their community to regain at least some of their lost prestige and power by their own exertions. Let our friends remember that it was bold self-reliance that raised the early leaders of Islam from the position of petty Arab Beduins to the position of conquerors of Persia, Turkey, Africa, Spain and India; and it will be by including habits of bold self-reliance alone that they can justify their descent from those warriors who conquered both men and hearts against, perhaps, braver and stronger enemies. These latter lost because they were deficient in that sterling quality, *self-reliance* which the former possessed." *Panjabee,* October 10, 1906, p. 3.

54. *Panjabee,* October 13, 1906, p. 3.

55. *Tribune,* January 6, 1907, p. 2.

56. See *Panjabee,* December 19, 1906, p. 5; December 22, 1906, p. 1; January 5, 1907, p. 5; and January 12, 1907, p. 6.

present day is composed of Hindus and Mussalmans both. Political bodies like the Congress and social bodies like the Indian National Social Conference look to the interests of both; and communal bodies like the Anjuman Himayat Islam look to the welfare of the Mussalman Branch of this ancient and holy banyan tree, but there is no particular care-taker of its Hindu Branch, and for want of that it is showing signs of slow decay and death."[57] Ram Bhaj Datta founded a Hindu Sahayak Sabha in Lahore and then set out with his wife, Sarala Devi Chaudharani, to organize other sabhas throughout the Punjab and the United Provinces. By the end of September, they established Hindu Sahayak Sabhas in Multan, Jhang, Gujranwala, Sialkot and Lyallpur.[58] Pandit Ram Bhaj, his wife, and his most ardent supporter, Rai Hari Chand of Multan, brought together members of the educated Hindu community, whether Aryas or orthodoxy, plus a number of leading Sikhs.

In order to celebrate this growing Hindu consciousness, Pandit Ram Bhaj organized a festival in honor of Hindu heroes and Hindu communal strength.

> The Vir Ashtami Festival or the Festival of Heroes is the latest institution in our midst, and this we own to the enthusiastic endeavours of Pundit Ram Bhaj Dutt Choudhri, and his patriotic partner Punditani Sarala Devi Choudhrani. . . . At the first celebration of the festival we were glad to notice men and women of all classes and persuasions looking at the admirable feats of Gymnastics, trials of strength, exhibitions of sword play, Gatka fights, and other interesting performances . . . . Sweet music suited to the occasion was admirably rendered and songs exhorted the assembled crowds to sink petty differences and unite in the service of the mother-land.[59]

Ram Bhaj Datta's campaign to unify Hindu politicians reached its culmination in December, with the founding of the Punjab Hindu Sabha. Intended to represent Hindus of the entire province, this meeting drew together leaders of the various factions within that community. Lala Lajpat Rai and Lala Harkishen Lal both agreed to serve on the Sabha's executive committee, along

57. *Tribune,* August 4, 1906, p. 3.

58. *Tribune,* September 8, 1906, p. 4; September 19, 1906, p. 4; September 23, 1906, p. 5; September 25, 1906, p. 5; *Panjabee,* September 8, 1906, p. 4; September 12, 1906, p. 4; September 19, 1906, p. 4.

59. *Tribune,* September 27, 1906, p. 1.

with Ram Bhaj Datta and his closest ally, Rai Hari Chand.[60] The Hindu Sabha posed as the spokesman of Punjabi Hindus, but in fact replaced no organization, no other faction; it simply added another voice in the diverse Punjab world. The Punjab Hindu Sabha, the Hindu Sahayak Sabhas, the new provincial Congress, and the older associations based on communal, sectarian, and secular interests were soon drawn into a vortex of unrest. The new year, 1907, would see Punjab plunged into its worst political crisis in half a century.

### RIOTS, THE RAJ, AND POLITICAL SUPPRESSION—1907

January began in the typical fashion with renewed interest in politics spurred by returned delegates from the annual Congress meeting. One hundred thirty-nine Punjabis attended the Congress meeting in Calcutta, the largest delegation ever sent from Punjab. On their return, attention focused on problems of organization. In the beginning of 1907, the Punjab Congress remained chaotic. Local Congress committees existed in some districts but not in others. Also no one knew how to fit political bodies such as the Indian Association into a provincial Congress organization. This confusion remained unsolved as the province found itself enmeshed in a swirl of converging political issues.

Rumors of further British legislation aimed at protecting peasants from exploitation by the moneylending classes proved true. The government proposed to amend the Land Alienation Act of 1900 in order to tighten its limitations on the sale, ownership, and mortgaging of land. Urban Hindus saw this as another attempt by hostile officials to reduce their prestige and to erode their economic base. Urban leaders quickly mobilized to protest the bill and if possible to prevent its passage. By February, anti-amendment meetings were held throughout the towns and cities of the province. Unlike earlier movements against the Land Alienation Act of 1900, this agitation was not limited to the urban elites; rural leaders as well joined the protest, not out of sympathy with the commercial classes but from a similar fear of bureaucratic tyranny.

Rural discontent stemmed from two separate points of conflict:

60. The Executive Committee included Sikhs and Bengalis as well; for a listing, see *Panjabee*, December 22, 1906, p. 4.

a sharp increase in the water rates on the land irrigated by the Bari Doab Canal, and the proposed Colonization of the Land Bill strengthening government control of the Chenab Colony. The latter issue proved far more contentious than the former. The Chenab Colony, begun in 1887, was considered an ideal example of Punjab administration. Wasteland, unfit for agriculture, was transformed by a system of canals linked to the Chenab River into fertile and productive farms. The government distributed over 2,000,000 acres of land to peasants and occasional landlords drawn from the crowded districts of central Punjab. The new colonies were carefully planned and controlled by local officials. The vast majority of peasants were in fact tenants to the government and held their land only as long as they fulfilled the stipulations of their grants. The Chenab Colony represented an ideal of governmental paternalism. Like the missionary land schemes, peasants lived under the constant tutelage of white "sahibs."

The growth of discontent among Chenab colonists challenged official paternalism. Canal officers had developed an informal system of fines for various breaches of regulations in a vain attempt to retain control. In 1903, colonists successfully challenged the legality of this system in the courts. They also founded a newspaper, the *Zamīndār*, to express their grievances.[61] The Punjab Government responded by drafting legislation, the ill-omened Punjab Colonization of Land Bill, to legalize the fine system and strengthen control of the Canal Officers. This legislation, hastily prepared and poorly timed, appeared to the colonists as a deliberate attempt to suppress their constitutional rights and to maintain a corrupt, oppressive system of administrative-rule.[62] As reaction to the proposed colonization bill gathered strength, the Punjab Government added further fuel to the growing conflagration. In November 1906, they raised the rates for water from the Bari Doab Canal, in some instances by as much as 50 percent. This affected landowners throughout the districts of Amritsar, Gurdaspur, and Lahore.[63] By early 1907, the three issues—the Colonization Bill, the Bari Doab water rates, and the Amendment to the Land

61. Barrier, "Punjab Politics and the Disturbances of 1907," Ph.D. dissertation, Duke University, 1966, pp. 358–361.

62. See Barrier, *Ibid.*, pp. 361–362.

63. Barrier, *Ibid.*, pp. 362–363.

Alienation Act—tended to unite rural and urban Punjabis in opposition to the government.

Agitation against the proposed bills began separately, yet simultaneously. Leading landowners, utilizing the Zamindar Association, inaugurated their campaign against the Colonization Bill with a "Grand Protest Meeting" of approximately 8,000 colonists at the Lyallpur Arya Samaj.[64] On the same day, Lahore was the scene of a "Monster Protest Meeting" against the Land Alienation Amendment Bill.[65] While Ram Bhaj Datta spoke at the Lahore meeting, Lajpat Rai, along with members of the Lahore Indian Association and the Indian National Congress, journeyed to Lyallpur.[66] The two movements linked, each reinforcing the other. Throughout February, anti-government activity gained momentum, as new meetings and the press continued their attacks.[67] Rising unrest stirred further hope of a new solidarity which would unite rural and urban areas, as well as Hindus and Muslims. February 27 saw the inauguration of a District Association in Multan, while the Rawalpindi Association under the leadership of Lala Hans Raj Sawhney became a center of a revived *swadēshī* campaign.[68]

In the midst of escalating political fervor, the government made its first counterattack. On February 20 the *Panjabee* announced the arrest of both its editor and proprietor under a section of the criminal code designed to punish "any act which promotes feelings of enmity or hatred between different classes."[69] Criminal charges against the *Panjabee* only increased popular anger. Throughout March, the temper of anti-government agitation mounted, culminating in a mass meeting in Lyallpur. The annual livestock show held on March 22 and 23 brought

64. *Tribune,* February 7, 1907, p. 3. Barrier gives the figure of 10,000; see Barrier, "Punjab Politics and the Disturbances of 1907," p. 365.

65. *Tribune,* February 5, 1907, p. 5.

66. Barrier, "Punjab Politics and the Disturbances of 1907," p. 365.

67. See *Panjabee,* February 9, 1907, p. 3; *Tribune,* February 15, 1907, p. 6; and February 19, 1907, p. 5.

68. See *Panjabee,* February 9, 1907, pp. 3–4; February 16, 1907, p. 3; March 6. 1907, p. 4; and, April 17, 1907, p. 2.

69. Section 153A of the Criminal Code. See *Panjabee,* February 20, 1907 p. 8. After an initial conviction, the case dragged on through postponements and appeals. See *Panjabee,* March 9, 1907, p. 3; and March 27, 1907, p. 3.

thousands of peasants into the city. They furnished an excellent audience for protests against the Colonization Bill. Lajpat Rai and Ajit Singh, an avowed revolutionary, spoke to a gathering of some 9,000 colonists. Carried away by his enthusiasm, Lajpat went beyond the bounds of his normal moderation, while Ajit Singh openly called for "bloody sacrifice."[70] Following this meeting Ajit Singh toured the Bari Doab countryside, organizing landowners to support *swadēshī* and to refuse payment of the new irrigation rates.[71] At last the Punjab seemed politically alive and unified in its opposition to paternal bureaucracy. Factional difference and normal divisiveness disappeared beneath a surface enthusiasm and emotionalism. The same rising political excitement which encouraged Hindu politicians perplexed and finally frightened the Punjab Government.

Officials discounted the early stages of unrest over both proposed bills. Evidence which initially linked urban politicians to rural discontent persuaded officials that there was little substance to this unrest. They saw it as the product of educated Hindus, the despised "Babu" and "Baniya," and concluded that it could be safely ignored. Plunging ahead with the Colonization Bill, Punjab administrators realized to their surprise that the passage of the bill did not end this unrest. Discontent did not evaporate as it had in earlier instances. Even the postponement of water rate increases brought more rural demonstrations, not less.[72] The *Panjabee* case ended in conviction when, on April 16, lengthy jail sentences were confirmed by the Chief Court; violence erupted in the streets of Lahore. A crowd of young men returning from an "indignation meeting" clashed with mounted police on Anarkali Road. "Young and old, sight-seers as well as innocent shopkeepers were trampled under the horses of the policemen and belaboured with *lathis* and butt-ends of muskets. The shops of a Hindu confectioner and another man were forcibly entered into and their furniture, cash and all things wantonly damaged or thrown away. I have seen with my eyes the gaping wounds in the scalp and fractured limbs of two or three innocent by-stand-

70. Barrier, "Punjab Politics and the Disturbances of 1907," p. 367.
71. Barrier, *Ibid.*, pp. 362–363.
72. Barrier, *Ibid.*, pp. 354–355 and 365–366.

ers, who had come in for this cruel beating at the hands of the guardians of the law."[73]

By late April, individual officials began to ban meetings and speakers.[74] On April 30, P. D. Agnew, District Magistrate of Rawalpindi, ordered a public hearing into the supposed seditious character of meetings and speeches in that city. This was quickly followed by the arrest of Lala Hans Raj Sawhney and four of his political associates, all lawyers, Aryas, and prominent men of the province.[75] News of the arrests and of British cavalry in the streets of Rawalpindi created anger, then violence. Amidst an atmosphere of suppression and arrests, official opinion, led by the Lieutenant-Governor Denzil Ibbetson, now viewed the growing political agitation as a plot to overthrow the British Government. He demanded special authority from the central government to suppress all seditious agitators before they succeeded in poisoning the peasantry against their paternal administrators.[76] After some confusion within official circles, the Punjab Government received permission to act and quickly did so.[77] They arrested both Ajit Singh and Lala Lajpat Rai and secretly deported them to Burma.[78] Shocked and dazed, urban leaders faced a determined Punjab Government which banned public meetings in crucial districts and arrested political leaders. Urban unrest brought mass trials, police, and the army. Ibbetson further warned his officials against employing Aryas because of their seditious nature and urged that they be "dismissed at the least sign of disloyalty."[79] Repression suc-

73. *Tribune,* May 5, 1907, p. 5.

74. *Panjabee,* April 24, 1907, p. 3. The District Magistrate of Multan prohibited Ajit Singh from addressing a meeting, while the District Commissioner of Lahore refused permission for a public meeting designed to show sympathy and solidarity with the *Panjabee* over its law case with the government.

75. *Panjabee,* May 1, 1907, p. 3; *Tribune,* May 5, 1907, p. 5; and Barrier, "Punjab Politics and the Disturbances of 1907," p. 369.

76. Barrier, "Punjab Politics and the Disturbances of 1907," p. 368.

77. Barrier, *Ibid.,* pp. 368–370. He has an excellent analysis of the British Government's decision to back Ibbetson in his proposed policy of suppression.

78. For an account of the arrest and deportation of Lajpat Rai, see the *Tribune,* May 11, 1907, pp. 3, 5. Also see Lala Lajpat Rai, *The Story of my Deportation* (Lahore: Punjabee Press, 1908).

79. Confidential circular 715, May 7, 1907, PGP 10/B, quoted by Barrier, "The Arya Samaj and Congress Politics in the Punjab, 1894–1908," p. 375.

ceeded in quieting the cities, while a policy of conciliation brought peace to the countryside. On May 26, Lord Minto vetoed the Colonization Bill and the Punjab Government postponed water rate increases on the Bari Doab Canal, claiming the need for further study of the question. Rural agitation disappeared immediately to be replaced by an outburst of enthusiasm for the British Raj. Cut off from their rural allies, urban politicians felt the full weight of governmental anger. The apparent solidarity among Punjabi Hindus vanished, as group after group sought to protect itself in a hostile world.

In the days immediately following Lajpat Rai's deportation, politics remained confused. One trend quickly developed, a defense against charges of disloyalty which necessitated either direct or indirect rejection of "seditious" leadership. In an article, "Spectre of Hindu Mutiny," the *Tribune* attempted to protect the Hindu community from general condemnation. "We know there are many, many loyal Hindus who have no sympathy whatever with unconstitutional agitation and who condemn it as strongly as we do, knowing that nothing is to be gained by it and that in consequence the Hindu cause must suffer."[80] Although many criticized the extremists and Lajpat Rai, the *Panjabee* attempted to defend him, maintaining that Punjab was not Bengal and that extremism as such found little relevance in the province.

No praise or defense of Lajpat Rai could negate the fact of his arrest and deportation. It hung like a cloud over educated Hindus and particularly the Arya Samaj. Many Aryas felt a desperate need to reestablish some working relationship with the government. Life under the pressure of official distrust and governmental discrimination was too fearful to contemplate. On May 22, 1907, a delegation of leading Aryas met with Denzil Ibbetson, the Lieutenant-Governor, in the hope of reassuring the government and in return being reassured by it that Aryas were loyal and eager to live in mutual peace. Led by Lala Hans Raj, the delegation declared that "the Arya Samajists as a body had nothing to do with the later disturbances, that the Samaj was an organization which had for its sole object the religious educational advancement of its members and that at the time of the last disturbance in Lahore the College was closed and he firmly believed that D.A.V College boys

80. *Tribune*, May 15, 1907, p. 2.

had no hand in it."[81] They received a chilly reply. Ibbetson pointed out that "he had been informed by every Deputy Commissioner in the Province that wherever there was an Arya Samaj it was the centre of seditious talk. . . . [and while] he was pleased to see them and to hear their earnest disclaimer as to any complicity of the Arya Samaj with the later disturbances but he thought it a great pity these disclaimers did not appear a little earlier." He ended with the admonition that " . . . it was the duty of the Arya Samaj to dissociate itself publicly from what has lately happened."[82] Failing to find a sympathetic response from the Lieutenant-Governor, Arya leaders of the D.A.V. College proceeded to accept his advice. The Arya Pradeshak Pratinidhi Sabha met on the following day, declaring that it and the ninety-five affiliated Samajes "Resolved that the Arya Samaj has always been and is now a non-political body and this fact the Arya Samaj has publicly declared and expressed in writings, but as some mischievous people have now here and there spread rumours to the contrary, this meeting of the Executive Committee of the Arya Pradeshak Pratinidhi Sabha, takes this opportunity to reiterate its old creed and declares that it has no connection of any kind with any political body or with political agitation in any shape."[83]

Leaders of the college party were not alone in their fears of official displeasure. In a letter to the *Panjabee,* Lala Munshi Ram reaffirmed the non-political status of the Samaj. He also faced the reality of Arya agitation and political participation. "It cannot be denied that some members of the Arya Samaj along with their brethren of other communities Hindus, Sikhs, Muhammadans and Christians have taken part in constitutional political agitation. . . . A few fanatics drawn from different classes have been preaching and writing sedition, and have brought troubles even upon those who were for constitutional agitation."[84] Munshi Ram did not criticize Arya politicians but instead attempted to defend them. "It is unfortunate that Lala Lajpat Rai, Lalas Hans Raj and Gurdas Ram (of Rawalpindi), prominent members of the Arya

81. *Tribune,* May 28, 1907, p. 1.
82. *Tribune,* May 28, 1907, p. 1.
83. *Panjabee,* May 29, 1907, p. 4.
84. Quotes given below from *Panjabee,* June 12, 1907, p. 5. Also see the *Ārya Musāfir,* June 1907, pp. 719–732; September 1907, pp. 963–967; and October 1907, p. 3.

Samaj, have been suspected of unconstitutional agitation. We believe that these gentlemen were advocates of constitutional agitation only, and that sedition had no place in their minds."

Not all Aryas were so gentle in their attempts to dissociate themselves and their factions from Lajpat Rai and other political activists. During May and June, a long, bitter, and degrading debate erupted in Punjab press over the role of Lajpat Rai in politics and particularly within the Dayanand Anglo-Vedic College movement.[85]

Anxiety expanded rapidly as Hindus in general felt compromised by Aryas, much as many Aryas felt condemned by a few activists. Hindu reactions varied from outright rejection of politics and complete protestations of loyalty to mild statements of unease. By the end of summer Aryas still looked out upon a hostile world. Neither protestations of loyalty nor deputations to the highest levels of officialdom eased Hindu fears; only the government could do so. During the summer and early fall it did nothing. Instead, new stories of official repression appeared throughout the press. Revived anxiety over Muslim competition haunted Hindu leaders. The hope of united political action now gave way to communal competition. "There are some Mahomedans who are anxious to make political capital out of the present state of things in the Punjab. They think that among European Officers there is some feeling against the Hindus and they are anxious to make the most of it."[86] Communal favoritism threatened Hindu interests directly, since government jobs, if granted on any basis other than merit, might go to Muslims rather than the educated Hindu classes. Hindus already under pressure from more Muslim competition for jobs could only see an escalation of that competition, aided now by official and unofficial policy.

Muslim attacks on the Congress and the Hindu community, led by Mian Shah Din, a Justice of the Punjab High Court and prominent barrister, added to Hindu bitterness. Throughout the summer and into the fall relations between Muslims and Hindus stead-

85. See Madan Mohan Seth, *The Arya Samaj, A Political Body, An Open Letter to Viscount Morley* (Gurukul Kangri: n.d.), Appendix B and Appendix C, pp. xxvi-xxix; *Panjabee,* May 29, 1907, p. 6; June 5, 1907, pp. 2–4; June 8, 1907, p. 2; June 12, 1907, p. 2; June 15, 1907, p. 2; June 22, 1907, pp. 1–2; June 19, 1907, pp. 1–2; *Tribune,* May 30, 1907, p. 3.

86. *Tribune,* July 26, 1907, p. 2.

ily degenerated.[87] By October, rumors of a Muslim boycott of Hindu shops reappeared in the press, as one Muslim extremist called upon his co-religionists: "O you slaves of the Prophet Mohammad and you followers of the sacred prophet: gird up your loins and like true Muslims take vow that we would not buy anything from the shops of Hindu brothers!" In response the *Tribune* warned that "if the Muslim Press in the Punjab by being patted on the back and supported by the Anglo-Indian press goes out of its way to preach openly the *boycott* of *Hindu* shops to the Mahomedans here in the Punjab, the authorities must prepare themselves to see new troubles ahead in the calm-settling-down-Punjab."[88] While Muslim attacks on Hindus continued even to this fundamental level of economic separatism, the government moved slowly to reassure Hindu leaders.

The first indication of a changed governmental attitude came on September 14 with the release on bail of the Rawalpindi prisoners. Totally surprised, Hindu leaders rejoiced at this decision,[89] but still remained uncertain as to any long-term implications of this act. At the close of October, discussion of proposed amendments to the Sedition Bill brought an official assessment of the political situation that stressed the tranquility of both Punjab and British India.[90] On November 18 the government presented its most dramatic evidence of a changed attitude. Lajpat Rai and Ajit Singh reached Lahore and were released unconditionally. They reappeared nearly as mysteriously as they had vanished. "All speculations as to the whereabouts and destination of Lala Lajpat Rai and Sardar Ajit Singh were set at rest in the morning, when about 7 o'clock the news spread like wild fire through the city that the deported gentlemen had just arrived and reached their respective quarters at Lahore."[91] While some met to honor the returned Lajpat, there remained a strong current of unease. No one knew what the government had in mind. Hope existed but little certainty.

Encouraged by a change of atmosphere, Punjabi Hindus organized another deputation to the Lieutenant-Governor. Led by Justice Chatterjee, this delegation met with a much more cordial

87. *Panjabee,* September 25, 1907, p. 3; September 28, 1907, p. 2.
88. *Tribune,* October 1, 1907, p. 5.
89. *Tribune,* September 17, 1907, p. 2 and *Panjabee,* September 18, 1907, p. 3.
90. *Tribune,* October 31, 1907, p. 2; *Panjabee,* November 6, 1907, p. 3.
91. *Panjabee,* November 20, 1907, p. 3.

reception than previously. Sir Denzil Ibbetson's reply hinted at an alteration in both attitude and policy. "There has undoubtedly been a feeling abroad that because much of the recent agitation has been promoted by Hindus as such, or at any rate educated Hindus as such, therefore the government views them with suspicion and disfavour. Now I want to tell you as Lieutenant-Governor that that impression is absolutely unfounded and mistaken. It would be grossly unfair to condemn a whole community because of the sins of some of its members. As I said to some gentlemen who met me at Kalka last May I am prepared to take men as I find them; and I am glad to think—nay I am glad to *know*—that there were very many thousands of Hindus, and of educated Hindus, in the Punjab who are true and loyal subjects of His Majesty."[92] Going beyond his own opinions, Ibbetson touched on what worried Hindu leaders most, the attitude of officials throughout the province who often acted out of their own conviction and prejudice. "I have seen it said in the Press that it is of but small avail for the Lieutenant-Governor to hold these views unless they are held by his officers also and I know that rumours have been spread about that my officers do not always share these views. Well gentlemen, we all know how rumour distorts and embroiders facts and I have no doubt that it has been done so in this case. But I may tell you that in order to make quite certain I have recently taken measures to convey my views in this matter to my officers, and to impress them upon them for their guidance."[93] The Governor's assurance of "recently taken measures" did much to ease the anxieties of educated Hindus.[94] The acquittal a few days later of those charged in the Rawalpindi riot case pointed to a policy of official conciliation.[95]

With the easing of tensions between Hindus and the government, symbolized by the return of Lala Lajpat Rai and the success of the Hindu deputation, Hindu leaders returned to their pre-1907 causes in both politics and religion. Lajpat Rai spoke at both Arya Samaj anniversaries in Lahore, appearing on the same platform as Lala Munshi Ram and Dayanand Anglo-Vedic College

92. *Panjabee,* November 27, 1907, p. 4.

93. *Ibid.*

94. *Panjabee,* December 7, 1907, p. 3; also see December 11, 1907, p. 3; December 14, 1907, p. 3; and December 21, 1907, p. 3.

95. *Panjabee,* December 4, 1907, p. 3.

leaders. The two wings of the Samaj declared their solidarity and reiterated the non-political nature of their movement.[96] By the end of December, Punjabi delegates to the annual Congress meeting marched off to Surat with an air of hopefulness that the difficult months lay behind them and they could once more participate in national politics. Harkishen Lal, Lajpat Rai, Ram Bhaj Datta, and the perennial Murli Dhar journeyed to Surat to find not a revived but a disintegrating Congress.[97] The growing rift within the Congress, between moderates and radicals, lay partially obscured by provincial problems, leaving little thought to the wider dilemmas of the National Congress. Punjabis hoped that somehow a compromise could be reached between the contending parties,[98] but all promise of unity proved false; the Congress split and 1908 saw Punjabi leaders faced with a bleak political world. The Congress was divided nationally and nearly paralyzed provincially. Past forms of politics seemed to offer little hope of alleviating the plight of educated Hindus. The old fears remained. Government suspicions continued, as did communal competition and the economic plight of the urban Hindus. Self-help, self-improvement, and communal solidarity offered the only basis for a rational program in the immediate future, for, if Punjabis believed in one maxim above all others, they knew that "God helps those who help themselves."

96. *Panjabee,* December 4, 1907, p. 4.

97. *Panjabee,* December 28, 1907, p. 4, gives a partial list of Congress delegates.

98. *Panjabee,* December 21, 1907, p. 3; for a lengthy discussion of the Congress difficulties, see *Tribune,* October 16, 1907, p. 3.

# Chapter X

# THE POLITICAL EXPRESSION OF HINDU CONSCIOUSNESS

> An attempt at unification has failed and failed miserably. Instead of the growth of one united nation, a sharp line of demarcation has been drawn and sanctioned by authority. In making their attempt the Hindus have lost ground and their interests have been pushed backward. There is surely time yet to turn round and try to recover lost ground. And this can only be achieved by asserting purely Hindu interest, and not by an Indian propaganda. The consciousness must arise in the mind of each Hindu that he is a Hindu, and not merely an Indian, and when it does arise the newly awakened force is bound to bring its results.
>
> LALA LAL CHAND

## TOWARD A HINDU POLITICS

The shadow of 1907 darkened the intervening years before World War I. Punjabi Hindus felt continual pressure from the government, from competing elites, and from declining economic opportunity. They searched for effective vehicles to protect their communal and class interest, but with little success. Aryas, who had led them into Congress, led them out again and into an explicitly Hindu politics. Finally, formal politics itself was abandoned, leaving only the older forms of communal and sectarian action and the institutions which supported this action. *Shuddhi, prachār,* education, and social uplift remained the only effective methods for the protection of urban Hindus and the broader religious community. After fifty years of history many Punjabi Hindus held a hierarchy of identities, Arya Dharm at the core, Hindu consciousness as an ideal of communal unity, and beyond that the vague, all-encompassing nationalism of a secular India.

In the opening months of 1908, three poles of anxiety delinated the world of Punjabi Hindus: the residue of fear and official hostility left from the unrest of 1907, the division of the Congress into two warring camps, and the impending reform legislation, which promised both hope for constitutional liberalization and the possibility of further governmental favoritism to the Muslim community. Around these points swirled new and old fears, as Hindu leaders sought some method of defense against their personal and communal opponents. Hemmed in by religious competition, an unfriendly government, and limited economic expansion, the educated Hindus of the Punjab continued to increase and to find diminishing opportunities within their world. A sense of impotency, of frustration, and insecurity haunted the urban elite, breeding as often factional strife as unity. National issues receded while Punjabi Hindus sought to bolster the fortunes of their own community.

The Surat Congress and its resulting chaos left Punjabis puzzled, angered, and confused. As they discussed both what had happened and what should be done, various factions advanced differing solutions from their own personal and ideological positions.[1] The Gurukul Aryas condemned Tilak and his extremist allies for destroying the Congress. They were an evil influence on Hindu youth and had infected them with "the poison of the 'New Spirit.'"[2] Members of the college party, who opposed Lajpat Rai, tried to bar from membership in either the College committees or staff anyone who had taken part in politics.[3] Although this attempt to purge politically active Aryas failed, it contributed to further factional and personal bitterness. Similarly, the appointment of Lala Harkishen Lal to the Punjab Legislative Council in February was condemned by followers of Lajpat Rai.[4] Politicians and the press still dreamed of an effective Congress organization throughout the Punjab, but there was little likelihood of this.[5]

With the Congress in disarray, Hindus felt a pressing need to create an organization which would speak for and defend their

1. See discussion in the *Tribune*, January 1, 1908, p. 2; January 2, 1908, p. 2.

2. *Sat Dharm Prachārak*, January 10, 1908, Government of India, *Selections from the Vernacular Newspapers Published in the Punjab, 1908*, pp. 39–40.

3. This motion was introduced by Lala Mulraj. *Sat Dharm Prachārak*, January 31, 1908, *SPVP 1908*, p. 84; and *Jhang Siāl*, February 8, 1908, *SPVP 1908*, p. 96.

4. *Jhang Siāl*, February 15, 1908, *SPVP 1908*, pp. 104–105; the *Tribune* was also brought into this quarrel, see *Aftāb-i-Punjāb*, February 23, 1908, *SPVP 1908*, p. 129.

5. *Parkāsh*, February 18, 1908, *SPVP 1908*, p. 101.

community. In the spring of 1908, Ram Bhaj Datta's earlier suggestion that the Hindu Sahayak Sabha fulfill a political role began to find adherents among Hindu politicians. By June, Lajpat Rai became convinced that Hindus needed to organize in order to defend themselves. The rapid expansion of the Punjab Muslim League and continued governmental hostility undergirded his arguments.[6] Hindu Sabhas were formed throughout the province during 1908–1909.[7] Aryas deserted the Congress, turning instead to the Hindu Sabha movement. The Hindu Sabhas still retained their religious and social overtones,[8] but given time and persistent anxiety, they gradually became as well a political tool of Punjabi Hindus.

During the spring and summer of 1908 governmental suppression of extremist politicians continued along with a revival of older, well-established nightmares. The drama of Tilak's arrest, trial and deportation not only cast a pall of gloom over Hindu leaders, but heightened tensions between those who supported and those who condemned political extremism.[9] Even from beyond the border of British India came news of arrests, discrimination and governmental suppression, this time from South Africa. Punjabis read eagerly of Gandhi's campaigns to save their brethren from white racism and its ally, colonial government.[10] The rights and dignity of Hindus appeared under attack wherever one looked.

In August, the Punjab Hindu Sabha presented an "address of welcome" to Sir Louis Dane, the new Lieutenant-Governor of Punjab.[11] Little resulted. The estrangement between government and

6. Barrier, "The Arya Samaj and Congress Politics in the Punjab, 1894–1908," *Journal of Asian Studies,* XXVI, No. 3, (May 1967), pp. 378–379.

7. Barrier, *Ibid.*, p. 379. He states that every district had a Hindu Sabha affiliated with the Punjab Hindu Sabha by June 1908. The Gurdaspur Hindu Sabha was founded, however, in June 1909. *Panjabee,* July 8, 1909, p. 5.

8. The Hindu Sabha began famine relief work in January 1908; *Tribune,* January 28, 1908, p. 6; it organized a school and even sponsored an occasional religious ritual. See *Tribune,* March 20, 1908, p. 4; May 3, 1910, p. 4.

9. *Tribune,* July 17, 1908, p. 2; August 1, 1908, p. 1; August 2, 1908, p. 1; and August 13, 1908, p. 1. Also see the articles on the Tinnevely Sedition Case and the Kol Sedition, *Tribune,* July 18, 1908, pp. 1–2.

10. See *Tribune,* January 14, 1908, p. 2; January 22, 1908, p. 5; September 13, 1908, p. 1; September 19, 1908, p. 1; and September 23, 1908, p. 1, for news items illustrating the Gandhian issue and Punjabi response.

11. *Panjabee,* August 19, 1908, *SPVP 1908,* pp. 509–510.

the Hindu community remained. Lajpat Rai noted that "The experiences of the past twelve months have thrown many people off their balance. Gigantic and stupendous efforts are being made to identify the refractory and the 'dangerous' and to hand them over to the hangman in the name of, and for, the safety of self and others. In such circumstances Aryas should hold to their beliefs, have nothing to do with the government, and never compromise their principles." For men of faith this answer sufficed, but for most Aryas and Hindus, incidents illustrating official tyranny remained more real and more relevant.[12]

The new year saw a continuation of Arya complaints over official harassment. The press carried stories of police spies, of official *zulum* (tyranny), as Aryas debated among themselves and factions accused each other of straying from the "true" Arya goals.[13] This debate proved inconclusive. It solved nothing. Arya fears remained as a subsection of greater Hindu anxieties. Looming over all and driving Hindus toward unity stood the proposed reforms. Hindu leaders reacted to two facets of these constitutional proposals: first, the degree to which they would be adopted within the Punjab, and second, to the principle of separate electorates. The Punjab Government seemed determined to limit the application of these measures. The province would receive only the most circumscribed use of election and elective councils. This offended Punjabi leaders, since it implied provincial backwardness and specifically threatened Hindus. It seemed as if the government would retain its powers of appointment and nomination using them to advance other communities ahead of urban Hindus. Even more frightening were the proposed separate electorates with their implied

12. For incidents of kine slaughter and Hindu response, see *Hindustān*, September 11, 1908, *SPVP 1908*, pp. 568–589; *Watan*, January 29, 1909, *SPVP 1909*, pp. 123–124; *Ārya Musāfir*, February 1909, *SPVP 1909*, pp. 192–193; *Rajput Gazette*, February 24, 1909, *SPVP 1909*, p. 192; *Jhang Siāl*, March 20, 1909, *SPVP 1909*, pp. 268–269; *Punjāb Samāchār*, April 3, 1909, *SPVP 1909*, pp. 319–320; *Hindustān*, May 14, 1909, *SPVP 1909*, p. 470; *Panjabee*, October 12, 1909, p. 4; November 6, 1909, p. 5; December 2, 1909, p. 5; December 7, 1909, p. 5

13. *Indar*, January 1909, *SPVP 1909*, pp. 137–139; *Ārya Musāfir*, March 1909, pp. 74–80; *Arya Gazette*, March 11, 1909, *SPVP 1909*, p. 244; *Prakāsh*, March 23, 1909, pp. 295–296; *Indar*, March and April 1909, *SPVP 1909*, pp. 217–218; *Prakāsh*, May 11, 1909, *SPVP 1909*, p. 466; *Prakāsh*, May 4, 1909, *SPVP 1909*, pp. 422–423; *Akāsh*, May 27, 1909, *SPVP 1909*, pp. 515–516; *Panjabee*, September 30, 1909, p. 1.

favoritism to the Muslim community, which in Punjab accounted for a majority of the population. For Punjabi Hindus this issue was communal, not national. Even the *Tribune* attacked separate electorates from a Hindu bias, pushed by events into the arms of its Arya enemies.[14]

In February, the first of a series of letters appeared in the *Panjabee* under the title "Self-Abnegation in Politics." These letters, by Lala Lal Chand, delineated the world of Hindu fear. They expressed vividly and accurately the base of Hindu ideology within the Punjab and later throughout much of British India.[15] Lal Chand's assessment of the Hindu community, its present plight and future prospects paralleled many later statements by the Samaj, the Hindu Mahasabha and the Rashtriya Swayamsevak Sangh. He explicitly rejected the Congress which repeatedly failed to support Hindu issues or even to discuss them. "If there is one thing which is strictly forbidden within the precincts of the Congress it is the term 'Hindu.' [A] resolution may be passed to favour purely Mohammadan interests but the Hindu is tabooed there." The Congress followed a dual set of values, ignoring Hindus interests while catering to the Islamic community.[16] The government demonstrated a similar discriminatory policy, vetoing the Chenab Colony Act but retaining the land Alienation Amendment. Both government and Congress tactics directly threatened the Hindu elite. "The Hindu middle class, which, as past history shows, is the real backbone of the community has now been driven away from one legitimate source of livelihood namely, the land. In the absence of any effective opposition the state of affairs has gone from bad to worse." Besides landownership, discriminatory policies hindered Hindu

14. They were discussed almost continuously in the pages of the *Tribune* from January through April. Some of the more valuable statements are to be found in the following issues: April 8, p. 1; January 9, p. 1; January 12, p. 1; January 13, p. 1; January 14, p. 1; January 15, p. 1; January 19, p. 1; January 26, p. 2; February 2, p. 2; February 19, p. 3; March 4, p. 2; March 16, p. 1; March 20, p. 2; March 28, p. 2; April 1, p. 2; April 9, p. 2; April 22, p. 3; April 27, p. 4; and April 28, p. 1.

15. Lal Chand's letters were later published in tract form; see *Self-Abnegation in Politics* (Lahore: The Central Hindu Yuvak Sabha, 1938), with a forward by Bhai Parmananda. Indra Prakash, in *A Review of the History and Work of the Hindu Mahasabha* (Delhi: Hindu Mahasabha, 1952), sees this statement as a foundation stone of the Hindu Mahasabha movement, pp. 9–11.

16. Lal Chand, *Self-Abnegation*, pp. 2–7.

advance in the governmental services. "Being driven away from the land, they are also being gradually ousted from Government service as a means of living. And, barring law and medicine, the only remaining source left is trade and industry where they are making a struggle."

Hemmed in by economic constriction, opposed by Muslims, Christians, and government, abandoned by the Congress, Hindus faced a hostile world. "The Hindus have no outside friends and sympathisers to look after and press their claims. Inside India they are helpless between the police and repressive measures, even if they give utterance to their grievances." A sense of impending doom ran through Lal Chand's assessment of his times. Hindus were weak, divided, and alone. "The result was that Hindu nationality and Hindu sentiments were being gradually obliterated and thrown in the background if not pushed out of existence."

The obvious strength of the Hindu community, its vast numbers, diminished upon closer examination. First the government intended to assist Muslims to overcome their numerical inferiority. The Morley-Minto Reforms proved this. "The Secretary of State speaks of the importance of Muhammadans as a community in the United Provinces in spite of their minor numerical strength, but he takes it for granted that the Hindu Minority of the Punjab is of no importance against the Muhammadan majority so that according to the Secretary of State where the Muhammadans form a majority they must get a lions share as a matter of course; and where they are in a minority, they will get it on the basis of their supposed importance."[17] Government would strip the Hindus of their right to dominance, while Christian missionaries would, in time, finish this task of destroying Hindu power. "Both in theory and in practice the Hindus have already been reduced to a position as if they formed 50 per cent of the population. They will soon be reduced to a position of one-third as another community of one kith and creed with the rulers is rapidly rising." The threat of Christian conversion still haunted Lal Chand after three decades as an ardent Arya. Hindus faced a future that promised gradual but inevitable diminution of their numbers. Perhaps in time they might disappear altogether. This nightmare was for the imaginative Hindu already taking place.

17. Quotes given below from Lal Chand, *Self-Abnegation*, pp. 12–13.

Muslims, even though a minority within British India, did not stand alone. Millions of Muslims bordered Hindu India. The followers of Islam with their heritage of warfare and unity stood ready to assist their brethren, while their mere presence in the world influenced the government. The British had already moved to strengthen this Islamic world and limit the geographical area of Hinduism. The partition of Bengal created a new Muslim province, as did the partition of the Punjab. "The Frontier Province, as it is called, was only a few years ago an adjunct of our Province but it was separated, . . . [creating] a province with exclusive preponderance of Mohammadan interests. . . ."[18]

Not only had the British aided Muslims while suppressing Hindus, they had in addition created the tension and communal mentality accountable for current religious strife. Lal Chand vividly described the town council of a Punjab city chosen by separate electorates. " . . . the members in the Committee meetings arrange themselves in two rows, around the Presidential chair. On the left are seated the representatives of the banner of Islam, and on the right the descendants of the old Rishis of Aryavarta. By this arrangement the members are constantly reminded that they are not simply Municipal Commissioners but they are as Muhammadans *versus* Hindus and *vice versa* . . . their activity is not so much to look after Municipal affairs, as to see that no advantage is gained by a Hindu or by a Muhammadan."[19] What was happening in a municipal council would now take place throughout British India as the government and Lord Curzon had decreed. "The fiat has now gone forth that there shall be separate electorates and separate representatives for the Hindus and the Muhammadans from top to bottom," a world divided, with one community set against all others, where Muslims were favored for their "importance." This seemed to characterize the future as determined by official policy.

Returning repeatedly to economics, to questions of employment, class legislation, educational policy and language, Lal Chand offered his program of action. "This then is the plan I advocate and the course I propose to adopt:—the substitution of Hindu Sabhas for Congress Committees, of a Hindu Press for the Congress Press, organisation of a Hindu Defence Fund with regu-

18. Quotes given below from Lal Chand, *Ibid.*, pp. 62–63.
19. Quotes given below from Lal Chand, *Ibid.*, p. 23.

lar office and machinery for collecting information and seeking redress by self-help, self-ameliorations and petitions and memorials supplemented by agitation in the Press and advocacy through trusted leaders in matters both special and common but dominated primarily by regard for Hindu interests."[20] Such an organization dedicated solely to the Hindu community could, he hoped, create unity. Not only would Hindu unity and Hindu political action save the community, it would in time bring about a reconciliation between Hindus and Muslims. "National" unity then could be achieved after communal unity, not through the false efforts of appeasement that characterized Congress policies. "My own belief is that if we succeed in establishing strong independent Hindu organisations, the Moslems would in course of time join us in making common demand or redress of common grievances." This argument enabled Lal Chand and those who would follow him to see communal loyalty as supporting nationalism, not negating it.

Lal Chand went beyond the immediate problems of the Hindu community to consider and then call for religious loyalty. "The point I wish to urge is that patriotism ought to be communal and not merely geographical."[21] Loyalty must be first to the community. "The idea is to love everything owned by the community. It may be religion, it may be a tract of country, or it may be a phase of civilization. But these are mere outward clothes of the inner feeling. This then is the fire I wish to rekindle." Communal unity, loyalty and patriotism offered hope for the future. The past offered vivid examples of communal death. "History bears ample testimony to how communities have been effaced and castrated. I will not go far but only refer to the case of Kashmir Valley, where, if my information is correct, the very dress was forced upon the people to make them effeminate." Lal Chand's letters marked a move from Arya Dharm to Hindu consciousness. They laid the foundation for Hindu politics as an alternative to the "national" politics of the Congress.

During July and August, leaders of the Hindu Sabha began

20. Quotes given below from Lal Chand, *Ibid.*, pp. 121–125; also see pages 123–124 on the Hindu Defence Fund, and pages 122–123 on the need for a Hindu press.

21. Quotes given below from Lal Chand, *Ibid.*, pp. 100–103.

planning for the first provincial Hindu Conference. At the end of August the Sabha announced that such a conference would meet over the Dussehra holiday on October 21 and 22. Sir Protul Chandra Chatterjee would preside. Lal Chand headed the reception committee which included Pandit Ram Bhaj Datta, Hari Chand of Multan, Lala Sukh Dial, and Lala Shadi Lal.[22] As preparations for the conference moved steadily forward, the writings of a Bengali Hindu reached Punjab and underscored Lal Chand's predictions, painting an even grimmer picture of the future disintegration of the Hindu community. Using census data, Lieutenant-Colonel U. N. Mukerji of the Indian Medical Service predicted the destruction of Hinduism as other religious communities through conversion and more rapid growth rates would submerge the once-dominant Hindus. His articles appeared in the *Bengalee* under the title, "A Dying Race," and vividly described the decline of the community. "The census report shows that within the space of 30 years from 1872 to 1901 the Mahomedans of Bengal proper, who were at the start in a minority of 4 lakhs, had not only made up the deficiency, but had become more numerous by nearly 25 lakhs than the Hindus. The increase had been steady and continuous, the Mahomedans having multiplied by 33 per cent and the Hindus only by 17 per cent." The declining Hindu population of Bengal pointed to a future of minority status of impotence and discrimination. It was as well the product of Hindu vice and Islamic virtue. "Various causes are at the root of this disparity—social, religious and economic—but the root cause is that while the Mahomedan aspiration is after strength and solidarity, the Hindu living for himself is without a broad outlook and therefore is declining. The former look for a united Mahomedan world, the latter are waiting for the nirvana of each and everyone of themselves. Thus while the one community grows in numbers, in strength, in

22. The committee personnel were as follows: Lal Chand, Advocate, R. B., M.A., Lahore, Chairman; Ram Saran Das, R.S., Reis, Lahore, Vice-President; Hari Chand, R.B., Reis, Multan, Vice-President; Meh Singh Chawla, M.C., Lahore, Vice-President; Shadi Lal, R.B., Bar-at-Law, Lahore, General Secretary; Gopal Chand, B.A., LL.B., Pleader, Lahore, Secretary; Roshan Lal, Pleader, Lahore, Financial Secretary; Sukh Dial, R.S., Advocate, Lahore, Financial Secretary; Ram Bhaj Datta, Chaudhari, B.A., Pleader, Lahore, Secretary, Organization Sub-Committee; Karam Chand Puri, M.C., Lahore, Secretary, Accommodation Sub-Committee; from *Panjabee*, August 28, 1909, p. 1.

material welfare and solidarity, the other is hastening towards disintegration."[23] "A Dying Race" soon became the symbol for the worst of the present, the grimmest of futures. Its vision added momentum to the proposed conference which would, it was hoped, provide an effective vehicle for unity and the preservation of the Hindu community.[24]

The conference in its organization and execution followed the pattern of the Indian National Congress. Local Hindu Sabhas met and chose delegates, while the reception committee prepared a program of resolutions for the assembly's consideration.[25] The proposed program followed a careful logic. After initial opening ceremonies and speeches, the delegate would consider a series of issues focusing on "feelings of Hindu Nationality and Hindu Unity." Grouped together were questions of language—Sanskrit, Hindi and Panjabi—the popularization of Hindu scriptures and literature, the celebration of Hindu festivals, the creation of a "true" Hindu history, cow protection, and the encouragement of traditional Hindu medicine. From problems of Hindu cultural unity the conference would consider relations between the Hindu community and the government, including resolutions on the Land Act, discrimination against Hindus in governmental service, the proposed reforms, and the problem of frontier violence. During their final session they would turn once more to internal problems, beginning with the overwhelming issue of numbers, the decline of the Hindu majority. From numbers they would consider

23. *Panjabee,* August 12, 1909, p. 3; see earlier statements in *Panjabee,* July 15, 1909, p. 3 and August 3, 1909, p. 2.

24. See *Panjabee,* September 4, 1909, p. 1; September 25, 1909, p. 3, and a reprinted article from the *Bengalee* in *Panjabee,* October 9, 1909, p. 1.

25. The *Panjabee* gave great attention to the Conference, to the founding of new Hindu Sabhas, the selection of delegates, the projected program and an account of the Conference daily proceedings. Two new Hindu Sabhas were founded in Lyallpur and Jhang, see *Panjabee,* September 7, 1909, p. 4 and October 7, 1909, p. 4; for the selection of delegates, see issues for October 2, 1909, p. 4; October 7, 1909, p. 4; October 9, 1909, p. 4; October 12, 1909, p. 4; October 16, 1909, p. 4; and for general comments on the Conference and the Hindu cause, see *Panjabee* for August 7, 1909, p. 4; August 17, 1909, p. 4; August 26, 1909, p. 4; September 7, 1909, p. 4; September 9, 1909, p. 4; September 18, 1909, pp. 1 and 3; September 25, 1909, p. 4; September 30, 1909, p. 4; October 5, 1909, p. 1; October 7, 1909, p. 3; October 12, 1909, p. 4; October 14, 1909, p. 3; and October 16, 1909, pp. 4 and 5.

various factors contributing to this phenomenon: physical degeneration, the question of widows, orphans, of low caste Hindus and their treatment, the multiplicity of subcastes, and the encouragement of technical education. Lastly, they would examine the feasibility of an All-India Hindu Conference and a proposed constitution for the Punjab Hindu Sabha.[26]

The conference moved through its program with little discord, as speech followed speech and resolutions were adopted in a steady stream. It appeared completely successful as delegates passed each resolution with unanimous acclaim, but underneath this surface unanimity remained acute differences over the degree to which the Hindu Sabha should be overtly political. Also the deep division between reformers and orthodoxy failed to appear due to a last minute change in the program. The final section of resolutions dealing with such issues as the declining number of Hindus and the depressed classes were never considered by the conference. Time ran out; the resolutions were deleted and controversy averted, but the accidental nature of this change itself became an issue, as militant reformers charged that the resolutions were deliberately removed to maintain an air of solidarity.[27] A seemingly minor issue, this reflected serious divisions which would haunt all efforts at creating an effective organization to represent Punjabi Hindus.

All differences, all difficulties disappeared, beneath a wave of enthusiasm and satisfaction as the conference closed. The conference drew wide praise from the provincial Hindu press.[28] The *Panjabee* proudly reprinted comments from throughout India, as paper after paper eulogized this new political creation.[29] The issue raised, speeches made, and resolutions passed provided topics for excited discussion, as Hindus hoped for a better future, one in which they could maintain their status and prevent further

26. *Panjabee,* October 14, 1909, p. 4.

27. See *Panjabee,* October 30, 1909, p. 3; for hints of disagreement over political issues, see October 26, 1909, pp. 5–6.

28. *Panjabee,* October 28, 1909, p. 3; November 2, 1909, p. 5; November 4, 1909, p. 3; *Tribune,* October 31, 1909, p. 2.

29. *Panjabee,* November 4, 1909, pp. 1–2; November 6, 1909, p. 2; and November 9, 1909, p. 2. Newspapers quoted included the following: the *Hindu, Indian Patriot, Amrita Bazaar Patrika, Indian Social Reformer, Hindoo Patriot, Indian Mirror, Advocate, Indian Spectator, Bengalee, Madras Standard;* unfavorable comments were no doubt ignored.

governmental action against their interests.[30] But enthusiasm soon dimmed as the old sense of helplessness returned. On July 30, 1909, the Punjab Hindu Sabha sent a memorial to the Viceroy detailing their fears and complaints. The Viceroy himself had invited this memorial after meeting with the Sabha deputation in Lahore.[31] On October 30, the *Panjabee* published the Viceroy's reply. It was a defense of the status quo and indicated official unwillingness to alter existing legislation and current practices of employment.[32] Punjabi Hindus had failed once more to move the government.

If an overtly and specifically Hindu politics did not bring immediate gains, it did further undercut Hindu interest in the Congress. Scheduled to meet in Lahore for its 1909 session, the Indian National Congress returned at an incredibly inopportune time. The proposed Congress meeting accentuated existing divisions among Punjabi Hindus and their diminished support for the Congress. As early as January 1909, militant Aryas condemned the Congress for its secularism. Such criticism was not new, but with the growing wave of Hindu consciousness, attacks on the Congress for forgetting religion and abandoning Hindu interests became general, spreading to many who once favored the Congress cause. By April, this anti-Congress feeling was painfully evident. The *Hindustān*, a pro-Congress paper, surveyed the political situation with a sense of desperation. "It was in an inauspicious moment . . . that the National Congress was invited to meet in the Punjab in December next. Opposition to the movement is fast gaining strength, which presages the failure of its next session. . . . Educated Hindus have grown lukewarm in their interests in the Congress, and have come to believe that a purely Hindu political movement is indispensable for safeguarding their interests."[33] After pointing out that both Muslims and Sikhs were unwilling to support the Congress, the *Hindustān* concluded gloomily that "if the Punjabis do not feel equal to holding its next session in a befitting manner, they had better proclaim their incapacity, so that

30. See *Panjabee*, October 26, 1909, p. 2; October 28, 1909, pp. 2, 5; November 2, 1909, pp. 2–4; November 4, 1909, p. 5; *Tribune*, October 31, 1909, p. 1; November 1, 1909, p. 1 and November 4, 1909, p. 1.

31. *Panjabee*, November 2, 1909, pp. 1–2, contains a copy of the memorial.

32. *Panjabee*, October 30, 1909, p. 2, text of the Viceroy's reply.

33. Quotes given below from *Hindustān*, April 23, 1909, *SPVP 1909*, p. 383.

some other province may come forward to discharge this national duty. Otherwise . . . there is a fear that the Congress may cease to exist and that the country's hopes from it may be dashed to the ground." Predictions of disaster aside, preparations for the coming Congress continued amidst increasing controversy.

Lajpat Rai turned from his past commitment to open condemnation. Previously Lajpat had occasionally differed with the Congress or simply abandoned it to more compelling causes; he now led an openly anti-Congress movement. He declared that "I am strongly of the opinion . . . that the efforts to hold the next session of the Congress at Lahore *in defiance of the best Hindu opinion of the Province* . . . are unwise and not in the best interests of the country, the Province and the Congress."[34] Lajpat's rejection of the Congress marked the departure of Aryas from Congress politics. It opened as well a sustained public debate which included a strong element of personal animosity between Lajpat Rai and Harkishen Lal. Past and present points of tension between these two leaders added fuel to the question of Congress acceptance among Punjabi Hindus.[35] Preparations for the meetings rested solely on Harkishen Lal and his allies. As the Punjab Hindu Conference drew near, it commanded the attention and energy of Punjabi Hindus. The Congress was nearly forgotten.

Problems plagued Congress organizers. As president both of the Punjab Congress Committee and the reception committee, Harkishen Lal carried the burden of organizing the Lahore session, a task of considerable difficulty and complexity. He found little assistance from within or beyond the Punjab. The choice of Congress president to preside over the session proved difficult. Finally in September, Ferozeshah Mehta agreed to act as president only to resign suddenly within six days of the actual meeting.[36] In desperation Harkishen Lal persuaded Pandit M. M. Malaviya to accept the Congress presidency. The session began in an atmosphere of chaos and anxiety. If any Congress was a failure, except for the disaster at Surat, it was this one. With the lowest attendance

34. *Tribune*, July 22, 1909, p. 5.

35. See *Tribune*, June 19, 1909, p. 1; July 3, p. 1; July 22, pp. 5–6; July 23, p. 1; July 27, p. 3; July 28, p. 1; July 29, p. 4; July 30, 1909, p. 1; August 1, p. 3; August 7, p. 2; August 11, p. 3; August 14, p. 3; August 15, p. 1; September 29, p. 2.

36. *Tribune*, September 29, 1909, p. 1; December 15, 1909, p. 1; also issues of December 17, p. 3; December 18, p. 4.

of its history, the third Lahore session indicated just how little interest it generated in the Punjab. Punjabi participation in the Lahore congress sessions fell from 481 delegates in 1893 to 421 in 1900 and a mere 76 in 1909.[37] The *Panjabee* assessed the 1909 meeting with brutal clarity. "Congress has come and gone. It came unwelcomed and departed unmourned . . . . It has given no new impulse to the political life of the country, inspired no new thoughts, [no] hopes, nor made the future of the movement any the brighter or smoother. It has perpetuated differences, made patent new lines of cleavage in the Indian community, and put off the realisation of national unity even to a greater distance than was ever imagined before: It has brought down Hindu sympathy with the movement almost to the freezing point, and made the Mahomedan estrangement from it complete."[38]

The Lahore Congress failed even to temporarily revive Punjabi enthusiasm for its cause. The *Tribune* duly reported on its speeches and proceedings, but within a month of the meetings even they turned their attention elsewhere.[39] During the next five years Punjabi delegations to the Congress sank to literally nothing.[40] Neither Lajpat Rai nor the Aryas returned to the Congress cause. It remained instead in the hands of a dwindling band surrounding Lala Harkishen Lal who lost much of his interest in politics as he became immersed in business and finally in the downfall of his economic empire. The reunion of Bengal in 1911 ended the great partition issue which had fueled much of the political life on a national scale and brought a drift toward unity among Muslims and Hindus. Disillusioned by reunion and anxious over the Balkan wars, Muslims sought a common ground with Congress leaders. This search was made easier by moderate control of the Congress. Extremism as a political creed was dormant and discredited. Tilak

37. Besant, *How India Wrought for Freedom: The Story of the National Congress Told from Official Records* (Adyar, Madras: The Theosophical Publishing House, 1915), pp. 162, 311, and 491.

38. *Panjabee,* December 30, 1909, p. 3.

39. See *Tribune,* December 28, 1909, p. 1; December 29, 1909, p. 1; December 30, 1909, p. 2; December 31, 1909, p. 2; and January 9, 1910, p. 1.

40. Punjabi deputations to the Indian National Congress fell steadily. In 1910 they accounted for 37 delegates out of 636; in 1911, only 3 out of 446; in 1912, 4 out of 207; in 1913, 10 out of 550; and in 1914, zero out of 866. Besant, *How India Wrought for Freedom,* pp. 509, 528, 552, 570, and 595.

was in jail, along with many others who had preached militancy, and the only alternative on the national scene remained the terrorism of young revolutionaries. Punjabi Hindus observed it all, but continued uninvolved. The *Tribune* faithfully reported each Congress session, but the few feeble attempts to revive Congress organizations in the province lacked both adherents and effectiveness.[41] Politics among Punjabi Hindus stayed in the hands of the Hindu Sabha and was overtly communal. Punjabi Hindus abandoned national politics.

### THE PUNJAB HINDU CONFERENCE, 1910–1914

In the years following its first meeting, the Punjab Hindu Conference and the Punjab Hindu Sabha replaced the Congress in the loyalties and expectations of educated Hindus. The annual conference expressed a generalized communal consciousness and also attempted to protect the community by winning redress for Hindu grievances and by providing leadership for Hindu projects. Yet effective action necessitated leadership and resources which in turn rested on a base of group identity. The degree to which Hindus saw themselves as such and were willing to submerge their existing loyalties, passions and diverse personalities delineated the effectiveness of the Hindu Sabha. Unity remained thin and tenuous, only occasionally effective during times of extreme communal stress. The sense of "Hinduness" proved strongest when action was merely symbolic, evoking the commonest symbols of communal pride or communal anxiety. Concrete proposals, whether political or social, threatened to accentuate deep differences within the Hindu community. The Sabha faced an ugly choice between unity and effectiveness. It drifted toward the former.

The Punjab of late 1909 and 1910 still lived under the fear of governmental suppression. The press talked of sedition, carried accounts of arrests and lengthy trials. The strong hand of government lay everywhere manifested in the C.I.D., punitive police, proclaimed districts and official lists of unreliable individuals and groups.[42] Overt political action seemed to offer little save con-

41. See the *Tribune* for December and January of the years 1910 through 1914. Little else can be found on the Congress during the rest of these years.

42. See the *Tribune*, December 1909 and January through February 1910 on the Lahore Sedition Case and the trials in Patiala; also June and July 1910 for the

tinued official hostility. Caught in a "Hamlet-like" dilemma, the Hindu Sabha did next to nothing. Even sharply worsening relations between the Hindu minority of the border districts and the surrounding Muslims failed to stir the Sabha.[43] In April, communal riots swept Peshawar, shocking the Hindu community as yet another example of Muslim violence.[44] The following month a deputation of leading Hindus met with the Chief Commissioner of the North-West Frontier Province to express Hindu grievances and concern. Led by Rai Bahadur Hari Chand, this delegation acted without reference to the Punjab Hindu Sabha.[45] They achieved little, and the plight of their brethren on the frontier remained a crucial, unsolved issue for Punjabi Hindus.[46]

In the wake of the Peshawar troubles and amidst worsening relations between Hindus and Muslims, leaders of the Sabha began plans for the second Punjab Hindu Conference. This would be held in Multan, with Bahadur Hari Chand chairing the reception committee and Sardar Gurbakhsh Singh Bedi as president. In the weeks before the conference the press discussed the advisability of political action. Should the conference become an openly political body or not? This question loomed over the conference unanswered, intrusive, and all-pervading.[47] The conference itself disappointed its leaders. In spite of considerable concern over the need for an all-India organization, prominent Hindus from beyond Punjab failed to attend. The response even among Punjabi Hindus did not reach expectation. Planning for 2,000 delegates

---

appeal of Bhai Parmanand, the placing of Rohtak under restrictive law, searches and arrests of Sanatanist leaders, and the extension of the seditious meetings bill. July and August brought news of Savarkar's arrest and escape which was followed avidly by Punjabi readers.

43. See *Tribune,* March 24, 1910, p. 1.

44. *Tribune,* April 5, 1910, p. 1.

45. Lala Harkishen Lal joined the deputation as did several leading Sikhs, including Baba Gurbakhsh Singh Bedi, but Lal Chand did not join nor Lajpat Rai, Ram Bhaj Datta or others closely associated with the first Punjab Hindu Conference. See *Tribune,* May 12, 1910, pp. 1, 4, 5.

46. See Tribune, May 15, 1910, p. 1; May 25, 1910, p. 1; June 1, 1910, p. 1; June 3, 1910, p. 5; June 10, 1910, p. 5; June 22, 1910, p. 1; July 28, 1910, p. 1; July 30, 1910, p. 1; August 11, 1910, p. 5; August 16, 1910, p. 2; August 30, 1910, p. 2; September 1, 1910, p. 1.

47. See *Tribune,* October 8, 1910, p. 3; October 15, 1910, p. 1; November 5, 1910, p. 1.

and visitors exceeded the 800 who actually attended; of that number only 150 were delegates and another 100 members of the reception committee.[48] The Multan Conference duly passed resolutions on much the same subjects as considered the year before.[49] This meeting took on a ritualistic quality devoid of intended action or concrete plans for the future. It fell into the same pattern of an annual show as the National Congress. Lacking in resources, the Hindu Sabha could do little else. Even Lal Chand noted its weakness in manpower but more critically in money.[50] The close of the conference left behind only a sense of disappointment.

During the remainder of 1910 and into 1911, the Punjab Hindu Sabha was attacked for its ineffective leadership and for eschewing politics, as it became embroiled in factional and personal struggles.[51] Its inaction spurred many critics and few defenders. "Rai Bahadur Lala Lal Chand, while answering the critics of the Hindu Sabha, stated at the Multan Conference that the Sabha had neither funds nor workers and that it was uncharitable to complain if it had not been able to work wonders within the short period of its existence."[52]

Underlying this dearth of support lay the Sabha's inability to end or even seriously mitigate the divisiveness of Punjabi Hindus. Lal Chand complained:

Some people, moreover, would not join the Hindu Sabha because they imagine its "sectional policy" is opposed to the national policy of the Con-

48. The districts and native states represented included: Multan, Lahore, Sialkot, Gurdaspur, Hoshiarpur, Lyallpur, Jhang, Jhelum, Wazirabad, Campbellpur, Rawalpindi, Chiniot, D.G. Khan, Bhakar, D.I. Khan, Ferozepore, Shahpur, and Bahawalpur. Prominent Hindus did attend, including Lal Chand, Shadi Lal, and Pandit Ram Bhaj Datta, while official approval was signified by the presence of the local District Commissioner and his assistant. *Tribune,* October 12, 1910, p. 2.

49. *Tribune,* October 12, 1910, p. 3; October 13, 1910, p. 2.

50. *Tribune,* October 12, 1910, p. 3.

51. The *Tribune* criticized the Sabha's lack of overt political action and the leadership ability of Lal Chand. *Tribune,* October 15, 1910, p. 2. The *Hindustān* also complained of similar failings in the Sabha, but remained wedded to the concept of a Hindu organization. See *Hindustān,* January 20, 1911, *SPVP 1911,* pp. 60–61; January 27, 1911, *SPVP 1911,* p. 80; February 3, 1911, *SPVP 1911,* pp. 131–132; March 3, 1911, *SPVP 1911,* p. 218; May 5, 1911, *SPVP 1911,* p. 444; June 2, 1911, *SPVP 1911,* pp. 615–616.

52. Quotes given below from *Panjabee,* June 6, 1911, *SPVP 1911,* p. 576.

gress. Others do not join because its politics is not as aggressive as they would like it to be. At the first Hindu Conference at Lahore several distinguished Hindus were sitting in the Conference only as sight-seers and positively declined to take any part in its proceedings because the programme of the Hindu Sabha was "too tame" for them. A third party does not join because in its opinion, it is the Arya Samaj that dominates the Hindu Sabha and nothing is apparently more distasteful to that party than co-operation with the Samaj. Some people connected with the Arya Samaj, on the other hand, think that the work of the Hindu Sabha would stand in the progress of their Samaj, and that Lala Lal Chand was doing disservice to the Arya Samaj by taking a leading part in the Hindu Sabha! These are some of the amenities to which the Hindu Sabha is subjected by educated Hindu separatists.

All too correct in his assessment, Lal Chand even omitted a few factional and personal differences plaguing the Sabha.[53]

Mutual quarrelling and a sense of hopelessness pervaded the Hindu press throughout the summer and into the fall of 1911. Continual numerical decline appalled Hindu leaders, but they had no ready solutions. The *Hindustān* lamented that Punjabi Hindus " . . . have decreased in number since the Census of 1901, and if they continue so at the present pace not one Hindu will be left in this province 70 years hence."[54] A lack of communal loyalty and a deficient sense of survival seemed to account for this drift toward group suicide. "Every promising Hindu young man makes up his mind to do good, not to his co-religionists, but to the whole world; and feels no shame in declaring that he looks with the same eye on the followers of different creeds." Even the impending Punjab Hindu Conference could not engender hope and unanimity among the Hindu community.

The third Punjab Conference met on September 29, 1911, in Amritsar with Lal Chand once more as president. The conference passed similar resolutions to the first two meetings. Its attendance proved no better, save for the presence of Pandit M. M. Malaviya. The conference lacked vitality while Lal Chand demonstrated "none of the old fire and the old reverberation."[55] The Sabha

53. The Gurukul wing stood in opposition to the Sabha and Lala Lal Chand. See *Tribune,* October 23, 1910, p. 3; also the *Jhang Siāl,* February 18, 1911, *SPVP 1911,* pp. 184–185.

54. *Hindustān,* June 30, 1911, *SPVP 1911,* pp. 70–71.

55. *Tribune,* October 1, 1911, *SPVP 1911,* pp. 444–445.

failed to mobilize either men or money, nor could Lal Chand provide effective leadership. He was an old man with but a few months to live. Furthermore, this scarcity of funds stemmed from a lack of commitment among Punjabi Hindus, not a dearth of resources. Within a few days of the conference, Pandit M. M. Malaviya and Babu Ganga Parshad Varma raised nearly Rs. 100,000 for the projected Hindu University at Benares. Large donations came from prominent Hindus, several of whom were connected with the Punjab Hindu Sabha.

The death of Lala Lal Chand in January 1912 removed the one consistent figure in the Sabha movement, which was to be characterized in the future by shifting, inconsistent leadership and factional struggles, as well as the older pattern of inaction. The fourth conference met in Delhi under the presidency of Lala Shadi Lal, considered the usual resolutions, and then disbanded. While the *Tribune* noted "enthusiasm" amongst the delegates and considered the conference a success, it also commented on "a paucity of delegates."[56] The 1913 conference, the fifth and last before World War I, demonstrated the weaknesses and difficulties that faced any attempt to bridge existing divisions within the Punjabi Hindu community. After a series of differences of opinion between Punjab Hindu Sabha leaders of Lahore and the reception committee in Ambala, the conference opened to a depressingly small audience.[57] The *Tribune* noted that "It is not very creditable that no more than 83 delegates from outside Ambala should respond to the call of the Reception Committee which had issued as many as 3,000 personal and individual letters to leading Hindus all over the province, and which had itself furnished about 150 members of the Reception Committee and delegates. The conclusion is irresistable that the movement has to contend against waning interest and solid apathy for which responsibility rests as much with the Punjab Hindu Sabha as with the Hindus of the Province."[58]

56. *Tribune,* October 19, 1912, pp. 2–3; October 22, 1912, p. 7. The Chief Commissioner of Delhi attended the Conference, again indicating government approval of the meetings. See *Tribune,* October 23, 1912, p. 2.

57. For reference to the internal difficulties of the Sabha and the Conference, see the *Tribune,* November 4, 1913, p. 3; November 9, 1913, p. 3; November 10, 1913, p. 1; and, December 3, 1913, p. 3.

58. Quotes given below from *Tribune,* December 17, 1913, p. 2; also see December 23, 1913, p. 2.

This lack of commitment was demonstrated most clearly by the absence of past leaders of the movement and the dearth of *mofussil* delegates who failed to attend. "None of the office-bearers of the Punjab Hindu Sabha, neither the president, nor its half-a-dozen Vice-Presidents, nor even its several secretaries, barring a solitary exception, attended the conference."

This fifth conference marked the lowest ebb of the Sabha since its founding.[59] A cycle of inaction leading to non-support, leading to further inaction, had not been broken. Lala Lal Chand had failed to bridge the deep divisions within the Punjabi Hindu community, nor had he been able to provide the Sabha with effective direction. His successors achieved less. The Punjab Hindu Sabha faced the future divided and devoid of dynamic leadership. Having expressed a general Hindu consciousness, the Punjab Hindu Sabha failed to give organizational life to that ideology. Action lay elsewhere at the level of sectarian commitment.

### THE ARYA SAMAJ AND THE GOVERNMENT

Within the Hindu community the Aryas retained both their leadership and their fear. A hostile government still suspected Aryas of seditious thought and seditious practice. Deputations to various officials had pleaded the case of both Aryas and the wider Hindu community but with little success. Throughout 1908 and 1909, this anxiety fed the cause of the Hindu Sabha and the Hindu Conference. Still, hope persisted for a calmer, more secure future, and a slow bettering of relations with the government. In October this illusion was smashed by frightening news from the Sikh state of Patiala. On the eleventh, the state police arrested 84 Arya Samajists and charged them with sedition. Later arrests brought the figure to 115, nearly all the leading Samajists within Patiala. Temples, offices, and homes were searched, publications seized, and all work of the Samaj brought to a stand-still.[60] The Patiala arrests shocked and horrified Aryas. The sudden and indiscriminate

59. For an account of its sessions, see the *Tribune*, December 6, 1913, p. 3; December 9, 1913, pp. 3–5; December 11, 1913, pp. 3–4; December 12, 1913, pp. 2–4.

60. See Munshi Ram and Rama Deva, *The Arya Samaj and Its Detractors* (Kangri, Hardwar: Satya Dharm Pracharak Press, 1911), pp. 62–63; also *Panjabee*, October 16, 1909, p. 4, for a slightly different account.

nature of this action seemed to endanger all Samaj leaders regardless of faction or political activism. Lala Munshi Ram and members of the Gurukul wing responded by organizing an Arya Defense Fund to assist those arrested, while all watched the trial with anxious fascination, as the state prosecution attempted to prove that the Samaj was dedicated to destroying the British Raj.[61] The case was lengthy but poorly constructed, more a statement of British fears and prejudices than evidence of concrete political agitation. Its hollowness became increasingly evident and finally on February 19, 1910, the Maharaja withdrew the prosecution. Its inconclusive ending left many Aryas still plagued with doubts, wondering what blow might fall next.[62]

In the interim, Lala Durga Prashad of the Gurukul wing wrote to the Lieutenant-Governor, claiming that the Samaj was not political and offered as well to assist in suppressing sedition.[63] In reply, the Lieutenant-Governor agreed that the Samaj was a religious and not a political organization. For Aryas this meant governmental acceptance of their claim to be solely a religious body, but it was a careful reassurance given only to the Gurukul wing of the Samaj, a fact that became evident in time. The *Ārya Musāfir* showed relief both at this interchange and at the militantly anti-political stance now taken by Lala Munshi Ram. "On this happy occasion, we should resolve that, if any member of the Arya Samaj expresses his revolutionary intentions through his word or action, his name would be struck off from the list of Samaj-members and that will be notified through Arya-papers and in future the Samaj would not have any connection with that man."[64] Fear of a general purge of Samajists undergirded this rejection of politics. Durga Prasad re-

61. See *Panjabee*, November 25, 1909, p. 5 and *Tribune*, November 27, 1909, p. 3, on the Defence Fund. Comments on the trial and its proceedings appear in the *Panjabee* and *Tribune* from October through February 1910. For comments on the Samaj and its plight, see *Panjabee*, November 30, 1909, p. 5, and December 2, 1909, pp. 1–2. Also see Valentine Chirol, *Indian Unrest* (London: Macmillan & Co., 1910). Chirol condemned "the political activities of the Arya Samaj, or at least a number of its most prominent members who have figured conspicuously in the anti-British agitation of the last few years" (p. 111).

62. See Munshi Ram and Rama Deva, *The Arya Samaj and Its Detractors*, for a fairly complete, although one-sided, account of the trial, pp. 62 through 126, and Appendix I, pp. 1–30.

63. *Ārya Musāfir*, January 1910 and *Tribune*, January 19, 1910, p. 1.

64. *Ārya Musāfir*, January 1910, p. 50.

ferred to a rumor "that the government of India will take the case of 'Patiala' as a reference to declare the Arya Samaj a revolutionary body and thus will crush the Arya Samaj."[65] This crisis seemed to demand a clear break with any and all political action as well as a rejection of those Aryas providing leadership in Punjab and national politics.[66]

During 1911 and 1912, the situation remained relatively static. The government had done nothing concrete to indicate a change in attitude or policy. Aryas remained anxious and fearful, but beginning in 1913, the government signaled a new policy by a series of apparently unconnected social acts. In March 1913, Sir James Meston, Lieutenant-Governor of the United Provinces, visited the Gurukul Kangri. Accompanied by various officials of the provincial government. Meston toured the college and at the end of his visit made a short but crucial speech. After a polite opening, he stated that "While at Hardwar I proposed myself a visit to the Gurukula for various reasons. The Gurukula is one of the most original interesting experiments carried on in these provinces, in fact in the whole of India. Again I wanted to meet a community which had been described in official papers as a source of infinite, terrible and unknown danger. (laughter). The best answer to this was to come myself (loud cheers). I have been more than rewarded by visiting one of the most wonderful, interesting and stimulating institutions." Meston saw not seditious agitators or secret conspirators but "a band of ascetics devoted to this duty, and working in the wilderness." As to politics, he dismissed the subject in a single sentence. "I will not talk of the political aspect of the question where politics are unknown."[67] Meston's visit put a seal of approval on the Gurukul; it also was but one such visit by Europeans both official and non-official.[68] Sir James Meston returned in February 1914, along with Lady Meston, remarking that the Gurukul was "my ideal of an educational institution."[69] In the meantime, the Lieutenant-Governor of the Punjab traveled to Jullundur for an official visit to the Kanya Mahavidalaya. In his speech, the Governor referred to his great privilege in visiting an "institution

65. *Arya Musāfir,* January 1910, p. 52.
66. See *Ārya Musāfir,* February 1910, pp. 15–22.
67. *Tribune,* March 11, 1913, p. 4; also see March 9, 1913, p. 1.
68. *Tribune,* April 30, 1913, p. 4.
69. *Tribune,* February 22, 1914, p. 4.

which had rendered an incalculable service to the cause of female education in the Punjab."[70] These visits and the words uttered in each institution signaled a new era of governmental approval and sanction for militant Aryas.[71] The government perceived that the religious orientation of militant Aryas did not threaten British bureaucracy, at least not in the same immediate manner as the more politicized Aryas for whom identity implied community and nascent nationalism.

Moderate Aryas, even when eschewing politics, presented two foci of anti-governmental feeling. First, the Dayanand Anglo-Vedic Schools and College were centers of anti-British sentiment and often, as in the 1907 unrest, became rallying points for agitation. Students supplied both manpower and leadership, as did Arya professors. Second, many of the most politically conscious leaders were associated with Lajpat Rai and the moderate Arya party. The government held out no olive branches to the college Aryas, but continued to be suspicious.[72] In February 1914, another series of arrests involving the superintendent of the Boarding House at Central Training College, Lahore, and a group of students reemphasized this official suspicion. Among the students were several Aryas, including Lala Bal Raj, eldest son of Lala Hans Raj.[73] Thus began another lengthy trial, one which ended with sentences for all concerned. This incident proved personally agonizing to Lala Hans Raj and his associates in the Dayanand Anglo-Vedic College. It also underscored the continual watchfulness of the government for any political action that seemed to smell of sedition.

Politics for the Samaj as for the general Punjabi Hindu community offered little hope. The dividends seemed small, while the penalties of offending official sensitivity were unpleasant and dangerous. The Congress and the Punjab Hindu Sabha both appeared impotent and irrelevant, unable to combat the most pressing single problem facing Punjabi Hindus, the decline in status

70. *Tribune,* August 13, 1913, p. 5. The visit took place on August 11.

71. Myron H. Phelps, *The Gurukula Through European Eyes,* 2nd ed., (Kangri, Hardwar: [1917]). This book carefully lists all such European visits as proof of the Gurukul's new respectability.

72. See the "Memorandum to the Lieutenant-Governor of the Punjab regarding the action necessary to check sedition in the Lahore College." Poll/June/12/ Deposit Govt. of India ItPHD (pol) 14, p. 67.

73. See *Tribune,* February 28, 1914, p. 1.

and numbers of their community. As a minority group whose leadership and centers of power lay in the cities, Hindus could not influence the government dominated, as it was, by a fixation on the peasant and his land. Instead, they fell back on the doctrine of "self-help." *Khandan, mandan, shuddhi,* and education were blended together as an antidote for the great overriding fear of numerical decline and the inevitable destruction of the Hindu race.

### ALTERNATIVES TO POLITICS: SHUDDHI, OUTCASTES, AND COMMUNAL DEFENSE

The *shuddhi* campaigns of 1900–1903 among Rahtias, Odes and Meghs provided Aryas with one of the few successful examples of action directly relevant to survival. It was controversial and socially dangerous, yet the "census mentality," which equated numbers with strength, impelled Aryas toward an increased use of *shuddhi* regardless of possible opposition either from Hindu orthodoxy or non-Hindu leaders. Having broken with their past allies among reforming Sikhs, Aryas now looked solely to their own resources and their own ideology in the performance of *shuddhi*. Conversely, members of the orthodoxy community viewed *shuddhi* with mixed feelings. At times it seemed to threaten the stability of tradition, and on a local level to undermine the social dominance of the clean castes; yet *shuddhi* offered to them the same hope for effective communal defense uppermost in the minds of many Aryas. Orthodoxy might condemn *shuddhi* but they had nothing else to offer against the continuing threat of conversion and shrinking numbers. For outcastes possessing a new sense of restlessness, *shuddhi* provided an alternative to continued social degradation and to the more traditional path of conversion. They could remain within Hinduism and yet become an honorable part of that community. Aryas pushed both by their own anxiety and the more restive outcastes continued *shuddhi* campaigns, extending them into areas beyond Punjab.

In 1905, the Sukkur Arya Samaj of Sind began purification of the Sheikhs of Larkhana. Technically, Muslims and low caste, the Sheikhs were raised in social status and also reclaimed to Hinduism.[74] Social reform and communal defense took the same form

74. See Graham, "The Arya Samaj," pp. 494–495.

and produced the same act. Not all mass *shuddhis* were from outcaste groups. Perhaps the most tempting targets of reconversion were Rajputs who had converted to Islam. Reclaiming these lost Kshatriyas would mean a great addition to the strength of the Hindu community and a moral victory of incalculable significance. During the years 1907–1910, Aryas saw this dream changing into reality, as they successfully purified Rajputs from the United Provinces, Baroda, and the Central Provinces. Joining with Aryas from these areas and working under the auspices of the Rajput Shuddhi Sabha, Punjabi leaders moved to purify Rajputs in a massive *shuddhi* campaign. The Rajput Sabha claimed to have reconverted 1,052 Muslim Rajputs by 1910.[75] This Arya campaign extended into Baroda reaching both Rajput and non-Rajput Muslims.[76] Muslims of the Punjab and the United Provinces reacted strongly to this new aggressiveness by initiating their own campaign of counter-agitation.[77] Formalized communal competition grew in widening circles from the Punjab, as Aryas extended the scope of their *shuddhi* movement.[78] This expanding *shuddhi* campaign reaching beyond the Punjab and into differing groups gained momentum during the year 1910–1911, as the next census loomed on the horizon, the next communal tally sheet.[79]

75. *Census, United Provinces Report 1911*, p. 134. The same figure is given in Lajpat Rai, *The Arya Samaj* (London: Longmans, Green and Co., 1915), p. 221, and Reid Graham, "The Arya Samaj as a Reformation in Hinduism with Special Reference to Caste," unpublished Ph.D. dissertation, Yale University, 1942, pp. 505–506.

76. *Census, Baroda Report 1911*, p. 56.

77. See *Ārya Musāfir* for March through July 1909 for accounts of the *shuddhi* campaign and for comments on Muslim reactions to it.

78. This is not to imply that communal competition failed to exist elsewhere prior to Arya and specifically Punjabi Arya penetration. The United Provinces had its own sizable Arya movement and its own forms of communal competition, some predating developments within the Punjab. What the Punjab did provide was leadership and institutional innovation that contributed to later intensification of communal tensions. In other areas such as Sind, Aryas were almost totally from Punjab as was their own modernized form of communalism. The specific impact of the Samaj and the degree to which it was Punjabi in origin or content would have to be studied in each area: such an analysis is beyond the scope of this volume.

79. The *shuddhi* campaign spread from the plains northward into the foothills; Aryas began *shuddhi* among the Doms or Dommas of the Kashmir Punjab and U.P. Hill tracts. While an outcaste group, they were not among the most despised.

The fear of Hindu numerical decline was initially created by Christian conversions, then fixed and substantiated by the census reports. Each decade saw the percentage of Hindus drop as other communities forged ahead, growing more rapidly by both conversion and reproduction. Hindus lost as well by redefinition. In the initial census of 1855 Sikhs were returned under the title of Hindus, giving the community its greatest strength. The loss of Sikhs after 1871 sharply cut into the size of the Hindu community. In 1910, the census administration appeared ready to once again redefine the classification of "Hindu" and in so doing strip the community of its outcaste population. On November 12, the *Tribune* published the Gait Circular, a note from the Commissioner of the Census, E. A. Gait, to his provincial superintendents. This circular began by noting that "the complaint has often been made that the Census returns of Hindus are misleading, as they include millions of people who are not really Hindus at all." It then went on to suggest that outcaste groups who could not really be considered Hindus be listed separately in a special table, although they would be retained as Hindus in the general tables.[80]

To Hindu leaders and Aryas in particular this was the first step in separating all Hindu outcastes from their community. They

"The hill 'Doms' are largely artisans, and many of them by their industry and enterprise have become well-to-do and even men of substance. But they still find themselves looked down upon by the hill Brahman and Rajput." Ram Bhaj Datta led in efforts to purify the Doms. He traveled with other Aryas from village to village preaching and, when possible, performing *shuddhi* ceremonies for those willing to risk the anger of the local high castes in the hope of achieving eventual social acceptance. The rising aspirations of Doms, plus their relative respectability among outcaste groups, facilitated this Arya campaign. During 1912 Aryas reported success in the purification of the Doms who at least nominally were raised to the level of pure-caste Hindus. This expanding *shuddhi* campaign reaching beyond the Punjab into differing groups gained momentum during the year 1910–1911, as the next census loomed on the horizon, the next communal tally sheet. See *Census, United Provinces Report 1921*, p. 56, and *Tribune*, September 15, 1912, p. 2; October 2, 1912, p. 2. During September and October, the *Tribune* carried a series of letters by Ram Bhaj Datta on the *shuddhi* campaign among Meghs, Doms, and other untouchables. Also see Ganga Ram and Charu Das, *The Uplift Movement at Sialkot Punjab: A Brief Report of the Working of the Arya Megh Uddhar Sabha (Aryan Mission for the Uplift of the Megh Untouchables) Sialkot, Punjab* (Calcutta: A. C. Sarkar, 1915) and Graham, "The Arya Samaj," p. 499.

80. *Tribune*, November 12, 1910, p. 5.

would gradually be brought into a new classification and would for all purposes, including the proportioning of political representation, be lost. This could hardly be accidental, not merely the action of a disinterested bureaucrat. It was instead another example of the government's pro-Muslim and anti-Hindu policy, another attempt to weaken the Hindu community. Earlier the Muslim League deputation to the Viceroy had claimed that outcastes were not Hindus and should not be considered as such for any purpose. Now it appeared that the government had accepted that claim and was acting to substantiate it.[81] The controversy over this Circular raged throughout November and December, arousing the worst fears of Hindu leaders[82] who turned to the Punjab Hindu Sabha for assistance. The Sabha protested to Mr. Gait but received little in return that either satisfied or relieved their concern.[83] Instead, Hindu anxiety led them to look in two directions, toward integrating outcastes more firmly into the Hindu community and toward the founding of an effective all-India Hindu organization.

The dream of an association which would unite Hindus under one common organization had existed since the founding of the Muslim League. Again and again Hindus commented that "they," the Muslims, were united and organized while "we," the Hindus, were not. This desire for a "national" Hindu organization found adherents both within Punjab and throughout British India. Babu Sarda Charan Mitra, its most outspoken advocate, toured northern India calling for Hindus to unite and defend their community. He became, along with the Maharaja of Dharbanga, an ardent exponent of Hindu unity.[84] Lala Lal Chand agreed enthusiastically with the need for such an organization.[85] In January 1911, Mitra at

81. See the *Tribune,* December 1, 1910, p. 2.

82. See *Tribune,* November 12, 1910, p. 5; November 18, 1910, p. 5; November 22, 1910, p. 1; November 27, 1910, p. 2; November 30, 1910, p. 3; December 1, 1910, p. 2; December 3, 1910, p. 6; December 13, 1910, p. 1; December 18, 1910, p. 7.

83. See *Tribune,* December 18, 1910, p. 5. Gait did answer an early statement from the Multan Hindu Sabha, but did not change the government's position, December 9, 1910, p. 1.

84. See the *Tribune,* July 16, 1910, p. 3; July 20, 1910, p. 1; October 7, 1910, p. 2; November 5, 1910, p. 6; and November 6, 1910, p. 2.

85. See *Tribune,* December 11, 1910, p. 3; December 17, 1910, p. 2. Durga Das criticized this proposal as he had nearly everything suggested by Lal Chand. See *Tribune,* December 20, 1910, pp. 3–4; and Lal Chand's letter on November 23, 1910, p. 2.

last succeeded in forming an All-India Hindu Association at Allahabad. He was joined in this by Lal Chand and other Punjabi Hindus, but the organization proved more difficult to sustain than it had been to create.[86] The same drive which led to the formation of this association gave continued life to the *shuddhi* movement and produced greater concrete results.

Annual *shuddhi* conferences had long been an integral part of the Gurukul anniversary celebrations. The Bharat Shuddhi Sabha met at Kangri in conjunction with the Gurukul festivities.[87] In an effort to bring together *shuddhi* leaders from Punjab and the United Provinces, the All India Shuddhi Conference was held in Allahabad just after the Hindu Conference. Both Ram Bhaj Datta and Sarda Charan Mitra addressed the meeting,[88] and as a direct result the All India (Bharat) Shuddhi Sabha was transformed into a formal organization registered with the government on June 23, 1911.[89] The Shuddhi Sabha expected to follow the goals laid down in the conference, which declared "that it is desirable and necessary to admit in the fold of Hinduism those non-Hindus who desire to be admitted after the performance of Prayaschitta and Homa." Expectations varied from those who wished simply to bring an end of the steady decline in the Hindu community to others who dreamed of converting to their Vedic faith all South Asia and even the world.[90]

This rising concern over Hindu survival fed new attempts at *shuddhi* and the continuation of existing reconversion and social uplift movements. The most successful by far was the Megh purification work of the Sialkot Arya Samaj and its subsidiary branch, the Arya Megh Uddar Sabha organized on April 21, 1912.[91] Aryas approached the Meghs much as Christian missionaries had, using itinerant preachers and the voluntary services of local Aryas. The Sialkot Aryas augmented their campaign by the establishment of new social institutions among the converted, and

86. See *Tribune*, January 4, 1911, p. 5.

87. See *Tribune*, April 4, 1908, p. 3.

88. *Tribune*, January 6, 1911, pp. 6–7.

89. *Tribune*, July 13, 1911, p. 3.

90. Ganga Ram and Charu Das, *The Uplift Movement at Sialkot Punjab*, p. 22.

91. For various concepts of *shuddhi*, its applicability and eventual goals, see the following: *Hindustān*, January 6, 1911, *SPVP 1911*, p. 35; *Vakīl*, January 21, 1911, *SPVP 1911*, p. 110; *Hindustān*, April 14, 1911, *SPVP 1911*, p. 397; *Tribune*, March 31, 1911, *SPVP 1911*, pp. 323–324.

by the creation of a Megh colony. In an echo of Clarkabad, they settled their converts on the land, organized them, dug wells, furnished assistance in housing, constructed a hospital, and provided basic education.[92] They attempted as well to create a new social structure among the converts by establishing "'Chaudhari Sabhas' comprising among themselves intelligent and influential Meghs . . . organised to serve as regulators of the lives of the purified Meghs."[93] "Arya Bhagats," the designation of the purified Meghs, would lead a paternally-directed life under the tutelage of their enlightened Arya brethren.

The forces which propelled both Aryas and outcastes to sustain the *shuddhi* campaign accelerated, but opposition appeared sporadically, particularly at the village level. Educated Hindus might be aware of communal decline and the broader issues of politics, but village elites felt threatened directly and reacted accordingly. Intimidation, occasional physical violence, and the inevitable recourse to the law courts typified much of this upper caste opposition. At times the dominant caste tried to prevent *shuddhi* ceremonies or even the preaching that preceded them. More often clashes occurred when the purified asserted themselves and insisted on the prerogatives of their newly-claimed status.[94] The degree of difference between pre-existing and claimed status contributed to the amount of upper caste reaction. In Hoshiarpur, when militant Aryas purified members of the Kabirpanthi sect who were sweepers by caste, and then publicly inter-dined with them, the local orthodox society led a movement to outcaste all Aryas. Unlike previous converts who were almost all weavers or from other relatively unobjectionable occupations, the Samaj was dealing here with the lowest of social groups, with the most demeaning of professions. Throughout May 1909, the Sanatan Dharm Sabha of Hoshiarpur mobilized public opinion against Aryas and their Chamar adherents. They succeeded in excommunicating the local Aryas, at least for a while.[95] In the long

92. See Graham, "The Arya Samaj," p. 521.

93. Ganga Ram and Charu Das, *The Uplift Movement at Sialkot Punjab*, p. 44.

94. See Ganga Ram and Charu Das, *Ibid.*, pp. 17–18.

95. For a record of this struggle, see the following: *Hindū Sanātan Dharm Gazette*, April 28, 1909, *SPVP 1909*, pp. 418–420; *Akhbār-i-'Ām*, May 1, 1909, *SPVP 1909*, pp. 421–422; *Paisā Akhbār*, May 4, 1909, *SPVP 1909*, *p. 420*; *Akhbār-i-'Ām*, May 5, 1909, p. 418; *Tilak*, May 6 1909, *SPVP 1909*, pp. 471–472; *Hindū Sa-*

run, however, they were unable to sustain this social boycott and gradually Aryas were readmitted to the normal world of social relations, while purified Chamars remained a part of the Hindu community. The Hoshiarpur experience rarely reoccurred, as Aryas refrained from purifying the lowest of the untouchables, and Sanatanists did not attempt to outcaste members of the Samaj. Neither side possessed the strength to alter existing social patterns in such a fundamental manner.

Orthodox leaders, who became increasingly aware of the need for communal solidarity, gradually accepted *shuddhi* as a necessary method of defense. They also could clearly see the need for retaining outcastes within the general outline of the Hindu community. In reaction to the Gait Circular, Sanatanists demonstrated this concern much to the relief of Aryas who could envision a future in which orthodoxy would meet their own program of untouchable uplift at least half way.

> . . . let the impartial observer see the attitude of the Pundits of Benares and other Sanatan Dharam Sabhas towards the untouchable in the recent Gait Circular controversy. The oracle of Hindu Society have declared it in bold and unambiguous terms that the Depressed classes are part and parcel of the Hindu body politic . . . . At the top of it, there comes the news of an establishment of a school for low classes in connection with Central Hindu College at Benares. The penitent convert is no longer kept at an arm's length. He is taken back into the bosom of the mother religion. Hundreds of cases could be cited showing how the Sanatan Dharm Sabhas are extending the right hand of fellowship to the outcaste and the renegade.[96]

Perhaps overly confident, the *Arya Patrika* did sense that in a world dominated by communal mobilization and a mentality which stressed the power of numbers, *shuddhi* would find tolerance among all Hindus.

*Shuddhi* produced serious tensions within the Samaj, raising problems among Aryas that proved nearly insurmountable. The question of integrating converts into the Samaj did not arise when large groups could be dealt with in a paternalistic manner; then leadership and power stayed in the hands of upper caste Aryas.

---

*nātan Dharm Gazette,* May 19, 1909, SPVP 1909, p. 500; *Arya Gazette,* May 20, 1909, SPVP 1909 pp. 500–502; *Tilak,* May 20, 1909, *SPVP 1909*, pp. 500–551.

96. *Arya Patrika,* January 14, 1911, *SPVP 1911*, p. 83.

The early experiences of *shuddhi* among the Rahtias, Odes and Meghs were handled thus. Individual or family purifications of Hindu converts created only the single problem of acceptance by the Hindu social world. Since these individuals were once Hindus, they moved back into their previous *jātis*. But integration either of non-Hindus or of outcastes who aspired to leadership within the Samaj presented difficulties of a different order. After the ***birādarī*** movement had collapsed, no institutional innovation existed or was even under consideration to ease this situation. From time to time Aryas discussed this situation, while urging their co-religionists to abandon their social exclusiveness, but the problem remained unsolved.

The *shuddhi* movement as well permanently altered the social composition of the Samaj. After a decade of near stagnation between 1891 and 1901, Samaj membership rose to 100,846 in 1911. *Shuddhi* campaigns contributed heavily to this rapid growth, shifting as well the geographic center of the Samaj. Sialkot contained the greatest number of Aryas, 27,910 individuals who were almost totally converted and purified Meghs.[97] From a movement overwhelmingly dominated by Vaishyas with a strong element of Brahmans and some artisans groups, the Samaj shifted its social composition to include 34 percent untouchables. The most numerical caste among Aryas changed from Khatris who had held that position since the movement's beginnings to Meghs.[98]

The heavy influx of Sudra and untouchable converts enabled the Samaj to grow rapidly, but would present difficulties within the movement over the readjustment of power relations between the dominant upper castes and the newly-won adherents from the lower levels of the social scale. *Shuddhi* had not, however, focused on the lowest levels of Punjab society, the sweepers and leather workers. The untouchable community could be roughly divided between those whose very touch polluted and who followed unclean professions, and those whose status was below the line of

97. *Census Punjab Report 1911*, p. 134. The census also gives the figure as 100,783 on p. 110.

98. The castes with more than 1,000 Aryas were listed as follows: Meghs, 22,115; Khatris, 17,237; Aroras, 10,547; Jats, 9,203; Brahmans, 7,240; Odes, 5,102; Rajputs, 2,403; Aggarwals, 1,983; and Sunars, 1,009. These figures are based on 82,488 of the total of 100,763 Aryas, since caste designations for all Aryas were not available. *Census, Punjab Report 1911*, p. 137.

pollution but whose occupations were not essentially unclean. Aryas concentrated on the latter, but aside from the one attempt to purify Kabirpanthis in 1909, refrained from *shuddhi* among the lowest of the untouchables.[99]

The *shuddhi* movement also provided impetus to Samaj growth beyond the Punjab. The number of Aryas in Kashmir rose from 79 in 1901 to 1,047 in 1911, and to 23,116 in 1921. Emigration of Punjabis into Kashmir State, particularly in the Jammu area, and *shuddhi* provided the foundation for this growth. The Megh uplift movement spread into Jammu and in 1913 another *shuddhi* campaign, this one to purify the Basiths, added over 9,000 converts to the Samaj by the next census.[100] A similar rapid expansion occurred in the North-West Frontier Province, though *shuddhi* played little part in this. It was largely a result of emigration by Punjabis in search of employment and business opportunities.[101] During this decade of growth the Samaj lost almost all of its Sikh supporters; those who saw themselves both as Aryas and Sikhs accounted for only sixty-three individuals.[102] The Samaj by 1911 remained the largest single block of educated Punjabi Hindus, save for that amorphous category of orthodoxy.

The Hindu Vaishyas still strong within the Samaj held much of the non-agricultural wealth through the Punjab.[103] Khatris maintained a crucial role in trade, banking and industry but were strongest in the professions where they accounted for more than one-third of the total assessment in that category.[104] This financial eminence of the Hindu elite was threatened both by new elites and also by a severe banking crisis during 1913 and 1914. During the last decade numerous new enterprises in finance and industry

99. See *Ibid.*, p. 151.

100. *Shuddhi* was also one of the major forces behind a remarkable increase in the Arya Samaj throughout the United Provinces. The Aryas of this province grew from 65,572 in 1901 to 131,638 in 1911. See the *Census, United Provinces Report 1911*, p. 105. For conversion of Meghs in Punjab and Kashmir, see *Census, Punjab Report 1911*, pp. 90–91; and *Census, Kashmir Report 1921*, pp. 59 and 62.

101. The Samaj went from 496 in 1901 to 4,140 in 1911, see *Census, North-West Frontier Provinces 1911*, p. 83.

102. *Census, Punjab Report 1911*, p. 134.

103. The Baniyas, Khatris and Aroras outranked all others in the possession of non-agricultural wealth. The Sheikhs came next, with less than one-quarter of the wealth held by the Aroras. *Census, Punjab Report 1911*, p. 527.

104. *Tribune*, June 15, 1913, p. 2.

were started throughout the province. Lala Harkishen Lal had led in this development and possessed an impressive array of businesses in insurance, banking and industry. During the closing months of 1912 and into 1913, rumors clustered around the People's Bank of Lahore, Harkishen Lal's primary financial institution. It was repeatedly attacked by the *Arya Patrika* and in September failed to meet a sustained run by its depositors. During September and October, the banking crisis deepened and threatened to engulf other major financial institutions and businesses. Hindu entrepreneurs felt their world threatened as the entire economic future of their enterprises seemed uncertain.[105] Business did not recover before it was engulfed in the world of war and change beginning in August 1914.

The banking crisis discredited Harkishen Lal as he fought desperately to save his economic empire. He would have little time or energy in the immediate future for politics and social reform. With Lal Chand dead and Lala Hans Raj deeply involved in his son's trial for sedition, the college Aryas used their talents and energies to sustain their already extensive institutions. Lajpat Rai left Punjab and sailed for England. He intended only a short visit but, trapped by the war, did not return until February 1920. Leaders of the Gurukul wing of the Samaj, having come to terms with the government, remained quietly involved in their own institutions, in *shuddhi* and *prachār*. During the last year-and-a-half before World War I the Punjab seemed strangely quiet, as if awaiting some great event. The historical process, which drove Punjabi, and particularly the urban Hindus, to come to grips with the British Raj was played out, completed; a half-century of change, of innovation, and creativity had constructed a new world from the old. The future would test the strength of that world as it was caught and finally torn asunder by the clash of competing ideologies.

105. For further developments on the banking crisis, see *Tribune*, September 25, 1913, pp. 2, 3; October 2, 1913, pp. 4–5; October 11, 1913, p. 2; and October 12, 1913, p. 5.

## Chapter XI

# IN SUMMARY: FROM IDENTITY TO CONSCIOUSNESS

> I am suggesting that in coming to new terms a person becomes something other than he once was. Terminological shifts necessitate, but also signalize, new evaluations: of self and others, of events, acts, and objects; and the transformation of perception is irreversible; once having changed, there is no going back. One can look back, but he can evaluate only from his new status.
>
> ANSELM L. STRAUSS

Interaction between British colonial culture as an extension of European civilization and the existent Punjabi society created a third world of marginal men. Both worlds were themselves dynamic, ever-changing, shifting universes with their own values, attitudes, and inner drives. No generalized impact of the British upon Punjab existed, but instead a highly selective merging of the two worlds came into being composed of those individuals who moved daily between two cultures, the colonial English and traditional Punjabi. The area of contact, and the number of individuals inhabiting that area, grew with the passage of time. New forms of occupation, communication and cultural interaction brought increasing numbers of Punjabis into the grey area of marginality which contained the seeds of a colonial culture, neither English nor Punjabi. Castes already possessing literacy provided the administrators and professionals demanded by the new order, while outcastes supplied both servants and Christian converts. The literate castes, with both existent and newly-acquired social prestige, became leaders of this expanding third world. They felt most its ambiguities, its alienation from existing traditions, and the humiliation of colonial rule. A compelling need for dignity and identity drove them to seek and accept new concepts and to make new commitments.

The creation of a third culture for northwestern India began first in Delhi during the 1830s and 1840s but was terminated abruptly by the Mutiny. The process began anew in the Punjab proper during the 1860s and 1870s, not so much as a group phenomenon but an individual one. Men such as Kanhya Lal Alakhdhari existed as loners, prophets of a future not yet arrived. They stirred other individuals but could find no group to support their drive for a reformed world. Not until the 1880s did the Punjab produce its first generation of marginal men, youths educated in the English language who supplied sufficient manpower to sustain movements for change. These young college students felt keenly the twin forces of cultural marginality and educationally-inspired alienation. They sought new ideas and found them in the Brahmo Samaj, the Dev Dharm, and Arya Samaj. They lived in a world of rapidly expanding occupational roles which demanded new social relations and lifestyles. Little in traditional society could provide them with either psychological or social guidelines. While British colonial life had found itself even to the point of social stereotypes, the life of an educated "native" remained in the process of formation.

Young Punjabi Hindus, after abandoning Brahmo ideals, seized the personal vision of Swami Dayanand, adapting it to their own particular needs, and transforming it into an ideology, a complex set of concepts that delineated the past, present, and future. They elaborated, debated, and differed on this new ideology, but they nonetheless found in this their lost dignity and sense of self. The ability of Arya ideology to explain the contemporary world, to provide a psychological foundation for contemporary life, established the authority of Arya ideas. Leaders who expounded this new ideology possessed authority drawn from its conceptual relevance.

The psychological peace, the balm to tormented souls, offered by the Samaj had its price. Ideological commitment limited possible action and channelled the energies of its believers in specific directions. Loyalty to a set of ideals and to the group that possessed those ideals heightened existing social divisions, setting one group against all others. The degree of commitment was reflected in the intensity of this divisiveness. For Aryas, their adherence to the Samaj set them apart from and in opposition to Hindu orthodoxy and to all other religious or reform groups within the Punjab. Similar processes of identity reformation and ideological commitment acted within the Muslim and Sikh communities with similar results. By the 1890s, the Punjab was divided into a series of aggressive organizations, each possessing its own ideology, each containing a unique sense of identity. To protect that identity and its base became the most fundamental drive for educated and marginal Punjabis.

The influence of the West remained ever present, but it could be met with a degree of dignity and honor. Punjabis knew who and what they were. They were still ruled by foreigners, but now could explain this condition in terms of an historic interpretation that soothed through visions of past greatness and by promises of a return to cultural eminence. Belief eased the pain of separation from their surrounding cultural norms, legitimized change, and fueled communal aggressiveness. It provided an identity to be maintained and defended. Yet the defense of identity meant increasing separation between religious communities, their mobilization, and bitter competition. Communal mobilization and communal strife grew out of this colonial dilemma and its solution, not from the unwillingness of individuals to transcend religious divisions. The process of ideological elaboration also produced rising tension among Aryas, as individual thinkers shaped this ideology to fit the reality each perceived.

The division of the Arya Samaj into moderate and militant wings represented two opposing interpretations of Dayanand's concepts. The former, deeply involved in the Dayanand Anglo-Vedic College movement, less devotional and more "secular," remained closer to the Hindus as a community and a people. Leading moderates, in their stress on education, and orphan and famine relief, served all Hindus regardless of sectarian commitments. They also led the way toward political action, first in the Indian National Congress and then the Punjab Hindu Sabha. Typical of such leaders, Lala Lal Chand and Lala Lajpat Rai stood foremost among politicized Aryas. They, like the Jewish intellectuals who founded Zionism, or the anglicized Muslims who dreamed of Pakistan, sought political solutions to the problems that faced the Hindu community. Their Arya Dharm merged with a broader Hindu consciousness. In contrast, militant Aryas retained a more religious and devotional vision of the Samaj and its mission. They sought to create a new man, the Arya Hindu, and a new world for him to inhabit. Their devotion to Arya ideology led them to challenge existing society in radical reform: *shuddhi* for conversion and as a vehicle of social uplift, widow marriage, higher education for women, and *prachār* for communal defense. These two orientations, moderate and militant, represented differing points on a continuum rather than separate categories. These views overlapped and at times converged, as issues of communal protection and communal unity brought both wings together to stand united.

By the twentieth century, Punjabi Hindus exhibited a complex pattern of loyalties based on various forms of identity. Beyond the levels of family and caste identification lay an awareness of being Aryas, or some other sectarian identity, Hindus, Punjabis, and even Indians. The stress and strain of various situations emphasized one or another sense of identity. At times the differing levels of identity and their concomitant loyalties clashed; occasionally they coincided. The fluctuating attachment to politics exhibited by many Punjabi Hindus illustrates this complex pattern of identities. The difficulties faced by the Punjab Hindu Sabha in creating any consistent unity among the Hindu community stemmed from the deep divisions which existed among Punjab Hindus. Symbolic unity drew wide support, but action did not. Repeatedly, the divisions within Punjabi Hindu society proved more compelling than the pleas for united action

The problem of unity appeared on a greater scale with the nationalism of the Indian National Congress. The identity "India" had to transcend all divisions within South Asia, but it could rarely do so. Punjabi Hindus joined the Congress when their own communal, religious or class interests converged with Congress goals. When the Congress joined in the struggle over the proposed Punjab Land Alienation Act, then urban Hindus united behind it. But in later years Congress seemed less and less willing to accept either the historical vision of Punjabi Hindus or their immediate causes. Aryas first and Hindus next, Punjabis left the Congress. For a few years the Punjab Hindu Sabha seemed to offer a new channel of political action and new hope. But once again divisiveness conquered action. The consciousness embodied in the Sabhas was not sufficiently strong to unite the Hindus of the Punjab into an effective political body. Punjabi Hindus abandoned explicit politics for older forms of religious, social, and economic action. They returned to the institutions and movements created in the 1880s and 1890s. The limited response of the Punjabis to the Indian National Congress and its secular nationalism stemmed primarily from the irrelevancy of that nationalism. It did not speak to their basic personal dilemmas, to their fundamental psychological needs, not in the 1890s, nor in the years before World War I.

During the second half of the nineteenth century, the British Indian government shaped historical change in Punjab through both direct and indirect action. Their displacement of the existing aristocracy and creation of a new bureaucracy opened the way for leadership as well as economic advance by the Hindu Vaishyas and Brahmans. This in turn provided concrete stimulus for Western education and the creation of a culturally marginal class. British law partly dictated form through its voluntary associations, although the models of such organizations were both British and Bengali. The government also provided form for social and religious change, and at times consciously initiated such change, as in the early drive against infanticide. Yet the government was often most influential when it lacked any intention to influence and was merely administering. Two excellent examples of such influence are the decennial census and the use of public commissions. The census created a mentality which equated numbers with strength. It became a communal tally sheet registering success or decline of one community against all others. The fact of listing people according to categories, whether communal, geographical or caste, furthered the process of institutionalization of all social divisions. The process of identity formation and the census reports each acted to reinforce the other. The use of public commissions provided an arena for expression of these identities and their concomitant loyalties. The Hunter Commission on Education exemplified this process. Occasionally the government consciously created new arenas of action as in the case of the elected municipal boards, but during the nineteenth century, the government first created a new administrative system and then concentrated on running it. Direct interference in the life of Punjabis remained at a minimum.

The decade of the 1890s marked the beginning of a long slow decline in the position of the British Raj, marked by a loss of confidence and a loss of power. The government increasingly began to manipulate the world around it to maintain as much support as possible. They would also consciously control change in search of the chimera of stability. This shift from indirect to direct manipulation of events took place through the 1890s and up to 1905. After the upheavals of 1905–1907, government stood at the forefront of events offering aid and support to those whom it favored and suppression for those deemed seditious. Loyalty was demanded and rewarded. The old game of charging one's enemies with disloyalty became both more dangerous and more attractive. No group, faction, community, or organization could exist without establishing some relation with the government. It loomed over all events, a deity no longer benign but alert, ready to strike those who would not follow the proper rituals of worship. The British provided a framework in which Punjabis acted, but this framework itself was dynamic and changed as the world of the ruler and ruled interacted through time. No constants existed, only a continual interaction between the British Raj, the new world of marginal men, and the older pre-British world of tradition.

The historical process which transformed attitudes toward caste, community, and nation also generated a vast change in life-style among the Punjabi Hindu elite as well as the elites of other communities. Punjabis accepted totally and with amazing rapidity many forms of social organization and interaction brought to their province from England. The voluntary association, with its annual gatherings, officers, executive committees, reports, proceedings, and budgets, was adapted directly into Punjabi life. Sabhas, samajes, clubs, anjumans, and societies proliferated with amazing speed. These associations in turn established schools, colleges, libraries, reading rooms, orphanages, publication departments, and presses—a universe of social organization. Battles were fought, victories won, and defeats suffered according to the proper forms of parliamentary procedure. The dominance of lawyers among educated Hindus contributed to the correctness of form even if the content was often traditional. Old games were played for status and power, but according to new rules. Both the effectiveness of these organizations and the degree to which foreign form was accepted illustrated an incredible cultural adaptation.

The lives of educated Punjabis became immersed in voluntary associations. For an individual seriously committed to a particular organization or organizations, his energies were demanded for writing, public speaking, committee meetings, demonstrations, missionary work—a whole host of activities which could and at times did consume the total personal resources of a given individual. Many abandoned their careers to devote themselves completely to a chosen movement. In so doing, they created the role of the modernized *sanyāsī* concerned with social reform, religion or politics. Social roles now existed for members of the newly-educated classes. By 1900, students in the English-language colleges could see around them the new lifestyles of the anglicized elite: doctors, lawyers, teachers, and businessmen, as well as a contemporary version of the ancient *sādhu* or holy man, now equipped with a printing press, Western dress, and fund drives to replace his traditional begging bowl. Never again would a single generation shape its own patterns of life anew as had the young men of the 1880s.

The social world of voluntary associations provided contacts with other educated men from various castes and subcastes. For those Punjabis stationed beyond their home area, voluntary associations often acted as a substitute *birādarī*, a mutual assistance group to replace the ties of family, marriage, and caste. They could also function as centers of interaction, of enjoyment or of gossip with other members of the educated elite. Businesses grew out of such contacts, as organizational expertise drawn from tradition and from experience in the new voluntary associations was applied to banking and joint stock ventures. Much as American clubs and lodges provided businessmen with personal contacts, so did these new associations. Both friendship and competition within the business world mirrored similar attitudes within the world of associations. A new society came into existence connected to but only partly enmeshed in the older social order.

Young men coming to maturity after 1900 found a set of social roles and practices befitting their new occupations. Punjab had been socially and culturally transformed within the term of a single generation. Those who came of age in the 1880s created this new world and left their stamp on the future. After 1900, change and innovation continued, but the fundamental shape of the colonial world was fixed. The rate of innovation slowed as did the pace of anglicization. The lifestyles, dilemmas, and ideologies created by educated, urban Hindus spread to others as the world of the marginal expanded. New groups pushed to be included in the elite, to become educated, to have a place in politics, but this was more a quantitative than a qualitative change. By 1914, the colonial world stood complete with the "Babu" and "Sahib." with Arya and Sanatanist, and it would remain so until torn by partition and reformed by independence. Even after, in post-independence India, identity and rival religious consciousness remained to clash and redivide in an after-shock of partition.

## Appendix I

# THE TEN PRINCIPLES OF THE ARYA SAMAJ

(1) God is the primary source of all true knowledge, and of all that is known by its means.

(2) God is All-truth, All-knowledge, All-Beatitude, Incorporeal, Almighty, Just, Merciful, Unbegotten, Infinite, Changeless, Without a beginning, Incomparable, the Support and Lord of all, All-pervading, Omniscient, Imperishable, Immortal, Exempt from fear, Eternal, Holy and the Maker of the Universe. To Him alone is worship due.

(3) The Vedas are the books of all true knowledge. It is the paramount duty of all Aryas to read them and to instruct others in them, to hear them read, and to recite them to others.

(4) All persons should remain ever ready to accept the Truth and to renounce untruth.

(5) All actions ought to be performed in conformity to virtue, i.e. after due consideration of right and wrong.

(6) The primary aim of the Aryasamaj is to do good to mankind, i.e. to ameliorate the physical, spiritual and social condition of all men.

(7) All ought to be treated with love, justice, and due regard to their merits.

(8) Ignorance ought to be dispelled and knowledge diffused.

(9) No one ought to remain satisfied with his own welfare. The welfare of the individual should be regarded as included in the welfare of all.

(10) In matters which affect the well-being of all, the individual should subordinate his personal likings; in matters that affect him alone, he is to enjoy freedom of action.

# Appendix II

## SCHEME OF STUDIES FOR EACH CLASS IN THE DAYANAND ANGLO-VEDIC SCHOOL

| *Lower Primary Department* | *Upper Primary Department* | *Middle Department* | *Upper Department* |
|---|---|---|---|
| *1st Class* | *4th Class* | *7th Class* | *9th Class* |
| 1. Hindi Reading & Writing | 1. Hindi | 1. Sanskrit | 1. Sanskrit |
| | 2. Sanskrit | 2. Arithmetic | 2. Mathematics |
| | 3. English | 3. English | 3. English |
| *2nd Class* | 4. Arithmetic | 4. Geography | 4. Geography |
| 1. Arithmetical Tables | 5. Geography | 5. History | 5. History |
| | 6. Urdu (Opt.) | 6. Physical Science | 6. Physical Science |
| | | 7. Urdu (Opt.) | 7. Sanitation (Opt.) |
| *3rd Class* | *5th Class* | *8th Class* | *10th Class* |
| 1. Hindi Reading & Writing | 1. Hindi | 1. Sanskrit | 1. Sanskrit |
| 2. Sanskrit | 2. Sanskrit | 2. Arithmetic | 2. Mathematics |
| 3. Arithmetic | 3. English | 3. English | 3. English |
| 4. Geography | 4. Arithmetic | 4. Geography | 4. Geography |
| | 5. Geography & Urdu (Opt.) | 5. History | 5. History |
| | | 6. Physical Science | 6. Physical Science |
| | | 7. Urdu & Sanitation (Opt.) | 7. Sanitation (Opt.) |
| | *6th Class* | | |
| | 1. Hindi | | |
| | 2. Sanskrit | | |
| | 3. Arithmetic | | |
| | 4. English | | |
| | 5. Geography | | |
| | 6. Urdu (Opt.) | | |

# Appendix III

## STATISTICAL ABSTRACTS

The majority of the following statistics are drawn from the decennial census reports. The figures should be taken with considerable skepticism and care. The censuses were plagued by both inaccuracies and inconsistencies. The resulting figures indicate general trends of historic development but are often unreliable in detail. For the purposes of this study, however, they carry great weight since Punjabis often accepted their statements as accurate and acted accordingly. The census reports reflected reality and also did much to create "subjective reality" as it existed in the minds of Punjabis. This literal reading of the census reports throughout the subcontinent provides much of their historical significance rather than the data which they contain.

*Reform Societies in Punjab*

Reform Societies' Membership in Punjab and Delhi, 1891–1921.
Major Castes of Punjabi Aryas in 1911.
Aryan Literacy by Caste in 1911.

## POPULATION TABLES

### Population for Punjab and the North-West Frontier Province 1881–1921

| *Year* | *Punjab** | *North-West Frontier Province* | *Total* |
|---|---|---|---|
| 1881 | 22,712,120 | — | 22,712,120 |
| 1891 | 25,130,127 | — | 25,130,127 |
| 1901 | 26,880,217 | — | 26,880,217 |
| 1911 | 24,204,814 | 2,196,933 | 26,401,747 |
| 1921 | 25,589,248 | 2,251,340 | 27,840,588 |

*Punjab includes the district of Delhi in all figures. *Census, Punjab Report 1881*, p. 21; *Census, Punjab Report 1891*, p. 93; *Census, Punjab Report 1901*, p. 169; *Census, Punjab Report 1921*, p. 98; and *Census, North-West Frontier Province Report, 1921*, p. 18.

### Population of Punjab by Religion 1881–1921

| *Year* | *Hindu* | *Muslim* | *Sikh* | *Christian* |
|---|---|---|---|---|
| 1881 | 9,252,295 | 11,662,434 | 1,716,114 | 33,699 |
| 1891 | 10,237,700 | 12,915,643 | 1,870,481 | 53,909 |
| 1901 | 10,478,721 | 14,141,122 | 2,130,987 | 71,864 |
| 1911 | 8,773,621 | 12,275,477 | 2,883,729 | 199,751 |
| 1921 | 9,125,202 | 12,955,341 | 3,110,060 | 346,259 |

Punjab includes the district of Delhi and excludes the North-West Frontier Province. *Census, Punjab Report 1891*, p. 93; *Census, Punjab Report 1901*, p. 169; *Census, Punjab Report 1911*, p. 97; and *Census, Punjab Report 1921*, pp. 34–42.

### Urban and Rural Population for Punjab and Delhi, 1891–1921 (in percentages)

| | *1891* | *1901* | *1911* | *1921* |
|---|---|---|---|---|
| Urban | 10.7 | 10.6 | 9.8 | 10.3 |
| Rural | 89.3 | 89.4 | 90.2 | 89.7 |

*Census, Punjab Report 1921*, p. 122.

## LITERACY

### Literacy in Punjab, 1891–1921

| *Year* | *Total Literates* | *Literates in English* |
|---|---|---|
| 1891 | 819,383 | 45,446 |
| 1901 | 976,663 | 98,831 |
| 1911 | 899,195 | 117,561 |
| 1921 | 1,020,401 | 168,759 |

Punjab includes the district of Delhi.

*Census, Punjab Report 1901,* pp. 263–264; *Census, Punjab Report 1901, Part II, Imperial Tables,* pp. 102–103.

### Literacy by Religion for Punjab and Delhi, 1891–1921

| *Year* | *Hindu* | *Muslim* | *Sikh* | *Christian* |
|---|---|---|---|---|
| 1891 | 530,875 | 161,365 | 85,007 | 29,661 |
| 1901 | 602,148 | 207,188 | 118,445 | 34,538 |
| 1911 | — | — | — | — |
| 1921 | 544,647 | 261,504 | 160,860 | 39,789 |

*Census, Punjab Report 1901,* pp. 263–264; *Census, Punjab, 1921, Part II, Imperial Tables,* pp. 102–106.

### Literacy by Major Castes in 1911: Number of Literates per Mille

| *Hindus* | | *Muslims* | |
|---|---|---|---|
| Khatri | 250 | Sayid | 83 |
| Aggarwal | 212 (Baniya) | Qureshi | 77 |
| Arora | 210 | Sheikh | 74 |
| Brahmans | 113 | Khoja | 58 |
| | | Pathan | 53 |

*Census, Punjab Report 1911,* p. 322.

### Number of Newspapers in Punjab—Five-Year Averages, 1880–1904

| *Years* | *Average Number of Newspapers* |
|---|---|
| 1880–1884 | 39.20 |
| 1885–1889 | 66.20 |
| 1890–1894 | 66.00 |
| 1895–1899 | 54.60 |
| 1900–1904 | 141.80 |

N. Gerald Barrier and Paul Wallace, *The Punjab Press, 1880–1905* (East Lansing, Michigan: The Research Committee on the Punjab and the Asian Studies Center, Michigan State University, 1970), p. 165.

## WEALTH

### Non-Agricultural Wealth in Punjab as Assessed from Income Tax Returns in 1911

| *Caste* | *No. of Assesses* | *Amount* |
|---|---|---|
| Baniya | 6,825 | Rs. 14,702,553 |
| Khatri | 5,136 | 10,832,621 |
| Arora | 7,037 | 9,688,365 |
| Sheikh | 824 | 2,104,207 |
| Brahman | 867 | 1,623,536 |
| European | 264 | 1,438,360 |
| Mahajan | 410 | 906,783 |
| Jat | 609 | 906,212 |
| Bhabra (Jain) | 404 | 895,947 |
| Sud | 285 | 802,306 |
| Rajput | 102 | 774,268 |

*Census, Punjab Report 1911*, p. 527.

### Industrial Leadership by Caste, 191

| *Factory Ownership* | | *Factory Managers* | |
|---|---|---|---|
| Khatri | 78 | Khatri | 80 |
| Arora | 52 | Arora | 52 |
| Sheikh | 34 | Sheikh | 35 |
| Aggarwal | 31 | Brahman | 35 |
| Jat | 20 | Aggarwal | 32 |
| Rajput | 15 | Rajput | 16 |
| Brahman | 12 | Jat | 10 |
| Kalal | 12 | Kalal | 9 |
| Kashmiri | 6 | Kashmiri | 7 |
| Pathan | 5 | Pathan | 7 |
| Mahajan | 5 | Arain | 6 |
| Sud | 5 | Mahajan | 5 |
| Khandelwal | 5 | Khandelwal | 3 |
| Others | 32 | Sud | 2 |
| | | Other | 2 |
| Total | 312 | Total | 301 |

*Census, Punjab Report 1911*, pp. 525–526.

## REFORM SOCIETIES IN PUNJAB

### Reform Societies Membership in Punjab, 1891–1921, and Delhi, 1891–1921

| *Year* | *Arya Samaj* | *Dev Dharm* | *Brahmo Samaj* |
|---|---|---|---|
| 1891 | 14,030 | 12 | 128 |
| 1901 | — | — | — |
| 1911 | 100,846 | 3,094* | 700 |
| 1921 | 223,153 | 3,597 | 305 |

*May include Devi worshippers in Hoshiapur District.

*Census, Punjab Report 1891*, p. 172; *Census, Punjab Report 1911*, p. 138; *Census, Punjab Report 1921*, pp. 181–182.

### Major Castes of Punjabi Aryas in 1911

| *Caste* | *Number* |
|---|---|
| Meghs | 22,115 |
| Khatri | 17,237 |
| Arora | 10,547 |
| Jat | 9,203 |
| Brahman | 7,240 |
| Ode | 5,102 |
| Rajput | 2,403 |
| Aggarwal | 1,983 |
| Sunar | 1,009 |

*Census, Punjab Report 1911*, p. 137.

### Aryan Literacy by Major Caste in 1911

| *Caste* | *Total Aryas* | *Literates* |
|---|---|---|
| Arora | 10,547 | 3,613 |
| Brahman | 7,240 | 2,077 |
| Khatri | 17,237 | 5,212 |
| Ode | 5,102 | 542 |
| Rajput | 2,403 | 421 |
| Aggarwal | 1,983 | 474 |

*Census, Punjab Report 1911*, p. 323.

## Appendix IV

# SELECTED SHORT BIOGRAPHIES

### DAYANAND SARASWATI, SWAMI

Born in 1824 at Tankara in the Kathiawar Peninsula; raised an orthodox Brahman; left home in 1846; took *sanyās* and the name Swami Dayanand Saraswati; became a disciple of Swami Virajanand Saraswati of Mathura in 1860; left Virajanand in 1863 to begin his career preaching a reformed Hinduism; held his first religious debate with Christian missionaries at Ajmer in 1866; visited the Kumbha Mela at Hardwar in 1867 and preached his Vedic faith while denouncing popular Hinduism; toured Utter Pradesh and reached Calcutta in 1872; in Calcutta met with Brahmo Samaj leaders Keshab Chandra Sen and Devendra Nath Tagore; met Sayyid Ahmad Khan in 1873; founded the first Arya Samaj in Rajkot, Gujarat, in 1875; founded the Bombay Arya Samaj on April 10, 1875; published the first edition of the *Satyārth Prakāsh* in Benares during that same year; traveled to Delhi for the Imperial Durbar in December 1876; met reform leaders while there; held a crucial *shāştrārth* at Chandapur with Rev. Scott, Rev. Noble and Maulvi Muhammad Kasim of Deoband in March 1877; reached Lahore on April 19, 1877; founded the Lahore Arya Samaj on June 24, 1877; published the *Sanskār Vidhi* in 1877; toured the Punjab founding Arya Samajes and left that province in July 1878; published the *Rigvēda Bhāshya Bhūmīkā* in 1878; visited Kumbha Mela again in February 1879; met with Colonel Olcott and Madame Blavatsky of the Theosophical Society at Saharanpur in May 1879; established the Vedic Yantralaya in Ajmer to publish his writings on February 12, 1880; wrote *Gōkarunānidhi* in 1881; second and revised edition of the *Satyārth Prakāsh* published in 1882; broke all connections with the Theosophical Society on March 28, 1882; reached Rajasthan in June 1882; founded the Paropkarini Sabha to publish his works after his death on February 27, 1883; died in Ajmer on October 30, 1883.

DITT SINGH GYANI, BHAI

Born in 1853 at Anandpur Kalaur in the Patiala State; a Mazhabi Sikh; became a Gulabdasi *sādhu;* joined the Arya Samaj at Lahore at the urging of Bhai Jawahir Singh; left the Samaj in November 1888 after Pandit Guru Datta and Pandit Lekh Ram attacked the Sikh Gurus; joined the Singh Sabha movement and became a supporter of Professor Gurmukh Singh; between 1880 and 1900 wrote forty books in defense of Sikhism; became a member of the Khalsa College Council and the Khalsa Diwan; died June 17, 1901.

GURMUKH SINGH, BHAI

Born April 1849 at Kapurthala, a Chandhar Jat; employed as a cook by the Maharaja of Kapurthala, given a stipend for his education; became the first professor of Punjabi at the Oriental College in Lahore in 1877; established the Singh Sabha of Lahore on November 12, 1879, to promote Sikh education and use of the Punjabi language; founded the Punjabi weekly, the *Gurmukhī Akhbār,* and the *Vidyārak* in 1880; helped to found the Khalsa Diwan in April 1883; started the newspapers the *Khālsā* in 1885, both the *Sudhārak* and the *Khalsa Gazette* in 1886; launched scheme to create the Khalsa College and saw its foundation stone laid on March 5, 1892; died at Kandaghat on November 24, 1898.

MUNSHI RAM, LALA (SWAMI SHRADDHANAND)

Born in Talwan, Jullundur District, of a Khatri family; father was a devout Shaivite and raised his son accordingly; family traveled throughout the United Provinces; Munshi Ram educated in a series of towns—Benares, Banda, Mirzapur, Benares again, and Prayag; began law classes at Government College Lahore in 1882; became president of the Jullundur Arya Samaj and began his law practice in that city in 1885; started campaigning to open a girls' school in 1888; succeeded in founding the Kanya Path Shala in 1890; became the leading figure in the militant party after the death of Guru Datta in 1890; established the Kanya Mahavidyalaya, a girls' high school, on June 14, 1896; founded the journal the *Ārya Musāfir* in honor of Pandit Lakh Ram in October 1898; led the drive to establish a Gurukul during 1899–1900; this drive culminated in the opening of the Gurukul Kangri on March

22, 1901; presided over the new Gurukul from 1902 to 1907; took *sanyās* with the name Swami Shraddhanand in 1917; supported Gandhi's non-cooperation campaign in 1919; participated in the Aryan Conference in 1924; assassinated by a Muslim in 1926.

### GURU DATTA, PANDIT

Born in Multan of a wealthy Arora family on April 26, 1864; original name Gurditta Mal Sadana; his father, Lala Ram Kishen, was a Persian scholar who worked for the Punjab Education Department; Guru Datta was educated first in Multan, then at Adhiwal High School in Jhang; joined the Multan Arya Samaj on June 20, 1880; left for Lahore where he joined the Government College in 1881; quickly became a leader among the students of the college; founded the Free Debating Club for college students; became attracted to atheism and the Brahmo Samaj; joined Lahore Arya Samaj by 1882; jointly edited the *Regenerator of Arya Varta* with Lala Hans Raj in 1882; stood first in his B.A. examinations; received his M.A. degree in 1886 and was appointed an assistant professor of science in the Government College; founded the *Vedic Magazine* in 1886; became leading figure in militant wing of the Arya Samaj, in the Dayanand Anglo-Vedic College movement; and in the drive to establish an Arya Pratinidhi Sabha; died March 19, 1890.

### HANS RAJ, LALA (MAHATMA)

Born on April 23, 1860, at Bajwara in the Hoshiarpur District; a Bhalla Khatri, father Lala Chuni Lal strongly influenced by Islam; family poor after his father's death on February 14, 1876; family moved to Lahore; Hans Raj entered Government College in January 1881; joined Free Debating Society founded by Pandit Guru Datta in 1882; also joined with others to start the *Regenerator of A.ya Varta* that same year; took his B.A. examination in 1885 and stood second; received his M.A.; offered to serve as principal of the proposed Dayanand Anglo-Vedic College without salary on November 3, 1885; became principal of the new high school on June 1,, 1886; principal of the new Dayanand Anglo-Vedic College in 1888; elected to the Dayanand Anglo-Vedic College Trust and Management Committee in February 1889; became one of two leading figures of the College Party; led a delegation of Aryas to call upon the Viceroy, May 22, 1907; retired from the college principalship in 1911; elected president of the Dayanand Anglo-Vedic College Trust and Managing Committee in 1912; his wife died July 7, 1914; retired from the presidency of the Managing Committee in December 1918; presided over the National Social Conference in December 1919; became deeply involved in the *shuddhi* campaigns of 1923; acted as president of the Aryan Congress held in Delhi November 4–6, 1927; died November 16, 1938.

### HARKISHEN LAL, LALA

Born at Leiah in the Dera Ismail Khan District on April 13, 1864; a member of the Arora caste; father a clerk in the British service; went to Lahore in 1882 for his college education; stood second in the province in his B.A. examination in 1886; received scholarship to Cambridge; traveled to England and returned to Lahore in 1890; served as professor of mathematics at the Government College and part-time professor in the Oriental College; helped to found the Punjab National Bank of Lahore in 1895; founded the Bharat Insurance Company in 1896; became a supporter of the Indian National Congress, playing a leading role in the 1900 Congress meeting in Lahore; 1901–1906 founded numerous businesses, including the Punjab Cotton Press Company, the People's Bank Ltd., Amritsar Bank Ltd., Cawnpore Flour Mills Ltd., and the Century Flour Mills Ltd.; acted as president of the Punjab Congress Committee and head of the reception committee for the Lahore Congress meeting of 1909; 1913–1914 severe economic crises caused the failure of several of his companies; began practice as a barrister in Dera Ismail Khan in 1913; arrested and put on trial before a special tribunal in connection with the Punjab Martial Law in 1919; served as a minister in the Punjab Government under the Montegue-Chelmsford Reforms; opened a new People's Bank of Northern India in 1925; died on February 13, 1937.

### JAWAHIR SINGH, BHAI

Born at Amritsar in 1859; took a position in the Accounts Department of the Sind, Punjab and Delhi Railroad in 1876; met Dayanand and joined the Arya Samaj in 1877; served as secretary of the Lahore Arya Samaj 1878–1883 and also as vice-president of the Paropkarini Sabha; worked to open the Dayanand Anglo-Vedic College after 1883; served as secretary to the College Fund;

claimed the position of Head Granthi at the Darbar Sahib of Amritsar in 1886; opposed Sikh participation in the Indian National Congress; left the Arya Samaj in 1888 after severe criticism of the Sikh gurus by prominent Aryas and joined the Singh Sabha movement; worked for education among the Sikhs and for the Khalsa College; served as secretary of the Khalsa College from December 1892 to December 1906; became a Fellow of the Punjab University, chief secretary and vice-president of the Khalsa Diwan and a member of the Punjab Text Book Committee; died on January 22, 1910.

### KANHYA LAL ALAKHDHARI

Born August 1809 in Agra; father was Diwan Dharm Das, an Extra Assistant Commissioner of the Inland Customs and also a wealthy merchant; Kanhya Lal studied in Calcutta from 1826–1829; served as an accountant and clerk to the Commissioner of British Burma from 1829–1834; returned to Agra; served in various posts at Saharanpur, Ambala, Simla, Shahpur, and Muzaffargarh sometimes for the British and at other times for Indian princes; established the Gyan Press in Delhi and published his first reform tracts in 1853; spent the period of the Mutiny working for the British at Ludhiana; following the Mutiny he returned to Agra; served in Kotla State from 1863 to 1870 when he transferred to Khalsia State; left Khalsia State service in October 1872, settled in Ludhiana, and founded the Niti Prakash Sabha and journal; clashed with Pandit Shraddha Ram Phillauri, leader of Hindu orthodoxy; died on May 1, 1882.

### LAJPAT RAI, LALA

Born on January 28, 1865, in the village Dhudike in Ferozepur District, a member of the Aggarwal Baniya caste; his father was Munshi Radha Krishna, a teacher of Persian and Urdu in the Government Schools; Lajpat's family moved often during his youth and was divided by religious antagonism; Lajpat joined the Government College in 1881; joined the Arya Samaj in December 1882 and worked with others on the *Regenerator of Arya Varta;* passed his *mukhtārī* examination in February 1882; returned to Jagraon to begin law practice and then moved to Rohtak in 1884; passed his *vakālat* examination; moved to Hissar where he prac-

## SHIV NARAIN AGNIHOTRI

Born December 20, 1850, at Akbarpur in the United Provinces; a Kanauji Brahman; entered the Government College at Rurki in 1866; became interested in Vedanta at college; strongly influenced by Kanhya Lal Alakhdhari; appointed Drawing Master at the Government School in Lahore in 1873; joined the Brahmo Samaj shortly thereafter; met and clashed bitterly with Dayanand in 1877; left the Lahore Brahmo Samaj for the Sadharan Brahmo Samaj in 1878; decided to become a Brahmo missionary in 1879; took Brahmo *sanyās* on December 20, 1878; gave up his post as Drawing Master to devote full time to religious work; founded a new religious organization, the Dev Samaj, on February 16, 1877; broke fully with the Brahmo Samaj in 1887; became known as Bhagwan Dev Atma; initiated policy of dual worship, of God and himself, within the Dev Samaj in 1892; eliminated the worship of God in 1895; died on April 3, 1929.

# BIBLIOGRAPHIC NOTE

Scholars interested in further enquiry into the Arya Samaj and related movements among Punjabi Hindus will find extensive references in the footnotes of this study. Those who wish to go beyond these references or who wish to have an overview of relevant secondary sources should see my bibliographic article, "Sources for Arya Samaj History," in W. Eric Gustafson and Kenneth W. Jones, *Sources on Punjab History.* (Delhi: Manohar Book Service, 1975). Unfortunately, little relevant literature exists in secondary sources either in English or in South Asian languages which might be useful to the general student of South Asian history rather than the more specialized scholar. Consequently, a formal bibliography, which would be a mere relisting of items already given in the footnotes, has been omitted from this volume.

# INDEX